STRATEGIC INFLUENCE

PUBLIC DIPLOMACY, COUNTERPROPAGANDA, AND POLITICAL WARFARE

Strategic Influence

Public Diplomacy, Counterpropaganda, and Political Warfare

J. Michael Waller, editor

THE INSTITUTE OF WORLD POLITICS PRESS
Washington

2008

Strategic Influence:
Public Diplomacy, Counterpropaganda,
and Political Warfare

Published by the Institute of World Politics Press
1521 16th Street NW, Washington DC 20036 USA
www.iwp.edu

Cover design by Bridget Sweetin
www.sweetin.net

Revised edition

ISBN-13   978-0-9792-2364-8

Other IWP Press titles by the same author

Fighting the War of Ideas like a Real War
The Public Diplomacy Reader

For Katie

*To the memory of Ed Waller
and all the other victims of the terrorist bombing in Bali,
October 12, 2002*

"Our arsenal of persuasion must be as ready as our nuclear arsenal and used as never before."

Edward R. Murrow
Director, U.S. Information Agency, 1963

Contents

Political Warfare

Toward the Future

Acknowledgements

This book is the product of the enthusiastic and diligent work of many people. First, I would like to acknowledge and express my appreciation for the research and editorial assistance of some of the graduate research associates currently or formerly at The Institute of World Politics: Mark Beall, Shawn Brimley, Erin Carrington, Jay Gress, Bryan Hill, Amleset Kidane, Mallorie Lewis, Brian Newsome Charles Van Someren and Nicole Villescas. They did the hard part: the copy editing, formatting and chasing down of details.

I would also like to thank Alex Alexiev, Jim Guirard, Stephanie Kinney, Michaelis Persianis, and IWP Professors Juliana Geran Pilon and Douglas Streusand for their many ideas, insights and expertise that helped shape the direction of this volume.

Professor Herbert Romerstein, author of two chapters on counter-propaganda, wishes to thank Dr. Klaus Kirchner for his valuable advice and for help in obtaining some or the rare World War II leaflets cited in Chapter 7. Dr. Kirchner is the author of 15 volumes on World War II leaflets and two on World War I. He donated all 17 volumes to the library of the Institute of World Politics. Prof. Romerstein would also like to thank Elinor and Tom Wright, Henry Durkin and Dick Markel for help with German translations, Dmitry Kulik for help with translation from Russian and Ukrainian, and Lawrence Peck for help with Korean translations.

Lastly, I wish to thank John Lenczowski, President of The Institute of World Politics, for his unfailing support of this project since it began as an idea exchanged in passing on the staircase.

Introduction

Why do we twist ourselves with angst at the thought of secretly placing truthful, positive stories about our military in the beleaguered newspapers of a country where we are at war? Why do innovations like "strategic influence" abroad to help our friends and defeat our enemies provoke such emotional opposition at home? Why is such outrage so much greater than the sorrow that our errant bombs or bullets kill innocent civilians in what we mechanically call collateral damage? Why do we prefer to have our troops killed than use strategic influence as an effective weapon?

Such disjointed logic defies human decency.

As the United States struggles to shape coherent messages to the world, it must form not only the means through which it delivers its ideas, but the very philosophy of how it wages a "war of ideas." The near-universal default is "more public diplomacy" – the U.S. government's communication with the publics of the world – without really knowing the limits of public diplomacy and the many other humane, non-lethal options available to assist our diplomats and warfighters. But saying we need more public diplomacy is like saying we can alleviate world poverty if only we spent more on foreign aid, or win wars through the application of greater military force. Sheer volume is not the answer.

Our public diplomacy approaches and applications are inconsistent with the realities of today's international environment. Advances in information technology and the proliferation of electronic media outlets have leveled the ground between the U.S. and small powers, non-governmental organizations, and even individuals, who can undermine Washington's carefully crafted messages rapidly and constantly, networking horizontally and virally, attacking in swarms and refuting, distorting and drowning out the American voice, and agitating increasingly shrill and even deadly opposition.

Public diplomacy and the far broader field of strategic communication, as developed, are missing key components and functions. Lacking are roles and capabilities between the soft policies of attraction and the lethal policies of military force. A wide void spans the two – a void easily filled, as it has been in the past, but with few trained practitioners and even fewer policy advocates. Yet that void is precisely where the enemy is fighting the war of ideas. Within that gray area the U.S. and its allies would be expected to wage counterpropaganda and political warfare to substitute or augment the military.

Military transformation has been a cornerstone of the United States' ability to fight the latest generations of terrorists and insurgents. The 9/11 Commission mandated a similar revolution in the intelligence community. Yet the owner of one of the key elements of fighting the war of ideas – the State Department – has made only the most rudimentary of attempts to transform its cumbersome diplomatic processes and its ineffective public diplomacy machinery since the 2001 attacks.

Mentalities and institutions that served well during the Cold War are not necessarily what the country needs today, but many of the tried-and-true Cold War strategies and tactics provide invaluable lessons that deserve careful – but quick – study and consideration. Many of the timeless means and methods used successfully in the last major ideological conflict can be applied to today's geopolitical changes, cultural shifts, technological advances, and asymmetries of insurgency warfare.

Which brings us to the purpose of this book. *Strategic Influence* is a collection of 19 essays meant to help orient a more integrated, holistic approach to winning the "battle of hearts and minds" and "war of ideas." Those terms have become clichés, but they accurately characterize the type of global conflict underway. That is why one finds it strange that the public diplomacy community has yet to engage as one would expect in time of battle or war; its leaders and its rank-and-file have done the political equivalent of getting themselves repeatedly wounded and killed in battle (when they have engaged at all), and frequently commit fratricide against the troops and themselves through a lack of urgency, poor planning, inadequately trained personnel, and a general approach more of trepidation than innovation.

One cannot consider public diplomacy strategy or strategic communications outside the context of diplomatic grand strategy. No grand strategy can exist apart from military strategy, and a military strategy with a weak information and influence component will fail in modern ideological warfare. In counterterrorism and counter-insurgency, most of the fight is psychological and political. "The political and military aspects of insurgencies are so bound together as to be inseparable," the U.S. Army says in its 2006 *Counterinsurgency* field manual. "Most insurgent approaches recognize that fact. Military actions executed without properly assessing their political effects at best will be reduced in effectiveness and at worst are counterproductive. Resolving most insurgencies requires a political solution; it is thus imperative that counterinsurgent actions do not hinder achieving that political solution," according to the manual. The Army's 2008 *Stability Operations* field manual integrates civil and military affairs even further, to win the peace after winning wars, and to prevent wars from taking place at all.

Like it or not, then, the U.S. must conduct its public diplomacy with war aims in mind – even though much of the activity will properly have little or nothing to do with the war at all. Diplomacy and public diplomacy must strongly support, to say nothing of not undermine, military actions. Military efforts, the *Counterinsurgency* field manual notes, "are only effective when integrated into a comprehensive strategy employing all instruments of national power."

Strategic communications, a means of exercising strategic influence, are for all the time, not simply in time of crisis or military conflict. Much remains before the United States and its allies develop a real strategic communication doctrine – or even better, a doctrine on strategic influence.

Until now, most official talk of *fighting* and *winning* a war of ideas as a national strategy has been little more than empty or misguided rhetoric. Public diplomacy, the art and practice of governments communicating with the people of other countries, is an important component of a comprehensive ideological strategy. As vital as it is, public diplomacy is commonly proffered as a throwaway recommendation or miraculous catch-all for what we need in the present conflict. But it is only a single tool in the arsenal of democracy. The State Department has flailed and floundered since 9/11 to dominate the public diplomacy function that its own foreign service neither wanted nor understood. Consequently the diplomatic corps has exhibited a pattern of success that generally is inversely proportional to that of the military. The military has done its job to neutralize and destroy the enemy. But the State Department has not done its job on the war of ideas front, despite the near-total bipartisan mandate and new laws for it to do so.

That fact was obvious from the beginning, which is why the Office of the Secretary of Defense took it upon itself a month after 9/11 to fill the void. Ultimately it settled for a "public diplomacy support" role (diplomatically pretending that there was much public diplomacy to support in the first place), but not before expanding a concept called "strategic influence." Recognizing in October 2001 that the war against Islamist extremism and next-generation conflict at large would be won or lost on the influence front, the Pentagon set up a small Office of Strategic Influence (OSI) to carry out influence operations abroad. OSI was meant not only to support combat operations, but ultimately to help limit the need for using military force, and even mooting the use of force at all. The Office was able only to launch a few initiatives, all with the support for the Under Secretary of State for Public Diplomacy, to limit the need for using military force and even to solve military problems without killing and destroying.

Yet woe to those who dared innovate in time of national emergency! OSI's creative efforts showed promise, for a brief moment, to work well in support of the war against the terrorists, receiving full interagency support. There was only one snag: A political appointee who admitted that she had no knowledge of the military, but who decided that the effort encroached on her turf.

That appointee was the Assistant Secretary of Defense for Public Affairs – the Pentagon spokeswoman herself. She leaked a misleading and inflammatory story to the *New York Times*, alleging falsely that OSI was in the disinformation business and that it would undermine the war effort. Abusing her authority, she forbade OSI officials from speaking to reporters while she spun her false version of the truth. The resultant one-sided controversy ballooned over a three-day weekend in early 2002. Neither the president nor the defense secretary was briefed to defend OSI, and the office, contaminated by the emotional controversy and barred from explaining itself, was promptly shut down. While the administration continued to support the concept of strategic influence, the bureaucracy and contractors scattered, and the initiative never fully recovered. An audit at Senator Carl Levin's request later disproved the *New York Times* story, but the damage was done.

Meanwhile, an independent Pentagon panel, the Defense Science Board, worked on a government-wide "strategic communication" concept. In 2004 the board issued an innovative report that stated in part,

> Strategic communication requires a sophisticated method that maps perceptions and influence networks, identifies policy priorities, formulates objectives, focuses on 'doable tasks,' develops themes and messages, employs relevant channels, leverages new strategic and tactical dynamics, and monitors success. This approach will build on in-depth knowledge of other cultures and factors that motivate human behavior. It will adapt techniques of skillful political campaigning...

The board's report continued, "We need to move beyond outdated concepts, stale structural models, and institutionally-based labels.

Public diplomacy, public affairs, PSYOP [psychological operations] and open military information operations must be coordinated and energized." The panel made recommendations for "changes in the strategic communication functions and structures of the Departments of State and Defense, U.S. embassies and combatant commands."

The State Department went along reluctantly, but came up with no transformational plan of its own. State's inaction made the Pentagon the chief innovator on strategic influence, though most public diplomacy professionals are adamant that the involvement of the armed forces in public diplomacy and related areas should be minimal. Many senior military officers seem to agree. Despite similarities and overlaps, there is a difference between civilian public diplomacy and military information operations – a difference to be maintained for the integrity and success of both. And both depend on the success of one another. Furthermore, both are but two elements of strategic influence as a whole, a field that also includes counterpropaganda and political warfare, as this book's title implies, as well as charitable, cultural, economic, ideological, legal and psychological means of influencing audiences around the world.

The Defense Science Board report was the most important first step the federal government took after 9/11 to improve the way the nation communicates with the world. However, even later versions miss some key elements for a successful strategic influence capability, showing the limitations of "strategic communication" without influence as the core principle. The Army's 2006 *Counterinsurgency Field Manual* thoroughly re-examines insurgents and the means of defeating them and includes elements of strategic influence as central components.

This book is a contribution toward broadening the understanding of strategic influence and filling the ideational void. Fourteen experts, all of them current or former practitioners in their fields or emerging scholars with innovative approaches, offer their own perspectives of various forms of strategic communication and influence. This book does not seek to ask all the questions or claim to have all the answers. Its purpose is to stimulate discussion, thought, and action, and serve as a general textbook reader on the subject.

The authors bring together a diversity of disciplines: diplomats, public diplomats, broadcasters, congressional and White House staff, military officers, intelligence and counterintelligence officers, journalists, academics, counterpropagandists, political and policy operatives, and leaders of non-governmental organizations. Some have backgrounds in psychology and law. Many have served on the ground and in the field in times of war and peace. Others bring experience from the national strategic level. Their service and experience ranges from the opening of the Cold War to present-day Iraq and Afghanistan. The views expressed in each chapter are those of the respective author, and do not represent the views of their employers, other authors, or this editor.

Public diplomacy, counterpropaganda, and political warfare are part of the American diplomatic and national security tradition. Their widespread use dates to the founding of the republic. In Chapter 1, the editor of this volume looks at the use of all three instruments in countering the might and wealth of the British Empire during the American Revolution, showing how a rather divided set of colonies lacking a strong military could take on and defeat the mightiest power in the world. The chapter not only puts the subject of the book into its proper historical context, but also illustrates how an inferior military force can use information, political, and psychological strategy to wage a successful asymmetrical warfare campaign. The study of the founding shows how a combination of gentle public diplomacy with tough political and psychological warfare at the heart of the American military and security tradition.

Carnes Lord, former national security advisor to the vice president of the United States and presently a professor of strategy at the Naval War College, sets the tone in the next two chapters, explaining in Chapter 2 what public diplomacy is, what it was and how it worked in its heyday, and how it should function as a strategic tool. Having been an author and practitioner on the subjects of public diplomacy and psychological warfare for more than two decades – he was the primary author of President Reagan's National Security Decision Directive No. 77 on the management of public diplomacy with regard to national security – Lord elaborates in Chapter 3 on public diplomacy and its relationship to "soft power," expanding the field by describing the difference between the policies of attraction and influence. These two chapters have appeared elsewhere in modified form but were commissioned specifically for this book.

In Chapter 4, John Lenczowski builds further on the architecture, commenting elegantly on cultural diplomacy, political influence, and integrated strategy. As an advisor to the undersecretary of state at the conception of the successful strategy to take down the Soviet Union, he was an early proponent of strategic cultural diplomacy as an instrument of friendship as well as a weapon to undermine adversaries through positive and peaceful means. He went on to serve seven years as director of European and Soviet affairs at the White House National Security Council before ultimately founding the Institute of World Politics, the graduate school that produced this book.

Moving into today's conflict versus Islamist extremism, Jennifer

Marshall devotes Chapter 5 to discussing the role of religion and civil society in public diplomacy, and offers a model to help the U.S. prevail in the war of ideas by understanding the role of religion in other cultures as well as our own. As director of domestic policy studies and director of the Richard and Helen DeVos Center for Religion and Civil Society at the Heritage Foundation, she oversees research and public policy programs that include religion and civil society.

Robert R. Reilly, a former senior official in the White House and Department of Defense who served as a director of the Voice of America, devotes Chapter 6 explicitly to "how to conduct a war of ideas." He was a contributor to the Defense Science Board's strategic communication reports. In Chapter 6, Reilly offers sharp but thoughtful criticism of how that war was – or was not – waged in the years following 9/11, discussing bureaucratic mentalities and structural dysfunctionalism, and explaining that our officials first must understand our own nation's ideas and the ideas of our enemies.

We then move from public diplomacy to the actual countering of adversarial and enemy propaganda. Here, history has much to teach us. During the Cold War years, the United States government did not regularly combat Soviet disinformation and active measures until 1981, after congressional committees forced the issue into the public. By then, for the first time since the Truman and Eisenhower administrations, U.S. leaders re-recognized the importance of challenging Soviet propaganda directly and at the highest levels. Herbert Romerstein, a professional staff member of the House Permanent Select Committee on Intelligence, later became head of the Office to Counter Soviet Active Measures at the U.S. Information Agency (USIA).

In Chapter 7, Romerstein describes the indispensability of counterpropaganda in the war of ideas, reaching back to World War II to look at ways in which the Americans and British countered Nazi propaganda, especially among troops and civilians on the ground, and later countered the Soviets. He reminds us that by our own bad policies and methods, we can unintentionally play into the propaganda campaigns of our enemies, only to become surprised that we have to counter so much hostility among the people we try to reach.

Fast-forward to recent years in Chapter 8, where Andrew Garfield assesses the war of ideas in Iraq. Garfield is a former senior advisor to the British Ministry of Defence and a senior fellow at the Foreign Policy Research Institute in Philadelphia, and a founding partner of Glevum Associates, an international communication consulting firm that is on the cutting edge of influence warfare theory and practice. He designed sophisticated information operations in Iraq, but found that the American and coalition approach to influence operations was short on creativity and long on excuses about why things cannot be done. Writing before the 2007 surge, Garfield says, "From firsthand experience in Iraq, I can only conclude that we are losing not simply the physical battle but perhaps even more importantly the psychological conflict." The success of the changed strategy in Al-Anbar province – the change that produced the counterinsurgency and stability operations doctrines – proved Garfield's points, but systemic challenges remain. Garfield makes a case for aggressive information operations and effective, properly coordinated counterpropaganda.

If the military has done its job from below, what can U.S. civilian leaders do from the top? Senior military officers tell this editor that they want and need more civilian leadership and direction in the influence field. Herb Romerstein is back in Chapter 9, describing how the U.S., in the last years of the Cold War, set up and ran a successful counterpropaganda process at the national strategic level. Based at the White House, the Interagency Active Measures Working Group was the Reagan administration's government-wide counterpropaganda coordinating body against the Soviets. Romerstein was there at the founding as USIA representative on the working group. Despite today's very different world circumstances, the working group provides insights into how a president can structure an effective counterpropaganda coordinator. Romerstein teaches defenses against foreign propaganda at the Institute of World Politics.

Merely countering what the enemy says and does would put the U.S. and its allies on the permanent defensive, leaving the initiative to the enemy. This is where political warfare, for lack of a better term, comes into play. Political warfare is the civilian analogue to the military's psychological operations (PSYOP) and information operations (IO). In Chapter 10, Boston University Professor Angelo Codevilla gives a primer on political warfare as both an instrument of power and an art form. "Political warfare," he writes, "is the art of heartening friends and disheartening enemies, of gaining help for one's cause and causing the abandonment of the enemies' through words and deeds."

To master the political, one must first know how others think, and how to take advantage of both universal human nature and specific cultural and even microcultural mindsets. That is why Michael Cohn in Chapter 11 advocates that American public diplomats, intelligence officers and warfighters master the use of psychology in waging the war for hearts and minds. Writing as a research associate at the Institute of World Politics, Cohn takes basic college psychology texts and applies them in his chapter to how the good guys can hearten friends and dishearten enemies through skillful mind-gaming.

The U.S. has succeeded in wartime psychological strategy, even against those who use terror. IWP Professor John J. Tierney provides case studies in Chapter 12 of two American success stories, both taking place in the Philippines. The first occurred in the early 20th century when obsolete military thinking and misperceptions helped give insurgents the edge in the Philippine Insurrection. Tierney shows how President William McKinley "had to fight a two-front campaign" – a political war against domestic anti-war groups and his opposition political party, and the Philippine insurgents themselves who, in 1900, tried to use the war to influence the American presidential election. The second took place after World War II when the Communist Hukbalahaps, who had been fighting the Japanese, turned on the United States. In both counterinsurgencies the U.S. used "policies of attraction" to win local support and defeat the guerrillas.

A successful policy of attraction depends on the judicious use of words. Words can have many meanings, and can be as repulsive as attractive. When not used wisely, words can be as destructive as any conventional weapon. In Chapter 13, this writer looks at how words are used as instruments of conflict and weapons of war, how meanings differ among languages and cultures, and sometimes within the same culture; how we unwittingly adopt the terminology of our adversaries to the detriment of our allies, and how we can take the vernacular back from the enemy and make it work for the present war effort and in the long-term.

America's adversaries have harnessed U.S. communication technology, using satellites and servers, to globalize their ideologies, spread their propaganda, and coordinate their operations. Hampton Stephens of WorldPoliticsWatch.com compares the agility and decentralization of terror networks and extremist movements and compares them in Chapter 14 with the centralized slowness of U.S. message-makers, remarking on the paradox that the highly authoritarian People's Republic of China has nimbly captured the power of the Internet to its advantage. Stephens argues that the only factors preventing the U.S. from reversing the problem are bureaucratic inertia and lack of political will.

The last six chapters look to the future. Chapter 15 takes low-intensity conflict theory and applies it to fighting enemy propaganda. Stephen C. Baker, who was with the Center for Security Policy and an IWP graduate student when he developed the theory of "low-intensity propaganda," argues that the U.S. and its allies must combat enemy propaganda on the civilian and politico-military levels with as much energy and drive as a traditional counterinsurgency force. This chapter should be particularly useful for those intending to expand new counterinsurgency doctrine, but is important for diplomats, public diplomats, and public affairs officers as well.

National Defense University Professor David Spencer follows with an analysis of certain terrorist insurgency doctrine and calls for the strategic communications community to "red team" their plans and theories. Red teaming is the term used by the U.S. when portraying adversarial forces in war games or simulations. The U.S. and its allies are blue, the enemy is red, and other parties and NGOs are green. Red teaming helps the U.S. understand the adversary and troubleshoot its own thinking and practices. Spencer argues in Chapter 16 that the State Department has been mistaken in not taking the lead in gaming and red teaming, choosing instead to leave the matter up to the military. He adds that the Pentagon should game out its own strategic communication and information operations. "We can see the results today," Spencer writes: "Superior military strategy and tactics over any foe, but grossly inadequate public diplomacy, political warfare, and information strategy at a time when warfare more than ever depends on communication."

In Chapter 17, Andrew Garfield offers a plan he developed at his international communication firm, Glevum Associates, for use in Afghanistan, Iraq after the surge, and elsewhere. As its "information operations" title implies, the chapter is oriented toward military support operations, but Garfield offers a lot for the reader in terms of ideas for the civilian and public diplomacy sides of the issue.

How does one coordinate the various tools of strategic communication and influence among different government agencies and even within individual departments and services? Juliana Geran Pilon gracefully explores the question in Chapter 18 on synchronicity. A veteran public diplomacy practitioner and Research Professor of Politics and Culture at the Institute of World Politics, Dr. Pilon critiques the policy since 9/11 for better and worse, and argues, "the right information delivered to the right audience in the right way is not only a nice idea, it is wise policy – and it should be the rule, not the exception." Having said that, she adds, "we seem not to know how to get it right. We engage in many important activities that we don't bother to talk about, or else we promise to do more than is possible and when the results don't match the rhetoric, we disappoint those we seek to help. Instead of winning friends we reap ridicule or worse." Her chapter offers positive solutions.

Few of the proposals in this book call for expensive and time-consuming structural changes to America's malfunctioning strategic communications machine. Most of the efforts discussed can be accomplished with no significant bureaucratic restructuring, at least for the short-term. What is needed is a change in thinking.

The last chapter focuses on such a change. The editor of this volume offers an immediate-term wartime message strategy in chapter 19 to accelerate "the tempo and intensity of the nation's conduct of the war of ideas and fighting it like a real war." As for developing a longer term strategy, we first must change our way about thinking about how our nation communicates with the world and why.

J. Michael Waller
Walter and Leonore Annenberg Professor
of International Communication
The Institute of World Politics
Washington, DC

1

The American Way of Propaganda: Lessons from the Founding Fathers

J. MICHAEL WALLER

Introduction

One of the most contentious debates in the war on terrorism centers on the "hearts and minds" aspect of the fight. Many argue for complete transparency in U.S. message-making, emphasizing the softer aspects of public diplomacy. A small minority argues that the United States must make greater use of edgier information instruments such as propaganda, political action, and psychological warfare.

Critics of the minority view say such actions are un-democratic and unworthy of serious consideration as instruments – let alone weapons – of American statecraft. Those critics are wrong. Such methods were part of the American founding. This chapter discusses how the founding fathers of the United States employed public diplomacy, propaganda, counterpropaganda and political warfare as instruments of democracy in the struggle for independence.

An American tradition

John Adams, Samuel Adams, Benjamin Franklin, Alexander Hamilton, Thomas Jefferson, George Washington and others recognized that the opinions and perceptions of foreign governments, publics, and armies mattered. They used public diplomacy, propaganda, counterpropaganda and political warfare as instruments of first resort in the American Revolution. They did it to seek support from elements within the British Empire and among Britain's European rivals. Their efforts led to a global coalition in support of American independence and democracy, though in reality the coalition was united not by democratic principles but by a common enemy.

They did not rely on appeals to goodness and virtue. The positive American messages of justice, equality, independence, and democracy had limited appeal at home as well as abroad. Often they conflicted with interests of potential or actual allies. American revolutionary leaders knew this, especially in France where they needed the financial and military support of the king but where their republican ideas were stridently anti-aristocratic, and indeed subversive to the French government. Among English Puritan and Presbyterian colonists, lingering hostility from the French and Indian War of a generation earlier, in which the Americans fought as British to force the French from North America, remained strong, to say nothing of anti-Catholic sentiment.

For all their mutual suspicions, the American revolutionaries and French monarchy found a common cause, if not in their ideals, in a common foe. Hopelessly outmatched against the world's most formidable military power, the American founders compensated asymmetrically with public diplomacy, propaganda, counter-propaganda, and political warfare. They never used those terms – all came into vogue as we know them in the twentieth century – but they employed all the measures, integrating them with domestic politics, secret diplomacy, intelligence, and warfare with decisive strategic effect.

Public diplomacy, according to an operating U.S. government definition, "seeks to promote the national interest and the national security of the United States through understanding, informing, and influencing foreign publics and broadening dialogue between American citizens and institutions and their counterparts abroad."[1] It consists usually of positive messages as a polite and nuanced form of propaganda.

Counterpropaganda is, literally, the act or product of countering the propaganda of one's adversary. *Political warfare* is the employment of aggressive and even coercive political means to achieve objectives, ranging from winning a tough campaign for public office to meeting military objectives through non-military means.[2] Closely related to political warfare, but almost purely military, is the discipline of *psychological operations* (PSYOP), which the military calls "planned operations to convey selected information and indicators to foreign audiences to influence their emotions, motives, objective reasoning, and ultimately the behavior of foreign governments, organizations, groups and individuals."[3] PSYOP is more manipulative than public diplomacy, and the U.S. generally uses it tactically, not strategically.

All these instruments bred the American Revolution. Massachusetts patriot Samuel Adams pioneered what a biographer called a blend of "philosophy and action in ongoing political struggles." A follower of 17th century English philosopher John Locke, Adams typically mounted a relentless negative political or ideological attack followed by a positive alternative solution that would keep the enemy on the defensive. The alternative was soundly based in philosophical and moral terms. Adams strategically integrated the negative and the positive with political action both at home and, when necessary and possible, abroad.[4]

The positive approach:
Promote ideas, values, and an image of victory

The American struggle for self-determination spawned the creation of a country based not on language, race, class, ancestry or geography, but a nation whose common bond was an idea. This transformational concept of nationality, derived from common ideas and values, embraced "self-evident" universal truths that "all men are created equal, that they are endowed by their Creator with certain unalienable Rights, that among these are Life, Liberty and the pursuit of Happiness."

The authors of the Declaration of Independence intended their words to go far beyond the American colonies and the king and parliament in London. They took their message to the world. Thus in the first action of its existence, the United States government initiated an international public diplomacy campaign.

Twice in the Declaration of Independence the Continental Congress appealed to international public opinion in support of the cause and principles of freedom. In the preamble explaining the need for severing ties to Britain, the founders noted that, "a decent respect to the opinions of mankind requires that they [the people] should declare the causes which impel them to the separation." To substantiate their philosophical and practical reasoning, the elected representatives of the people said they would "let Facts be submitted to a candid world."

Their message-making campaign was global. Being morally right was insufficient, especially among European leaders who saw no moral superiority among the ragtag Americans or who viewed the conflict with Britain on traditional, great-power terms. Those leaders influenced or controlled the cash, the material supplies, the munitions, and the military forces that the outmatched Americans desperately needed. The colonial rebels had to project an image of strength and invincibility. Against the British who out-powered them in seemingly every way, building that credible image would take time and sacrifice. It would also mean waging constant political and psychological attacks on the crown and its agents to undermine Britain's will to fight.

The negative approach: "Put and keep the enemy in the wrong"

The second and inseparable track of the founders' public diplomacy and political warfare strategy was to wage a relentless propaganda attack on the enemy. All forms of warfare need an enemy, including any good political campaign, and so vilification of the British government was at least as strong as positive messages in early American public diplomacy.

Samuel Adams, the earliest proponent of secession, and an author and signatory of the Declaration, consistently pursued the two-track campaign. The first step, he argued, must be the negative attack, couched when possible in comity and amity by allowing the adversary's misconduct to speak for itself, but always attacking. He counseled in 1775, "It is a good Maxim in Politicks as well as in War to put & keep the Enemy in the Wrong."[5]

Leading Bostonian opposition to the Stamp Act and other laws Parliament imposed on the colonies in the 1760s, Adams pioneered new methods of democratic political warfare, combining scandal, outrage, and demands for justice with public accountability and transparency, ridicule, shame and personal abuse.

He worked through the English constitutional and legal system, using the system as a weapon against its very self, exploiting laws, procedures and precedents to his revolutionary advantage. As he orchestrated political takeovers on the inside, he attacked the system as politically and morally illegitimate from the outside to show that the crown could do nothing to meet the people's fair demands against taxation without representation. He worded legislative resolutions and other pronouncements in ways designed to put the local royal authorities, as well as parliament and the king, in impossible situations, placing them in lose/lose positions for which to attack them no matter what decision they made. Taking advantage of the crown's own mis-steps and the dislikable traits of colonial authorities in Boston, Adams built parallel political and administrative structures that mocked and negated British rule while creating new, legitimate democratic formations that demonstrated both the limits of the crown's power and the new powers of the people.[6]

Crowds made effigies of royal officials and hanged them from the branches of the Liberty Tree before thousands of enthralled Bostonians. A weak speaker, Adams understood the integration of oratory with the written word and the visual image. Recruiting a young, wealthy merchant named John Hancock, he ensured that protesters were outfitted with elaborate costumes, props, and musical instruments to lead protest songs in harborside demonstrations and parades through Boston's streets. He filled broadsheets with news of events that he created or orchestrated. Newspapers throughout the colonies and in London reported about the brash and colorful spectacles that energized crowds and made stories interesting and exciting to tell and retell. They reinforced the fears and hopes of political figures in other colonies, warning them that if the people of Boston were threatened, the people of all the colonies would be threatened.

Adams defined his enemy early and kept that enemy in the wrong for decades, relentlessly and often single handedly, provoking, alerting and educating the people about the dangers of a king's rule and a parliament in which the far-flung subjects could never be truly represented.

1775: British saw political warriors more dangerous than soldiers

Throughout the American independence period, the British repeatedly complained about revolutionary propaganda, and often viewed the political warriors as more dangerous than the shockingly unconventional warriors on the battlefield. For the Americans, propaganda and political action would compensate in the asymmetrical war ahead – areas where the British were not as competent as their wayward colonies – and the British knew it.

King George III was well aware of Samuel Adams from his briefings on political unrest in the colonies. The king, his ministers and parliament were so clumsy in reacting to Adams' agitprop that they unwittingly allowed the upstart Bostonian to goad them into taking the very repressive actions about which Adams had warned the public. General Thomas Gage, named royal military governor of Massachusetts in 1774, considered Adams and Hancock as the most dangerous men of the nascent rebellion. On receiving orders to arrest the entire elected political leadership of the colony, Gage focused on those two, marching 800 troops to Lexington where his spies reported they were hiding. Lexington sat astride the road to Concord, where Gage intended to capture a rebel powder magazine. Paul Revere foiled the plan on his famous Midnight Ride, helping Adams and Hancock escape as the British approached the town. The war began literally as a British attempt to capture the colonial propagandists.

As volunteers massed around Boston to fight what would become the Battle of Bunker Hill and the Continental Congress named 43 year-old George Washington as commander of the new Continental Army,

Gage issued a proclamation to pardon any and all American rebels who had opposed, fought or even killed the king's forces. In capital letters he made only two exceptions: "SAMUEL ADAMS and JOHN HANCOCK, whose offences are of too flagitious a nature to admit of any other consideration than condign punishment."[7]

A winning combination

Neither man would hang; both would be re-elected to the Continental Congress and, with Hancock as Congress President and Adams operating behind the scenes, help craft the Declaration of Independence. As the unanimous bedrock statement of principle of the United States of America, the declaration illustrates the founding fathers' three-part approach to communicating their message.

The document begins with repeated positive statements of rights, ideals and obligations, including the right to oust repressive governments. Second, it resists Britain's divide-and-conquer colonial strategy and aims at attracting other large powers as allies by showing inter-colonial unity. Finally, it vilifies the repressive government, while sparing the British people and even parliament, laying all blame on the king: "The history of the present King of Great Britain is a history of repeated injuries and usurpations, all having in direct object the establishment of an absolute Tyranny over these States."

For good measure, the Founders – 32 year-old Thomas Jefferson mainly, influenced by Samuel Adams[8] – substantiated their accusations with a litany of crimes that reads like an indictment of the king, accusing him of everything from arbitrariness, illegality, abuse and neglect to hinting that His Majesty was not only a tyrant, but unwholesome, criminal, and possibly even unmanly. The king refused to approve necessary local laws, respected only those who signed away their rights, and harassed legislative assemblies "for the sole purpose of fatiguing them into compliance."

George III dissolved public legislatures and blocked the people from electing new lawmakers, prevented the states from determining their own population policies, obstructed justice and manipulated judges, and "erected a multitude of New Offices, and sent hither swarms of Officers to harass our people and eat of their substance." The king kept standing armies in local communities without the people's consent, and outside the control of civil authorities. He waged economic warfare on the colonies, cutting off their trade, taxing the people arbitrarily, and denying them jury trials. Indeed, he abolished English law and replaced it with arbitrary government. Now, the framers said, the king "has abdicated Government here, by declaring us out of his Protection and waging War on us." The king was preying on his own subjects.

"He has plundered our seas, ravaged our coasts, burnt our towns, and destroyed the lives of the people," according to the Declaration, in a reference to British punitive attacks on civilian populations. The document refers to the anticipated arrival of Hessian troops: "He is at this time transporting large Armies of foreign Mercenaries to compleat [sic] the works of death, desolation and tyranny, already begun with circumstances of Cruelty and Perfidy scarcely paralleled in the most barbarous ages, and totally unworthy the Head of a civilized nation." That was certainly putting the enemy in the wrong. For the purposes of discussing public diplomacy, propaganda, and political warfare, we see that these words comprise the first official document issued by the United States of America.

Targeting British audiences

Well before the revolution began, colonial leaders targeted British public opinion and elites to push for changes that they were powerless to influence within parliament. They took advantage of the often freewheeling English newspapers' substantial coverage of colonial politics and developments, and produced declarations and domestic news stories that they believed would be picked up in the British press. The newspaper industry of the time depended on contributed letters and essays, which were often published anonymously or pseudonymously, and American patriots wrote prolifically.

Without their own representation in parliament, American anti-tax advocates ran campaigns to pressure the British legislature indirectly. Their successful boycotts forced parliament to repeal the Stamp Act of 1765. With the imposition of the Townshend Duties in 1767, Boston, New York and Philadelphia led a "non-importation" effort and public boycotts, a form of economic warfare. They would make English merchants feel the pain. The efforts succeeded with the repeal of the Stamp Act, but they soon found a far more determined British government of Prime Minister Frederick "Lord" North.

Colonial legislatures circumvented the royally appointed governors and named their own agents to represent their interests in London. Four of them hired Benjamin Franklin of Pennsylvania. Known for his charm and quick wit, Franklin was a popular figure in London where he had lived for years, all the more respected for his reputation as a political philosopher, an inventor, and a cutting-edge scientist experimenting with electricity. Franklin was probably the most famous American in Europe and the colonies.

Like most colonists at the time, Franklin considered himself an

Englishman from America. He arrived late to the cause of independence. He wrote influential articles in London against the Stamp Act and against the crown's abuse of its colonial subjects. Like nearly all the Founding Fathers at that point, he merely sought to extend all the rights of English subjects, so he naturally was positioned to fuel internal British opposition to the ruling Tories. Franklin worked with pro-American groups like the Society of 13 and the Society of 1774, exploited the opposition press, and blamed Lord North for failures to work out reasonable agreements with the colonies.

Pointing to Samuel Adams and other radicals who wanted independence, Franklin and other agents attempted to warn the British that they risked antagonizing the thirteen colonies forever. Sometimes they tried to mediate between sides. Franklin often used satire. He penned a pamphlet in 1773, "Rules By Which a Great Empire May Be Reduced," a tongue-in-cheek guide to destroying the British imperium that showed that the king and parliament were following directions perfectly.[9]

The Continental Congress began issuing resolutions to the king, the British public, Canadians and others in respectful tones. The public petitions to George III were deferential, befitting of English subjects making appeals to their king. Bureaucrats and appointed officials, not the sovereign, were to blame. That would change over the next two years.

A year before declaring independence, on July 6, 1775, the Continental Congress explained colonial grievances in a "Declaration of the Causes and Necessity of Taking Up Arms." News of Bunker Hill was just reaching British shores. The declaration was an eloquent explanation from Americans who still considered themselves Englishmen, who feared a trans-Atlantic civil war (not dreaming of independence), and sought to save the union with London. It was also a propaganda document, addressing "our friends and fellow subjects in any part of the empire," as well as "before God and the World."[10]

Twelve months later, in the Declaration of Independence, the Continental Congress explained the colonists' diligent attempts to communicate with their royal brothers in private diplomacy as well as public using Adams' messaging formula.

Targeting Canada, Bermuda and Ireland

As a major British possession adjoining the colonies, Canada presented both a dangerous enemy rearguard and an opportunity. The Americans and the crown both vied for the loyalty of Quebec, the French-speaking Catholic colony that had been won from France a half-generation earlier. After the war broke out, the First Continental Congress voted in 1775 to invade Canada to cut off British supplies and replenish troops from Quebec and Montreal. Via the Boston Committee of Correspondence, Samuel Adams directed U.S. propaganda operations in Canada. He appealed for a combined North American front against the British.

Gen. George Washington wrote a specific letter "To the Inhabitants of Canada" and another to the people of Bermuda, calling for their support. Formerly a part of the Virginia colony, Bermuda had strong political, familial and economic ties to the American mainland, and was the site of a poorly guarded British arsenal that the colonists could use. Washington's letter to the Canadians said, in part:

> Come then, my Brethren, Unite with us in an indissoluble Union. Let us run together to the same Goal. We have taken up Arms in Defence of our Liberty, our Property; our Wives and our Children: We are determined to preserve them or die. We look forward with pleasure to that day not far remote (we hope) when the Inhabitants of America shall have one Sentiment and the full Enjoyment of the blessings of a Free Government.[11]

The Congress soon authorized a propaganda operation to urge Canadians to join as a "sister colony" against the British. After Franklin returned from England and was elected to the Continental Congress, he and a few others made up a small Committee of Secret Correspondence, considered the nation's first foreign intelligence agency. The committee sent a French printer to Quebec "to establish a free press... for the frequent publication of such pieces as may be of service to the laws of the United States." The committee also recruited French Catholic priests to promote Canada's secession to the rebel cause. The effort failed, however, due to French-Canadian antipathy toward the openly anti-Catholic New Englanders on their border who had been their enemies in the French and Indian War, a hostile Canadian clergy, the excesses of American troops who attacked the province, occupied Montreal and attempted to take Quebec city, and Congress's inability to deliver more than promises.[12]

While the Continental Congress failed to gain the Canadian provinces' secession from Britain, the British decried the effectiveness of American propaganda efforts. The British colonial secretary in Canada complained that unrest was growing with "the minds of the people poisoned by the same hypocrisy and lies practiced with so much success in the other provinces, and which their emissaries and friends here have spread abroad with great art and diligence." British General

John Burgoyne blamed his recruitment woes in Canada "to the poison which the emissaries of the rebels have thrown into their mind."[13]

Coordinating secret intelligence and message-making

The American founders sought to coordinate the collection of secret intelligence with public message-making. Thanks to Franklin's fortuitous and well-exploited intelligence collection in England, the patriots knew in advance that the crown would send thousands of mercenaries from the German principality of Hesse to augment its own Redcoat regulars. That knowledge, combined with the Americans' instincts for psychological warfare learned during the French and Indian War, enabled the Continental Congress and General George Washington to run successful PSYOP against the Hessian troops and divide thousands of them from the British.

Franklin began the effort in London in September 1775, before his return to America. He warned the Continental Congress that the German Prince of Hesse was visiting to sign an agreement with George III to hire Hessian mercenaries. "The leading people, among the Germans of Pennsylvania, should likewise be consulted," he said in his secret letter. The British king signed the agreement in November 1775, Congress found out quickly in January 1776, and by the spring the Americans had already devised a psychological warfare effort to divide the Hessians from the British army and discredit the British government.

Thanks to Franklin's secret work, the Continental Congress received copies of the British-Hessian treaties in May. General Washington asked Congress President Hancock about raising German-American groups to promote Hessian desertions, while the Congress appointed John Adams, Jefferson and others to a new committee to make propaganda of the treaties (in its words, to "extract and publish the treaties") and to "prepare an address to the foreign mercenaries who are coming to invade America."

Events quickened their pace and bear recounting to illustrate how the Americans operated. In June, a Samuel Adams protégé in Congress, William Henry Lee of Virginia, introduced the resolution to declare independence. Under Hancock's leadership, continental lawmakers unanimously adopted the declaration on July 4, in which they referred to the incoming troop fleets of "large Armies of foreign Mercenaries." With his distinctive penmanship Hancock signed the document immediately. The rest signed it on August 2. A week later, Congress set up a committee to devise a plan to encourage Hessian desertions. Three days afterward, on August 12, the Hessians landed in New York.

By this time, Franklin had returned to Philadelphia and joined Adams and Jefferson on the Hessian desertion committee. The Continental Congress resolved to protect non-English deserters from the British forces (Hessians mainly, but Irish, Scots and others) and give each 50 acres of land to start a new life as free Americans. It ordered leaflets printed in English and in German, and sent copies to General Washington in New York. The congressional desertion committee issued its report on August 14; on the 18th, Washington summoned Christopher Ludwick, a Continental Army cook born in Hesse, to be his agent to infiltrate Hessian ranks. Franklin had the leaflets printed at his shop and sent them to troops in New Jersey on August 24.

Two days later, Washington reported that his agents successfully disseminated the leaflets among the German troops. That same day, Franklin and John Adams wrote a congressional resolution to non-English officers in the British military, offering a sweeter deal of hundreds of acres of land to each deserter. Congress instructed that the resolution be immediately translated into German and printed the night of August 26-27.

The Battle of Long Island (Battle of Brooklyn) raged on August 27 and 28, ending in a quick British victory before Franklin could send the congressional pamphlets to New York. Washington wrote to Hancock on the 29th, "As to the Encouragement to the Hessian Officers, I wish it may have the desired effect, perhaps it might have been better, had the offer been made sooner."

The British soon occupied New York City. Washington learned in mid-October that a Hessian deserter said his comrades had not been receiving the leaflets, and that the British had filled the Hessians with fear of surrendering to the Americans. Later Washington and other military commanders learned that British officers told their Hessian mercenaries that if they deserted, the "shaggily clad" Americans would cannibalize them, so the Hessians would have to "exterminate first" if they were to live. It was easy for the Hessians to believe, as many American troops wore tattered and filthy civilian clothes unbecoming to any European soldier, and U.S. sharpshooters, who had the bad form to shoot enemy officers, were dressed as "savage Indians."

With time and patience, the strategy to divide the Hessians worked. One in six of the 30,000 Hessians ultimately deserted. Playing up the use of professional German mercenaries among British troops also paid dividends to the United States, not only to discredit the empire, but to show the great odds against which the heroic Americans would fight. When news of British General John Burgoyne's surrender at Saratoga reached Europe in late 1777, the French realized that the American irregulars, against troops of two of the world's best armies, had a fighting chance. In Paris, Franklin was prepared for the moment.

Secret and public diplomacy in France

Nearly a half-year before the first shots at Lexington and Concord, French Foreign Minister Charles Gravier, Comte de Vergennes, noted the increasing friction between most of the thirteen colonies and what he called the metropolis in London. With the loss of nearly all France's North American territories in the Seven Years' War (French and Indian War) still fresh, Vergennes observed the tension with anticipation. "The quarrel between the colonies and the British government seems to grow more serious every day," he wrote in late 1774. "It may prove the most fatal blow to the authority of the metropolis." The rift was an opportunity for France – if the upstart Americans had a chance of winning.[14]

The armed combat began in April 1775. King George III declared the colonies in rebellion in August. Franklin's return to Philadelphia after a decade in England took place in October, after he realized that the Anglo-American political break was irreconcilable. During Franklin's long sailing journey home, the French ambassador in London, the Comte de Guines, proposed to Vergennes that he send a secret agent to Philadelphia to collect intelligence on the capabilities and needs of the revolutionary American government and its military. He dispatched a young retired military officer who had recently returned from the colonies for the job. Shortly after Franklin, the agent, disguised as a merchant from Antwerp, set out to sea.

As happened so often, despite the length of transatlantic journeys and the slowness of communication, events moved quickly. The citizenry almost immediately elected Franklin to the Continental Congress upon his landing in Philadelphia in October. In November, Congress established the five-man Committee of Secret Correspondence intelligence service. Franklin was the only committee member who was familiar with Europe, and was well known and well regarded across the continent for his scientific, diplomatic and philosophical works.[15] He also spoke some French. And he enjoyed a well established reputation for creativity as a political thinker, activist, networker and yarn-spinner.

To conceal the dire conditions of the American military, Franklin appears to have exaggerated the force's strengths to French intelligence, just as Washington had been doing in an elaborate deception operation against the British military. The French agent, Bonvouloir, filed a hugely inflated report on December 28, saying that

"Everyone here is a soldier, the troops are well clothed, well paid and well armed. They have more than 50,000 regular soldiers and an even larger number of volunteers who do not wish to be paid. Judge how men of this caliber will fight." In truth, only about five thousand poorly paid, ill-trained, hungry cold men comprised Washington's army.[16]

Bonvouloir apparently never second-guessed Franklin, and Vergennes did not question Bonvouloir. The false report persuaded King Louis XVI and his divided court to aid the Americans, covertly at first, and with the secret assistance of Spain. By early 1776, Vergennes secured funding from the French and Spanish kings to set up a front company, Hortalez & Cie, to provide weapons and other material assistance to the Americans while officially maintaining their neutrality.[17]

After the signing of the Declaration of Independence, with France now secretly aiding the Americans in the war, the Continental Congress returned Franklin to Paris, where he would attempt to negotiate a formal military alliance against the British. The struggling United States had little to offer the cash-strapped French for such a high-risk venture. The strategy was for the U.S. to check British imperial expansion, in this case by American diplomacy and political action backed by French wealth and military power. London deemed the septuagenarian Franklin, crossing the Atlantic with his two grandsons, as one of its greatest threats.

British Ambassador Lord Stormont, who also headed the king's secret service station in France, wrote less than admiringly to the Foreign Secretary in London: "I cannot but suspect that he comes charged with a secret Commission from Congress ... and as he is a subtle, artful Man, and void of all Truth, he will, in that Case, use every means to deceive... He has the advantage of several intimate connexions here, and stands high in the general opinion.... In a word, my Lord, I look upon him as a dangerous engine and am very sorry that some English frigate did not meet him by the way."[18]

British agents spread rumors in Paris that Franklin had given up the revolutionary cause as lost, enriched himself with 30,000 pounds of gold, and sought asylum from the king. Stormont made the mistake of ridiculing Franklin's humble beaver-skin hat, not appreciating the adoring Parisians who swooned over the American's exotic back-woods appearance. In response, Franklin coined a French verb, *stormonter*, meaning to lie, and the word instantly went vogue.[19]

Franklin was hugely popular in France, where the Age of Reason had begun to eclipse that of the divine right of kings. French journals already had published his works on science and theory. Parisians bought engraved and painted portraits of him and set them on their mantels. Franklin's distinctive profile decorated snuff boxes. Deliberately trading his Philadelphia silk clothes for his hat and rustic "Quaker" attire, he personified the American Revolution.[20]

In the course of making the rounds of Parisian society and cultivating support in Spain, Franklin prepared action plans well in advance so that when the opportunity presented itself, he could act instantly. The moment came in December 1777, when news reached Europe that in October General Burgoyne had surrendered to American troops at Saratoga. Franklin knew his next move: a proposed Treaty of Amity and Commerce with France, part of which included an American military alliance with France and Spain against the British. He had already prepared a draft in anticipation. Within two months he facilitated a Franco-American military alliance. The army and navy of King Louis XVI formally engaged in the war, ultimately sealing defeat for the British.[21]

Counterpropaganda in Europe

Well before war for independence began, American influence operations in Europe responded mainly to aggressive and sophisticated British propaganda. Thanks to the regular reports on British attitudes that Benjamin Franklin and others supplied the colonies from London and elsewhere, the patriots knew what was being said about them and how to counter the negative publicity.[22] Samuel Adams was concerned that the Massachusetts royal governor's portrayal of the colony would legitimize the deployment of a large occupation force to Boston.

When the Redcoats were provoked and fired on Bostonian civilians in the March 1770 incident known as the Boston Massacre, the patriots wanted to make certain that the world viewed the dead not only as martyrs for the colonies, but as martyrs with whom British society would identify. Paul Revere's famous engraving that depicted the event, portrayed the British soldiers as coldly and ruthlessly firing point-blank into a crowd of fashionably dressed ladies and gentlemen. In reality, however, the victims were members of social classes that would evoke the least sympathy in England: dock workers, sailors, a runaway Afro-Indian slave and Irishmen. Bostonians raced a boat to England so their version of the event reached London first. Adams found a local lawyer who would defend the British soldiers in court without besmirching the reputation of Boston: his second cousin, John.[23]

When the war finally broke out, the Americans needed a good information operations capability on the continent to present their view and wage counterpropaganda against the British. Coordination fell to the Committee of Secret Correspondence of the Continental Congress. The committee, whose function, according to the resolution that formed it, was to correspond "with our friends in Great Britain, Ireland and other parts of the world."[24] John Adams, later sent as a U.S. emissary to the Netherlands, wrote to Franklin in Paris, "It is necessary for America to have agents in different parts of Europe, to give some information concerning our affairs, and to refute the abominable lies that the hired emissaries of Great Britain circulate in every corner of Europe, by which they keep up their own credit and ruin ours."[25]

Franklin recruited a Swiss journalist friend in Holland, Charles Dumas, as a secret agent for the Committee of Secret Correspondence to collect intelligence and run propaganda operations in Europe. Among his activities, Dumas "planted stories in a Dutch newspaper, *Gazette de Leide*, intended to give the United States a favorable rating in the Dutch credit markets."[26] Soon, the U.S. had secret agents in Spain, Portugal, Berlin and Tuscany.[27]

The American way of propaganda

America's success in the Revolution can be largely attributed to the extremely well fought war of ideas, proving indisputably that the many tools of statecraft – diplomacy, public diplomacy, propaganda, counterpropaganda, political warfare, and psychological warfare – have been an integral part of America's strength since the nation's origin. The founders' strategy in this respect was simple: Relentlessly express the best about the American cause and the worst about the enemy by almost any means possible. This, naturally, is not always a positive and gentle undertaking, calling into question whether such actions are consistent with the American ethos. Who better to look to for the answer than America's founding fathers, who provided the nation and the world with the first principles in the Declaration of Independence and the Constitution. Through both words and deeds, the founders endowed their successors with the diplomatic and political tools necessary to promote and defend the nation's interests around the world. Those tools, properly used, meant the margin of victory for America's first strategic hearts-and-minds campaign: They provided life-saving ways of achieving military objectives by political means – and hold the key to future success against a constantly transforming, unconventional, and ruthless global adversary.[28]

Notes

---

[1] United States Information Agency (USIA) definition, cited by USIA Alumni Association, on its PublicDiplomacy.org Website, accessed 21 November 2005. Public diplomacy has many variations, according to the government agency involved, as well as to independent observers and practitioners.

[2] Political warfare, according to a National Defense University publication, is "the use of political means to compel an opponent to do one's will, political being understood to describe purposeful intercourse between peoples and governments affecting national survival and advantage. Political war may be combined with violence, economic pressure, subversion, and diplomacy, but its chief aspect is the use of words, images, and idea, commonly known, according to context, as propaganda and political warfare." Paul A. Smith, *On Political War* (National Defense University, 1989), p. 3.

[3] Joint pubs 1-02, Department of Defense *Dictionary of Military and Associated Terms* (1994)

[4] John K. Alexander, *Samuel Adams: America's Revolutionary Politician* (Rowland & Littlefield, 2004), p. 12.

[5] Samuel Adams, letter to Richard Henry Lee, March [21], 1775, Samuel Adams Papers, Lenox Library; a shorter text is in Force, *American Archives*, 4th ser., vol. ii., p. 176; portions of the letter are printed in W. V. Wells, *Life of Samuel Adams*, vol. ii., pp. 256, 257, 281.

[6] Alexander recounts Adams' political maneuvering throughout his book. In his critical 1935 biography, heavily sources with primary materials, John C. Miller shows Adams as a skilled backdoor political maneuverer. See John C. Miller, *Samuel Adams: Pioneer in Propaganda* (Stanford University Press, 1966; reprint of Little, Brown edition of 1936), *passim.*

[7] Gen. Thomas Gage, "A Proclamation," *Philadelphia Evening Post,* June 14, 1775, pp. 1, 2, and 3. This document is in the author's personal collection.

[8] Samuel Adams had more of a role in authoring the Declaration of Independence, both intellectually and operationally, than many historians credit. Though Jefferson physically wrote the Declaration, much of the wording is from Samuel Adams, who had been using the rhetoric for a decade or more. Rep. Richard Henry Lee of Virginia, a close Adams ally who was considered as radical as the Bostonian, introduced the resolution for the Continental Congress to declare independence while Adams, seeking unanimity, tried to limit dissent. Alexander, pp. 154-155.
Lee introduced the resolution on June 7, 1776. Congress, under the presidency of Adams protégé John Hancock, established a panel comprised of Benjamin Franklin of Pennsylvania, Robert Livingston of New York, Roger Sherman of Connecticut, and Thomas Jefferson of Virginia to write the declaration. Jefferson, at age 32, was a compromise member. Fellow Virginian Lee was considered too militant, while the other, Benjamin Harrison, was too conservative for Lee's supporters. Some saw Samuel Adams in one of Jefferson's writings, and while the young Virginian was very quiet, he privately shared Adams' sentiments. John Adams persuaded Jefferson to join the committee because he was a Virginian and because "you can write ten

times better than I can." A. J. Langguth, *Patriots: The Men Who Started the American Revolution* (Simon & Schuster, 1988), pp. 344-345.

[9] Benjamin Franklin, "Rules by whick a Great Empire may be reduced to a Small One," *The Public Advertiser* (London), 11 September 1773, in Walter Isaacson, ed., *A Benjamin Franklin Reader* (Simon & Schuster, 2003), pp. 240-248.

[10] Continental Congress, "Declaration of the Causes and Necessity of Taking Up Arms," 7 July 1775, from Library of Congress.

[11] George Washington, "To the Inhabitants of Canada," September 6, 1775, in *George Washington: A Collection,* comp. and ed. W. B. Allen (Indianapolis: Liberty Fund, 1988).

[12] Central Intelligence Agency, "Intelligence and the War of Independence," undated. Electronic version accessed on CIA Website at: http://www.cia.gov/cia/publications/warindep/frames.html.

[13] Philip M. Taylor, Munitions of the Mind: A History of Propaganda from the Ancient World to the Present Day (Manchester University Press, 1990, 2003), pp. 134, 135-136.

[14] Eric Niderost, "Revolutionary Spymaster: Benjamin Franklin," *American History,* February 2006, p. 56.

[15] G.J.A. O'Toole, "Intrigue in Paris," in Edmond R. Thompson, ed., *Secret New England: Spies of the American Revolution* (Provincial Press, 2001), pp. 68-69.

[16] Langguth, pp. 325-326.

[17] O'Toole, p. 71.

[18] Ibid., p. 67.

[19] Langguth, 433-434.

[20] Taylor, 140.

[21] O'Toole, pp. 77-78.

[22] In October, 1769, the Boston Town Meeting approved a long essay that Samuel Adams principally authored, titled "An Appeal to the World; or a Vindication of the Town of Boston, from Many False and Malicious Aspersions" that the royally appointed governor of Massachusetts had been reporting to the crown.

[23] Alexander, 77-86.

[24] Niderost, p. 54.

[25] Taylor, p. 141.

[26] CIA, "Intelligence in the War for Independence."

[27] O'Toole, p. 75.

2

What "Strategic" Public Diplomacy Is

CARNES LORD

Public diplomacy is so fundamental to defending and spreading the ideas of America that on the first day of the nation's existence in 1776, the Continental Congress twice appealed to world opinion in the Declaration of Independence. Oddly, more than two centuries would pass before public diplomacy would return as a central component of a national strategy to subdue a foreign foe.

After World War II, when the U.S. found itself faced with an ideological opponent that it could not fight with military means, public diplomacy became an important part of the American defensive arsenal. It become a core component of national strategy in the 1980s, when President Ronald Reagan employed public diplomacy as a weapon of first resort not to defend against Soviet expansionism, but to defeat the Soviet Union as an empire.

Public diplomacy has many meanings, but for the purposes of introduction, we will use the official State Department definition from the height of the offensive against the Soviets: "Public diplomacy refers to government-sponsored programs intended to inform or influence public opinion in other countries; its chief instruments are publications, motion pictures, cultural exchanges, radio and television."[1]

There is in this definition, however, a (perhaps calculated) ambiguity that points to a long-standing uncertainty over the nature of public diplomacy. To inform – or to influence? The first alternative implies an approach to international communication not far removed from the venerable "public affairs" function of government agencies, or indeed from the commercial media. The second, however, underlines public diplomacy's character as a strategic instrument of national policy. It is important to understand properly the term "strategic" in this context. The practice of "spinning" the news to create immediate benefit for individuals or organizations (politicians or corporations, for example) is a well-known aspect of the contemporary media environment. Public diplomacy is too often confused with such essentially tactical manipulation of the interpretation of events.

Though it is indeed concerned with placing the United States and its policies in a favorable light, public diplomacy achieves its most important effects not by this kind of manipulation, but rather by the cumulative impact of its presentation of news and other information or interpretative commentary over time. Public diplomacy is therefore perfectly compatible with a straightforward approach to presenting the news that is not very different from what many would regard as the model provided by the commercial media. It differs from that model by tailoring the information it provides to the needs and concerns of particular audiences, and by engaging in proactive and sustained efforts to shape foreign perceptions and attitudes in ways supportive of American interests and policy.

After the collapse of the Soviet Union in 1991, many in Washington felt that America's venerable public diplomacy machinery had outlived its mission and could be scaled back significantly in its operations and levels of funding. The 1990's saw consistently stagnant or declining budgets for the United States Information Agency (USIA) and the various U.S. international broadcasters. So-called surrogate broadcasting to Eastern Europe came under particular pressure, as three services (the Polish, Czech, and Hungarian) of Radio Free Europe/Radio Liberty (RFE/RL) were soon abolished and others reduced sharply.

In 1998, in one of the most dramatic bureaucratic reorganizations within the U.S. government in decades, and with strong bipartisan leadership, USIA was formally abolished. While the State Department absorbed most of USIA's functions and personnel, it soon became evident that State was far from wholly committed to the public diplomacy mission, and significant capabilities were eroded or lost both in Washington and the field. Moreover, White House (above all, presidential) involvement in public diplomacy, which had reached a postwar peak under Reagan, declined markedly under George H. W. Bush and virtually disappeared in the Clinton years.

During the presidency of George W. Bush, this situation did not change appreciably, in spite of the rise of a new ideological challenge to the United States and its allies in the form of Islamist terrorism and the nation's interventions in Afghanistan and Iraq. Both the Pentagon and the State Department launched promising initiatives that for various reasons proved abortive. The White House created a new Office of Global Communications that brought a measure of improved coordination to the U.S. government response to media coverage of the terror war, but the scope and intensity of this effort left much to be desired. The office was run more like a domestic public relations campaign than a real global communications shop, and was quietly abandoned. Several high-visibility broadcasting initiatives directed at the Arab world proved both expensive and of dubious strategic benefit, while existing broadcasting capabilities were attrited. Interagency cooperation in the public diplomacy arena, rarely smooth, suffered debilitating setbacks as a result of the open warfare between Defense and State that complicated U.S. policy toward Iraq, and was never effectively managed by the White House; at the time of this writing, it remains for all practical purposes in suspended animation. Finally, few senior administration officials, including the president himself, showed much interest in the public diplomacy instrument. The post of under secretary of state for public diplomacy underwent a succession of occupants punctuated by long vacancies in between, and never broke out from being a creature of the recalcitrant bureaucracy.

This cumulative neglect and mismanagement, coupled with occasional spectacular gaffes (perhaps most notably, the president's use of the term "crusade" in the context of the terror war, Secretary Rumsfeld's distinction between "old" and "new" Europe, and a stream of unfortunate pronouncements from the State Department's own public diplomacy leadership) and the fallout from the Iraq war that itself lacked a coherent communication strategy in its planning and execution, have arguably contributed in a major way to a disastrous decline in the image and reputation of the United States around the world.

Since the abolition of USIA, public diplomacy alone among the elements of our national security policy lacks a core institutional base, an established infrastructure of education and training, a stable cadre of policy-level officials with recognized career tracks, a generally accepted doctrine, or roles and missions that national decision makers and the public agree with and accept. Not coincidentally, it tends to be chronically underfunded, and much of the inadequate resources is misspent, misallocated, or otherwise wasted. Given all this, it can hardly be surprising that public diplomacy has great difficulty sustaining itself and being effective in the absence of high-level political attention.

Further, public diplomacy operates in a uniquely challenging domestic environment in the United States, one centrally shaped by the fundamental hostility of the commercial media and much of the general culture toward any government involvement in the management of information. This situation is only aggravated by the fact that a large percentage of those who operate or oversee public diplomacy organizations are in fact journalists or identify strongly with the profession and its characteristic outlook – and not necessarily with the strategic approach and sense of mission that real public diplomacy requires. Public diplomacy is necessarily in the position of competing with the commercial media and tends to measure itself according to standards prevailing there, which have little to do with the strategic requirements of the United States. This imperative in turn creates tensions with policy officials elsewhere in the government, and at the extreme makes it necessary to raise the question of whether public diplomacy is a business the government should really be in at all. This question seems increasingly legitimate in an era of rapidly expanding global communications and increasing openness in most societies to multiple sources of information.

The lamentable condition of American public diplomacy today is widely acknowledged. A raft of studies and reports over the last several years by a variety of official, semi-official, and independent bodies has told a broadly similar story of institutional ineffectiveness, lack of strategic direction, and insufficient resources.[2] Prior to September 11, the Bush Administration's top defense agenda was to force a revolutionary transformation upon an often unwilling and adversarial bureaucracy. Few dispute the need to continue the defense transformation process today. But it took 9/11 to prompt the elected leadership of the nation to summon the political will to make the most far-reaching changes in the national security bureaucracy in more than half a century in order to enhance the security of the American homeland in the face of the terrorist threat. At the present time, a similar national commitment to institutional change seems to have emerged in the area of intelligence.

However, such a commitment does not exist in the area of public diplomacy, or in the area of diplomacy, period. There are a number of reasons for this, but two are critical. Not only is there no real consensus among practitioners or critics of American public diplomacy as to what needs to be done to fix it, but the nature of the pathologies afflicting it are themselves not well understood. In what follows, we offer an analysis of the key problems that limit the effectiveness of American public diplomacy today, with some suggestions for solving them.

On the utility of public diplomacy

It may be helpful to begin by stating the case for the utility of public diplomacy as a strategic instrument of American statecraft today.

The unprecedented dominance of American military power throughout the world after the end of the Cold War makes it easy enough to underestimate the importance of other instruments of traditional statecraft, or for that matter the global impact of elements of our national power not generally thought of in such terms. Education, science and technology, and popular culture fall into this last category. Joseph Nye coined the term "soft power" to designate aspects of American power not encompassed by military force or the economy, and made the case for its relative importance.[3] This concept evolved into what Nye and others call "smart power." Americans will be quick to acknowledge the power of advertising in today's commercialized world, even as we are perfectly aware of the limitations of advertising in terms both of the superficiality of the message and the credibility of the source. The United States "advertises" itself to the world both directly, through public diplomacy, and indirectly, through the impact of aspects of American life that the government itself controls little if at all – especially popular culture in all its dimensions, but also the American political system and tradition. While it is admittedly difficult to measure this impact, there is no question that it can be at least as powerful as bombs or dollars, the harder coin of U.S. international influence.

Clearly, care has to be taken not to oversell the virtues of public diplomacy. In the twentieth century, the unprecedented scope and success of Nazi and Soviet propaganda for a time convinced many social scientists and other observers in the West that state-sponsored information programs could be dramatically effective in shaping not only the political environment both domestically and abroad but ultimately human nature itself. That totalitarian propaganda could persuade its own citizens that "war is peace" and "ignorance is strength" – the mantras of the Ministry of Truth in George Orwell's classic novel *1984* – seemed not at all implausible. But ordinary persons would prove more resistant to propaganda even in closed or totalitarian societies than had been initially supposed, as various popular uprisings against Communist rule in Eastern Europe throughout the 1950s, vibrant dissident movements, clandestine samizdat literature and essays, and underground jazz and rock cultures clearly attested. The thirst for the forbidden in political theocracies like Iran and Saudi Arabia manifests itself today through satellite dishes and online linkups with expatriate websites in California.

At the same time, there are many reasons for thinking that the impact of public diplomacy during the Cold War was greater than many in the West even today seem prepared to admit. Indeed, an excellent case can be made that the peaceful ending of the Cold War had a great deal to do with the cumulative impact of Western broadcasting and other public diplomacy programs targeting the East Bloc. The loss of faith in Communism as an ideology that was so obvious not only among the mass of the people but even among the very functionaries of the Communist system itself, unarguably played a key role in the lack of serious resistance to the revolution from above launched in the Soviet Union in the mid-1980s by President Mikhail Gorbachev.

Propaganda versus public diplomacy

Perhaps ironically, part of the secret of the West's success in the decades-long war of ideas between Communism and democratic capitalism lies precisely in its gradual but finally decisive rejection of the tone, style, and approach of classic "propaganda" and its replacement by what has come to be known (since the mid 1960s) as "public diplomacy." Some will say that this is a distinction without a difference, and that the term "public diplomacy" is simply a euphemism to disguise what remains a fundamentally sordid business of manipulation and deception. This is to misunderstand fundamentally the reality of the issue we are dealing with. The nub of the case is nicely stated by Aristotle in his *Rhetoric*, the oldest treatise on this subject and one that is still worth reading: "The things that are truer and better are more susceptible to reasoned argument and more persuasive, generally speaking."

The fact of the matter is that the argument for Western-style liberal democracy was and remains a stronger one than the argument for Nazism, Communism, or radical Islamism. This means that public diplomacy need not rely on distortion and manipulation of inconvenient facts to achieve its strategic effect. Much of the power of contemporary public diplomacy in the West can be traced precisely to its known commitment to convey the truth of world events even at some occasional tactical cost to the conveyor. Thus the central importance for American public diplomacy practitioners is maintaining the "credibility" of their programs – and the success they have generally enjoyed in facing down occasional interference in them by policy officials. By contrast, Soviet information efforts were critically hampered until the end not only by a filter of ideological language increasingly remote from the real world, but by a routine resort to classic propaganda techniques laden with what Soviet tradecraft knew as "disinformation."

Arguments against public diplomacy

Two arguments are sometimes made nowadays to disparage public diplomacy as a tool of statecraft. One is that the proliferation of channels of overseas communication in the world today, coupled with the opening up of formerly closed societies in the wake of the fall of the Soviet empire, have essentially made obsolete the information programs of Western governments.

The second is that at the end of the day the source of problems for the United States in its relationships abroad is not what the nation is or says, but what it does; hence its attention and resources should be concentrated on fixing poor policies, not on rhetorically defending them. In the context of the current low standing of the U.S. in public opinion in the Arab and Muslim world, for example, it is frequently asserted that nothing can truly remedy this problem apart from a basic shift in U.S. policy toward the Arab-Israeli conflict in a direction more favorable to the claims of the Palestinians.

There is no simple answer to this latter argument. At a minimum, it is obviously important to consider the impact of particular policies on public opinion abroad before they are adopted: as USIA Director Edward R. Murrow once famously phrased it after having to deal with the failed Bay of Pigs invasion of Cuba in 1961, "If they want me in on the crash landings, I better damned well be in on the take-offs."[4] It is fair to say this has never been done in any systematic way within the U.S. government. On the other hand, public diplomacy surely cannot be allowed to wag the policy dog if the policy is merely unpopular but sound and necessary. And while it is possible that there may be policy choices so misguided that nothing useful can be said in defense or mitigation of them, this is surely the exception rather than the rule.

Decisions generally have contexts that are more transparent to American policymakers than to foreigners on their receiving end; these contexts can be identified and explained. In other cases, it will be a question of making appropriate distinctions, signaling intentions, and providing assurances. Public diplomacy, like diplomacy itself, has an important role to play in smoothing the inevitable rough edges of a nation's foreign policy.

In the Arab-Israeli example, a good case can be made that the United States has in fact committed a major strategic error over the years in essentially conceding the public diplomacy field to those hostile to Israeli policies, while allowing those forces to portray the U.S. as unfairly biased toward Israel if not being its tool. Meanwhile, the U.S. has done little to showcase the large amount of development and humanitarian aid it has given the Palestinians. Correcting false perceptions has to be seen as an indispensable piece of our larger war on terror.

At the same time, it has to be admitted that public diplomacy is most effective when it is closely tied to policy – that is, when it is seen as an integral element of a larger policy initiative or campaign, not simply a *post hoc* rationalization for something an administration has decided to do on other grounds. This is a crucial lesson of some of the signal successes of American public diplomacy in the past (for example, its nuclear and arms control public diplomacy in the early 1980s), one too often overlooked in current discussions of these issues.

As to the first argument, there can be little question that proliferating global communications, and in particular growing access to satellite radio and television, cable TV and the Internet, are creating a very different and in many ways less welcoming environment for American and other government broadcasting services abroad. The collapse of the East Bloc greatly weakened if not entirely negated the rationale underlying Radio Free Europe and Radio Liberty historically – that they function as "surrogate" broadcasting operations in the absence of free domestic media in the target countries. But those who argued for the radios' closure were not thinking in strategic terms. They seemed to be caught up in the optimism of a democratizing Russia while dismissing, even scorning, those who were concerned that Russia had not shed many of its totalitarian institutions and attitudes. They watched silently, if they watched at all, as a former KGB officer took power and began systematically to emasculate the country's free press. The surrogate radios would soon be needed again.

In the case of all U.S. broadcasters, the availability of CNN and other sources of more or less objective news around the world raises a legitimate question as to the extent to which the reportage of news as such should continue to be seen as government broadcasters' priority mission. Having said this, two points need to be made. First, foreigners look and have always looked to U.S. international broadcasters – particularly but not only the Voice of America – not merely as sources of news but as an authoritative guide to understanding American intentions and actions. This will not change with increasing competition from commercial media. Second, the commercial media for the most part lack any incentive to invest large resources in addressing foreigners in their own languages. Nor do they invest in programming about the less sensationalist and more esoteric issues that the U.S. government can properly and usefully address with foreign audiences. They value their full editorial independence, which in American journalistic culture tends to be adversarial – not a trait that necessarily advances the national interest when a particular message needs to reach the world. Few can argue that the voice of the American government should be placed in the hands of Ted Turner or Rupert Murdoch. U.S. international broadcasters will and should have the capability to reach not only a global English-speaking elite (as CNN does) but mass audiences everywhere.

Problems of definition and scope

It was suggested earlier that it is a fundamental mistake to equate "public diplomacy" as practiced by the United States and others today with "propaganda" in the classic sense that term acquired in the practice of Nazi Germany or the Soviet Union. Yet the problem of defining or characterizing public diplomacy hardly ends there. Central to an effective public diplomacy effort is a clear understanding of the scope of public diplomacy and its relationship to kindred disciplines, but the United States has never had anything approaching an operationally adequate doctrine that provides this. The result has been continuing uncertainty and confusion over the roles and missions of public diplomacy and the institutional responsibilities that flow from them.

The most commonly invoked terms bearing on the central meaning of public diplomacy are "information" and "communications." Both of these terms have become seriously overworked in recent years, and in any case do not fully capture this meaning. "Psychological warfare," a term once used virtually synonymously with "propaganda," is now unfashionable if not obsolete; but the term "psychological operations" (PSYOP) remains in use as the technical expression for communications activities carried out by uniformed military personnel under combat conditions. PSYOP tends to be tactical or, as its name implies, operational in nature and therefore not strategic. "Public affairs" is another bureaucratic term of art for the public relations activities of government agencies, with their principal focus being the handling of the domestic media. And finally, there is the term "public diplomacy" itself, which is suggestive of a further dimension of the field, one that has been very inadequately discussed or analyzed.

The idea of diplomacy, whether carried out publicly or in private, involves not simply words but actions – and actions that are designed not simply to inform or communicate but to have certain measurable political effects. Public diplomacy frequently addresses a generic global audience, yet it may also be specially targeted. Public diplomacy directed toward well-identified political groups within or across national boundaries – women, youth, religious or business leaders, legislators, political parties, and the like – and generally involving face-to-face dealings with them is sometimes referred to as international "political action." We adopt this usage here for want of anything better, in spite of its lingering association with certain categories of covert intelligence operations, and with domestic political activity among private citizens and politicians.

Finally, public diplomacy is now generally considered to incorporate the mission often referred to as "educational and cultural affairs," distinguished from its other missions by a longer-term and less policy-relevant focus. There continue to be those who view educational and cultural affairs as sharply distinct from public diplomacy as a strategic instrument of government policy, and would prefer to have this aspect of public diplomacy handled by a separate agency or even entirely devolved to the private sector.

But the fallacy of a sharp separation between educational and cultural affairs and "policy" is if anything even clearer today than it was in the 1970's. In the context of a conflict that is not merely ideological in nature but a "clash of civilizations," in Samuel Huntington's well-known phrase, education and culture are front and center in a way they were not during the Cold War. Hence the idea that education and culture represent an arena for essentially non-political interaction with adversaries simply cannot be sustained today, and it becomes difficult to see what advantage is gained from assigning a separate organization to oversee that arena. This is by no means to argue that educational and cultural public diplomacy must in all cases be carried out by a government agency; indeed, there may be very great advantages in giving the private sector the lead in many of them. It is only to argue that there is a compelling argument for retaining a measure of policy control over these activities. (Editor's note: John Lenczowski treats cultural diplomacy at length in the fourth chapter of this volume.)

"Strategic communications" is a term that originated recently in the Department of Defense (DoD) as part of a larger effort to improve coordination between military PSYOP, public diplomacy, and public affairs.[5] Problems have bedeviled DoD in this area for many years, but became acute in the context of the terror war and most recently the war in Iraq, where the communications component of coalition post-combat operations has generally and rightly been viewed as disastrous. Again, issues of definition and jurisdiction have been key. Public diplomacy has never had a well-defined, permanent niche within the defense bureaucracy, and existing PSYOP doctrine and practice tends to blur the distinction between these functions. Meanwhile, State Department officials have expressed concern about Pentagon encroachment on their diplomatic turf, or on the militarization of public diplomacy.

Public diplomacy verses public affairs

What precisely is the distinction between public diplomacy and public affairs? In the most general terms, public diplomacy may be said to be more strategic and proactive, public affairs more tactical and reactive. Public affairs is mainly concerned with domestic audiences, and sees as its highest priority maintaining a good press for its organization and leaders, and good relations with those who write and announce the news. Therefore, the care and feeding of the domestic media tends to preoccupy it. Rarely does it seek to shape the news in any sustained or strategic way, given the sensitivity of the media to anything perceived as attempted manipulation, though it will certainly cultivate and favor individual reporters and seek to shape their coverage of stories on a day-to-day basis (sometimes through the release or leak of privileged information).

Public diplomacy by contrast is concerned with international audiences. It too is concerned with breaking news and media coverage, but its focus is the foreign press (though this function has sometimes tended to blur with the domestic media). But, at least in theory, public diplomacy is interested more in the strategic impact of the news on foreign audiences than in providing news for its own sake; it is therefore willing to tailor its news coverage in some measure to the interests, needs, and limitations of its diverse audiences. In addition, of course, it provides various kinds of thematic programming designed, again, for longer-term or strategic effect.

Having said this, a case can also be made that this situation is in fact not ideal, and that public affairs itself needs a strategic component. The arguments that apply to public diplomacy as a strategic instrument for addressing foreign audiences also apply to public affairs in its relationship to domestic audiences, at least to the extent that the American media cannot be relied on to satisfy fully the government's requirements in this regard. One must reach back more than two decades to find such an integrated strategy in place. In the 1980's, the Reagan administration created within the State Department an "Office of Latin American Public Diplomacy" of which the primary function was to inform and educate the broad public concerning the threat to American interests in the hemisphere posed by the Soviet-backed Sandinista regime in Nicaragua and its proxy, the Marxist FMLN guerrilla movement in El Salvador. This effort was much criticized at the time as an improper if not actually illegal intervention in the public or (more to the point) the congressional debate then underway on these issues. Yet at a time when wild charges intended to undermine U.S. policy were being generated by organizations of very dubious credibility, some fronting for the Sandinistas, FMLN and others, and then retailed uncritically in the American press and in Congress, it is not at all clear that the government should have been enjoined from defending itself through such means. Shaping domestic public opinion to confront unrecognized threats to the national security or to accept other desirable if unpopular measures (consider the Carter administration's efforts to "sell" the American people on the Panama Canal treaty or the Clinton White House's promotion of multilateral intervention in the Balkans) seems a perfectly legitimate activity, and indeed, a positive obligation of government, especially when needed to counter foreign propaganda.

Public diplomacy and traditional diplomacy

Let us return to the question of the relation between public diplomacy and diplomacy proper. To repeat what was said earlier, public diplomacy is most effective when it is closely integrated with policy, rather than being simply an afterthought or *post hoc* justification of policy. Public diplomacy can and should be supported by diplomacy. Ambassadors, for example, can lend their personal presence and voice in their particular countries to public diplomacy campaigns; diplomatic demarches can be crafted to reinforce in private with foreign governments the arguments made in public statements emanating from officials in Washington. (Moreover, though this point is not often enough made, public diplomacy can support diplomacy. A difficult negotiation can sometimes be made easier by ratcheting up public pressure on a foreign government through public diplomacy channels or the domestic media.) At times in the past, American administrations have launched diplomatic initiatives whose fundamental purpose was to affect international opinion rather than to reach agreement. Dwight Eisenhower, who was keenly attuned to this dimension of diplomacy through his involvement in psychological warfare during World War II, launched the Atoms for Peace and Open Skies initiatives in the 1950's primarily for reasons of psychological-political strategy, as a way of gaining the moral high ground relative to the Soviet Union and enhancing the standing of the United States in the contest with the Soviets in the Third World.

This leads to a further point concerning the direct role of the White House and the president himself in public diplomacy. Presidents are a very important public diplomacy asset. Even when presidents address domestic audiences, as they do most of the time, they are covered by foreigners, so that they and their speechwriters need to keep in mind the sensitivities of foreign audiences. Occasions for addressing foreign audiences directly (for example, interviews with the foreign press or speeches given on overseas trips) should be sought out and used for strategic public diplomacy purposes. Further, what presidents do often matters as much as what they say. Presidents engage in a varied array of symbolic behaviors (laying of wreaths, reviewing troops, and the like) that need to be seen as an integral part of American public diplomacy. Reagan's extraordinary speech in France on the fortieth anniversary of the Normandy invasion exemplifies these too often forgotten or missed opportunities.

A final point concerns the relationship between public diplomacy and American "soft power" generally. There are certain activities of the United States government that clearly are beyond the purview of public diplomacy in its most expansive sense, and yet are important assets in the projection of American influence around the world. Humanitarian operations and economic and development assistance are foremost among these. The Agency for International Development (USAID) has in recent years become increasingly sensitive to the psychological impact of its work and begun producing public diplomacy-style materials, and it is active in areas that border public diplomacy closely, especially assistance to education programs abroad. It is probably too difficult and unnecessary to try to draw precise lines of demarcation between such activities and public diplomacy; but it is certainly true that too little attention has been paid in the past to integrating all such issues in a single bureaucratic framework or even a strategic vision.

Problems of organization: The bureaucratic context

Since the outbreak of World War II, there has probably been more instability in the strategic communications sector of the American national security bureaucracy than in any other. During the war itself, long-running and bitter disputes over roles and missions marked relations between the three organizations with responsibilities in this area, the Office of War Information, the Office of Strategic Services (forerunner of the CIA), and the psychological warfare branch of the Army. A residual information service was kept after the war as a semi-autonomous bureau of the State Department, but the Voice of America came close to being abolished. With the outbreak of the Korean War, interest in public diplomacy revived within the Truman administration and in Congress, but there was little consensus on how it should be organized. In 1953, after much internal study, the United States Information Agency was created by Eisenhower, but largely because of the reluctance of Secretary of State John Foster Dulles to have his department run what he saw as an operational or programmatic function. The Voice of America joined the new agency, but the education and cultural affairs function was rather illogically retained by State. Meanwhile, the newly formed CIA had set out to create its own broadcasting empire with the creation of Radio Free Europe (1950) and Radio Liberty (1953) as "surrogate" radios targeted at Eastern Europe and the Soviet Union respectively, and in addition sponsored an array of political action campaigns directed against the growing threat of Soviet Communism. The military too maintained a foothold in this arena, though its psychological warfare capabilities had declined greatly from their wartime heights.

The involvement in public diplomacy of a variety of very different and potentially competing organizations raised the question of coordination, and hence in particular the question of the White House role in public diplomacy. As a Defense Department official lamented at the time, "Our psychological operating agencies are like bodies of troops without a commander and staff. Not having been told what to do or where to go, but too dynamic to stand still, the troops have marched in all directions." In response to the Korean War, the Truman administration created a Psychological Strategy Board under the auspices of the recently established National Security Council (NSC) to organize and spearhead this effort, but it was able to make only limited headway, and was abolished near the beginning of the Eisenhower administration. The reorganized NSC system of the Eisenhower years included an Operations Coordinating Board that was assigned public diplomacy and related tools as part of its responsibility for interagency coordination of foreign and national security policy generally, but its public diplomacy focus seems gradually to have dissipated. While journalist Edward R. Murrow is remembered as a great USIA leader under President John F. Kennedy, crystallizing the ethos of public diplomacy as we know it today, even some supporters acknowledge that he "never fully mastered the bureaucracy of public diplomacy."[6] Only in the Reagan administration was an effort later made to reestablish an interagency coordinating mechanism for public diplomacy under NSC auspices, but again with only limited success. The problem remains a fundamental one that must be addressed in any rethinking of the public diplomacy architecture of the U.S. government.

The 1970's again saw major organizational change. Following the exposure of the CIA connection to RFE and RL on the floor of the U.S. Senate in 1971 and the resulting threat to the radios' continued existence, a new oversight mechanism, the presidentially-appointed Board for International Broadcasting (BIB), was created by Congress in 1973. In 1976, the two radios and their respective corporate boards were merged into a single entity, RFE/RL. Then it was the turn of USIA. In 1977, in the wake of a number of outside studies of the organization of the foreign affairs agencies of the government, the Carter administration decided to merge the State Department's Bureau of Education and Cultural Affairs (ECA) into USIA, while also changing the name of the parent agency to the U.S. International Communications Agency. At the same time, the administration also promulgated a new mission statement for the agency. It was enjoined first "to tell the world about our society and policies – in particular our commitment to cultural diversity and individual liberty," and second, "to tell ourselves about the world, so as to enrich our own culture as well as to give us the understanding to deal effectively with problems among nations." This so-called "second mandate" was a startling innovation that seemed to turn on its head the entire purpose of public diplomacy and to call for the establishment of an altogether new bureaucratic entity to carry it out. Though its polling data have been useful to monitor public opinion for U.S. policymakers, in practice, the second mandate amounted to very little.

In the most influential of the studies just mentioned, the report of the so-called Stanton Commission, several recommendations were made which, though not adopted at the time, would shape in important ways the future course of the debate on these issues. Going back to fundamentals, the Stanton Commission identified the core missions of public diplomacy as follows: exchange of persons, general information, policy information, and policy advice. It then pinpointed as the key problem "the assignment, to an agency separate from and independent of the State Department, of the task of interpreting U.S. foreign policy and advising in its formulation." It also noted "the ambiguous positioning of the Voice of America at the crossroads of journalism and diplomacy."

This analysis led the commission to the findings that (1) USIA should be abolished and replaced with a new, quasi-independent Information and Cultural Affairs Agency which would "combine the cultural and 'general information' programs" of both USIA and State's ECA bureau;" (2) State should establish a new "Office of Policy Information, headed by a deputy undersecretary, to administer all programs which articulate and explain U.S. foreign policy;" and (3) the Voice of America should be set up as an independent federal agency under its own board of overseers.

These Stanton Commission recommendations responded to two very different if not contradictory requirements. The first was a perceived need to enhance the "credibility" of American public diplomacy by increasing its distance from the government. The second was to fix what the Commission saw as an artificial and ultimately dysfunctional organizational separation between the State Department, the agency responsible for formulating U.S. policy, and USIA insofar as it was responsible for defending U.S. policy and disseminating it abroad. In a sense, this reform too was intended to enhance the credibility of U.S. overseas information programs, but it would do so by narrowing their distance from government policy, not increasing it. Henceforth, the State Department would speak for itself – and thereby necessarily assume greater responsibility for the accuracy, timeliness and effectiveness of its information efforts, or so it was hoped.

As it turned out, the next stage of public diplomacy reorganization in the mid-1990's, culminating in the merger of USIA with the State Department in 1998, largely embraced the Stanton Commission approach. Though its vision for USIA itself was not realized, the information functions of the old USIA were indeed folded into State, while the Congress created a new Undersecretary for Public Diplomacy and Public Affairs designed to give public diplomacy new visibility and clout within the department. At the same time, significant steps were being taken toward autonomy for U.S. international broadcasters. Under the International Broadcasting Act of 1994, a new oversight board, the Broadcasting Board of Governors (BBG), replaced the Board for International Broadcasting, and was assigned responsibility not only for RFE/RL and the more recently created surrogate radios (Radio Marti and Radio Free Asia), but for the Voice of America itself. Severing the Voice from the direct control of a policy agency was a major step.

It is certainly true that VOA had enjoyed much *de facto* autonomy when it reported to USIA; at the same time, the Secretary of State was made an *ex officio* member of the BBG, with the under secretary of state for public diplomacy physically representing the secretary. Nevertheless, the stage was now set for the eventual liberation of all U.S. overseas broadcasting from U.S. government strategic direction or control. And it soon became clear that this was indeed the direction the newly empowered BBG intended to take it.

This much abbreviated history is essential background as one tries to come to grips with the various deficiencies of American public diplomacy today, and the struggle the U.S. has had with strategy in the past. There can be little doubt that American public diplomacy is broken, both organizationally and in terms of its fundamental conceptual underpinnings. Any rethinking of public diplomacy as a strategic instrument in the global war on terror and other needs must address the problem at both of these levels. Central to the organizational dimension is the question of whether the merger of

USIA and the State Department in 1998 was a mistake and whether and how it might be undone without creating bureaucratic havoc. In the broadcasting arena, it is necessary to ask whether the turn toward greater autonomy makes sense in the context of what promises to be an extended period of quasi-war for the United States. At the same time, the U.S. must adapt from its rigid vertical hierarchies that discourage innovation and prevent the immediate anticipation and response that the Internet, global satellite television, and other information technologies require.

The Department of Defense needs as an urgent matter to sort out the precise roles and relationships of military PSYOP (strategic, operational and tactical), defense public diplomacy, and defense public affairs. Finally, the White House needs to review and redefine its own role here, for one of the chief lessons of the history of American public diplomacy is the indispensability of political leadership – and strategic thinking – from the highest levels of our government.

Notes

---

[1] U.S. Department of State, Dictionary of International Relations Terms, (1987), p. 85.

[2] See especially *US Advisory Commission on Public Diplomacy, Consolidation of USIA Into the State Department: An Assessment After One Year* (October 2000); Stephen Johnson and Helle Dale, "How to Reinvigorate US Public Diplomacy," Backgrounder No. 1645 (The Heritage Foundation, April 2003); Council on Foreign Relations Task Force, *Finding America's Voice: A Strategy for Reinvigorating U.S. Public Diplomacy* (Council on Foreign Relations, 2003); Advisory Group on Public Diplomacy for the Arab and Muslim World, *Changing Minds, Winning Peace: A New Strategic Direction for U.S. Policy Diplomacy in the Arab and Muslim World* (October 2003), *Report of the Defense Science Board Task Force on Strategic Communication* (Department of Defense, September 2004), and Public Diplomacy Council, *A Call for Action on Public Diplomacy* (The Public Diplomacy Council, January 2005)

[3] Joseph S. Nye, Jr., Soft Power: The Means to Success in World Politics (Public Affairs, 2004).

[4] Crocker Snow, Jr., "Murrow in the Public Interest: From Press Affairs to Public Diplomacy," USINFO.State.gov, April 2006. Snow is director of the Edward R. Murrow Center of Public Diplomacy at the Fletcher School, Tufts University.

[5] Defense Science Board, *Report of the Defense Science Board on Strategic Communication,* Office of the Under Secretary of Defense for Acquisition, Technology and Logistics, September 2004.
[6] Snow, op cit.

3

Public Diplomacy and Soft Power

CARNES LORD

A major factor contributing to the relative neglect of the study and practice of public diplomacy in the United States and elsewhere is the tendency to view it through the prism of the small and often under funded and otherwise marginalized agencies that are responsible for it. From this point of view, it is seen as the last and least of the various instruments of national power. Yet this reflects a fundamental misapprehension.

Public diplomacy derives much of its efficacy from the fact that it forms part of a larger whole. This larger whole encompasses not only public words but public deeds – that is to say, government policies and actions. What is more, it extends beyond the operations of government altogether, to the activities of the private sector and to society and culture at large. A great deal of the work of public diplomacy agencies consists of mobilizing and deploying private sector resources. Public diplomacy is enabled, and its effect enhanced, by the larger society and culture. At the same time, public diplomacy helps to amplify and advertise that society and culture to the world.

"Soft power," a concept popularized in recent years by political scientist Joseph Nye, is useful for understanding the larger context in which public diplomacy functions. Defined as "the ability to get what you want through attraction rather than coercion or payments," soft power means "getting others to want the outcomes that you want."[1] Soft power has been a strong suit for the United States virtually from its inception – certainly long before the country became a recognized world power in the twentieth century.

American "exceptionalism" – the nation's devotion to freedom, the rule of law, and the practice of republican government, its openness to immigrants of all races and religions, its opposition to traditional power

61

politics and imperialism – has had a great deal to do with the rise of the United States to its currently dominant global role. However, other great powers throughout history have also been adept at exploiting the advantages of soft power.   The Roman and British empires, for example, were both able to control vast territories with very limited military forces through the appeal of the civilization they spread before them and the relatively benign character of their rule.

Today, there are signs that a number of countries besides the United States are becoming more conscious of their own soft power resources and seeking more actively to take advantage of them. Perhaps the best example is the People's Republic of China, which has undertaken a major effort over the last few years to improve its image as a responsible member of the international community and to promote Chinese culture and Chinese language instruction around the world

At the same time, voices both at home and abroad have expressed concern that the United States, with its increasing reliance on unilaterally-exercised military power, is in danger of forgetting the lessons of its own past by failing to safeguard its soft power resources. Such critics call attention not only to the current low standing of the United States in public opinion in many parts of the world, particularly following its invasion of Iraq, but more fundamentally, the apparent insensitivity of the United States government to foreign perceptions of a range of current American policies – domestic, such as adhering to the death penalty, as well as international.   In particular, the United States stands accused of failing to take sufficient account of the views and interests of its traditional allies and of international institutions such as the United Nations. The result, it is argued, is what might be described as a "crisis of legitimacy" in the exercise of American power and the American global role generally.

Point of departure

Nye's book is an appropriate point of departure. *Soft Power* analyzes the relationship with public diplomacy and other instruments of national power in the contemporary context of the global war on terror and the United States' new quasi-imperial role in the Middle East. The Harvard professor and former top Pentagon official begins by rightly stressing the elusive nature of the term "power" itself. Many people, he argues, identify the exercise of power with command or coercion, but the exercise of such power immediately raises questions on the receiving end about motivation. Identifying power with measurable resources such as a large population and territory overlooks the importance of the intangibles of leadership and strategy in deploying such resources effectively. Soft power underlines the intangible dimension of power. Hard power is preeminently military or economic power, operating through threats ("sticks") or inducements ("carrots"). But,

> a country may obtain the outcomes it wants in world politics because other countries – admiring its values, emulating its example, aspiring to its level of prosperity and openness – want to follow it. In this sense, it is also important to set the agenda and attract others in world politics, and not only to force them to change by threatening military force or economic sanctions. This soft power – getting others to want the outcomes that you want – co-opts people rather than coerces them.[2]

People thus cooperate because they want to, rather than because they are forced. Submission or resistance are not products of soft power.

Soft power is not the same as influence, since men are influenced by hard power as much as they are by soft; nor is it the same as persuasion through argument. "Simply put, soft power is attractive power." This could seem to suggest that soft power is purely passive in its mode of operation; but Nye hastens to correct this impression. Soft power can also rest on "the ability to manipulate the agenda of political choices in a manner that makes others fail to express some preferences because they seem to be too unrealistic." Nye does not give a great deal of emphasis to this agenda-setting aspect of soft power, or for that matter any illustration of it; and his use of the term "manipulation" in this context conjures up a picture somewhat at odds with the notion of soft power as attraction.[3] What he seems to have in mind is the ability of the United States in particular to shape the agenda of world politics through projecting an image of societal success and responsible international leadership.

Nye identifies three broad categories of soft power: "culture," "political values," and "policies." Culture includes high culture and popular culture; both can have potent effects, but the appeal of American popular culture throughout the world probably puts it in a category of its own. The United States also enjoys valuable advantages in terms of political values, as the world's oldest constitutional democracy and an impressive, if far from perfect, showcase of good governance and the rule of law. Finally, the policies of governments, both domestically and abroad, are an obvious source of soft power. America's early commitment to religious toleration, for example, was a powerful element of its overall appeal to potential immigrants; and

American aid in the reconstruction of Europe after World War II was an advertisement both of the prosperity and the generosity of the people of the United States.

Ironically, a nation's soft power can be undermined by these same factors. American popular culture can be feared and resented in many places abroad. It can often act at cross purposes with government policies that seek to cultivate traditionalist allies in the Islamic world and elsewhere. At home, American soft power has variously been tarnished by policies such as racial segregation, the death penalty and gun control issues; abroad, recent American policies toward the global environment, the World Court and the Arab-Israeli dispute, among others, are widely said to have fostered a damaging image of reckless American "unilateralism" – a charge echoed by Nye throughout his book.

A few remarks may be added on the limitations of Nye's analysis of soft power. It can be argued that in spite of everything he has to say about the importance of culture and other societal forces not under the control of governments, Nye in the end significantly understates the contribution of these forces to national power; and this is true above all in the case of the United States. In their outstanding study *America's Inadvertent Empire*, William E. Odom and Robert Dujarric provide a more satisfying analysis of what they call "the sources of American power," emphasizing in particular the international impact of American science and technology, higher education, and media.[4] It is striking that opinion polling in different regions of the world suggests that America is most admired for its scientific and technical achievements.[5]

Also striking, and little understood is the extent to which American higher education and American scholarship outclass and dominate those of the rest of the world. The United States continues to be a magnet for foreign students and is able in this way to exert immense influence over the rising generation of intellectual and political elites throughout the world, though post-9/11 visa restrictions have unintentionally undermined higher education as a public diplomacy asset. Finally, American commercial media have penetrated foreign markets to a perhaps surprising extent.[6] Moreover, an aggregate effect of all these developments is to further cement the role of English as the dominant global language.

A second issue concerns the relationship between soft and hard power. Nye admits that this relationship is complex:

> Hard and soft power sometimes reinforce and sometimes interfere with each other. A country that courts popularity may be loath to exercise its hard power when it should, but a country that throws its weight

around without regard to its effects on its soft power may find others placing obstacles in the way of its hard power. No country likes to feel manipulated, even by soft power. At the same time... hard power can create myths of invincibility or inevitability that attract others.[7]

But it is not clear whether Nye has thought through sufficiently the ways in which hard power may be said to function like soft power – that is, to cast an aura of attraction. This is especially true in the economic area where it becomes especially difficult to distinguish between compulsion and choice in the economic decisions made by individuals or states. The American economic model is surely one of the great sources of the nation's international attractiveness (or in some quarters, opprobrium); this is quite distinct from the question of how the United States government uses its economic resources to wield power and influence over others.

In the case of military force, however, there would seem to be an important soft power dimension that calls for further analysis. Even countries that oppose U.S. policy paradoxically derive security, comfort and economic prosperity from the very military capability or presence that they so bitterly denounce. Heroic or romantic myths can strongly color the way national or transnational military forces are viewed by others, and exercise a strong attraction. Consider the flow of would-be terrorists to the banner of Al Qaeda in Iraq. They seek their status not so much in fighting for Islam, as they twist and trample Islamic laws, customs and mores; but in fighting the United States and its allies.

All of this can lead one to raise a more fundamental question concerning the adequacy of Nye's understanding of soft power in terms largely if not wholly of "attraction." Perhaps the term "influence" is better after all at capturing the overall phenomenon we are dealing with. Many French, for example, may be less attracted to the United States than they were in 1945, but this does not necessarily mean that American soft power is ineffective in France. To the extent that the widely discussed process of "globalization" is fundamentally a manifestation of American soft power, it can be argued that American soft power is inexorably shaping the behavior of peoples and governments around the world whether or not they are sympathetic to the United States – or indeed, whether or not they are fully aware of the ways in which they are being influenced.

Consider in this regard the undeniable success the United States has had in promoting democracy and societal reform in Afghanistan and Iraq, in spite of the virulent hostility of much of the region to the United States and all it stands for. Irrespective of whether they like the U.S. or agree with the occupations, most Afghans and Iraqis want

American and coalition troops to stay in their countries or, more subtly, want them to leave, but not just yet. And their vision of the political future of their countries seems largely to coincide with the American vision, not with the theocratic model offered by radical Islamism, in spite of the formidable obstacles to its implementation under current conditions.

What bearing does all of this have, then, on how we should think about public diplomacy, and in particular its role in the global war on terror? Nye argues that soft power is a more difficult instrument for governments to wield than hard power for two reasons: many of its critical resources are outside the control of governments; and soft power tends to "work indirectly by shaping the environment for policy, and sometimes takes years to produce the desired outcomes."[8] This seems broadly true. Some have held for these reasons that public diplomacy is an instrument of very limited utility. In our contemporary information age, it is commonplace to hear criticism of government-sponsored information programs as obsolete given the proliferation of commercial and other private sector media, and particularly the internet. Yet another line of argument calling into question the utility of public diplomacy is that its effect on foreign opinion is marginal in relation to the impact of a nation's foreign policy, and that current American foreign policy in particular has rendered public diplomacy essentially a futile exercise.

There can be no question that public diplomacy is limited in what it can do by itself, and that it is helped immeasurably by a diplomacy that is sensitive to its requirements. As Nye rightly indicates, diplomacy properly understood is an important source of soft power; too often, however, diplomats (and the political leaders they report to) see themselves rather as facilitators and beneficiaries of the hard power instruments of force and money. Having said this, it is probably also true that a public diplomacy that adroitly leverages the cultural resources of its society can under some circumstances afford to do without effective top cover from its nation's diplomacy.

In the 1970's, for example, when the American government pursued a policy of "détente" with the Soviet Union, U.S. public diplomacy receded in some measure in its engagement with the Eastern bloc at a political level. Yet it maintained steady pressure against the Soviets at the societal and cultural levels. For several crucial years, the population of the Soviet Union, and even elements of the ruling *nomenklatura* class, looked toward the United States as an ally to liberate them from the regime and to help them assert their national identities. The actual liberation came about after the Reagan administration designed and implemented an integrated strategy to bring a peaceful end to the Soviet

Union, through a combination of military modernization, economic pressure, public diplomacy, counterpropaganda and political warfare.[9]

The limited control that a government exercises over its soft power resources has both advantages and disadvantages. Wholly controlled public diplomacy outlets such as state broadcasting operations have the obvious advantage that they are more easily aligned with a government's policy and diplomacy. To the extent that such control is lacking or very loose, on the other hand, there may be significant net gains in terms of the "credibility" of the public diplomacy activities in question and hence their effectiveness with the intended audience.

But it is a fallacy to elevate "credibility" to the ultimate touchstone of the merits of particular public diplomacy efforts. Many people, including foreign policy elites, in countries lacking a free press have a great deal of difficulty understanding the extent to which the American media operate independently of the United States government, and are no doubt less sensitive than we tend to imagine to nuances in the formal relationship between the government as a whole and the entities that conduct its public diplomacy.

A 2005 exchange between President George W. Bush and Russian President Vladimir Putin illustrates the problem. When Bush chided Putin for cracking down on democratic movements and leaders, Putin acidly retorted that Bush had no moral authority to criticize, as he had gotten Dan Rather fired as CBS News anchorman.[10] Moreover, it is also the case that foreigners often turn to official American public diplomacy outlets not because these are credible sources of independent news, but because they want to know what the United States government thinks about issues of current concern.

While public diplomacy programs are notoriously hard to measure qualitatively and often have very indirect and long-term effects, it is easy to overstate the difficulty. Studies of American broadcasting into the Soviet bloc, and testimonials from Czech President Vaclav Havel, Polish President Lech Walesa, and Russian President Boris Yeltsin confirm that the public diplomacy efforts of the United States and its allies during the Cold War were hugely successful in creating the favorable conditions that led to the collapse of the Soviet empire in the late 1980's.

Relatively direct and short-term results produced by intensive public diplomacy campaigns include the successful American-led effort to counter the Soviet propaganda offensive against NATO's deployment of theater nuclear missiles in Europe in the early 1980's. In that instance, the Soviets deployed medium-range SS-20 ballistic missiles to threaten the Western European democracies. In response, Germany and other countries backed the U.S. deploying similar Pershing II missiles on their soil, upping the ante because the Pershings were capable of hitting Moscow. To prevent that deployment, the Soviets launched a massive active measures campaign in Europe and the United States, which, as Herbert Romerstein explains in the counterpropaganda chapter of this book, the U.S. and NATO successfully countered. The happy result: Moscow agreed to remove its missiles if the U.S. would do the same.[11]

In the area of strategic political change, American broadcasting into Soviet-occupied Europe, particularly Poland, contributed massively to the rise of the Solidarity movement there and ultimately to the collapse of the Soviet-backed regimes there and in the rest of the Warsaw Pact alliance. The extent to which the Polish service of Radio Free Europe played a virtually operational role in mobilizing the Polish resistance is still not widely understood or appreciated in America, though the documentation is extensive.[12]

Radio Liberty played a vital role inside the Soviet Union – so much so that opposition leaders in the different republics used officials at the radio as confidential advisers to plan their secession from the USSR. Many of those leaders became the presidents of their countries. So great an importance did the Czechs place on the radios that the government of post-communist President Havel gave Radio Free Europe/Radio Liberty the use of the former communist parliament building in Prague as its new global broadcasting headquarters.

Simply having ongoing electronic public diplomacy machinery in place can have decisive effects in unforeseen circumstances. At a time when some in Washington thought Radio Liberty's broadcasts into Russia had outlived their usefulness in the late 1980's, reform-minded Russians hosted the first-ever Radio Liberty bureau in Moscow. Radio Liberty then was perhaps the single most trusted source of news and information in Russia. When the KGB led a coup against Gorbachev in August 1991, Radio Liberty was the main place where people turned for information. In the early hours of the coup, dozens of correspondents and stringers fanned across Moscow to report on troop movements, barricades and other activity, and played up the young people – including troops – camped out in the streets to defy the junta. RL correspondents in other Russian cities reported on troop movements, including the special units flown in from outside Moscow. Civilian resisters to the coup, from the mayor of Moscow to the Russian president, relied on the American radio to spread their message, help inspire and organize resistance, network resisters across their continent, and give people hope. President Yeltsin openly thanked Radio Liberty for its role in helping Russia put down the coup.

Too soon for despair

It can certainly be argued that it is much too soon to despair of American public diplomacy efforts in the Middle East and in the global terror war more generally. For one thing, the United States has been very late getting into this game. But it is also essential to realize that the long isolation of the peoples of the Arab world from the global information grid is only now coming to an end, and with effects little short of spectacular.

In spite of all the problems it has caused the United States, the Al Jazeera satellite television operation and its increasingly numerous imitators have brought about an irreversible revolution in the regional media environment. In the long run, this revolution seems certain to prove a net benefit to the United States. Already, Al Jazeera's constant challenge to established authority throughout the Arab world, its extensive coverage of the Iraqi elections, its willingness to give air time to Israeli officials, and even more significantly, the serious attention it is now giving to covering and explaining the American political process, have arguably transformed it from a liability to a major asset in some ways for the United States. Indeed, Al Jazeera's BBC-trained editors have complained bitterly about the reticence of American officials to appear on their programs. While serving, according to some U.S. officials, as a willing outlet for al Qaeda propaganda, and with a distinct editorial bias against the United States, the fact is that Al Jazeera can serve U.S. interests as long as American officials are adept, flexible and creative enough to try.

Satellite TV is actively promoting American soft power in the Arab world in ways that the United States has been incapable of doing. The launch of the Arabic-language Alhurra satellite channel in early 2004 to provide news and entertainment in ways more beneficial to the U.S., marked an important turning point in U.S. public diplomacy development. Though it calls itself the largest Arabic-language news organization in the world, the Virginia-based Alhurra lacks the cache and brand recognition of Al Jazeera, but its balanced presentation of news has earned it a small but significant viewership. Controversial innovations in radio broadcasting that target young mass audiences through a mix of light news and mild American popular music – Radio Sawa in Arabic and Radio Farda in Persian – have captured a substantial market share in their target regions. The design of their programming is not intended to produce immediate, measurable results but to gain listener loyalty and spread a message with short, twice-hourly headline news updates.

Education and training

How can American strategists leverage public diplomacy and soft power generally in order to advance the nation's security interests? This is really the key question facing American policymakers at present, given the time and effort likely to be required in order to put in place credible and effective channels of communication from Washington to Arab publics and to the Muslim world more generally. A fundamental issue, though one that has not been very much discussed at least in public, is what overall posture or policy the United States should adopt regarding Al Jazeera and other regional and local media.

Though the United States has chosen to compete against or circumvent them, a more promising strategy may be simultaneously to develop cooperative relationships, while at the same time putting significant resources into the training of Arab journalists in professional standards and practices. The Voice of America already partners with AM and FM stations around the world, providing free content in the increasingly competitive broadcasting business. There are also many possibilities for program placement or even collaborative programming on existing Arab-language media outlets, especially given the shaky financial condition of many of these broadcasting operations.

A second area of strategic importance and great promise is education. As noted earlier, Nye has surprisingly little to say about the education component of American soft power. It has been widely recognized that perhaps the most serious long-term challenge facing the United States in the war on terror is to reverse the trend in the Islamic world toward the domination of its institutions of higher education by various forms of radical Islamism. There are obviously many sensitivities to be faced here, particularly if the United States is seen as in any way shaping or suppressing the way Islam is taught in the Islamic world. Yet the baleful influence of religious dogmatism and its direct contribution to terrorist recruitment is not the only shortcoming of much of contemporary Arab education. The lack of attention to science and technology, to economics and the other social sciences at all levels of education is a major contributor to the underdevelopment of Arab societies, an irony since so much of modern science was brought to the West from Arab and Muslim lands. The lack of knowledge of recent history and politics, coupled with regionalist and ideological biases in teaching, feed the various pathologies of contemporary Arab opinion – for example, relating to the Arab-Israeli conflict. These problems are not unrecognized in the Arab world, and American assistance in addressing them is apt to be more welcome.

Even such simple measures as book translation programs could have a very significant impact on the next generation throughout the region.

Third, and most obvious, is the area of democratization and political reform. Again, there is always the danger that active promotion of democracy throughout the Middle East by the United States will be seen as part of a larger imperial project and prove counterproductive in terms of influencing opinion and changing attitudes. And, as critics have frequently pointed out, there are still serious questions as to whether or to what extent the growth of democracy in the Middle East is really in American interests, since at least in some countries it may well lead to an upsurge of popular anti-Americanism and prove politically beneficial to radical Islamist parties. In Iraq, despite all the setbacks, the images of enthusiastic voters with purple thumbs, risking death as they waited to vote, sent powerful messages around the world. Enter, then, the attractive role of soft power.

The United States has been better at organizing "coalitions of the willing" to promote democracy in the Middle East than to wage war there. This is particularly true of the Europeans, who have been generally supportive of American reform initiatives in the region and thereby have largely undercut charges of American unilateralism or imperialism. Of course, a great deal remains to be done on this front. But the overall political climate in the region seems much more favorable to democratic reform than ever before. The case of Iraq certainly shows that democracy has proven attractive enough to broad segments of the population in a country that has never known it. The prospect of functioning democracies in Iraq and Afghanistan is certain in turn to have an enormous long-term effect on political attitudes and behavior throughout the entire region.

Conclusion

The days are over when millions of people would cloister themselves eagerly to hear the latest American radio broadcasts. The proliferation of news, the information technology revolution, ideological propaganda from Saudi Arabia, the emergence of broadcasting giants as the People's Republic of China and small but wealthy troublemakers like Venezuela, mean that the U.S. will have to compete more aggressively and creatively to win the world's eyes and ears. Old public diplomacy models are vital to study, but not always relevant to replicate.

For largely bureaucratic reasons, much of what the United States government has done in the areas of foreign media support, education reform, and democratization has not been viewed as "public diplomacy" proper and has mostly been carried out by agencies other than those explicitly dedicated to public diplomacy. With the abolition of the United States Information Agency (USIA) and its absorption into the State Department, no U.S. government agency has a public diplomacy ethos or mission. In the vacuum, the Agency for International Development (USAID) has been and remains in the forefront in programming traditionally considered public diplomacy. Given its humanitarian mission, USAID is a major soft power asset. The publicly-funded National Endowment for Democracy is an independent body that provides focused support for specific programs around the world, but its funding level is minuscule in comparison to USAID. Scattered programs in other agencies perform public diplomacy functions, with the Department of Defense taking a greater role, including an attractive soft power dimension in its own right among military services around the world, and among the millions of people who benefit from the U.S. military's humanitarian relief work.

Nowhere was this last feature more visible than in Indonesia after the 2004 tsunami, where anti-submarine warfare helicopters of the *USS Abraham Lincoln* aircraft carrier fleet became humanitarian relief choppers, ferrying relief and medical personnel, food, water, supplies and even toys to the stricken Muslim communities. Local Muslims, traditionalists who lived under shar'ia law, begged American forces to stay.

Soft power, then, is not simply an appendage of public diplomacy, nor is it a private reserve of the State Department or, for that matter, the government. The range of soft power instruments is broad and deep, waiting for the right leadership to use it well.

Notes

---

[1] Joseph S. Nye, Jr., *Soft Power: The Means to Success in World Politics* (Public Affairs, 2004), p. 5. Nye and others updated the concept as "smart power." See Richard L. Armitage and Joseph S. Nye, Jr., Co-Chairs, *A Smarter, More Secure America: Report of the CSIS Commission on Smart Power* (Center for Strategic and International Studies, 2007).
[2] Ibid., pp. 2-5.
[3] See notably William Riker, The Art of Political Manipulation (Yale University Press, 1986) and The Strategy of Rhetoric: Campaigning for the American Constitution (Yale University Press, 1996).
[4] William E. Odom and Robert Dujarric, *America's Inadvertent Empire* (Yale University Press, 2004).

[5] Nye, *Soft Power*, pp. 69-72, reports polling results to this effect by the Pew Global Attitudes Project in four regions of the world in 2002, though oddly, without acknowledging this.

[6] The global presence of CNN is well known; but few are aware that *Forbes, Foreign Affairs, Fortune,* the *Harvard Business Review, National Geographic, Newsweek,* and *Time* are all available in Japan in Japanese translation – an extreme but revealing case. Odom and Dujarric, *America's Inadvertent Empire,* p. 197.

[7] Nye, p. 25.

[8] Ibid., p. 99.

[9] Norman Bailey, The Strategic Plan that Won the Cold War: National Security Decision Directive 75 (Potomac Foundation, 1998).

[10] John F. Dickerson, "Vladimir Putin: CBS News Loyalist," *Time,* March 7, 2005.

[11] Alex R. Alexiev, "The Soviet Campaign Against INF: Strategy, Tactics, and Means," *Orbis,* Summer 1985, pp. 319-50; Hans Tuch, *Communicating with the World: U.S. Public Diplomacy Overseas* (St. Martin's, 1990).

[12] Arch Puddington, Broadcasting Freedom: The Cold War Triumph of Radio Free Europe and Radio Liberty (University Press of Kentucky, 2003).

4

Cultural Diplomacy, Political Influence, and Integrated Strategy

JOHN LENCZOWSKI

Cultural diplomacy is one of the most strategic and cost-effective means of political influence available to makers of U.S. foreign and national security policy. Because of neglect and misunderstanding, however, this powerful tool of statecraft has been vastly underutilized, its absence the source of numerous lost opportunities in our dealings with other countries.

Definition

What is cultural diplomacy? The definitions in the literature on the subject are remarkably consistent. Representative is that of Milton Cummings, Jr., the Johns Hopkins University political scientist: "the exchange of ideas, information, art, and other aspects of culture among nations and their peoples in order to foster mutual understanding."[1] Culture and ideology critic Frank Ninkovich speaks of cultural diplomacy as "promoting an understanding of American culture abroad."[2]

A related definition says that "cultural diplomacy has long served to foster understanding of America and our culture around the world...

Cultural diplomacy, in particular, can help to bring people together and develop a greater appreciation of fundamental American values and the freedom and variety of their expression."[3] Harvard's Joseph Nye recognizes culture as an important component of public diplomacy and what he calls "soft power."[4] A definition from an earlier era describes cultural diplomacy as:

the act of successfully communicating to others complete comprehension of the life and culture of a people. The objective of American cultural diplomacy is to create in the peoples of the world a perfect understanding of the life and culture of America... it is the requirement of mutual understanding which is the basis of successful cultural diplomacy, and it is this requirement which helps make cultural diplomacy so vitally important today.[5]

Helena Finn, a longtime senior State Department cultural affairs practitioner, states that cultural diplomacy consists of, "efforts to improve cultural understanding" and, "winning foreigners' voluntary allegiance to the American project..."[6]
Most of these definitions stress the role of cultural diplomacy in producing greater foreign understanding or appreciation of the United States and American culture, or greater mutual understanding. While all these definitions are accurate, most of them do not reflect either the other functions of cultural diplomacy or the alternative interpretations of those who do not share the consensus cited above.
Finn, for one, does introduce one of the missing dimensions linked to mutual understanding – its link to national security, a goal rarely and only implicitly acknowledged as a purpose of cultural diplomacy:

history is a useful reminder of how seriously [the United States] once took the promotion of mutual understanding through cultural exchange. Policymakers understood the link between engagement with foreign audiences and the victory over ideological enemies and considered cultural diplomacy vital to U.S. national security.[7]

In his history of cultural diplomacy, Richard T. Arndt introduces greater complexity to the definition than is found in most other places:

Most thoughtful cultural diplomats use 'culture' as the anthropologists do, to denote the complex of factors of mind and values which define a country or group, especially those factors transmitted by the process of intellect, i.e., by ideas. 'Cultural *relations*' then (and its synonym – at least in the U.S. – 'cultural *affairs*') means literally the relations between national cultures, those aspects of intellect and education lodged in any society that tend to cross borders and connect with foreign institutions.

Cultural relations grow naturally and organically, without government intervention – the transactions of trade and tourism, student flows, communications, book circulation, migration, media access, inter-marriage – millions of daily cross-cultural encounters. If that is correct, cultural *diplomacy* can only be said to take place when formal diplomats, serving national governments, try to shape and channel this natural flow to advance national interests.[8]

Arndt, a veteran public diplomacy professional at the former U.S. Information Agency, also defines cultural diplomacy from another perspective – that of the cultural diplomats themselves:

> Quietly, invisibly, indirectly, my cultural colleagues and I spent our lives representing American education and intellect, art and thought, setting foreign ideas about America into deeper contexts, helping others understand the workings of the peculiar U.S. version of democracy, combating anti-Americanism at its taproots, linking Americans and foreign counterparts, helping the best Americans and foreign students study somewhere else – in short, projecting America, warts and all.[9]

British scholar David Caute, while not endeavoring to produce a definition of cultural diplomacy *per se*, describes the uses of cultural instruments as implements of war. The Cold War was not a traditional political-military conflict, but an "ideological and cultural contest on a global scale and without historical precedent."[10] Caute argues that for all of the Soviet Union's failures to be economically competitive or to sustain its vast military establishment, "the mortal 'stroke' which finally buried Soviet Communism was arguably moral, intellectual, and cultural as well as economic and technological."[11] For all their books, ballets, scientific advances, chess champions, Olympic athletes and so forth, the Soviets "were losing the wider *Kulturkampf* from the outset because they were afraid of freedom and were seen to be afraid."[12]

In this war, then, cultural diplomacy took the form of "cultural promotion" and "cultural offensives" designed to compete with similar campaigns by the Soviets to "prove their virtue, to demonstrate their spiritual superiority, to claim the high ground of 'progress,' to win public support and admiration by gaining ascendancy in each and every event of what might be styled the Cultural Olympics."[13] What distinguished this conflict and its use of cultural instruments as weapons of war from religious and cultural conflicts of earlier centuries, according to Caute, was the presence of "the general public" as a theater of conflict, due to the emergence of mass media. Here, war was disguised as cultural "exchange" or "diplomacy."[14]

The use of cultural instruments as implements of war is not the preferred understanding of what cultural diplomacy is or ought to be among most cultural diplomats or students of the subject. Nevertheless, given the history of their use in this way, there is no escaping this dimension of the definition.

Under the circumstances, cultural diplomacy may be defined as the use of various elements of culture to influence foreign publics, opinion makers, and even foreign leaders. These elements comprehend the entire range of characteristics within a culture: including the arts, education, ideas, history, science, medicine, technology, religion, customs, manners, commerce, philanthropy, sports, language, professional vocations, hobbies, etc., and the various media by which these elements may be communicated. Cultural diplomacy seeks to harness these elements to influence foreigners in several ways: to have a positive view of the United States, its people, its culture, and its policies; to induce greater cooperation with the United States; to change the policies of foreign governments; to bring about political or cultural change in foreign lands; and to prevent, manage, mitigate, and prevail in conflicts with foreign adversaries. It is designed to encourage Americans to improve their understanding of foreign cultures so as to lubricate international relations (including such activities as commercial relations), enhance cross-cultural communication, improve one's intelligence capabilities, and understand foreign friends and adversaries, their intentions and their capabilities. Cultural diplomacy may also involve efforts to counter hostile foreign cultural diplomacy at home and abroad.

In short, cultural diplomacy, being designed not only for mutual understanding but for these other purposes as well, has as its proper end the enhancement of national security and the protection and advancement of other vital national interests.

Note that the this definition, in addition to those cited earlier, contains enough references to foreign publics, foreign opinion makers, foreign cultures, and "Americans" in general, that cultural diplomacy fits principally within the sphere of public diplomacy, which involves principally relations with, and influence over, foreign publics, with a result being greater understanding by Americans of foreign cultures and policies as well. While it does comprehend influence and relations with governments, the primacy of its public diplomatic effects is worth stressing because some cultural diplomats, as discussed below, have been known to subordinate cultural diplomacy to the exigencies of traditional government-to-government diplomacy.

Integration with other arts of statecraft

Properly speaking, cultural diplomacy is an element of national security policy in general and public diplomacy in particular. Cultural diplomacy can be integrated with other elements of these activities whether they be in the realm of information policy, ideological competition, countering hostile propaganda, foreign aid policy, religious diplomacy, or establishing relationships of trust. In these capacities, cultural diplomacy can have positive effects on foreign cooperation with U.S. policy.

Foreigners who trust the United States, Americans in general, or even merely certain individual Americans, and who feel that Americans respect them and are willing to listen to their point of view, are more likely to help those whom they trust with sustenance, safe haven, information, and communications in wartime. They are more likely to help establish relations with others, build coalitions, collaborate with U.S.-sponsored political arrangements, and so forth during times of peace making and peace keeping. They are also more likely to do business with Americans.

Cultural diplomacy is an important ingredient in the collection of secret intelligence and open-source information of a political, diplomatic, or other national security-oriented nature. This is not to say that participants in cultural diplomatic activities are, or should be, intelligence collectors. In fact, as in the case with Peace Corps volunteers, it is more effective that such participants should stay clear of intelligence activities precisely in order to maximize the beneficial effects of their activity. Nevertheless, cultural diplomats and participants in cultural diplomatic activities often have insights into foreign political conditions and foreign public attitudes that embassy political officers do not. Yet, rare is the occasion when they are debriefed by our traditional diplomats or policymakers for these insights.

Cultural diplomatic participants also establish and develop relationships with individuals who are not likely to be sources of intelligence or other information, but whose networks of personal relationships can lead to such sources. The best human intelligence collection and operations were accomplished through the broadening of personal relationships. Collection is also successful when there are significant numbers of foreigners who sympathize with American ideas and ideals. Insofar as cultural diplomacy involves the effective promulgation of those ideas and ideals, it increases the pool of potential sources.

Cultural diplomacy can also be integrated with political action, political warfare, and subversion. It can be part of strategic psychological operations.

It can be integrated with these other arts and dimensions of statecraft by being overtly political or, in most cases – and most effectively – by avoiding association with politics altogether. Its effectiveness in the latter case results from the fact that many forms of cultural activities do not have political or strategic strings attached and are authentically aboveboard. And yet, paradoxically, they have tremendous positive political effect. Thus, cultural diplomacy, like other forms of public diplomatic outreach such as Peace Corps volunteerism, foreign medical assistance, disaster relief, and the like, can be undertaken effectively by various governmental and non-governmental participants in many cases without their being aware of strategic integration or the political/psychological methods and effects associated with it.

Why cultural diplomacy is neglected

With all these possibilities, why is cultural diplomacy ignored or relegated to tertiary status in U.S. foreign and national security policy? Part of the explanation derives from the nature of the two principal perspectives in policy making: that of the defense community and that of the traditional diplomatic community – the communities representing "hard" and "soft" power respectively.

The defense community is that which conceives of its role in "national security" terms more so than the diplomatic community (notwithstanding the latter's oft-articulated role as the "first line of defense"). Similarly the defense community tends to think in "strategic" terms more than the diplomatic community does. However, it sees strategy as a matter involving armed forces, physical battlespace, geo-strategic opportunities and constraints, intelligence concerning these matters, and sometimes even a limited view of the psychological element of strategy, insofar as it involves such things as deterrence and depriving the enemy of his will to resist. This community, which can be said to be concerned with "hard power," historically has tended not to think of the other psychological elements of strategy, such as public diplomacy, which, after all, is not its principal professional focus. Occasionally, this community does consider such activities as aid programs and their role in winning hearts and minds in the context of counterinsurgency warfare. The U.S. military has a substantial soft power dimension of its own, and since 9/11 arguably has taken a lead in public diplomacy innovations which, out of deference to the State Department, it calls "public diplomacy support." However, the potential fruits of cultural diplomacy almost never enter into the military community's strategic calculus.

The traditional diplomatic community, exemplified by the Department of State, has traditionally treated cultural diplomacy as an afterthought. This has been aggravated by the fact that it does not conceive of diplomacy in grand strategic terms that incorporate a variety of instruments of statecraft. During the early years of the Cold War, this was less the case, as the Department included its own Bureau of Educational and Cultural Affairs. Subsequently, however, this bureau was shifted to the U.S. Information Agency, which became the main public diplomacy agency of the government.

Meanwhile, primacy in the Department was placed on traditional, government-to-government diplomacy, including consultations, dialogue, demarches, negotiations, peace processes, agreements, and reporting on political conditions affecting the foreign governments in question. This diplomatic culture has traditionally placed its emphasis on negotiations and reporting and rarely on influence in the largest sense of the term. These emphases derive principally from a longstanding bureaucratic culture that has placed no career incentives on influencing non-governmental figures and larger publics. One can even say that it is a culture that discourages such influence insofar as it has become risky and certainly profitless to one's career for an American diplomat to speak, for example, to the foreign media or to endeavor in other ways to shift foreign public attitudes.

When American career diplomats speak publicly, they use a language of caution and rarely a language of persuasion and advocacy – the art of rhetoric that can be used to sway large numbers of people. The diplomatic culture in this sense cannot be called an influence culture, and thus it does not think of all the ways influence can be exercised.

After years of separation of public (and cultural) diplomacy from the Department's direct purview, these functions became not simply subjects of neglect, but even irritants to the smooth running of the diplomatic process. Some public diplomacy initiatives – particularly targeted toward publics living under tyrannical regimes – would irritate those regimes and thus produce mild disruptions to traditional (i.e., government-to-government) relations. Telling the truth to truth-starved populations denied a free press cannot easily be reconciled with withholding such truth in the interest of harmonious relations with censorious regimes. The genetic impulse among State Department policymakers was to attempt to suppress those initiatives that risked "rocking the boat." Because of the primacy of the State Department in policy making, whereby country desk officers exercised a trump over public diplomacy policy that might be attempted at USIA or other public diplomacy agencies, more than a few public diplomats acceded to smooth relations with tyrannies rather than improved relations with oppressed publics.[15]

One of the most breathtaking examples was the opposition by the leading staff members of the Board for International Broadcasting to a major modernization plan and budget increase (totaling $2.5 billion) proposed in 1982 for Radio Free Europe/Radio Liberty (as well as the Voice of America). This program, part of President Reagan's strategy to dismantle the Soviet Union, had been initiated in response to the deterioration and obsolescence of the radios' equipment, to the extreme scarcity of programming funds, and to the KGB's proxy operation to bomb RFE/RL's Munich headquarters. That it should have been opposed by the very agency responsible for funding and overseeing these radios' work is contrary to every law of nature and bureaucratic behavior.

Similarly, a coalition of USIA cultural affairs officials and State Department officials who fashioned the first draft of an exchanges agreement (including cultural exchanges) with the USSR in 1985 was so bent on avoiding any disagreement with the Kremlin that this initial bargaining position contained 21 violations of a Presidential directive (NSDD 75) requiring full reciprocity in exchanges.[16] The spirit of this draft agreement was to make preemptive concessions to Moscow on every matter of sensitivity to the Kremlin, the net effect of which would have been to minimize the extent of cultural outreach to the Soviet public.

It should not be surprising, then, that, the nation's message-making will suffer when public diplomacy and cultural affairs officials are co-opted by the government-to-government diplomatic priorities of a State Department that has long since shed any inclination toward adopting a culture of influence towards foreign publics.

Another reason why cultural diplomacy is neglected is because it is a long-term endeavor requiring a long-term strategic vision. As Winston Churchill noted in *The Gathering Storm*, democracies have congenital difficulty in pursuing a consistent policy for more than five years at a time. Changes in administrations, and in cabinet and sub-cabinet positions all make for short-term thinking in foreign policy.

Finally, cultural diplomacy is neglected because it, along with other arts of statecraft, is not studied by aspiring or current diplomats and strategists in their academic preparation or mid-career training. Where there is little understanding gained through on-the-job training of the integration of cultural diplomacy with other arts of statecraft, there has been little or no education on this integration in existing professional schools in or out of government. This includes, not remarkably, the State Department's Foreign Service Institute, whose training in public and cultural diplomacy historically has been superficial and management-oriented.[17] While the defense and intelligence communities depend and ought to depend on the success of cultural diplomacy undertaken by other agencies, there is sufficiently little comprehension of this dimension of statecraft in those communities that they fail to demand its inclusion in national strategy.

The tools of cultural diplomacy

While every element of what can be considered part of the culture of a nation has been used in cultural diplomacy, some have been used more regularly and intensively than others. The literature in this field is replete with examples of these instruments. It may be useful to summarize them as briefly as possible here, before showing how they work.

The Arts

Both the United States and other powers have made significant use of the various arts to great effect in cultural diplomacy. These include the performing arts such as theater, film, ballet, and music, the fine arts such as painting and sculpture, and an art that can be considered *sui generis*: architecture.

Exhibitions

While exhibitions can be considered an art unto themselves, they harness a variety of other elements of culture, such as science, technology, folk and ethnic culture, commercial products, and the activities of various professions, including charitable work, as well as hobbies. They can convey American customs, manners, and the enthusiasms of popular culture. They can be used to teach and convey interpretations of American, regional, and world history as well as ideas.

Exhibitions can be huge, World's Fair-type displays. They can be as small as a poster outside the U.S. embassy in Moscow, portraying Rev. Martin Luther King's struggle for civil rights. In this one example, our cultural diplomats conveyed: the history of King's struggle and the success of that struggle; the fact that there was sufficient freedom in America for him to conduct that struggle in the first place (implicitly in contrast with political conditions in the USSR); that America celebrates that struggle as a reflection for its concern about the dignity of the human person and human rights both at home and abroad (including implicitly the USSR); and American honesty about the adverse conditions of American blacks ceaselessly highlighted by Soviet propaganda (this honesty being implicitly in contrast with Soviet official mendacity about political and human rights conditions both in the U.S. and the USSR). None of these points was conveyed in a way that directly attacked the Soviet government or its policies.

Exchanges

Exchanges with foreign countries have included every imaginable field. The most common have been educational, scientific, and artistic. However, there are many other fields that have also been covered including professional, labor, sports, youth, and religious exchanges.

Educational programs

Educational programs abroad can incorporate: the establishment of American universities abroad (e.g., the American University in Beirut, the American University in Cairo, Robert College in Turkey, etc.); sponsorship of American studies programs at universities around the world; the dispatching of American authorities (professors, teachers, experts working in private industry and government) abroad to teach or conduct lecture tours; the sponsorship of conferences; scholarships, both for Americans studying abroad and foreigners studying in America, (such as Fulbright Scholarships); etc.

Literature

While the distribution of some kinds of literature can properly be considered to be in the realm of information policy, the distribution of books and other periodicals that do not relate specifically to official information policy is a form of cultural diplomacy. The establishment of libraries abroad for use by foreign populations is one of the most effective means of conveying ideas, history, and other elements of culture, whether to generate understanding or to persuade.

Language teaching

Teaching foreigners English is the key to giving them access to American literature, film, broadcasts, and other media and the information, ideas, and other messages they carry. Similarly, the American study of foreign languages is the key to opening up understanding of foreign cultures.

Broadcasting

American broadcasts abroad by radio and television, and related multimedia, are among the most important media of cultural diplomacy. These are the only means by which unfiltered information and ideas can be conveyed to foreign audiences that live in countries where media access is restricted either by market realities or official censorship. The Voice of America has traditionally served not only as an instrument of U.S. information policy (as the voice of the U.S. government), but also as the voice of the American people and their culture. Other radios, such as Radio Free Europe and Radio Liberty have broadcast respectively to the countries of East-Central Europe and the former Soviet Union acting as "surrogate domestic free presses" for those countries, especially when they were under communist rule and had no free press. Other U.S.-sponsored radio and television media have undertaken similar roles in recent years, including Radio Marti, Radio Free Asia, Radio Free Afghanistan, Radio Sawa, Radio Farda, and Alhurra satellite television.

These various media have broadcast, among other things, news, music, literature, and poetry, whether American or native to the audience's country, programs on alternative ideas, historical programs, and religious programs — all concerning subjects that may be unknown or forbidden in the target countries.

Gifts

The giving of gifts has been a perennial staple of cultural diplomacy. It is a sign of thoughtfulness, of respect, of care about others. Its psychological and political effects can be long lasting.

Listening and according respect

The simple tools of dialogue, listening to others, expressing interest in and solicitude toward others, and according them respect are such obvious instruments of any kind of diplomacy that it would seem unnecessary to mention them. Yet, given the lack of integrated strategic thinking within the larger foreign policy and national security communities, and one may add, the lack of contact with foreigners among too many foreign and defense policy makers, it is clear that these most elementary tools are often neglected, and their power not appreciated or misunderstood.

According foreigners respect merely by listening and endeavoring to understand their perspectives breeds such good will that it is amazing that these instruments are not emphasized in every dimension of security policy.

Promotion of ideas

While most of the previous instruments can be described as vehicles or media for the transmission of cultural products and influences, the role of certain elements of culture should be included in this list for purposes of emphasis, despite the risk of violating a consistency of categories. The promotion of ideas is arguably the most important of these cultural elements. In the American case, this has meant the explanation of such American ideas as: the inalienable rights of the individual and the source of those rights; the rule of law; political and economic liberty; our Founders' view that since men are not angels there is a need for government and also for limits on government, including checks and balances; the dignity of the human person, no matter what his or her background or condition; democracy and representative government; the freedoms of speech, press, assembly, association, and religion; and other ideas central to our political culture.

The use of ideas as an instrument of cultural diplomacy may involve the gentle explanation of unknown or misunderstood ideas or the attempt to undermine hostile ideological currents abroad.

The question arises as to who in the U.S. government should be involved in the promotion and articulation of ideas. Given that developing and maintaining literacy in the realm of ideas is virtually a full-time occupation, it is questionable whether the vast majority of those whose profession is traditional diplomacy, strategy, or information policy will ever have the time to cultivate the necessary intellectual skills to double as competent professionals in this field. The only practical answer as to who should undertake the job of promoting and articulating ideas or arranging that this task by done by non-governmental organizations or individuals with maximum competence to do so, is: cultural diplomats.[18]

Promotion of social policy

Among the ideas American cultural diplomacy has promoted in recent years are those whose cultural effects are so notable that they merit individual attention. The United States has promoted contraception and abortion as part of both a policy of population control and "reproductive rights," sexual abstinence and marital fidelity (as part of a campaign against HIV/AIDS), and women's rights. Some of these policy positions are controversial not only in the United States but also in many of the countries to which they are targeted.

The controversial – and, in some countries, even offensive – character of these positions raises questions central to cultural diplomacy: to what degree should such diplomacy respect the customs and mores of often fragile foreign cultures, and to what extent should it attempt to disrupt these cultural patterns? The answers to these questions must be informed by prudential judgments that balance the need to build good will toward America and support for U.S. interests on the one hand, and a desire to promote social agendas worldwide in spite of the effects such promotion may have on other U.S. foreign policy interests. Such judgments cannot be made by those whose sole interest is in an ideological or social agenda. It must be made with the perspective of the entire array of U.S. interests.

History

The writing and interpretation of history has long been the object of political controversy and struggle, not only domestically but internationally. The distortion of history (marked principally by the deliberate neglect or suppression of significant facts and evidence) has been a staple of the proponents of political ideologies whose extreme political ends justify the use of any means, including dishonesty in historical interpretation. Typical examples were communist movements and regimes, which used historical revisionism to re-shape national memory and national identity in an effort to create a "new communist (or "Soviet") man."

It is the province of cultural diplomacy to enter into historical controversy in ways that advance U.S. national interests. This may mean disseminating historical facts that have been flushed down what George Orwell called the "memory hole." Or it may mean correcting historical distortions that have captured the minds of foreign populations or leaders, and which serve to inspire hatred, resentment, and desires for justice that are not merited by the true historical evidence.

In the case of communist historical revisionism during the Cold War, U.S. cultural diplomacy consistently and faithfully endeavored to supply accurate history to populations subjected to intellectual oppression and denied access to a free press, and historical archives. The good will toward the United States engendered among millions of people behind the Iron Curtain from this cultural diplomatic effort alone was of strategic proportions. When Vaclav Havel, as the first president of post-communist Czechoslovakia (and later the Czech

Republic) visited the United States, he made a special visit to the Voice of America to thank its personnel for keeping his national flame alive for half a century.

Religious diplomacy

Religion has long been, and continues ever more visibly to be, a central element of international relations and foreign policy. Yet, in the U.S. foreign policy culture over the past few decades, policy makers and governmental structures continue to pretend it does not exist. This is partly the result of cultural illiteracy due not only to secularization but to a precipitous decline in the study of history, philosophy, and religion in American colleges. It is also the result, in more recent times, of an ill-informed attitude that any use of religion by U.S. officialdom represents a violation of the First Amendment.

Religion, however, has for years been both the medium and the subject of cultural diplomacy not only by foreign powers but also by the United States as well, albeit in less visible corners of the U.S. foreign policy community. For example, U.S. international broadcasting has regularly included religious programming, including actual religious services, for populations where freedom of religion has been suppressed. For years such programming was conducted with no hesitation, and completely in conformity with Constitutional law, since it had nothing to do with the First Amendment proscriptions against Congress establishing an official religion in the United States. Such programs involved different religions, depending on the target audience.

A key element of religious diplomacy has involved inter-religious dialogue. Such dialogue has been used in recent years to overcome hostility and mistrust between Moslems on the one hand, and Christians and Jews on the other, by stressing their common Abrahamic tradition, monotheism, and subscription to the idea of a transcendent, universal, objective moral order, in contrast to modern relativism and materialism and their contemporary cultural fruits.

Knowledge of religion and its attendant philosophical categories of thought is a necessary professional skill for at least some cultural diplomats. In the contemporary period, we have been witnessing a struggle between traditional Islam and "Islamism" – which is arguably one of two things: either (1) not a pure religion, but rather a political ideology that attempts to harness religion to serve its worldly ends; or (2) a version of a religion that has a strong political-ideological agenda. Is it the business of traditional government-to-government diplomacy to affect this struggle? Are traditional diplomats equipped to do so? Is this the province of information diplomacy and "public affairs officers"? We hear constantly about how the United States is in a "battle of ideas" with extremist, terrorism-prone Islamism. So, once again, who within the U.S. government is to affect or conduct this battle of ideas? The main answer is cultural diplomats. It is they who must either be actively involved or who must have at least the adequate intellectual preparation to identify private sector individuals or non-governmental organizations who are equipped intellectually to conduct these affairs with some level of competence. They must be accompanied by people with the same skills in our intelligence community who are capable of conducting political action and political and ideological warfare.

How cultural diplomacy works:
Political and psychological effects

The ways by which cultural diplomacy achieves its desired objectives are little studied and little known in the larger foreign policy community. They include the palpable political and psychological dynamics and effects as well as less obvious ones.

Enhancement of international relations

The most widely acknowledged way by which most cultural diplomatic tools work is by promoting cross-cultural communication and mutual understanding. Cultural diplomatic tools are methods of having relations with influential groups in foreign countries outside the purview of normal diplomatic or commercial channels (although commerce can be considered a "cultural" activity in the broader understanding of the term). They can significantly ameliorate relations with foreign publics, opinion makers, influential groups, and even governments by bringing to light and strengthening cultural affinities and thereby inspiring relationships of trust. This happens, for example, when, through artistic performances or exhibitions, our cultural representatives speak to foreigners in a "universal language" of art or music. This language serves as a vehicle of cross-cultural communication that highlights commonalities of aesthetic sensibility – particularly a common appreciation of beauty, which contains an element spiritually related to truth. The discovery of such aesthetic commonality can, in turn, inspire respect and trust.

Cultural diplomacy, when conducted with respect for foreign cultures and in ways that minimize disruption of foreign cultures, can inspire first the obvious mutual understanding but also ever greater relations of trust. It is a way of conducting international relations without a *quid pro quo*, without a direct political agenda, without specific diplomatic, commercial, or military goals. This breeds such good will that it can, over time, translate into better relations on a political level. The establishment of this good will and trust, however, is a long-term endeavor the beneficial effects of which cannot be realized overnight. The oft-entertained idea of public diplomacy as the equivalent of "crisis public relations" whereby a poor corporate public image can be reversed through a skillful short-term public relations campaign could not be more inapplicable here.

It is difficult to overemphasize the strategic value of respect for foreign cultures. In recent years, much of the world has perceived the United States as having a unilateralist foreign policy that is disdainful of the views of the international community and even culturally imperialist. Attendant to this is the feeling that American policies are based on an underlying lack of respect for other cultures and a lack of willingness to listen to other points of view. As cultural diplomacy can initiate and broaden cross-cultural communication, two worthwhile results can emerge: 1) it can mitigate the existence of any extant American lack of respect for foreign cultures and sensibilities; and 2) insofar as Americans do respect foreign cultures yet are perceived by foreigners as not doing so, cultural diplomacy can disabuse such perceptions or at least lessen their intensity.

Finally, cultural diplomacy produces those levels of mutual understanding, trust, and comfort by contact with foreign cultures that promotes better international relations in other fields, such as commercial, diplomatic and military.

Immunization against, and cure for, the effects of hostile propaganda

Cultural diplomatic tools, particularly those in the realm of the arts, exhibitions, and sports, can have the effect of immunizing foreign audiences from hostile propaganda, and even reversing the effects of that propaganda. Exposure to inspiring cultural products, displays, and performances have the effect of creating curiosity about, and appreciation for, the United States that may not have been there before. Indeed, the witnessing of even a single artistic performance can have instantaneously positive effects on foreign attitudes.

For example, during the Cold War, the Indian subcontinent was the target of the greatest investment of Soviet anti-American propaganda. In spite of the affinities that India and the United States might be thought to have had as the world's largest and oldest democracies respectively, relations between the two countries were considerably strained for various reasons, not least of which was the adverse effect of Soviet propaganda, which portrayed America as materialistic, imperialistic, rapacious, militaristic, aggressive, and unjust in its policies. When audiences in New Delhi witnessed performances of an American college choir, many of these images were erased. As with G.K. Chesterton's description of art as a reflection of the soul,[19] the Americans' performing art revealed the existence of a spiritual component to the American character that many in the audience had never seen. This spiritual element had the effect of melting hearts hardened by the distortions of hostile propaganda.

The very establishment of personal relations of trust, developed as a result of any number of different types of cultural relations, can have an immunizing effect. Foreigners who know, like, and trust individual Americans are less likely to believe hostile portrayals of America simply because they could not imagine their American friend being guilty of the opprobrious behavior or attitudes alleged of Americans in general.

Conditioning for subsequent political messages

Baruch Hazan has dissected a related dimension of the dynamics of cultural diplomacy. He describes it as a form of conditioning propaganda: whereby cultural diplomatic tools induce sufficient curiosity or appreciation for their users that they have the effect of breaking down the barriers that foreigners erect to prevent themselves from receiving messages from sources they do not trust. The cultural influences "impregnate" those barriers, poking holes in them, increasing the likelihood that the audience will listen to political messages that follow.[20] Thus, cultural diplomacy can set the stage for political communications and even serve as a cover for them.

Psychological disarmament

A related effect of cultural diplomacy is psychological disarmament. This is a tool used principally by powers posing a political or strategic threat to others and which use cultural diplomacy as a means of disguising the threat.

Again, recent history provides us with insights. The USSR was a master at this form of psychological disarmament. During the latter stages of the Cold War, Moscow launched a multi-faceted campaign directed toward the psychological disarmament of the United States so as to remove the competitive military pressure that had contributed to the crisis in the Soviet military economy and the larger crisis of the legitimacy of the regime.[21] The key objective of this campaign was revealed publicly by Kremlin representatives as an endeavor to "deprive you [the United States] of an enemy image."[22] A key part of this effort was the launching of a huge cultural offensive targeted against the United States and the West in general.[23]

This campaign was accompanied by propaganda efforts to demonstrate that the Soviet Union had changed its political genetic code, that it had in effect, ceased to be Marxist-Leninist in character, and therefore, ceased to have, by definition, unlimited global political-strategic goals. The larger propaganda campaign also included a campaign of military *glasnost* (a term designed to be understood as "openness" but really meaning "publicity," or perhaps "controlled openness with manipulated truth") – a campaign of partially opening up formerly secret military facilities to show that military secrecy was no longer a strategic priority.[24]

The cultural component of the campaign involved dispatching every imaginable cultural product, from ballet companies and jolly balalaika-playing sailors on naval port visits to films and Olympic gymnasts. They were specifically designed to have a psychologically disarming effect. When the Red Army Chorus gave a concert at Washington, D.C.'s Kennedy Center for the Performing Arts, and included a stirring rendition of the American National Anthem, it received an enthusiastic standing ovation.[25] Only a couple of years before, the Chorus' parent institution had been involved in creating and disseminating butterfly toy bombs, designed to be picked up by small children in Afghan villages so that their hands and arms would be blown off, thus inducing their parents and neighbors to flee the villages, depriving the anti-Soviet *muhajeddin* warriors of safe haven in the countryside. Contemporaneous with that concert, Soviet armed units invaded Azerbaijan ostensibly to create inter-ethnic peace after the KGB had inspired Azeri communist pogroms against Armenian citizens in Baku, but in reality, as the Soviet defense minister publicly admitted, to prevent political power from slipping from the hands of Moscow's local communist authorities.

When regaled with the inspiring choral strains thundered by the Soviet army's *bassos,* who could be reminded of such events? Well into Moscow's cultural and psychological disarmament offensive, it became clear that Mikhail Gorbachev's military buildup considerably exceeded that of President Reagan in *eighteen of twenty* categories of armament.[26]

Political power projection

Cultural diplomacy is a form of demonstrating national power – by exposing foreign audiences to every aspect of culture that reflects such power, including the advancement of science and technology, a nation's quality of life, a nation's wealth (as reflected in the development of those elements of a civilization that can only come from wealth), its competitiveness in everything from sports and industry to military power, and its self-image of cultural and civilizational confidence. Some tools, such as a scientific and technological exhibition, accomplish this purpose directly; others, such as architecture, do so symbolically. The skillful use of these cultural tools can thus project a nation's power politically and thus have strategic effects ranging from inspiring confidence among allies to enhancing the deterrence of adversaries.

Inspiration for political change

Cultural diplomacy is a method of inspiring political change in foreign countries. When targeted toward states representing a political, strategic, or cultural threat, it can serve as a form of warfare. In this connection, the use of cultural vehicles and the seizure of cultural institutions by one's political allies is a well-known form of subversion.[27] By creating a climate where certain thoughts and ideas become reinforced by cultural tools, whether through artistic or intellectual fashion or even in the realm of etiquette, cultural instruments can shape political attitudes and conditions. Typical targets of such cultural influence are film, literature, theater, popular music, educational institutions, the mass media, religious organizations, and even charitable organizations.

Counteracting atomization

One noteworthy effect of cultural diplomacy when utilized by the United States against the Soviet Union during the Cold War was the undermining of the Soviet regime's atomization of society. Atomization was the attempt to separate people from one another, to make each individual isolated from others so as to prevent people from organizing in groups beyond the control of the regime. The principal technique was to prevent people from trusting each other. This was done mainly by recruiting and co-opting even unwilling individuals into the internal security apparatus. People were thus pressed against their will into this service by being required to inform on their neighbors, co-workers, and even family members. Failures to report and denounce infractions of Soviet laws resulted in punishment of the coerced "informer." The climate of mistrust thus engendered became pervasive.

Contributing to political and ideological warfare

When cultural categories, notably ideas, are used as instruments in political and ideological warfare, they can be critical to achieving several of the classic goals of these forms of war. They can be used to persuade or co-opt publics, opinion makers, or leaders in allied, neutral, or adversary countries. They can be used to isolate extremist and adversary forces by exposing and discrediting them or their ideas, polarizing and splitting contending factions within an adversary's camp, or even demoralizing such adversaries.

Cultural diplomacy includes political and ideological argument. It uses the language of persuasion and advocacy. This is not the kind of language that is associated with traditional diplomacy, which, as mentioned earlier, stresses diplomatic caution and endeavors to smooth rough edges rather than accentuate them in political debate. Traditional diplomats rarely learn the language of persuasion and advocacy and almost never use it in public fora, as there is no career incentive to do so. In fact, it is a career-threatening move to use such language when speaking to foreign media. Who, then, should use such tools in service of U.S. strategic interests? The answer, again, is: principally cultural diplomats.[28]

Cultural instruments as double-edged swords

Cultural products and instruments are not uniformly effective in achieving the many beneficial political, psychological, and strategic effects our foreign policy seeks. Some of these products can be offensive to foreigners. U.S. popular culture, for example, contains numerous attractive products that have captured the imaginations of people around the world, whether it be music, film, technology, or many other examples. However, there are dimensions of this popular culture, such as the pornographization of American cinema, dress, and music and the treatment of women (and men) as objects rather than persons, that many traditional foreign cultures find offensive and subversive of national cultural mores. Ordinary American television programs broadcast on American Forces Radio and Television Service (AFRTS) to American armed forces stationed abroad have been seen as sufficiently offensive by allies as close to the United States as South Korea that the governments of such countries have endeavored to prevent these shows from being viewed by their own populations.

Similarly, American and other Western attempts to export various social policies have been viewed in other countries as culturally imperialist and lacking in respect for the moral and cultural arrangements painstakingly worked out over centuries in their lands. The perception of the lack of respect has alienating effects among foreigners as great as the beneficent effects that derive from their feeling that Americans treat them with respect.

The question thus arises as to how U.S. cultural diplomacy should be involved in tempering the adverse effects of those elements of American popular culture that are widely perceived in foreign lands as toxic and subversive. There may not be consistency, of course, in how American cultural products are perceived in a given country. Religious and political leaders in a given Muslim country, for example, may view such products (or policies, such as women's rights) one way, while the youth of their country may view them otherwise. Even in such cases, cultural diplomacy can find ways of mitigating the adverse effects of American culture among the members of one group while enjoying their benefits among the members of another. In the case of foreigners being offended by the pornographic character and sexually libertine values portrayed in American films, cultural diplomacy can educate the concerned foreign audience about the existence of American constituencies that find such fare equally offensive and explain the existence of cultural conflict in America and how it is a feature of a free society.

Cultural diplomacy with adversary states can have a multiplicity of effects. The usual desired effects are to appeal to the people of such states over the heads of their (usually tyrannical) governments, to neutralize adversary governments, or to persuade them to change their attitudes and policies. Cultural interactions and exchanges arranged with adversary governments pose certain risks, however. Insofar as they principally involve U.S. exchanges with representatives of that government, they can have various adverse effects.

For example, they can legitimize illegitimate institutions thus serving the adversary government's efforts to achieve political-strategic deception. For example, during the Cold War, exchanges were arranged between the American Bar Association (ABA) and the Association of Soviet Lawyers (ASL). An exchange of this type gives Americans the impression that an organization like the ASL is the functional and moral equivalent of the ABA: in other words, a professional association representing the interests of a membership of independent lawyers who work in an analogous legal system. Such an exchange would have been more accurately portrayed if it were described as being between American lawyers and official prosecuting agents of the Communist Party's system of arbitrary legal repression who double as official propagandists.

Similarly, "inter-parliamentary" exchanges between members of the U.S. Congress and members of the USSR Supreme Soviet gave similar legitimacy to the latter, by portraying them as having been legitimately democratically elected by citizen constituents whom they represent. Again, truth in advertising would describe such an exchange as being between U.S. elected representatives and Communist propagandists disguised as elected representatives. By portraying the Supreme Soviet as a putatively legitimate parliament, an exchange of this type serves to send the message that the Soviet state is a state like any other (particularly like other democracies) with a parliament like any other. By portraying a system of government that is familiar and non-threatening, such an exchange reinforces illusions about the systemic requirements and, therefore, strategic intentions of a state with a radically different genetic code.[29]

Exchanges with foreign adversary governments can present the (usually oppressed) population of their country with an image of cozy relations between their oppressive government and the United States. Little can be more demoralizing to a suffering people, yet it is the objective of tyrannical government precisely to produce such demoralization so as to prevent internal political resistance to its rule.

Yet another risk of exchanges with adversary states is that such exchanges can be used by them to serve strategic purposes such as psychological disarmament, intelligence collection, and technology acquisition. Under such circumstances, it should occur to U.S. policymakers to erect defenses against such purposes. Insofar as the threat may be intelligence collection or technology theft, the relevant counterintelligence and defense agencies must be involved. But in cases where psychological disarmament is the purpose, who exercises responsibility for defense against this? In one sense, this is a function of strategic counterintelligence. However, since most counterintelligence in the United States is conceived of principally as an exercise in tactical counterespionage and almost never a task of countering foreign political influence operations, cultural diplomats must be involved.

Here such involvement must include, at minimum, briefing participants in cultural exchanges about the potential threats and strategic purposes of their exchange counterparts and their official sponsors. The construction of such exchanges must also avoid political symbolism that reinforces the strategic purposes of those governments. The days of exchanges between uninformed, naive Americans and well-briefed official propagandists from adversary countries must end.

A final consideration relating to the double-edged nature of cultural diplomacy is in order: the role of American participants who do not share a given administration's policy positions, especially when the country is at war. Americans who dissent from administration policy can most assuredly undermine national policy objectives when speaking abroad in the context of whatever cultural activity they maybe pursuing. However, it is also true that dissident voices can nonetheless serve longer-term American interests especially if their foreign audience also disagrees with the current administration policy in question. Under such circumstances, the portrayal of an America where there is free debate and where dissident voices are not suppressed can mitigate hostile attitudes of foreign audiences who oppose U.S. policy by giving those audiences hope that U.S. policy can change or at least be informed by views that seem more respectful of their own.

Conclusion

Given the vast array of activities included in cultural diplomacy, it is obvious that the U.S. government has ignored the many possibilities they offer to influence the world in ways that promote U.S. national interests and higher moral purposes. There is no genuine career track leading to positions of high influence in the Department of State for experts in these matters. Nor are there career incentives for foreign affairs personnel to apply their talents to this field. There is no serious professional education for cultural diplomats within the government. Nor are cultural diplomats sent to outside educational institutions to develop the knowledge and intellectual skills necessary to succeed in this most sophisticated of political influence activities.

Meanwhile, despite the utterly strategic nature of this form of influence, no resources – neither human nor financial – commensurate with this strategic character are devoted to cultural diplomacy.

For all the specific policy recommendations one might make in concluding this analysis, and for all the recommendations that have been made in a slew of worthy reports on the subject, as a realistic matter, none will be seriously considered by either the executive or legislative branches until two prerequisites are realized:

First, there must be a conceptual revolution in the character of American statecraft. This must involve the adoption within the broader diplomatic and national security communities of an influence culture, to complement the culture of government-to-government dialogue, consultations, and negotiations on the one hand, and the culture of material power, be it military or economic, on the other. A culture of influence can only come about with the merging of both these cultures so that the ministers of "hard power" recognize the value of "soft power" and that the diplomatic culture recognizes the existence of one of its critical dimensions that make "soft" instruments powerful. What this means is that there must emerge a new culture of *integrated strategy* that refuses to abandon instruments critical to a successful foreign policy and grand strategy.

Second, determined leadership is necessary if existing patterns of bureaucratic practice and budgeting are to be overcome and cultural diplomacy is to secure its place at the strategic table. The existing advocacy by proponents of cultural diplomacy is weak. This is so because it is almost always divorced from integrated strategy. Its strategic value and its indispensable character have remained unsatisfactorily explained. Ironically, those whose business ought to be the arts of capturing attention and of persuasion have failed both to capture national strategic attention and to persuade. Existing national leadership in both political parties remains oblivious to the enormous gap that must be filled. And given how difficult it is for existing leaders to acquire intellectual capital while in office, it seems quixotic to hope that they will undergo the necessary conceptual revolution, become enthusiasts and advocates for a necessary structural and bureaucratic revolution within the government, and then go about implementing such change with strategic and tactical determination.

The realistic conclusion to be drawn from this is that the fruits of this extraordinary instrument of national influence will have to be picked up by a new generation. But time flies and a new generation is in formation.

Notes

[1] Milton C. Cummings, Jr., *Cultural Diplomacy and the United States Government: A Survey* (Center for Arts and Culture, 2003), p. 1.
[2] Frank Ninkovich, "Arts and Minds: Cultural Diplomacy Amid Global Tensions," a paper based on a conference by the National Arts Journalism Program, Arts International, and the Center for Arts and Culture, 2003, p. 26. Also see Ninkovich, *U.S. Information Policy and Cultural Diplomacy* (Foreign Policy Association Headline Series No. 308, 1996).

[3] Cultural Diplomacy: Recommendations and Research, Center for the Arts and Culture, July 2004, p. 7.

[4] Joseph S. Nye, Jr., *Soft Power: The Means to Success in World Politics* (Public Affairs, 2004), passim.

[5] Robert H. Thayer, "Cultural Diplomacy: Seeing is Believing." *Vital Speeches of the Day* (October 1, 1959), Vol. 25 Issue 24, pp. 740-744.

[6] Helena K. Finn, "The Case for Cultural Diplomacy," *Foreign Affairs*, November-December 2003, Vol. 82 Issue 6, pp. 15-20.

[7] Ibid.

[8] Richard T. Arndt, The First Resort of Kings: American Cultural Diplomacy in the Twentieth Century (Potomac Books, 2005), xviii.

[9] Ibid., x.

[10] David Caute, The Dancer Defects: The Struggle for Cultural Supremacy During the Cold War (Oxford University Press, 2003), p. 1.

[11] Ibid.

[12] Ibid., p. 2.

[13] Ibid., p. 3.

[14] Ibid., p. 6.

[15] This author personally witnessed examples of this phenomenon while in and out of government. He served in the Department of State and the National Security Council from 1981 to 1987, working on U.S.-Soviet relations and public diplomacy.

[16] This is the judgment of this author, whose 1985 memorandum on this issue to the National Security Advisor to the President documents each violation.

[17] There is some evidence, at this writing, of greater sensitivity to public and cultural diplomacy within the Department in response to the extraordinary harvest of U.S. anti-Americanism around the world in reaction to the U.S. occupation of Iraq.

[18] There is a role here as well, under certain unavoidable circumstances, for intelligence personnel charged with covert intelligence operations.

[19] G.K. Chesterton, *The Everlasting Man* (Ignatius Press, 1993).

[20] Baruch Hazan, *Soviet Impregnational Propaganda* (Ardis Publishers, 1982), p. 17.

[21] John Lenczowski, *The Sources of Soviet Perestroika* (Ashland University: John M. Ashbrook Center for Public Affairs, 1990).

[22] John Lenczowski, "Military Glasnost and Soviet Strategic Deception," *International Freedom Review*, Winter 1990, pp. 6-7; as quoted in "Increasing Realism in U.S.-Soviet Relations," *Nepszabadsag*, June 4, 1988, Foreign Broadcast Information Service *Daily Report-Eastern Europe*, June 8, 1988.

[23] John Lenczowski, Soviet Cultural Diplomacy: A Multi-faceted Strategic Instrument of Soviet Power (IWP Press, 2008).

[24] Lenczowski, "Military Glasnost and Soviet Strategic Deception."

[25] Lenczowski, Soviet Cultural Diplomacy.

[26] Lenczowski, *Sources of Soviet Perestroika*, p. 27, based on a chart compiled by Jim Guirard, *West Watch*, January-February 1990 (data based on U.S. Department of Defense, *Soviet Military Power*, 1989).

[27] See, notably, the works of Antonio Gramsci, as compiled in David Forgacs, ed., *The Antonio Gramsci Reader: Selected Writings 1916-1935*, (New York University Press, 2000).

[28] Again, there is an important role to be played here by similarly qualified covert intelligence personnel responsible for influence operations.

[29] For an elaboration of how Soviet institutions served purposes of strategic deception, see my "Themes of Soviet Strategic Deception and Disinformation," in Brian Dailey and Patrick Parker, eds., *Soviet Strategic Deception* (Lexington Books, 1987), pp. 55-75.

5

Mediators of the Message: The role of religion and civil society in public diplomacy

JENNIFER A. MARSHALL

In the fall of 2006, foreign policy opinion leaders Madeleine Albright and Walter Russell Mead turned their attention to religion as a factor in international relations.[1] Articles by these and other writers recognized the geopolitical significance of global Islam and the need for serious reconsideration of religion in world politics. Such attention to religious dynamics, both at home and abroad, was a promising development as the United States continued to come to grips with the clash of beliefs at the heart of the war on terrorism. As these articles appeared in print, President Bush was reaffirming the ideological nature of the clash at hand: "The war we fight today is more than a military conflict; it is the decisive ideological struggle of the 21st century."[2]

That recognition and rhetoric have yet to be converted into a coherent formulation of policy, strategy and tactics for waging and winning a war of ideas. While international engagement on material grounds – military and economic – is familiar to U.S. policymakers, ideological confrontation has proven much more challenging, in part because American foreign policy has discounted the power of ideology and not adequately reckoned with the power of religious beliefs in world politics.[3]

"[T]he most critical aspect of American disposition toward non-Western societies ... is a pronounced inability or unwillingness to come to terms with religions, philosophies, ideologies, and other bodies of beliefs that have decisively shaped the foreign mind-sets but which continue to baffle Americans," wrote the late Adda B. Bozeman, whose work focused on the interrelation of culture and statecraft.[4] "America's failures in the conduct of foreign affairs must thus be ascribed in no small measure to slipshod treatment of values."[5]

Effective ideological engagement requires an accurate concept of the role of religion in the United States as well as accurate perceptions about the beliefs that motivate foreign publics. That begins with mustering the full force of the ideas on which the United States is founded. A hallmark of the U.S. constitutional order has been its success in balancing the dual allegiances of spiritual and temporal realms without emptying either's authority or significance. Today, however, the religious roots of the American order and the role of religion in the continued success of the American experiment are poorly understood by the general public and policymakers alike.

This leads to a lack of facility in grappling with cultures in which religion plays a dominant role, and an even greater difficulty in communicating with such audiences. America's official awkwardness with religion and ambivalence about its significance hinder U.S. policymakers from reaching and winning hearts and minds abroad.

"Our failure to take seriously religious motivations for public human behavior, at least as seriously as we do the incentives of power, politics and material gain, has placed at risk the security of the American people," says former Foreign Service officer Thomas F. Farr, who directed the State Department's Office of International Religious Freedom.[6]

Among the many disciplines of statecraft, public diplomacy in particular must grapple with religion as a fact of life. Religion is one of the strongest determinants in both the life of the community and the life of the individual; hearts and minds are never more deeply affected than by religious belief. Religion defines the worldview of many whom U.S. public diplomacy seeks to influence. For public diplomacy, finding the appropriate means to appeal to these touchstones and to employ the services of those who can engage on these levels is essential.

To overcome this deficit, American foreign policymakers in general and public diplomats in particular must systematically analyze and address religious factors as a powerful motivating force in human behavior, from the individual to the community, nation and culture. Specifically, U.S. policymakers must:

- understand the role of religion and civil society in the American constitutional order
- improve articulation of the essential elements of religious liberty and civil society both at home and abroad

- guard against the distortion of such ideas (whether by friends or foes)
- recognize the perceptual barriers, including religious beliefs and traditions that prevent more widespread understanding of the ideals we hold to be universal
- identify and confront (and where possible, influence) the sources of opposition to these ideals.

Understanding the role of religion in the American order

The United States can expect to be endlessly engaged in cold wars of ideas. America is a nation built on an idea, specifically, the principle "that all men are created equal, that they are endowed by their Creator with certain unalienable Rights, that among these are Life, Liberty, and the pursuit of Happiness." That idea had its enemies in 1776, and it continues to have them today.

Cold "wars of ideas are fought in terms of ideas and for the sake of ideas. It follows that ideas ... must be in good fighting shape," wrote Bozeman.[7] Today, a number of the ideas essential to the American order are not in prime "fighting shape," including those about the importance of religion and civil society in relation to freedom. That leaves the United States vulnerable in its ideological engagements abroad.

If U.S. public diplomacy aims to impart to foreign audiences an understanding and appreciation of American founding principles, institutions and policy, it must begin with an adequate self-concept of the same. This is not merely the task of public diplomacy; it is also the task of self-government in general. Democracy demands a high degree of social self-consciousness when it comes to the ideas that sustain the order: the principles and institutions of a free society are inherently more susceptible to corruption of purpose and meaning than are those of more authoritarian states.[8]

Despite this imperative of self-government, Americans have not been consistently diligent in defending the ideas at the heart of the American order. Americans' disinclination to study their own history and founding principles, or the history of foreign cultures and thought, has "gradually made for a crippled, decidedly unconvincing national self-image," exposing America's defining attributes to mischaracterization at home and abroad.[9]

Such a vague, "unconvincing" national identity makes it difficult to build a foreign policy, let alone a rhetorical defense for that foreign policy and national identity. It follows that confusion about foreign policy goals is linked to confusion about who we are as an American nation.[10]

Civil society in America has been marked by a strong tradition of religious belief and practice and by active civic associations. These features characterize the American order as much as its political system or market economy and serve to sustain them.[11] Religion has been a dominant theme in American civic life, from the earliest 17th century settlements founded for religious reasons to the great social justice causes led by religious congregations in the late 19th century to the current day charitable giving of religious individuals. This has not translated, however, into an adequate comprehension of American religious freedom and practice in U.S. foreign policy and public diplomacy.

Part of the confusion stems from prevailing assumptions about the direction of the Western world and modernity in general. It has widely been assumed that over time, scientific knowledge tends to displace faith resulting in a society becoming less religious. While evidence from around the world as well as emerging data on religious belief and practice in the U.S.[12] suggest that secularization[13] is not the trend of history, official secularism has been the inclination of policy for some time.

This has led to an expansive "separationist" mentality in which the constitutional idea of non-establishment of religion is interpreted to mean that the government must have nothing to do with religion - to the extent that religion is perceived as a personal, private affair, inconsequential for the purposes of public policy, and of negligible social significance. In addition to the moral framework that religion offers for understanding human motivation in the political sphere, this conception overlooks the wealth of data indicating that religious practice yields significant positive goods for society, including high levels of civic engagement.[14] Still, according to veterans, "secular myopia" dominates at the State Department.[15]

"While most American and European foreign-policy elites may hold a secular worldview, much of the rest of the world lives in one of the great religious traditions," according to Andrew Natsios, former chief of the U.S. Agency for International Development (USAID). By contrast, faith-based organizations "have much more in common with the rest of the world and thus may understand ethnic and religious conflicts, political movements driven by religious devotion, and the way in which the religious mind functions, better than secularized foreign-policy practitioners."[16]

Understanding the role of religion in world politics

The lack of acknowledgement and understanding of religion's
relevance domestically contributes to the failure to recognize religion's
importance as a motivating factor in world politics. Increasing
secularization in the West has also resulted in a greater psychological
distance from societies dominated by religious institutions, traditions,
and symbols. Without the capacity to conceive of the beliefs and
motivations of the religious individual, policymakers will be ill-
equipped to imagine how to communicate with him most effectively.

Both the realist and idealist traditions have underappreciated the
power of values and beliefs. Realism, as George Weigel has noted,
needs "a more comprehensive theory of moral reasoning applied to
world politics [to] take more seriously... the truth that ideas have
consequences."[17] On the other hand, a foreign policy that simply
repeats an "unresearched trust in the universal validity of such basically
Western values as law, democracy, and peace,"[18] overlooks the foreign
belief systems that hinder the reception of and resonance with
American rhetoric on universal ideals.

The religion deficit in U.S. public diplomacy is nowhere more
apparent than in the case of Islam: "Western policymakers have let
their dedication to a vigorous separation of church and state become an
excuse for failing to comprehend – and understand how to deal with –
the worldview of Islam," writes Douglas Johnston of the International
Center for Religion and Diplomacy.[19]

Strict separationism combined with the "mirror-imaging" tendency
result in a failure to perceive the need to more deeply investigate the
interaction of religion and politics in Muslim societies. Without
adequate appreciation of the role of religion, one cannot begin to
comprehend the complexity of Muslim experience with concepts
Westerners take for granted, including the state and the notion of a
political space (as distinct from the religious or personal). Nor can one
proceed to make critical distinctions between Muslim (religious) and
Islamist (political ideological) thought.[20]

Religious analysis helps to illuminate such differences and avoid the
trap of thinking of Islam as a monolithic faith and culture. Just as sharp
domestic political strategists understand the American electorate well
enough to know that a national candidate's message must reach
Baptists in Oklahoma as well as Roman Catholics in Massachusetts, the
challenge of public diplomacy is to develop methods and messages that
discern among the sects of Islam and its various cultural and political
contexts from Iran to Iraq to Indonesia to Pakistan.

Individuals who understand the religious mindset are best equipped to tackle that challenge. While a secularist viewpoint is antithetical to the Muslim worldview, Western religious believers – evangelicals, conservative Catholics, and Orthodox Jews, for example – can understand and appreciate Muslims' belief in a supernatural reality, adherence to a comprehensive moral code, and concept of a well-ordered interior life. This appreciation is what diplomats, intelligence officers, and policy practitioners operating from a secular viewpoint lack. "As the rising evangelical establishment gains experience in foreign policy, it is likely to prove a valuable - if not always easy - partner for the mostly secular or liberal Christian establishment," observes Walter Russell Mead.[21] One way in which that cooperation could prove beneficial is in encouraging a richer understanding of democratic order in the United States as well as abroad.

A civil society approach to public diplomacy

Democracy is more than electoral machinery. It is the governmental expression of civil society. Civil society is the network of mediating structures – like family, neighborhood, religious congregation, or clubs – that link the individual in his private life to the state and major institutions of public life.[22] These mediating structures generate and sustain values in a society. As mediating structures are eroded or eliminated, values are increasingly determined by the state.[23] As a state tends toward the extreme of totalitarianism, civil society institutions are under siege or wiped out; the religious faithful are often persecuted and private associations are typically outlawed or highly suspect. The constriction of civil society is one of the most striking differences between an authoritarian state and free society.

In America, civil society has been marked by a strong tradition of religious belief and practice. The moral authority exercised by religious congregations, family, and other private associations is fundamental to maintaining limited government. The American Founders frequently asserted that virtue and religion are essential to maintaining a free society because they preserve "the moral conditions of freedom."[24] Man is capable of both justice and evil, they believed, and he needs to be inspired to love his neighbors and be restrained from harming them by a moral authority beyond government edict.

U.S. foreign policy that aims at democratization or advancing freedom globally must include strategies for cultivating civil society institutions that are adequately robust to support those ends. "Without institutionally reliable processes of mediation," write Peter L. Berger and Richard John Neuhaus, the political order becomes detached from the values and realities of individual life. Deprived of its moral foundation, the political order is 'delegitimated.' When that happens, the political order must be secured by coercion rather than by consent. And when that happens, democracy disappears.[25]

The context of Berger's and Neuhaus' comments is the United States, but these and other lessons from domestic discussions of civil society have international relevance as well. Domestically, the civil society dialogue arose out of a concern for cultural erosion in American society. Not only were government programs unable to stop it, they seemed often to contribute to the erosion. The civil society movement focused attention on the limits of government and, by contrast, the power of private sector institutions – including family, religious congregations, and other community-based organizations – in creating social stability. Religious congregations and faith-based groups in particular have offered solutions to seemingly intransigent problems like prisoner recidivism, gang warfare, and welfare dependency. Where government programs have failed, religious groups have been effective in dealing with matters of the heart. In short, religious groups have won hearts and minds where the welfare state was unsuccessful.

Could religious groups also have a strategic advantage in the contest for hearts and minds internationally? What would a civil society approach to public diplomacy look like?

A civil society approach to public diplomacy would begin with greater clarity about the role of religion and private associations in the continued success of the American experiment in ordered liberty. It would accurately assess the persistent significance of religious belief and practice and display a deferential rather than dismissive attitude toward religion in America and abroad. Government spokesmen, public diplomats and others would be less visibly awkward in discussing religion and religious issues.

This approach would highlight America's network of mediating structures as a distinguishing feature of the American constitutional order and as an essential support for its system of democratic capitalism. Such a strategy would tap the potential of civil society groups, including religious groups, to communicate and model civil society to their counterparts abroad who could fill similar functions. It would aim to transform hearts and minds among foreign audiences by targeting those cultural and religious gatekeepers who influence community sentiment and allegiance.

This civil society approach to public diplomacy would look beyond both government and market for its message as well as its method. It would contest the idea that global mass communications through corporate marketing or the news media are an adequate substitute for strategic communication about American ideals. From Madison Avenue and Wall Street to Hollywood and Silicon Valley, American businesses and their marketers have global communications agendas that serve their own ends. These are not inherently at cross-purposes with strategic public diplomacy messaging; marketing messages about the "American way of life" can portray aspects of the civil society ideals that a public diplomacy campaign might aim to communicate.

The proliferation of global communications does pose challenges for a civil society-focused public diplomacy strategy. The distaste of many Americans for some of the sexually explicit or crass mass media messages can serve as a warning system for similar responses on the part of foreign audiences. Such cases demand, at minimum, a more representative portrayal of American life through public diplomacy projects. Not everyone lives like the characters on popular television shows.

Winning the war of ideas is more than a marketing challenge. A corporate model for public diplomacy will not adequately sustain U.S. foreign policy objectives. Selling "brand America" is insufficient. When Condoleezza Rice took the helm at the State Department in 2004, one commentator highlighted the need to remake public diplomacy away from this corporate model. The secretary of state, he argued, "must reinvent our public diplomacy, articulating abroad the values for which the U.S. stands, using not the techniques of Madison Avenue executives (one of the failures of the first part of the administration) but speech rooted in America's history and politics."[26]

When public diplomacy is enlisted in support of democratization, a civil society approach is imperative: civil society is a prerequisite of democracy. Public diplomacy aimed at promoting democracy should be strenuously focused on explaining the role of religious liberty and freedom of conscience as the cornerstone of limited government while cultivating the civil society support system necessary to sustain the consent for the emerging democracy.

Freedom of conscience is a means of preserving the integrity of religion. Far from demoting religion to a lesser status, constitutional religious liberty frees religious institutions, leaders, and individual believers to exercise their "prophetic voice," appraising government actions for their attention to morality and justice without fear of reprisal. In this way, religious institutions and individuals can exercise a check on government claims and actions.

Where civil society has been stifled or never existed, such a model of religious engagement will be quite foreign. Therefore, another element of this approach to public diplomacy should be the identification of religious intermediaries, both individuals and groups, who can model and teach civil society functions or who have already undertaken such projects. In addition to the technical skills they impart, these religious believers' endorsement of civil society processes conveys an important message to religious communities in the target audience.

Finally, a civil society approach to public diplomacy should target leaders of mediating structures in the foreign culture. This approach would look beyond state structures and political leaders to actual or potential civil society leaders, including religious and community leaders. Robert L. Woodson, Sr., founder of the Center for Neighborhood Enterprise, has this to say about domestic civil society strategy: "because their constituents trust them and seek them as a source of support and guidance, indigenous community leaders should be considered the primary vehicle for the delivery of services and resources to their neighborhoods."[27] Just as domestic community leadership efforts have looked beyond formally titled roles to detect the indigenous authorities in a neighborhood – the pastors or matriarchal activists of the inner city, for example – such an approach applied to foreign policy would seek to identify the culturally authoritative figures in a society.

In his book, *What Went Wrong?* Bernard Lewis discusses the notion of civil society in the Muslim world:

> In the Islamic context, the independence and initiative of the civil society may best be measured not in relation to the state, but in relation to religion, of which in the Muslim perception, the state itself is a manifestation and instrument. In this sense, the primary meaning of civil is non-religious, and the civil society is one in which the organizing principle is something other than religion, that being a private affair of the individual.[28]

This assessment challenges the Westphalian concept of nation-state that provides the framework for U.S. diplomacy and most international politics. It argues for a civil society strategy for public diplomacy that is centered around a clear understanding of religious liberty based on freedom of conscience. Such a campaign must be waged not *against* religion, but *in the interest of* the integrity of religious belief. In other words, public diplomacy directed to Muslim audiences should not be based on a crusade of secularization or Westernization. Both can serve to exacerbate extremism and give occasion or protest against the United States.[29]

In assessing Islam's record of tolerating non-Muslim minorities, Lewis finds greater accommodation prior to the end of the 17th century, from which time Islam has been in retreat. "The emergence of some form of civil society would therefore seem to offer the best hope for decent coexistence based on mutual respect."[30]

A former Iraqi government official advocated the same in a 2006 speech: "Civil society in Iraq... is a question of reconfiguring the age-old structures that kept society intact." Major differences "were resolved in history by smoothing out the edges that allowed for a large common space between Arabs and Kurds, between Shi'ites and Sunnis, between various minorities and the majoritarian perspective of Islam." Dictatorship cut off this tradition and the insurgency in Iraq represents "an attempt to re-write the history of Islam and its sects by a narrow group of people who have perverted the idea of modernism and have perverted the ideal of the identity of Islam."[31]

Specific proposals for a civil society public diplomacy agenda

Ensure that key personnel have an understanding of the role of religion in the U.S. and abroad.

This should include the recruitment of personnel and advisory networks who have experience working for or alongside religious or civil society groups. U.S. public diplomacy specialists should understand and be able to articulate the significance of religion in the American constitutional order and within civil society. They should also be equipped to appreciate the role of religion in the individual lives and societies of foreign audiences.

In regions of the world where religion is a dominant force in politics, the U.S. must staff its diplomatic posts with individuals who have a deep understanding of the religious dynamics at issue. From ambassadors to Foreign Service officers, the selection of individuals who appreciate the significance of religion will enhance communications potential and contribute to the credibility of the United States. The president would not select an individual with a dismissive attitude toward Catholicism to be U.S. Ambassador to the Vatican; nor should he appoint someone who lacks a significant understanding of Islam to be ambassador to a predominantly Muslim country.

To further this end, the U.S. must designate personnel to provide analysis of religious dynamics to U.S. missions. Because of the complexity of religious situations in many places around the world, Douglas Johnston of the International Center for Religion and Diplomacy estimates that about 30 U.S. missions – including those in the Middle East, Southeast Asia, and the Balkans – would benefit from a religion attaché. The qualifications of the attaché would include an expertise in the religious complexities of the location and an understanding of religious beliefs on the individual and societal levels. The attaché would build relationships with local religious leaders to gain knowledge and trust in dealing with the particular situation at hand.[32]

The U.S. should make the message faithful to its tenets of religious liberty.

Public diplomacy exists to promote the understanding of America's founding principles among foreign audiences. A major component of the message must be an explanation of the nature of religious liberty and the significance of religious belief and practice in America's civil society. At the same time, this requires an understanding of the political claims of Islam and other religions that may present obstacles to the resonance of such ideas.

One way of accomplishing this is to better integrate the on-going work of two important aspects of the international freedom agenda – the promotion of religious liberty and democracy. The 1998 International Religious Freedom Act states: "It shall be the policy of the United States… to condemn violations of religious freedom, and to promote, and to assist other governments in the promotion of, the fundamental right to freedom of religion."[33]

The law calls for a wider view of the mandate of the religious liberty office at the State Department. Created by the 1998 law, the office annually reports on religious freedom around the world, identifying those countries that are the worst offenders in persecuting religious believers as well as noting any that have made improvements in their treatment of religion. This role as human rights monitor has represented an important step, but foreign policy engagement on religious liberty should go further. Particularly as U.S. foreign policy advances democracy, the religious liberty mandate should be construed more broadly so that the office serves as a resource and offers strategic input in the essential task of establishing freedom of conscience as the foundation of democracy.

A decade after its creation, however, the International Religious Freedom office still was not integrated into an overall democratization strategy, according to former director Thomas Farr. Instead, it addresses religious liberty primarily "as a sequestered, humanitarian problem."[34] Farr argues for expanding that vision: "If the United States is to encourage the spread of democracy, it must learn to engage and influence powerful religious communities."[35]

In accordance with these goals, the U.S. must investigate the political claims of Islam and determine their implications for the United States' national security objectives and constitutional commitment to religious liberty. This amounts to an inquiry into theology to which policymakers are generally not accustomed. However, as former secretary of state Madeleine Albright has written, "the constitutional requirement that separates state from church in the United States does not also insist that the state be ignorant of the church, mosque, synagogue, pagoda, and temple."[36] The inquiry into Islamic political claims will help identify potential points of conflict with the claims of the West (e.g., the U.S. constitutional guarantee of civil liberty independent of citizens' religious profession). The challenge for public diplomacy is to distinguish essential elements of the American order from incidental features of 21st century American culture, committing to the promotion of the former without letting the latter create distracting friction.

Indeed, American history is replete with examples of the way in which religious principles have contributed to the shaping of the American republic and society. These include, the Catholic principle of subsidiarity,[37] the Protestant work ethic, the Lutheran concept of sphere sovereignty, and the general Christian principle of "just war," which defines the legitimate use of force.[38] U.S. public diplomacy specialists must tap religious tradition for such principles that support civil society and limited constitutional government. Similarly, they must seek out Muslim principles that promote charity and other civil society ideas and amplify the messages of those who most effectively promote them.

While doing so, however, the U.S. must be sure to confront politicized factions as distinct from religious. American deference to religious freedom should not extend to politicized ideologies acting under the guise of religion. Domestically, the U.S. constitutional guarantee of free exercise of religion does not go so far as to allow those acting in the name of religion to destroy the order that ensures their freedom. Internationally, U.S. officials should not shrink from denouncing violent action or speech that incites violence, even when veiled in religious terms such as "holy war" (*jihad*) or "holy warriors" (*mujahideen*).[39] This includes the need to recognize political propaganda disguised as religion, such as the Guantanamo Bay prisoner claims of human rights abuses and religious liberty violations that track with instructions in an al Qaeda training manual. Discovered during a raid of an al Qaeda member's apartment in Manchester, England in 2000, the 18-chapter manual gives explicit instructions for carrying out terrorist operations, complete with directives in the case of capture. In that event, terrorist trainees were told to claim mistreatment and torture.[40]

The U.S. has ample precedent, consistent with internationally recognized norms, for making distinctions between religion and ideologies that use religion to legitimize violence and political power. General Douglas MacArthur set one of the most important precedents when he handled Shintoism in post-World War II Japan. Shinto, nationalized in 1884, was "what National Socialism would later be to Germany, an indigenous folk creed promoting the national character, the martial virtues, and the inferiority of other races," according to MacArthur's biographer, William Manchester. MacArthur treated Shintoism as a political cult that had fueled Japanese opposition to surrender. Under the U.S.-dictated terms of surrender in 1945, the Emperor renounced his claim to deity and the state ended its support for Shinto shrines of which there were 110,000 at the time. This was a momentous break. The end of the state support for Shintoism was directly related to the launch of a democratic order, with Japanese political leaders consenting to the transition: "The Diet [parliament] agreed that Shinto (the way of the gods) should be replaced by Minshushugi (the way of democracy)."[41]

Enlist civil society mediators of the message.

"Public diplomacy," as a former government advisory commission chairman defined it, "is promoting U.S. interests and security through understanding, informing, and influencing foreign publics and broadening dialogue between American citizens and institutions and counterparts abroad on a long-term basis."[42] Religious citizens and institutions can further the work of public diplomacy by reaching their counterparts abroad in ways that the U.S. government cannot.

As such, the U.S. should seek the counsel of religious individuals and groups with experience in the target cultures. Christian missionaries serving foreign communities through schools and hospitals are one example of largely harmonious interaction between the United States and non-Western cultures.[43] Missionaries who have participated in such outreach efforts glean valuable insights into the culture and religious beliefs of people and groups that continue to confound many U.S. officials. Similarly, military chaplains stationed with units in critical locations could provide insight and assistance in communicating with religious audiences.[44]

With such insight, it becomes increasingly possible to encourage and build upon "faith-based diplomacy." Douglas Johnston defines faith-based diplomacy as a type of Track II unofficial diplomacy that combines insights drawn from religious faith with the practice of international relations.[45] The faith-based diplomat (Pope John Paul II was the preeminent example, but others would include less public religious leaders) has moral authority and engages in conflict resolution by appealing to transcendent spiritual resources, including sacred texts and prayer. At the same time, such diplomacy recognizes "the profound and irreconcilable differences between religious traditions;"[46] to minimize them would threaten the credibility of faith-based diplomats. Instead, they appeal to a religious tradition's own tenets. Of particular importance for conflict resolution is the capacity of religious traditions to "(1) reflect on their history in a redemptive manner, (2) bring meaning and dignity to the suffering, and (3) to hold out the promise of genuine healing."[47] Johnston's International Center for Religion and Diplomacy has conducted such conflict resolution projects in places like Sudan and Pakistan.

An important part of such conflict resolution is the encouragement and promotion of religious leaders who refute the violent politicization of their faith and practice. Is Islamic orthodoxy moderate or aggressive? Western policy circles have debated the question, but the struggle over the direction of Islam goes on within the faith. U.S. policy and public diplomacy should continue to seek out and strengthen non-violent, moderate voices in the Muslim world.

While government officials can condemn violence by religious extremists, religious leaders can speak with spiritual authority that will command far more attention among believers. It is the hearts and minds of these believers – caught between calls for political moderation and violent extremism – that are particularly at stake, and mainstream religious leaders can carry significant weight with them. U.S. officials and their surrogates should work with leaders who are urging temperance to encourage and reinforce their condemnation of the extremism that distorts their religion. Examples of such refutation include the following:

Radical Islam

The July 2005 *fatwa* against terrorism issued by U.S. and Canadian Muslim leaders is one example of orthodox religious leaders condemning extremists' perversion of their religious tenets. This statement was an official judicial ruling of the Fiqh Council of North America, a group of 18 Islamic scholars that decides Muslim judicial issues. Citing passages from the Koran that urge peace and justice, the ruling forbids acts of terrorism and cooperation with terrorists. It also reminds Muslims of their "civic and religious duty… to cooperate with law enforcement authorities to protect the lives of all civilians." It closes with the following:

> We pray for the defeat of extremism and terrorism. We pray for the safety and security of our country, the United States, and its people. We pray for the safety and security of all inhabitants of our planet. We pray that interfaith harmony and cooperation prevail both in the United States and all around the globe.[48]

Liberation Theology

The "revolutionary Christian" participation in Marxist-Leninist insurgencies in the 1980s is an example of a political movement exploiting religion. Christians adhering to liberation theology, which emphasizes socioeconomic redemption and political power rather than individual spiritual transformation, were attracted to the Marxist revolutionary ideas of the Sandinista leaders in Nicaragua and the FMLN guerrillas in El Salvador. While some may have had ideas of merging their Christian faith with Marxist politics, as one member of the movement said, "'I consider myself a Christian, but I am clear that if at some point in time I would have to choose between religion and the revolution, I am with the revolution.'"[49]

For many Christians who joined the Sandinistas and FMLN, Marxism became the faith to which they sought to convert their former fellow believers. "[The revolutionary Christians] do not preach to Marxists in order to attract them to Christ, but to Christians in order to draw them to Marx," explains one observer whose conversion took him the opposite direction.[50] The U.S. government actively combated liberation theology as an international political movement, sponsoring defectors from the movement to tour the world as part of an aggressive public diplomacy effort.

In an example of how a faith community can call on its own to avoid political temptation, the Catholic Church in Nicaragua spoke out against the Sandinistas, as well as their one-time fellow believers who had joined them. Pope John Paul II publicly rebuked priests who made common cause with the Marxist Nicaraguans. Church leaders criticized the human rights abuses and the militant atheism of the Sandinista regime. While these religious leaders did so actively and of their own initiative, the United States magnified their message around the world, occasionally assisting and promoting their publications, and facilitating as much media exposure as possible. Congress held hearings to expose the extremism of the ideology.

"It is one thing to call a priest to exercise his ministry [within the political arena] and another very different thing to insert himself into a system in order to justify it or give it religious legitimacy. Religion cannot be at the service of partisan interests," wrote the Nicaraguan bishops in response to the claims of a few priests who said they were doing their civic duty by serving in the senior ranks of the Sandinista government.[51] "The church is at the service of the people, but not at the service of power."[52]

As policymakers seek out the voices of moderation in religious circles, it is important to make a distinction between political moderation and religious or doctrinal moderation; they are not necessarily synonymous, though a secularist perspective tends to conflate them. For the purposes of international politics, the political expression of a religious group's beliefs is the major concern, not the mere fact that they profess deeply held beliefs. A society can be strongly religious and politically moderate – the United States is a prime example. The genius of the American founding was that it balanced citizens' dual allegiances to God and to earthly authorities without forcing believers to abandon or to compromise (or "to moderate") their primary loyalty to God.

Conclusion

The United States will be prepared to wage a war of ideas only when it understands the role of religion. Founders carefully poised the new American order in relation to religion, producing a constructive tension between church and state rather than the radical separation sometimes implied by today's circuit-shopped court decisions. Many U.S. officials, as well as the public at large would be hard-pressed to define religious liberty and to discuss its role in American civil society. Yet an understanding of America's pioneering approach to religious liberty and the reasons for its continued success, both for the maintenance of a healthy state and for a thriving religious culture, are critical to the success of U.S. public diplomacy. Only by understanding the role of religion in the American order can U.S. public diplomacy begin to place adequate significance on religion's role in foreign societies and work with it effectively.

A civil society approach to public diplomacy should begin by recognizing the fundamental relationship between religious liberty and democracy. It should recruit the assistance of religious groups and individuals who can encourage the mediating structures that will support self-government in foreign societies. It should also identify and cultivate the potential leaders of civil society, including religious leaders, among such populations.

Because religion speaks so loudly to thoughts and sentiments and can move people in ways that no temporal ideology can, violent extremists have used it for their own ends to incite terrorism. U.S. policymakers must disentangle themselves from apprehensions that prevent them from grappling with the religious dynamics of the war on terrorism and learn how to engage the debate in civil society terms, tapping the strength of religious practice in American society and the history of religious liberty in the American order. They will then realize that Americans have more in common with other civilizations than they ever imagined.

Notes

[1] See Madeleine Albright, "Faith and Diplomacy," *The Review of Faith and International Affairs*, Fall 2006; Walter Russell Mead, "God's Country," *Foreign Affairs,* September-October 2006.

[2] President George W. Bush, Remarks to American Legion National Convention, Salt Lake City, Utah, August 31, 2006.

[3] That is not to say that religious considerations are absent from U.S. foreign relations. The question is *how* religion is considered and whether this is adequate to current challenges. Clearly, religious understanding informed the moral framework and rhetoric of the Bush administration's foreign policy (as it had previous administrations). Likewise, Members of Congress pay heed to their religious constituents' global interests, particularly with regard to persecuted believers abroad, as in the International Religious Freedom Act of 1998. But this has not translated into the systematic practice of assessing religious belief as a motivating factor in geopolitics.

[4] Adda B. Bozeman, "Knowledge and Method in Comparative Intelligence Studies," in *Strategic Intelligence & Statecraft*, (Brassey's, 1992), p. 191. Though the essay was originally published in 1988, Bozeman's analysis of America's strategic intelligence deficits remains *apropos* to the present situation.

[5] Bozeman, "American Policy and the Illusion of Congruent Values," in *Strategic Intelligence,* op cit, p. 220.

[6] Interview and subsequent correspondence with Thomas F. Farr, July 2005.

[7] Adda B. Bozeman, *Strategic Intelligence and Statecraft*, (Brassey's, 1992), p. 19.

[8] Peter L. Berger and Richard John Neuhaus, "Mediating Structures and the Dilemmas of the Welfare State," in *To Empower People: From State to Civil Society,* Michael Novak, ed. (American Enterprise Institute, 1996), p. 160.

[9] Bozeman, "American Policy and the Illusion of Congruent Values," *Strategic Intelligence*, p. 216.

[10] Samuel P. Huntington, Who Are We? The Challenges to America's National Identity, (Simon & Schuster, 2004), p. 10ff.

[11] As Michael Novak describes, democratic capitalism is a three-part system: "Not only do the logic of democracy and the logic of the market economy strengthen one another. Both also require a special moral-cultural base." Michael Novak, *The Spirit of Democratic Capitalism* (Madison Books, 1991), p. 16.

[12] "American Piety in the 21st Century: New Insights to the Depth and Complexity of Religion in the US," Selected Findings from the Baylor Religion Survey, September 2006, pp. 7-8, 12.

[13] Peter Berger defines *secularization* as "the process by which sectors of society and culture are removed from the domination of religious institutions and symbols." Peter L. Berger, *The Sacred Canopy: Elements of a Sociological Theory of Religion*, (Anchor Books, 1990) p. 107.

[14] Patrick F. Fagan, "Why Religion Matters: The Impact of Religious Practice on Social Stability," *Backgrounder #1064*, The Heritage Foundation, January 25, 1996.

[15] Thomas F. Farr, "The Diplomacy of Religious Freedom," *First Things*, May 2006.

[16] Andrew Natsios, "Faith-Based NGOs and U.S. Foreign Policy," *The Influence of Faith: Religious Groups & U.S. Foreign Policy*, Elliott Abrams, ed. (Rowman & Littlefield, 2001), p. 200.

[17] George Weigel, "Comment on Chapter 3: Religious Persecution and Religious Relevance in Today's World," *The Influence of Faith: Religious Groups & U.S. Foreign Policy*, Elliott Abrams, ed. (Rowman & Littlefield, 2001), pp. 65-66.

[18] Bozeman, Strategic Intelligence, p. 5.

[19] Douglas Johnston, *Faith-Based Diplomacy: Trumping Realpolitik* (Oxford University Press, 2003), p. xii.

[20] Social scientist Olivier Roy distinguishes between the terms *Muslim* and *Islamist*, the former designating the religious tradition and the latter referring to contemporary political ideological movements heavily influenced by Marxist patterns of thought and action. See Olivier Roy, *The Failure of Political Islam* (Harvard University Press, 1996), p. ix.

[21] Walter Russell Mead, "God's Country," *Foreign Affairs*, September-October, 2006.

[22] Peter L. Berger and Richard John Neuhaus, "Mediating Structures and the Dilemmas of the Welfare State," in *To Empower People: From State to Civil Society*, Michael Novak, ed. (American Enterprise Institute, 1996), p. 158.

[23] Ibid, p. 163.

[24] Thomas G. West, "Religious Liberty: The View from the Founding," The Claremont Institute, January 1997, at http://www.claremont.org/writings/970101west.html (August 18, 2006).

[25] Berger and Neuhaus, pp. 159-160.

[26] Elliott Cohen, "From Colin to Condoleezza," *Wall Street Journal,* November 17, 2004.

[27] Robert L. Woodson, Sr., "Success Stories," in *To Empower People,* p. 108. Editor's note: The American and British militaries have been remarkably successful at the local level by using similar tactics in Afghanistan and Iraq.

[28] Bernard Lewis, What Went Wrong? The Clash Between Islam and Modernity in the Middle East (Perennial, 2002), p. 112.

[29] See for example, Lewis, pp. 104-107; Olivier Roy, *The Failure of Political Islam* (Harvard University Press, 1996); and Anna Simmons, "Making Enemies, Part Two," *The American Interest,* September-October, 2006.

[30] Lewis, p. 115.

[31] Ali Abdul Ameer Allawi, Former Minister of Finance of the Republic of Iraq, "Civil Society in Iraq at Work Amid the War," Address at The Heritage Foundation, April 26, 2006.

[32] Douglas M. Johnston, "The Case for a Religion Attaché," *Foreign Service Journal* (February 2002), pp. 33-38. At http://www.afsa.org/fsj/feb02/johnston.cfm, August 1, 2005. Johnston put a $10 million price tag on the training, payroll, and operating costs of such an effort.

[33] The International Religious Freedom Act of 1998, Public Law 105-292, Sec. 2(b)(1).

[34] Thomas F. Farr, "The Diplomacy of Religious Freedom," *First Things,* May 2006.

[35] Ibid.

[36] Madeleine Albright, "Faith and Diplomacy," *The Review of Faith & International Affairs,* Fall 2006, p. 8.

[37] See discussion in Michael Novak, "Seven Tangled Questions," in Berger and Neuhaus, p. 139.

[38] See for example, James Turner Johnson, *Morality and Contemporary Warfare* (Yale University, 1999), and Jean Bethke Elshtain, *Just War Against Terror: The Burden of American Power in a Violent World* (Basic Books, 2003).

[39] Editor's note: We discuss this subject at length in Chapter 13.

[40] Donna Miles, "Al Qaeda Manual Drives Detainee Behavior at Guantanamo Bay," *American Forces Information Services,* June 29, 2005, at http://www.pentagon.mil/news/Jun2005/20050629_1901.html, August 1, 2005.

[41] William Manchester, *American Caesar: Douglas MacArthur, 1880-1964* (Little, Brown, 1978), p. 462.

[42] Edwin J. Feulner, "American Public Diplomacy: Roadmap to Recovery," Opening Remarks at The Heritage Foundation, June 14, 2005. Feulner was Chairman of the U.S. Advisory Commission on Public Diplomacy from 1982-1991.

[43] See Walter Russell Mead, "God's Country," *Foreign Affairs,* September-October 2006, p. 42.

[44] Johnston, *op cit,* pp. 24-25.

[45] Douglas Johnston, *Faith-Based Diplomacy: Trumping Realpolitik* (Oxford University Press, 2003) pp. xii, 15.

[46] Ibid., p. 17.

[47] Ibid, pp. 16-17, 19.

[48] Jason DeRose, "U.S. Muslim Scholars Issue Edict Against Terrorism," *All Things Considered*, National Public Radio, July 28, 2005, at http://www.npr.org/templates/story/story.php?storyId=4775588, August 1, 2005. Editor's note: The fatwa was long in coming. It did not materialize without nearly four years of pressure on American Muslim leaders to take a clear stance against terrorism.

[49] Quoted in Humberto Belli, Breaking Faith: The Sandinista Revolution and Its Impact on Freedom and Christian Faith in Nicaragua,(Crossway Books, 1986), p. 163.

[50] Ibid.

[51] Ibid, p. 186.

[52] Ibid, p. 187.

6

Conducting a War of Ideas with Public Diplomacy: An insider's view

ROBERT R. REILLY

The purpose of U.S. public diplomacy is to reach the audiences of key foreign countries, outside of the bilateral channels of traditional diplomatic relations, with ideas that are powerful enough to form their disposition toward the U.S. and its ultimate objective of advancing freedom and democracy in the world. This broad objective, emanating from the Founding documents of the U.S., encompasses the promotion of U.S. policies as they are related to it. However, public diplomacy is, essentially, the defense and promotion of the Founding principles of America. Anything less is an exercise in public relations related to the advancement of a particular policy at a specific time, for example, a free trade agreement or an arms control measure. This is why, at times of national peril, the call goes forth not for more public relations, but for a public diplomacy that can engage in the war of ideas. It is vital to get public diplomacy right because modern wars are most often manifestations of wars of ideas. The final victory takes place not on the battlefield, but in the human mind.

How to conduct a war of ideas

There are several fundamental maxims for the successful conduct of a war of ideas. In order to fight a war of ideas, one has to have an idea. This is not as simple as it may sound. A war of ideas is a struggle over the very nature of reality for which people are willing to die. Therefore, the first thing one must do is formulate the ideas that are so central to one's life that one is not willing to live without them. For a nation successfully to project such ideas, there must be a broad consensus within it as to what those ideas are.

Second, one cannot go into a war of ideas until one understands the ideas with which one is at war. Such wars are always conducted in terms of moral legitimacy. The defense of one's ideas and the attack on those of the enemy are conducted with moral rhetoric. "Axis of evil" is a perfect example, as is "the great Satan." All moral differences are at root theological, even if secular society pretends that they are not.

Third, wars of ideas, by definition, can only be fought by and with people who think. This defines the natural target audience for this war, the so-called "elites." The term "elite" is not determined by social or economic status, but by intellectual capabilities. Trying to use ideas to influence people who do not think is an exercise in futility. Such people are led and influenced by those who do think. The effort to reach these people is more properly the purview of public relations. This is not to demean that necessary effort but to define it and to distinguish it from public diplomacy.

Fourth, along with a consistency of purpose, one must have the organizational and financial means for conducting a war of ideas over the course of generations. Ideas, when they are profound enough to form the basis of a civilization, have a prolonged gestational period. K.P.S. Gill, India's foremost authority on counter-terrorism, has said that, in Kashmir, radical Islamists taught their doctrines in madrassas for two decades before the occurrence of any terrorist acts. After this period of gestation, *the war of ideas was already won* in the minds of the students who then formed the cadre of Islamist terrorist organizations. The same is true in other parts of the Islamic world. The war of ideas requires institutions that are capable of countering this kind of indoctrination over similarly lengthy periods, i.e. decades.

The United States is currently bereft of such institutions. A few private foundations do what they can on private donations. Since the elimination of the U.S. Information Agency, the government has lacked a platform from which to conduct a war of ideas in any consistent way. What passes for public diplomacy seems more preoccupied with short-term public relations problems than with the long-term inculcation of the principles of freedom.

How we got it wrong

Today, U.S. public diplomacy is in disarray, failing in some essential way to observe each of these maxims. Both President George W. Bush and Secretary of State Condoleezza Rice admitted that U.S. public diplomacy performed poorly on their watch. One reason for the failure was dramatically illustrated by the testimony of Margaret Tutwiler, during her six month stint as Under Secretary of State for Public Diplomacy and Public Affairs, before the House Appropriations Subcommittee, on February 4, 2004. Though occupying the senior appointed position in the U.S. government for the conduct of the war of ideas, Tutwiler failed even to mention the war of ideas or the global war on terrorism. Her testimony consisted of a litany of State Department programs without an enunciated purpose beyond that of demonstrating how nice Americans are, so as to clear up the misunderstanding that Americans are not so nice. If you get the war of ideas wrong at this level – the level of principle – you will certainly get it wrong at the level of execution. This chapter examines how we got it wrong in both respects, and then suggest how we can get it right.

Let us take the first maxim. What is the American "idea" over which the war of ideas is being fought? How do we formulate the view of reality over which we are willing to fight and die so we can communicate it to the world? How, to put it vulgarly, do we "advertise" ourselves to the world?

Unfortunately, American advertising is not only the primary means by which we present ourselves to the world, but the preferred model for doing so. And after 9/11, it is to the advertising world and its executives, including from MTV, that the State Department and U.S. international broadcasting first turned to meet the enemy in the war of ideas. Surely, it was thought, the country whose commercial brands dominate the world economy can, with the same means, promote the cause of freedom. Typically, this approach was translated into TV commercials showing happy Muslims in the United States, under the rubric of "Shared Values," and new radio stations playing pop music to Arabs and Iranians, under the same assumption of whatever "shared values" such music expresses.

While advertising techniques have valuable contributions to make in pubic diplomacy and may be particularly useful in tactical situations, the general approach of advertising is aimed at influencing an audience with a short attention span with subliminal messages to affect short-term behavior. In other words, the means of advertising determines the message. It reduces the war of ideas to slogans that are of marginal use in persuading thoughtful people concerning matters of life and death. The advertising approach shows a misunderstanding of the nature of this war. It assumes that the war of ideas is based upon a misunderstanding. If we can only convey a more favorable impression of our "brand," the problem will go away.

Not only do the means restrict the message. The message itself is wrong. When the rainbow of diversity that is popularly celebrated in

America leads the message, it leaves the impression upon foreign audiences that the United States is indifferent to the various claims to ultimate truth that its assorted representatives put forth. Islam is just another item on the shelf of American consumer society, chosen for its level of personal satisfaction. The happy Muslims are simply happy shoppers in the cafeteria of religions. The implied demotion of the importance of what is believed to be true inadvertently inflames the believers. America is seen as shallow.

The objective of the TV ads presenting happy Muslims in the U.S. was laudable in so far as it intended to demonstrate tolerance and the fact that the U.S. does not consider itself at war with Islam, both important points. However, it was the wrong message for the audience. The fact that Islam is tolerated here is not a particularly persuasive message to a Muslim who thinks that Islam is true. In fact, it is likely to be seen as condescending. Also, a demonstration of tolerance is not a convincing message to those who do not think tolerance is a virtue, but a sign of indifference. In fact, tolerance is taken by many in the audience as a sign of our moral decline. What we see as a virtue is perceived as a moral failing.

Because of their inherent limitations, these ads could not begin to suggest the moral principles from which such tolerance is drawn. Muslims are not free in the United States because the United States thinks Islam is the source of happiness, but because the United States recognizes Muslims as human beings with inalienable rights. It is precisely that recognition that is absent in many of the Muslim countries that deny such rights to its heterodox Muslims and non-Muslim citizens. The sanctity of the individual and the inviolability of conscience are not doctrines necessarily recognized by an audience that does not have a framework in which to receive them. That is why several Muslim countries prohibited the ads. The problem has to be addressed at a higher level.

In other words, contending claims to truth are often incompatible. That is why there is a war of ideas in the first place. It is a mistake to fudge this issue and to offer a derivate virtue – tolerance – in place of the larger truth from which it stems. If there is to be a war, let it be of one truth against another – not of a seeming indifference to truth on our side against an absolute claim to it on the other. For if it be the latter, the former will lose.

Another example of the failure to formulate and convey ideas in a compelling way was manifested by the changes in U.S. international broadcasting after 9/11. This is particularly important since broadcasting absorbs roughly half of the U.S. public diplomacy budget of around $1.2 billion. At a time during which Americans showed their

willingness to die for their country and what it represents, how did
government broadcasting portray the U.S.?

The Voice of America (VOA) is the premier broadcasting arm of
the U.S. government. VOA's mission is to express and serve the
enduring interests of the United States, which includes, most
importantly, the spread of its democratic principles. A Broadcasting
Board of Governors, which exercises executive powers, oversees it. Its
members are largely drawn from journalism and the U.S. commercial
broadcasting industry. To their credit, the members successfully sought
the funds to update the obsolete broadcasting infrastructure to the
Middle East, which had consisted almost solely of short wave, so that
radio could be heard in AM and FM.

Since 9/11, the board has spun off from VOA several of the
language services especially critical to the war of ideas, Arabic and
Farsi, and transformed them into primarily music stations, Radio Sawa
and Radio Farda. The model for doing so is commercial. The most
successful members of the board made their millions in U.S. domestic
broadcasting and they are only doing what they know. Large
audiences, demographically defined in the Arab and Persian worlds as
youth audiences, are attracted by popular music formats, like youth
audiences everywhere. Since numbers mean survival for a commercial
broadcaster, it is hardly strange that this perspective was brought to
bear on U.S. international broadcasting. However, this approach shares
the same faulty assumptions of the "Shared Values" TV ad campaign,
albeit in a different manner.

Numbers of listeners certainly matter, but not as much as *who* is
listening – and to *what*. The Voice of America was designed to operate
without the financial pressures of commercial media in order to be able
to afford to tell the whole truth about the United States, including its
full cultural depth and spiritual resonance. VOA has always used
music to attract audiences. For example, Willis Conover's jazz
program broadcast on VOA to Soviet audiences during the Cold War
was one of the most successful radio programs in history. However, it
was offered within a format devoted mainly to substance – news,
editorials, and features. That ratio has now been reversed with music
occupying as much as, or more than, 80% of the hour in Radio Sawa.

The more like commercial radio U.S. broadcasting becomes, the
less reason it has to exist. After all, the image of America created by
the popular media is the cliché that often repels much of the world.
U.S. broadcasting has the duty to portray the character of the American
people in such a way that the underlying principles of American life are
revealed. Music with a sprinkling of news cannot do this. U.S.
broadcasting owes it to its listeners to show how a free people live –

and to correct the image of the U.S. that our own popular culture has sometimes created in their minds, a false image that has often helped fuel anti-Americanism.

However, the level of confusion on the Board has been so profound that its leading members do not even consider broadcasting to be part of U.S. public diplomacy. At a town hall meeting at the Voice of America on September 10, 2002, Chairman Ken Tomlinson told the employees, "You can't intertwine public diplomacy with broadcasting." Board member Ted Kaufman responded, "I couldn't agree with the chairman more... we've got to start thinking about ourselves separate from public diplomacy." This loss of a sense of mission has been reflected in the changes the board has made.

Radio Sawa, for example, has two brief, bulletin-style newscasts in the hour. The rest is American pop and Arabic music, including, according to Sawa's progenitor, Governor Norman Pattiz, "everyone from Eminem to J.Lo to Britney Spears." Mr. Pattiz told the *New Yorker* magazine that "it was MTV that brought down the Berlin Wall," a statement of breathtaking ignorance. In October 2002, Chairman Tomlinson approvingly quoted his Naval Academy graduate son: "her [Britney Spears'] music represents the sounds of freedom." Based upon this extraordinary assumption, the Board of Governors transformed the substantive programming of VOA's and RFE/RL's Farsi services into another mostly music station modeled on Sawa. The war of ideas has been demoted to the battle of the bands. Will MTV help win the war of ideas?

Instead of appealing to reason as recommended by the Declaration of Independence, "out of a decent respect for the opinions of mankind," the new nearly all-music formats pander to another part of the human anatomy. The act of condescension implicit in this new format is not lost on the very part of the audience that we should wish to influence the most – those who think. Only those who think have the potential of affecting the future of their societies.

The change in format has provoked questions from the Middle East: is America playing music because it has nothing to say to us? Alternatively, others who believe that the United States is a degenerate country suspect that the U.S. is consciously attempting to subvert the morals of Arab youth through this kind of music. As one Islamic scholar put it, American pop exemplars are "torchbearers of American society with their cultural and social values . . . that are destroying humanity. They are ruining the lives of thousands of Muslims and leading them to destruction, away from their religion, ethics, and morality." Curiously, when American journalist Charles Glass was kidnapped by Hezbollah in 1987, he reported that his young captors "liked Michael Jackson and Madonna." Apparently, MTV and terrorism are not necessarily incompatible.

Another irony was noted by Abdallah Schleifer, director of the Adham Center for TV Journalism at the American University in Cairo. In August 2003, he noted that "MTV, which may get to their kids, appalls them [the Muslims]. This is one of the weird things, to hear the U.S. administration – which rests on a silent majority of churchgoers – talking about American culture in its Hollywood and New York television manifestations, which is utterly devoted to undermining the values of a conservative Christian society." If it can undermine a Christian civilization, why not a Muslim one? This is the antithesis of a "shared values" campaign.

One of the facile explanations for why U.S. government broadcasting has been reoriented to huge youth audiences and away from elites is because "democracy is a mass movement" – a tautology that overlooks the fact that mass movements are formed and led by leaders who think. *The Federalist Papers* were not the result of a mass movement, but the foundation for one. Would someone immersed in Eminem ever consider reading *The Federalist Papers*, or even know what they are? Those who worry over the moral health of their own societies despise the vulgar part of American popular culture. Since that part of American culture is already available in their societies, why should it be officially reinforced by a U.S. government broadcast? Becoming the caricature of ourselves is bad U.S. public diplomacy. Rather, the job of VOA is to present *before* a 9/11 what much of the world saw only after it – the sacrifice, bravery, charity and piety of the American people as part of a complete picture. By presenting this picture, VOA might even prevent the miscalculations of those who believe they can attack the U.S. with impunity because they have been led to believe, often by our popular media, that it is a weak and morally corrupt country.

The success of Radios Sawa and Farda should be tested by more than sheer audience numbers among the youth. After several years of broadcasting Brittany Spears to the Levant, did the average radical mullah die of apoplexy and the average Abdullah come to love democracy and forsworn all but internal jihad? Apparently, not. According to a State Department draft report on Radio Sawa by the inspector general, cited in the October 13, 2004 *Washington Post*, "it is difficult to ascertain Radio Sawa's impact in countering anti-American views and the biased state-run media of the Arab world." Or, as one expert panel assembled to assess its value concluded, "Radio Sawa failed to present America to its audience." This is not to say that Radio Sawa has not done some good. Ensuing years saw few very encouraging changes. Certainly, it is better if some Arab youth listen to Sawa's non-toxic news broadcasts rather than to their own highly toxic state media. But if the price for this small accomplishment is the elimination of all other U.S. radio broadcasting in Arabic, and other languages like Russian and Chinese, it is too high a price to pay.

Radio broadcasting is needed in the war of ideas, but it has to deal in ideas to be effective. The "MTV message" is not only something that commercial broadcasting can do, it can do better than government-funded radio. Government broadcasting is needed when the United States must communicate an important message to a key audience that it would otherwise not hear. Music, appealing to the emotions, may have a role in this kind of broadcast mission, but only if it is part of a larger idea-based strategy. Commerce-based strategy is profit dominated. Government-based strategy is policy and idea dominated. Only when the policy is to make a profit are the two the same. Combating terrorism and winning the war of ideas are altogether about something other than profit. As broadcast journalist and former USIA chief Edward R. Murrow said, when someone changes his mind, the cash register does not ring.

Structural dysfunctionalism

As mentioned before, engagement in a protracted war of ideas requires institutions that are capable of countering radical Islamist indoctrination and other ideas inimical to democracy over lengthy periods, i.e. decades. Today, there is no single government institution whose sole responsibility is the conduct of the war of ideas. As a result, no government agency feels responsible for it. This mission used to belong to the United States Information Agency, which at the height of the Cold War had some 10,000 employees and a $1 billion budget. After the Soviet collapse, USIA's functions were dispersed to the State Department and the Broadcasting Board of Governors. Within the State Department, public diplomacy functions were further dispersed to regional and other bureaus, making coordination and control by the new Under Secretary for Public Diplomacy problematic.

This is structurally dysfunctional in several ways. Diplomacy and public diplomacy often conflict. Diplomacy may at times require tacit support for an authoritarian government, while at the same time public diplomacy may be reaching out to its citizenry to support democracy. In one infamous episode, VOA created a diplomatic furor by broadcasting an editorial listing Iraq as one of a number of "police states." Saddam Hussein, who was being courted at the time of the Iran-Iraq war, complained bitterly to the State Department. This is not likely to be the only time that principle-based public diplomacy and diplomacy will collide. For that reason, the two missions should not reside in the same institution. The State Department does not, and should not be expected to, give priority to public diplomacy. Even a spike in funding for public diplomacy programs in the Near East and South Asia bureau at State since 9/11 has not produced discernable results. The State Department should concentrate on the implementation of the broad range of the President's policies. Public diplomacy should concentrate on the longer-range goal of winning the war of ideas.

Another consequence of the dissolution of USIA, of which VOA was a part, is that the Broadcasting Board of Governors was left virtually as a freestanding institution with little accountability. Though it meets only once a month, the board was invested with executive powers. As a result, broadcasting is ruled by eight part-time CEOs, with all the attendant chaos such an arrangement would bring to any organization. Board members horse-trade with each other, peeling off favorite parts of the agency, which they then run as personal fiefdoms.

Also, because of the emphasis on appointing members with domestic broadcasting experience, few have any in-depth knowledge of foreign policy, much less of the war of ideas. For example, in 2002, the board attempted to eliminate the Turkish, Thai, Uzbek, and Portuguese to Brazil language services of VOA. The political implications of eliminating broadcasts to Turkey, a key U.S. ally and the premier Muslim democracy, while retaining the Greek service, are staggering to contemplate. Thailand is the most important U.S. ally in Southeast Asia, with its southern most region seething with Islamist activity. Uzbekistan is so centrally located in Central Asia that, within months of the board's attempt to kill the service, U.S. servicemen were posted there. The Secretary of State, who is an *ex officio* board member, tried to intervene. The chairman of the board sent Secretary Colin Powell a condescending letter telling him to come to the next meeting where his views would be considered along with everyone else's. Sanity finally prevailed, and the board was only successful in eliminating Portuguese to Brazil, South America's largest country and the world's 11th largest economy, awash in anti-American sentiments.

All of this happened because there is no central U.S. government institution within which policy, personnel, and budget can be deployed coherently to implement a multifaceted strategy to win the war of ideas over an extended period of time. As a result, the U.S. is largely absent from the field. Tinkering with the current system will not work because it is not set up to work. In the case of broadcasting, the lawyers at the USIA General Counsel's office, which was tasked with drafting the legislation for establishing the Board of Governors, told the staff of the National Security Council that the proposed structure would not work. They were told to draft it anyway because it reflected a compromise agreement that had been reached on Capitol Hill.

How to get it right

Understanding our ideas

To repair the damage, we must return to first principles. Though its form has changed, today's war of ideas is not new. On our side, it has its provenance in the American Founding, at which time our Founding Fathers explicitly declared the source of our moral legitimacy. Why did the Founders of the United States feel it necessary to address the Declaration of Independence to the entire world? After all, a revolution against the British Crown in 13 small colonies on the eastern seaboard of North America would hardly seem to have been an event requiring the world's attention. The Founders were bold enough to turn to the world in setting forth the justification for their undertaking because the principles to which they were appealing are based upon truths that they claimed to be universal. By universal, they meant true everywhere, at all times, for everyone. These self-evident truths are the God-given, inalienable rights that each human being possesses and that governments are instituted to guarantee and from which alone they derive their just powers. Somehow, our public diplomacy people have difficulty with that message.

In effect, the Declaration of Independence was the first public diplomacy document of the United States. Everything done in U.S. public diplomacy is, or should be, an elaboration of this pronouncement. For instance, the U.S. government's radio and TV broadcasting efforts are an outgrowth of the Declaration in their efforts to address the world as to the moral legitimacy of the United States. The underlying presumption is that members of the audience possess these rights no less than we, and that is why we speak to them with respect and without condescension. It is why we appeal to their reason in our attempts to present, "out of the decent respect for the opinions of mankind," our case before them. The case now, as it was then, is for freedom and democracy, for the exercise of those inalienable rights for all people. President George W. Bush was referring to this mission when he said in his first inaugural address, "Our democratic faith is more than a creed of our country... Now it is a seed upon the wind, taking root in many nations."

This message has inspired and given hope to millions of people around the world. However, the people who hate the United States understand it as well, and deeply fear it. The last thing they wish their people to hear is that they, too, possess these same God-given, inalienable rights and ought to have the free exercise thereof. The enemies of freedom find this truth to be the most dangerous weapon we employ. It is far more powerful than a cruise missile. And that is why U.S. broadcasting continues to be jammed by totalitarian and authoritarian regimes, such as North Korea, Iran, China, Cuba and Russia, which understand wars are really won or lost in the minds of people.

Since 1776, the nature of that war has changed in terms of the character of the enemy opposing these truths. For a large part of the last century, it was totalitarian ideologies that dehumanized people: because of their race, in the case of Nazism; because of their class, in the case of Communism. Now, it is through a perverted deformation of a great religion that people are dehumanized as infidels. We have to recall that it is the same self-evident truths that have upheld this nation that remain our greatest weapons against this latest lie about humanity.

Understanding their ideas

In this particular war, the character of the enemy is defined by a new term, *Islamism*, as distinct from Islam. Like all "ism"s, this term indicates a transmogrification of reality. Islamism is the political ideologization of Islam. Drawing on several of the many strands of Islamic tradition (among them Kharijites, Asharites, al-Ghazali), radical Islamists reduce God to his omnipotence, concentrating exclusively on His unlimited power, as against His reason. God's "reasons" are unknowable by man. God rules as He pleases. There is no rational order invested in the universe upon which one can rely, only the second-to-second manifestation of God's will. This view results in anti-rationalism, which, in turn, produces irrational behavior.

For these theological reasons, radical Islamist fundamentalists reject the relationship of cause and effect. This denial has undermined the foundations of modern science and aborted the development of natural law thinking that is necessary for constitutional, democratic government. It is the principal reason that parts of the Islamic world have become a backwater. Several years ago, an Imam in Pakistan instructed physicists there that they could not consider the principle of cause and effect in their work. Many people in the Muslim world who still refuse to believe men have been to the moon do so not because they are ignorant, but because it is theologically unacceptable to them.

Radical Islamists translate their version of God's omnipotence into a politics of unlimited power. As God's instruments, they are channels for this power. As the former deputy prime minister of Malaysia, Anwar Ibrahim, put it: "By juxtaposing the exercise of state power with the sovereignty of God, this view confers on tyranny the mantle of not only worldly legitimacy but divine ordination." The primacy of force, on which their endeavor is based, necessitates the denigration of reason as a means to know the world or God. Once the primacy of force is posited, terrorism becomes the next logical step to power, as it did in the 20th-century secular ideologies of power, National Socialism and Marxism-Leninism. This is what led Osama bin Laden to embrace the astonishing statement of his spiritual godfather, Abdullah Azzam, which Osama quoted in the November 2001 video, released after 9/11: "Terrorism is an obligation in Allah's religion."

The direct link between the denial of causality and the development of terrorism is illustrated in the bedside reading of Hasan al-Banna, founder of the Muslim Brotherhood in 1928 and an admirer of the Nazi Brownshirts. His daily reading included the works of Abu Hamid al-Ghazali, author of the eleventh-century work *The Incoherence of the Philosophers*, written to rebut the Mu'tazilite school and its successors who fought for the primacy of reason. Ghazali insisted that God is not bound by any order and that there was, therefore, no "natural" sequence of cause and effect, as in fire burning cotton.

The radical Islamists are the new totalitarians, with the ironic twist that, unlike 20th-century totalitarians, they are not secular. However, this is a distinction without a difference because they share with atheist ideologues the belief that power is the primary constituent of reality. Every totalitarian program flows from the premise that unlimited will is the basis of reality. The Arab jihadist volunteers who went to Iraq to fight for the fascist regime of Saddam Hussein – a cynical secularist who simply manipulated Islam for his own purposes – did not do so simply because they shared his anti-Americanism. Saddam Hussein and the Islamist fighters met at the nexus at which the secular and the theological views of unlimited power coincide. Like 20th-century totalitarians, radical Islamists also use this shared view of reality to dehumanize large portions of mankind, justifying their slaughter – albeit in their case as "infidels," rather than as non-Aryans or bourgeoisie.

Because democracies base their political order on reason and leave in play questions radical Islamists believe have been definitively settled by revelation, radical Islamists regard democracies as their natural enemies. No amount of aid to persecuted Muslims in Bosnia, Kosovo, and Afghanistan or changes in American foreign policy can remove this stigma.

The response: Judeo-Christian belief holds that the natural order in the universe is a reflection of God as reason, not some blasphemous restriction of His omnipotence, and thus an invitation to explore the universe as a means of knowing Him. The primacy of reason in Western thought is the principal cause for its success in developing science and constitutional government, both of which emanate from natural law. The primacy of reason is also the source of tolerance, as it is only within this worldview that one can "reason" together over even fundamental differences with an adversary.

Reason is compatible with many strains and schools of Islam that share this point of view (indeed, this view was often dominant during Islam's golden age) and that comprehend why some areas of the Islamic world have been frozen in time. The single most important thing is to support their advancement and encourage, through third parties (since non-Muslims are not welcome as direct interlocutors in this debate), the resuscitation of natural law thinking. This may sound like an abstruse endeavor, but without it, as many Muslims know, there is no hope for the Islamic Umma to enter the modern world. The radical Islamists are violently opposed to Muslim thinkers who espouse a development of Islam's dormant natural law tradition because it represents a potent threat to them from within Islam itself.

Ironically, an unprecedented act of terrorism by radical Islamists may have helped move things within Islam in a direction exactly opposite to the terrorists' intentions. As Turkish intellectual Haldun Gulalp told the *Washington Post* in February 2003, "September 11 came as the turning point that sealed the end. It is perfectly all right to recognize Islam as a cultural, religious identity but quite another to build a political project based on it, because it reduced a diverse group of people to one meaning. People in Islamist movements started saying: 'This has nothing to do with us. We have to dissociate ourselves from September 11.' It is not an accident that a lot of people are talking about liberalism in Islam. Liberal elements have always been there; what is politically significant is what you make of it now, how you teach it."

It is exactly based upon such thinking that we must facilitate the creation and reinforcement of an anti-totalitarian social and intellectual network throughout the Islamic world. A microcosmic example of what can be accomplished was offered by Judge Hamoud al-Hitar in Yemen. He and four other Islamic scholars challenged Yemen's Al Qaeda prisoners to a theological contest. "If you study terrorism in the world, you will see that it has an intellectual theory behind it," said

Hitar. "And any kind of intellectual idea can be defeated by intellect." Hitar won the debate and the terrorists renounced al Qaeda. Since December 2002, Yemen has used this approach successfully with more than 360 young men.

Afghanistan demonstrated the impact of military victory as a powerful rebuttal to radical Islamism, and Saddam's defeat disillusioned some of his Islamist allies. Within their theological viewpoint, defeat by a superior power must be interpreted as a judgment from Allah that they have deviated from his path. Therefore, when necessary, the United States must not hesitate to use force to eliminate opponents on the battlefield. However, the ultimate victory in the war of ideas, as Hitar demonstrated, will only be won by ideas. Many in the West seem not to have a clue as to the nature of the struggle at this level. They had better learn fast. Otherwise, our military victories will turn out to be hollow indeed.

Organization

"I think one of the things that we will want to look harder at is how we do better on the public diplomacy side. We are obviously not very well organized for the side of public diplomacy."
Secretary of State Condoleezza Rice, August 19, 2004

In this time of crisis, a new USIA-like organization should be created that can articulate and promulgate American ideals and institutions to the world and counter hostile propaganda. A new cabinet-level "Strategic Communications Agency" could maintain a strategic focus on aiding Muslim liberals and moderates, and not get lost in daily "spin" control. As stated, it should be independent of the State Department, which may be inclined to downplay differences for the sake of overall relations with a particular state or group of states. It should also be independent of the Defense Department and the CIA in order to avoid entanglement with their respective missions. Its director should report to the President.

This new agency should have the funds to promote the free exchange of ideas in the Islamic world (and elsewhere) and to support our friends there. Currently, U.S. public diplomacy expenditures approximate McDonald's corporate budget for promoting its burgers globally, and roughly half of what Saudi Arabia has spent yearly for the past two decades to spread Wahhabism around the world, including in the United States. The $1.2 billion budget is 1/450th of the Pentagon's budget. It is grotesquely inadequate and needs to be trebled for starters.

There should be grant mechanisms within this new agency, like the National Endowment for Democracy, but far better "endowed," that would provide concrete support to Islamic liberals and moderates, and even non-extreme traditionalists, as well as to others in vital regions of the world. This would allow others, such as private foundations both here and abroad, to make approaches by providing them with the financial means for their programs. This one (or two)-step removed approach would raise the comfort levels for some overseas partners whose effectiveness might be compromised by a closer U.S. government association. The new agency should have the authority and funds to purchase and provide to responsible broadcast and print journalists in Muslim societies the equipment and operating funds to initiate news and features broadcasts via, for example, FM transmitters, or to start up newspapers or journals with the necessary print equipment.

The organization needs to be staffed by people who know substantively what the "war of ideas" is about and have the regional expertise to operate across the Muslim world and in other vital regions. All involved must get over the self-imposed paralysis that has made current message-making so ineffective: the official squeamishness about dealing with religion. In earlier wars of ideas where religion was an issue, the U.S. handled the problem directly and without apology, whether destroying Europe's most powerful Catholic monarchies in the early 20th century, subduing Muslim guerrillas in the Philippines, re-casting the Shinto religion by forcing the Japanese emperor to renounce his claim as a deity, defeating an adulterated Christian-Leninist "liberation theology" in Latin American counterinsurgency operations of the 1980's, or openly battling the Roman Catholic church head-on in 1990's abortion battles at the United Nations conferences on population and development.

A new Strategic Communications Agency could be organized functionally, as was the USIA, into four separate bureaus, with additional offices arranged regionally. The regional offices would replicate the State Department geographic bureaus: African; European and Eurasian; Near Eastern; Western Hemisphere; East Asian and Pacific; and South Asian. These offices would coordinate with the field public affairs officers (PAOs) and civic affairs officers (CAOs) in each region to insure they received appropriate support from the functional bureaus. They would also coordinate with their counterparts in State, Defense, Homeland Security, and the intelligence community.

The Educational and Cultural Affairs Bureau would oversee all exchanges: academic (Fulbright), cultural, and the International Visitors Program. If we wish our ideas to win, or think they deserve to win, we must at least present them, if not inculcate them. This requires recruiting suitable candidates and exposing them to coherent programs that are intellectually substantive enough to change their lives and create long term relationships. Indiscriminate exposure to the U.S. is not sufficient to influence "youth" in a way favorable to us. (Sayyid Qutb, the chief ideologist of the Al Qaeda movement, was the product of a teacher program in Colorado where he deepened his intense dislike for the U.S.) A great deal of effort is required to identify the potential intellectual and political leaders in Muslim societies and to reach them. Influencing people without any influence is a waste of time and resources.

More important than the quantity of exchanges is the quality and substance of what is exchanged. These exchanges should include an in-depth explication of the ideas of the American Founding, to include the development of the Declaration of Independence and the Constitution, and an examination of *The Federalist Papers*. Exposing visitors to "a slice of life" in the U.S. is often insufficient to have a profound influence. It is necessary to make clear the moral and philosophical principles that allow life in the U.S. to be lived as it is, or as the Founders believed it should be.

The Information Bureau would supervise: overseas American Centers; press guidance and the wireless file; foreign press centers; the speakers program; and research and evaluation for press reaction, opinion research and resource research, print presses for books, magazines, and newspapers; and Internet-related resources.

The Private Sector Programs Bureau would engage private sector organizations both here and abroad to undertake and coordinate public diplomacy projects on the Agency's behalf through grants and/or contracts. This bureau would be able to act fast to get specific programs in the field.

The Broadcasting Bureau would subsume all non-military government broadcasting (radio, TV and Internet) and maintain the distinctions between VOA and surrogate broadcasters, such as Radio Free Asia and RFE/RL, as appropriate. The Bureau should resume VOA's mission to explain and promote U.S. foreign policy.

The only effective way to combat the biased media coverage in the Muslim world is to offer our own alternative media (but with substance, not an overdose of music) or, if the country in question legally allows free media, to support the start up of an indigenous broadcaster or media outlet that will provide a more accurate portrayal of the U.S.

Conclusion

The United States is conspicuous in its absence from the war of ideas. If the U.S. sent its troops into battle without armor or ammunition, there would be a political outcry, as there was when that was thought to be the case in Iraq. Such negligence would be deadly. If our soldiers are willing to die, we ought to be able to explain to others what they are dying for. Our failure to do so has not provoked a similar outcry. Why? The question is particularly poignant in that, if we were able to do so effectively, fewer Americans would have to die abroad – or in possible terrorist attacks here at home. One reason for this failure is that, within the scope of the federal budget, the size of the budget for public diplomacy is so small that not much attention is paid to it. Also, public diplomacy has no domestic constituency that lobbies on its behalf. Those who do lobby, such as members of the Broadcasting Board of Governors, have vested interests that they are able to bring to bear with the members of Congress to whom they have given generously over the years. Therefore, their well-intentioned but profoundly mistaken views are able to prevail.

The only other possible reason for failure is that we do not have a consensus in this country over what it represents – that we are so confused over essential issues concerning the meanings of life, family, and moral worth that we cannot coherently articulate a set of ideas to project. Some of the debates in the worlds of academe and politics make this explanation unfortunately plausible – plausible, but not persuasive. Threats to national existence have a marvelous way of concentrating the mind on exactly why we do have a moral right to exist, in fact, an imperative to exist in a certain way. A President of the United States can effectively articulate these reasons as well in the short space of a speech. But a president is only the tip of the spear. Where is the rest?

7

Counterpropaganda:
We can't win without it

HERBERT ROMERSTEIN

Anti-American propaganda and disinformation are powerful weapons in the hands of our rivals and enemies. Counterpropaganda is our defense. Much of what we know, including the terminology, about propaganda and disinformation is derived from our experiences in both world wars and the Cold War.

The manipulation and shrewd molding of information to suit a political purpose is the hallmark of modern conflict. Disinformation and propaganda campaigns threaten the image and effectiveness of the United States abroad in peacetime and in war, and are among the most important weapons in the arsenals of our militarily weaker adversaries. Despite the difficulty the U.S. has had in the face of such weapons, there is no mystery to them, and our democracy need not let its institutions serve as delivery systems for enemy propaganda. As it has in the past, the U.S. and its allies can neutralize the threat through counterpropaganda.

The roots of modern disinformation and propaganda campaigns can be traced to the end of World War II. Until the early part of the last century the term "propaganda" was neutral. It simply meant propagating some one's viewpoint. However, revelations of the extent of propaganda intended to draw the United States into World War I, and the later work of the Nazi Propaganda Ministry and Soviet Propaganda Department, loaded the term with heavily negative connotations. Counterpropaganda is carefully prepared answers to false propaganda with the purpose of refuting the disinformation and undermining the propagandist. The Nazis and the Communists were masters of false propaganda and carried out effective counter-propaganda against one another and against the democratic world.

During World War II, the United States developed considerable expertise in propaganda but remained ineffective at counterpropaganda. Although the Cold War provided an excellent laboratory to study, develop and refine techniques of counterpropaganda, the U.S. started to lose its knowledge, and the practice of it, in the late 1960's and 1970's. By the 1980's it was possible, by examining the experiences of the past, to develop an effective counterpropaganda campaign against the Soviets' strategic propaganda offensives. In a repetition of history, however, this ability atrophied in the 1990's after decision-makers saw no more need to retain the knowledge or ability. New adversaries placed great value on the Soviet technique, while the U.S. has yet to rebuild its counterpropaganda capabilities for the post- 9/11 world.

This chapter is designed to provide the historical and intellectual background for a comprehensive study of Soviet propaganda techniques and the means by which the United States countered them. While many of the examples are from the battlefield and could be classified as psychological operations (PSYOP), they illustrate points that are soundly applicable to civilian public diplomacy and strategic communication. The examples also show the need for integration from the president on down, where one rhetorical slip or a single lazy, timid or disloyal official can alter events in ways as deadly as any bomb.

'A well-arranged orchestra'

The Soviets used propaganda both to spread their own ideology and to undermine their enemies. In 1983 Soviet Communist Party Politburo member Konstantin Chernenko told a Central Committee meeting,

> Comrades, our entire system of ideological work should operate as a well-arranged orchestra in which every instrument has a distinctive voice and leads its theme, while harmony is achieved by skillful conducting. The main demands on party leadership of ideological work are constantly to check the tone of propaganda against our policy goals and people's interests, and to ensure that 'word becomes deed,' as Lenin put it. Propaganda is called upon to embrace every aspect of social life and every social group and region and to reach every individual.[1]

In 1992 the former head of KGB foreign intelligence, Leonid Shebarshin, explained to a London-based Arabic-language newspaper the role of Soviet intelligence in propaganda and disinformation. He described one objective as "to strengthen Soviet influence and to destroy positions of the forces that we considered unfriendly... through what we called in intelligence terms 'effective movement,' i.e. influencing government, political circles, and public opinion. Toward this end, we used our relations with politicians and the press... The objective was to harm the United States, Israel, or Arab leaders whose relations with the West 'exceeded the limit,' in our opinion."[2]

The East German Ministry for State Security, the security and intelligence service known as MfS or Stasi, played an important role in Soviet disinformation strategy. An official report to Minister Erich Mielke in 1969 explained, "One can select actual events, problems etc. using a mixture of truths, half-truths, fiction and other purposeful, well crafted interpretations which seem credible to the recipient and [thus] attain the desired impression. Exact knowledge of conditions within the particular government in the operational area is imperative. Absolutely necessary is thorough knowledge of western language use, as well as psychological, sensitive tactic in approach."[3]

Soviet training of foreign Communists in overt and covert propaganda started in the early 1920's in what was then called the Lenin School. Although closed in the late 1930's, it was reopened after World War II as the Higher Party School. Its cover was the Institute of Social Sciences. An English textbook for training foreign Communist propagandists at the school was published in Moscow in 1985. The textbook explained to the propaganda trainees,

> Situations sometimes arise in practical propaganda in which the logical mode (arguments *ad rem*) do not produce the necessary effect, despite the convincingness of the arguments and correctness of the propagandist's propositions. The psychological mode (arguments *ad hominem*) prove to be more effective, for the propagandist takes into account the usual course of reasoning and conclusions to which the listener resorts proceeding from his interests and convictions. Psychological arguments make the propagandist's words more convincing, comprehensible, and clear... Particularly great is the significance of the emotional predisposition in youth audiences. Creating a favourable emotional mood in the audience is one of the essential conditions for raising the effectiveness of propaganda actions.[4]

Understanding the techniques to counter them

A democratic society must understand the techniques of disinformation in order to develop effective counterpropaganda. However, a democratic society cannot use disinformation not only for moral reasons but for practical ones: in our open society the truth would soon come out. Although this appears to be a weakness, in fact it was a strength when we refuted Soviet disinformation. America's reputation as a truth teller and the Soviet reputation as a lie teller helped us refute their propaganda themes and discredit the Soviet Union for using them.

As early as the 1980's, but even more so in our present information age, when disinformation is spread to one audience it can be replayed to a more sophisticated audience to the detriment of the disinformer. The United States was able to show European audiences examples of Soviet disinformation targeting the Third World. The Europeans easily saw through the lies. That exposure helped damage the image of the Soviet Union at the time when Moscow desperately wanted to look good to the Western democracies. The exercise sensitized the West Europeans to Soviet disinformation and propaganda directed at them.

Nazi Germany entered World War II with intensive experience in propaganda and counterpropaganda. In 1939, the British tried every way they could to convince Hitler not to start the war. Nazi Propaganda Minister Joseph Goebbels authored Berlin's reply. He said, "Your English propaganda tricks are absurd. There was a time when we National Socialists possessed no power, and yet we were able to overcome our political opponents at home. That trained us in the work of propaganda."[5] The British responded with both overt (white) propaganda (signed by the British government) and unsigned (gray) propaganda. Later in the war, they dropped falsely attributed (black) propaganda over German lines. Black, white and gray are terms developed during World War II. They only refer to the attribution not the truth of the data. For the most part, British propaganda to Germany was true regardless of the attribution. Two gray booklets were printed in England for distribution to publications in neutral countries. Although not officially attributed to the British government, they exposed specific Nazi propaganda claims as being false.[6]

Leaflet warfare

Leaflets are among the simplest of propaganda and counterpropaganda devices, and the Internet affords all sides with easy and cheap means of leafleting targets electronically. Examples of leaflet warfare from pre-electronic conflicts is instructive. In August 1940 the Germans dropped a four-page, newspaper-sized leaflet over southern England titled *A Last Appeal to Reason by Adolf Hitler*. While in Germany keeping British propaganda leaflets was forbidden, the British collected copies of the Nazi leaflet and sold them to raise money for the Red Cross and buy cigarettes for soldiers. The British press published pictures of people reading the Nazi leaflet. The British had no fear of the German propaganda since the Hitler speech had already been reported in the British press and thoroughly discussed. Britain's democratic society was sufficient counterpropaganda in this case.

Nazi propaganda had always argued that German-Americans would support Nazi Germany in war. In March 1941, British counterpropaganda responded with a leaflet, dropped by balloon, "7,000,000 German Americans Accuse." Although America was not yet at war, President Roosevelt's sympathy for the English cause was well known. This leaflet showed a picture of Wendall Willkie, his Republican opponent in the 1940 election. Willkie, speaking for German-Americans, made it clear that they were anti-Nazis. The leaflet concluded "With us the free world!"[7]

In 1943 a small group of students, the White Rose issued leaflets in Munich condemning the Nazi regime and particularly the political and religious persecution. The students were arrested and executed. However, British Intelligence was able to secure one of the leaflets. It was reprinted with an introduction that said the RAF was now dropping on the Germans "a German leaflet."[8]

With American entry into World War II much of the propaganda and counterpropaganda activities were coordinated with the British. In early 1944 American troops in Italy captured a German headquarters and secured a document that had been sent to a German infantry division by higher headquarters. The document headed "Treatment of Prisoners of War" said, "The troops are to be advised that messages of atrocities and murder of German prisoners of war committed by Allied troops arrive in steadily growing numbers. Such actions are inconceivable to German military thinking. The facts are documented and these crimes can be explained by the bestial cruelty and hatred of the Jews who incited the underworld of the Anglo-Saxon cities." The document was dated April 24, 1943. At that time, the Americans and British were battling the Germans in North Africa.

The allegations were false, but the German troops who were told this story had no way of knowing the truth. The British prepared and airdropped leaflets to the German troops starting on the night of February 15-16, 1944. The leaflet reproduced the German document with its false charge. It also showed a picture of German POWs eating. The problem was that the picture showed German prisoners eating from plates filled with food. The picture was accurate, but German prisoners, who indeed were being fed that well, told their interrogators that the German troops would never believe that prisoners would be treated with such generosity. The British then printed a new version of the leaflet showing German prisoners eating, but the amount of food was not quite as obvious.[9]

Knowing the audience and learning from mistakes

The American psychological operations personnel learned from the prison food incident. Lies can be easily refuted but where the audience has a predisposition to believe the lies, it is not easy to change their views. A heavily propagandized audience is difficult to convince. A decade of Nazi propaganda against the Jews and against the United States was hard to overcome. In addition even the truth may be hard to believe if it is contrary to the experience of the audience.

One clever British black leaflet addressed the same problem. Supposedly distributed by the nonexistent Red Circle, a supposed underground anti-Nazi group in the German Army, it reported the wonderful living conditions of the German prisoners of war who had been sent to Canada. It purported to be a message from the POWs to their former comrades at the front. The message included the claim that breakfast included tea or real coffee with milk and sugar, and bacon and eggs. Lunch was soup, meat, two vegetables, dessert of fruit and cheese. For afternoon snack they were fed coffee or tea, bread, butter, and marmalade. For dinner soup, meat, two vegetables, fruit and cheese. At any time the prisoners could have beer and lemonade, cigars, cigarettes and tobacco.[10] It was logical to the German reader that someone thousands of miles outside of the combat zone might indeed be well fed. Dr. Klaus Kirchner, the leading authority on World War II propaganda leaflets, said that the term *Kanadastimmung* ("satisfaction as if in Canada") was used by World War II German soldiers for a good experience.

The most effective British-American leaflet addressed to the German troops was a Safe Conduct pass signed by General Dwight D. Eisenhower. It was distributed from early September 1944 until the end of the war. More German troops surrendered carrying this leaflet than any other. The statement by Eisenhower said in German and English, "The German soldier who carries this safe conduct is using it as a sign of his genuine wish to give himself up. He is to be disarmed, to be well looked after, to receive food and medical attention as required, and to be removed from the danger zone as soon as possible."[11]

When the enemy counters counterpropaganda

After D-Day all German propaganda against the Allies was assigned to the SS Standarte "Kurt Eggers" headed by Gunter d'Alquen, a veteran SS propagandist. The SS unit also called itself Skorpion. The SS soon thought up an answer to the Allies' Safe Conduct leaflet. The front of the leaflet looked almost the same, but Eisenhower's statement was changed to "The German soldier who carries this safe conduct is using it as a sign of his genuine wish to go into captivity for the next ten years, to betray his fatherland, to return home a broken old man and very probably never to see his parents, wife and children again."

The reverse of the Allied leaflet was an excerpt from the Geneva Convention in German. The reverse of the SS leaflet was a taunting note to the Allies. It began "Dear Friends, We are returning your age old dodge, after having made the necessary rectifications, with sincerest thanks... It should be obvious to you that the ideals for which 90 Million Germans have fought (according to Churchill) 'like lions' for over five years cannot be so very rotten that we could be lured into surrender through mere ham and eggs." It ended "Heil Hitler." Apparently the Skorpion remembered the Red Circle black leaflet, only changing bacon and eggs to ham and eggs.[12]

Skorpion also issued a leaflet to explain to German troops how they had answered the Allies leaflet. The front was the same as the leaflet dropped on the Allied troops. The reverse said in German, "Mr. Eisenhower thought it to be effective to supply our soldiers with permits for surrender. The thing looks like this scrap of paper. The rag is copied exactly as it came, with signature, etc. by Skorpion. The text is altered a little on the front." There was also a translation of the message to the Allies, albeit somewhat more scatalogical. Skorpion went on to say, "This 'copied' Safe Conduct pass was then shot back to the enemy," and asked "We are asking you, comrades: Would you have answered the same way? Has Skorpion stung back correctly? Is something missing? Or does it say it all?"

When personnel are disloyal or inept

Despite Skorpion's intention German soldiers continued to surrender carrying the Safe Conduct leaflet until the end of the war. Not all Allied leaflets were that successful. One of the most useless leaflets was called "My Name is Joe Jones." It combined the concept of the American soldier being "just like you" with threats to punish those Germans who resist. It ended "Those who understand these things will be able to get along with the Americans. Those who do not want to get along with the Americans must remember... As one makes his bed so will one sleep." The leaflet was written by Stefan Heym, who would later become a well-known novelist.[13]

While the leaflet was little more than an inept product, the Heym case demonstrates the importance of screening personnel who work on message-making programs. Stefan Heym was born Hellmuth Flieg in Germany in 1913. He fled Hitler and came to the United States and in 1943 became a United States citizen. However, he joined the American Communist Party in 1937 and remained a member until 1939. He served in the United States Army in a psychological warfare unit in World War II where he reached the rank of lieutenant. In addition to the "Joe Jones" leaflet, Heym also wrote articles for the 2-page leaflet/newspaper, *Frontpost*, which came out every few days and was air dropped on the German troops. When the Korean War broke out in 1950, Heym renounced his US citizenship and went back to East Germany. There he got into difficulty with the East German government for expressing disagreements while claiming that he was an "undogmatic socialist" and a Marxist.[14] After the fall of the Berlin Wall, he went back to his communist origins and became a leading figure of the PDS (Party of Democratic Socialism), which replaced the official East German Communist Party, the SED (Socialist Unity Party).

Perils of presidential proclamations:
Some slogans that sound good at home can help the enemy abroad

As we shall soon see, there were other cases where our propaganda was counterproductive. In addition, propaganda slogans designed to raise morale at home could have an undesired effect on enemy troops. President Roosevelt's slogan "Unconditional surrender" sounded good to the American and British public. To the German public it was frightening concept. The same was true with Japan.

Frontpost, a series of newspaper-style leaflets, tried in its October 25, 1944 issue to soften the concept of unconditional surrender in a front page story telling the Germans that Roosevelt had said that "The enslavement of the German people stands in opposition to the war goals for which the United Nations are fighting." In January 1945 the British dropped a leaflet, signed by Winston Churchill, on German troops that said, "We demand unconditional surrender, but you are aware that we have set ourselves narrow, morale limits we will not exceed. We do not exterminate nations. We do not slaughter whole peoples."[15]

A propaganda slogan that has to be explained does more harm than good. Even the pro-Roosevelt Robert E. Sherwood in discussing the unconditional surrender slogan in his 1948 book *Roosevelt and Hopkins* admitted, "There were many propaganda experts, both British and American, who believed that the utterance of these words would put the iron of desperate resistance into the Germans, Japanese and Italians and thereby needlessly prolong the war and increase its cost; there are some who still believe that it did so. These critics were not necessarily opposed to the principle of total defeat – but they considered it a disastrous mistake for the president to announce it publicly."[16]

In mid-1943, with Allied armies fighting on Italian soil, American and British propaganda told Italians that they had no part in Hitler's war and should surrender. On July 25, Benito Mussolini was ousted and Field Marshall Pietro Badoglio was appointed by King Victor Emmanuel III. This was a tremendous opportunity for the Allies. If Italy made a separate peace before the Germans were able to reinforce their army in Italy, the Western Allies would be in the position to move from Italy to liberate the Balkans. This was Churchill's concept of moving through the "soft underbelly of Europe." The Soviets had their own plans for the post-war Balkans and had no desire for the Allies to move in. The week before Mussolini's ouster Churchill and Roosevelt had prepared an appeal declaring that "Italy's sole hope of survival lay in 'honorable capitulation to the overwhelming power of the military forces of the United Nations.'"

On July 25, the British propaganda radio hailed Mussolini's downfall as the end of both fascism and the war in Italy. This indicated that the Western Allies were ready to make peace. But an American propaganda broadcast took a different line. Instead of reaching out to the Italian king to make peace, the broadcast announced, "the moronic little king who has stood behind Mussolini's shoulder for twenty-one years has moved forward one pace." The radio blasts referred to Badoglio and the king as fascists. The words were personally approved at the Office of War Information New York Control Desk by Joseph Barnes.[17] The bureaucratic excuse for the "moronic little king" incident was that it was a quotation from *New York Post* columnist Samuel Grafton and therefore was not the fault of the Office of War Information.

The explanation did not help. The confusion created by the broadcast helped prevent an Italian surrender. The Germans were able to build up forces in Italy who fought until 1945. The delay cost the lives of thousands of American troops and many thousands of others. How could such a colossal propaganda blunder have such devastating military consequences? The insults against the Italian field marshal and king were not a blunder at all. Barnes was an agent of Soviet GRU military intelligence, and had been since the 1930's.[18] With Italy continuing to bog down Western Allied troops, it became impossible for American- and British-led forces to liberate the Balkans. Thanks to a Soviet agent in the U.S. Office of War Information, the Balkans fell to Stalin's Red Army instead.

Embarrassing allies

Having the Soviet Union as an ally often proved embarrassing to the Americans and British and created serious problems for those assigned to answer Nazi propaganda. In April 1943, the Nazis discovered the bodies of thousands of Polish officers in Katyn Forest. They had been captured by the Soviet Army when Nazi Germany and the Soviet Union had divided Poland pursuant to the Soviet-Nazi Pact. The Soviets, of course, accused the Nazis of murdering the Poles.

The Office of War Information pressured Polish-language radio stations and newspapers in the United States to support the Soviet version of the story. An OWI official threatened the Polish-American journalists that the Federal Communications Commission (FCC) would take away the licenses of the radio stations and the newspapers would not be supplied with paper if they accused the Soviets of committing the crime. The OWI official was Alan Cranston, head of the foreign languages unit, who would later become a U.S. senator from California.[19] The Polish government in exile in London asked the International Red Cross to investigate the Katyn massacre. The Soviets used the request as an excuse to break relations with the Polish government and provided a pretext for Moscow to establish a post-war government of Communist Poles.

As late as 1946 a newspaper called *Main-Echo* licensed by the Allied military governments published a front page story reporting from the Nuremberg War Crimes Trials that evidence had been presented that the Germans were responsible for the massacre of the Polish officers at Katyn.[20] It was not until 1952 that the United States Congress, prodded by journalist Jules Epstein, investigated the case and concluded from the overwhelming evidence that the Soviets had committed the massacre of eleven thousand Polish officers.[21] After the collapse of the Soviet Union, the Russian government publicly admitted responsibility and released documents showing that Stalin had ordered the killings.

Soviet behavior provided the Nazis with grist for truthful anti-Allied propaganda. In October 1944, Soviet troops broke through the German lines and occupied the East Prussian village of Nemmersdorf. Two days later, the Germans counter attacked and retook the village. They found twenty-four people murdered, among them twelve women, a 19 and a 15-year-old girl, a baby, three school children and six old men. Both of the girls as well as two of the women were raped and then murdered.

The Nazi propagandists of Skorpion took advantage of this incident. The SS took graphic, shocking pictures of the victims and printed them on leaflets spread to the American troops showing the action of their Allies.[22]

A similar situation took place in Hungary in February 1945. Skorpion sent a radio message and issued a leaflet with an open letter to General Eisenhower:

> In the name of the German Wehrmacht and the European forces allied with it, we solemnly and officially invite General Dwight D. Eisenhower, commander-in-chief of the United Nations forces, to appoint a delegation composed of from six to ten officers, noncommissioned officers, or enlisted men, with their own interpreters.... They will be transported by the quickest possible means to Stuhl Weissenburg area of Hungry, where they may remain for any length of time they choose up to a week, and speak in absolute freedom with the civilian victims of the Bolsheviks. They will then be returned safe and sane [sic] to the allied lines. We are awaiting General Eisenhower's answer upon reception of this message. Arrangements will immediately be agreed upon for the sending and the reception of this delegation. COME AND SEE FOR YOURSELVES... what your Bolshevik allies are like![23]

Countering this Nazi propaganda theme was very difficult, because it was true. However, the GIs ignored the evidence because, as they had begun liberating the death camps, they saw the unimaginable, industrialized brutality of the Nazis. American troops were not receptive to anything the Nazis said. But the German population did believe the stories of Soviet atrocities. The leaflet/newspaper *Frontpost* published by the 12th Army Group of Patton's Third Army, and air dropped over the German lines, tried to respond with a defense of our Soviet ally. In issue No. 49 (No. 1 for March 1945) appeared an article titled "Keine Rache" (No Revenge) which quoted a Moscow report from the Soviet Army newspaper *Red Star* saying that "We don't rape German women, not because of pity, but because of dignity..." *Frontpost* also published the false Soviet denial of plundering German property.[24]

Denying what was obviously true did not improve the image of the American propagandists as truth tellers. For the most part, American propaganda leaflets stuck to the truth and told the German soldiers and civilians things that they knew were true. For example another leaflet newspaper *Feldpost* also published by the 12th Army Group of Patton's Third Army, in January 1945 had true stories about the Americans crossing the German-Belgium border and the Russians in the city of Brandenburg.[25]

Spies and leakers

Even more damaging to the Western attempts to convince the German troops not to fight was the surfacing of the "Morgenthau Plan." On August 7, 1944, Henry Morgenthau, Jr., the U.S. Secretary of the Treasury, meet with General Dwight Eisenhower. Accompanying Morgenthau at the meeting were two Treasury Department officials, Harry Dexter White and Fred Smith. What we know of the meeting comes from an article that Smith later wrote. Eisenhower had expressed concern that Germany would not suffer sufficient punishment after its defeat. White responded "We may want to quote you on the problem of handling the German people."

With White's encouragement, Morgenthau later told British officials, "I think we could divide Germany into a number of smaller provinces, stop all industrial production, and convert them into small agricultural land holders." Morgenthau then allowed White to develop the details of the plan that would de-industrialize Germany and convert one of the world's most technologically advanced countries into a pasture, indeed to make it, in White's words "a fifth-rate power."[26] Unknown to Morgenthau, Harry Dexter White was a Soviet agent. He had been an agent of Soviet military intelligence (GRU), reporting to Whittaker Chambers and J. Peters, since the mid-1930's. In the late 1930's, the Soviets transferred White to the NKVD (later called KGB), after Chambers' defection from the Soviet service.[27]

Although Roosevelt and Churchill liked the Morgenthau Plan at first glance, after careful study they rejected it. However, the plan was leaked to the American press on September 23, 1944, apparently from the Treasury Department. The leak suggested that the plan was official government policy. This story was of great help to the Nazi propagandists. They could then say that the Jew Morgenthau wanted Germany to be destroyed. Therefore Germans had to resist the Allied forces in every way possible. This helped the Soviets by encouraging resistance in the West while the Red Army came in from the East.

Even after the defeat of the Nazis, the East German Communists picked up the theme that Morgenthau planned Germany's destruction. A pamphlet called *The Enemy of the German Nation*, published by an official East German publishing house in 1952 referred to "the proposed plan of destruction by Henry Morgenthau." It quoted extensively from the Morgenthau Plan without revealing that the American British governments had rejected the scheme. According to this pamphlet only the Soviet Union was concerned with protecting Germany and the German people. The pamphlet quoted Stalin as saying, on February 23, 1943, "Hitlers come and go, but the German people, the German State remains."[28] The Stalin statement was widely used during the war in Soviet propaganda leaflets to imply that the Soviets would give Germany a "soft" peace while the West would give Germany a "hard" peace.[29]

Bad policies, bad propaganda

The name of Morgenthau was of use to the Nazis in attacking another foolish Western policy. The Nazis got hold of a notice from General Omar Bradley on December 4, 1944 ordering that GIs not fraternize with German civilians. According to Bradley, "we are not just fighting Hitler and his crowd; we are fighting the whole German nation." He GIs were not supposed to talk to Germans. The non-fraternization order held only until the GIs realized that among the Germans they were not permitted to talk to were girls. By fall 1945, GIs were marrying German girls. But in the meantime, the non-fraternization orders reached the ridiculous point. One instruction pamphlet for the GIs concerning treatment of the Germans issued by the 12th Army group explained that the GIs should not give chewing gum and candy to German children because "A kid can shoot you just as dead as a grown man." It told the GIs "Don't believe there are any 'good' Germans in Germany."[30]

While the GIs tended to disbelieve Nazi propaganda, this non-fraternization policy directly affected them. The SS issued a leaflet titled *Brain Splitters... For Suckers Only!* They reprinted the General Bradley order and said, "Mr. Morgenthau and his fellow-kikes preferred to concoct a series of imbecile plans dictated merely by hate. These plans left the Germans *no* chance to survive. The German people and especially the German soldier have taken these plans serious and have acted accordingly. Since that time, the American Armies have lost no less than 150,000 men and losses are increasing tremendously day by day." Here, Nazi propaganda combined its normal anti-Semitic theme with two that resonated with the ordinary GI. One was non-fraternization; the other was that Allied losses were the result of such Western policies.

There was a similar problem with our propaganda to the Soviet prisoners of war who had volunteered to fight on behalf of the German forces. This included not only the Vlasov Army (Russian POWs who volunteered to serve in the German forces against the Soviet Union) and the Ukrainian National Army but even the former Soviet citizens who had been taken to Germany as slave labor.

One U.S. leaflet was addressed *Fighting Men!* It said, "Russian, Ukrainian, and Georgian fighting men of eastern battalions: why do you continue to fight us? Why do you spill your blood for nothing? It is not your war. We know that you were forced to fight against us....Many of your comrades are already in safety with us. We treat them well; we feed them as if they were our soldiers, and we immediately send them to a safer place."[31] This leaflet did not deal with the subject on the minds of the former Soviet citizens – would they be returned to the Soviet Union after the war? Having experienced life in Soviet Russia, they knew that even if they had not served in the German forces, they would be punished if they were returned home.

Col. James Monroe was an American propaganda officer and inventor of the Monroe leaflet bomb that was widely used during the war. In one of his reports, he revealed an incident in August 1944 when the American 12th Army Group came upon a group of Russian soldiers serving in a German artillery unit. A leaflet was air dropped on them saying that if they surrendered they would be treated as Prisoners of War and would not be returned to the Soviet Union. Over a hundred of them surrendered, leaving the way clear for the Americans to advance without hindrance. Instead of being treated as POWs, as promised, they were returned to the Soviet Union and executed.[32]

Soviet propaganda also promised that if former Soviet citizens serving in the German forces surrendered they would not be punished. A leaflet dropped by the Soviets on the Ukrainian Insurgent Army, a guerrilla force that fought against both the Soviets and the Germans, was addressed to "To Armenian, Turkmen, Kazakh, Chechen, Tatar, Russian, and other soldiers of the Ukrainian Insurgent Army." It urged them to "come over to our side and fight against the leaders of the Nationalist gangs. Do what many of our colleagues... did and join us. We treated them as our friends. The Motherland has forgiven them for their previous mistakes. And it will forgive you as well if you come over to our side." The Soviet leaflet went on to say that if they came over "the 'black spot' of traitor to the Motherland will be removed from you and your families."[33] In addition to recognizing that many non-Ukrainians were serving with the anti-Soviet Ukrainian forces, the leaflet falsely claimed that if they surrendered to the Soviets they and their families would not be punished. In reality not only were they punished, but their families who under Soviet law were held responsible for their actions, even if they knew nothing about it, were also punished. The entire nations of Chechens and Crimean Tartars were removed from their homes and sent to Siberian exile.

An elaborately printed American leaflet titled *Instructions* was addressed to "Allied Nationals in Enemy Countries." It was in thirteen languages including German, Russian and English. It said in part, "Plans of the Allied Governments to care for you and to return you to your country are ready and will be put into force at once. These plans will be carried out with much greater speed if you obey my instructions. *Obedience will hasten your return home.* Disobedience will mean delay and unnecessary hardship to you."[34] The leaflet was never distributed. It would have resulted in even more resistance from the former Soviet citizens who did not want to be returned to the Soviet Union. As it was, former Soviet citizens resisted being returned. They fought against the American and British troops who tried to turn them over to the Soviets. Some committed suicide. The British code word for the forced repatriation was "keelhaul."

In the 1970's, Julius Epstein, the journalist who had embarrassed the U.S. government into investigating the Katyn Forest massacre, demanded a congressional investigation of forced repatriation. He did not succeed but he did write a book in which he protested the policy.[35] A strong civil libertarian, Epstein argued that the West had no right to forcibly repatriate the former Soviet citizens as under the Geneva conventions they could not look behind the uniform of a captured soldier.

Although the United States government did not publicly admit it made a mistake by forcibly repatriating former Soviet citizens, it showed it had learned its lesson during the Korean War.

The Soviets did not share the American concern for truth in propaganda. One leaflet told the German troops that foreigners were sleeping with their wives. It said that while the German soldiers were fighting in Germany, "foreigners Frenchmen, Italians, Slovaks, Hollanders, etc." were sleeping with their wives.[36]

In addition to leaflets, the Soviets used loud speakers on the front line, as well as radios aimed at both the German troops and the civilian population. The Soviets issued special leaflets to the German Communists who maintained the audio propaganda operation and served as announcers. One of the leaflets said, "Hitler propaganda is serving you up the most extravagant stories regarding the behavior of the Russian troops in German cities and villages. ... The Red Army is fighting only against those who offer resistance. The occupied areas of Germany are in the rear areas of the Red Army. The Red Army is interested in a peaceful rear area. Therefore the Soviet administration is doing everything so that law and order exists and that work continues as normal."[37]

German soldiers and civilians knew too much about the actual conduct of the Red Army to believe this propaganda. In mid-1944, the Communist International Intelligence had an agent in Germany reporting on the effect of its propaganda radio transmissions. On June 29, 1944, Moscow broadcast to the German agent, "Inform us by return whether you get good reception of the German 'People's Transmitter' at the transmitting periods (BERLIN Summer-time) 9 and 19 hours on wave-length 25, and 22 and 23 hours on wave-length 48."[38]

The agent radio in Berlin responded on July 7, "We reported to you in detail about the 'People's Transmitter' in March. Nothing has changed in the meantime. Audibility of the People's Transmitter good to very good, but it is often drowned out by a jamming transmitter. The subject matter is much discussed, but often to the effect that it does not correspond with the facts."[39]

On July 9, the agent radio responded to a Soviet propaganda broadcast of June 24/25 that reported anti-Nazi demonstrations in Berlin on June 21.[40] The Gestapo was attempting to locate these radios. When they found them, the radio operators were executed. The Soviet agent in Berlin risked his life to tell Moscow that its propaganda report was false.

Bad slogans in the Pacific War

In the Pacific War the unconditional surrender slogan was likewise a problem. On May 8, 1945, President Harry S Truman issued a statement to Japan saying,

> The more the war is prolonged, the greater will be the suffering and hardship of the Japanese people. Moreover, this is entirely in vain. Until the Japanese Army and Navy throw down their arms and surrender unconditionally, America will continue her fierce attacks. What effect will the unconditional surrender of the military authorities have on the Japanese people? It means the end of the war and the end of the power of the military leaders who have now brought Japan to the brink of destruction. It also means the return of soldiers and sailors to their families, to their farm villages, and to their various occupations. More, it means not prolonging the pain, suffering, and slave-like status of the Japanese people, who cling to the vain hope of winning this year.[41]

A short time later the U.S. dropped another leaflet on the Japanese, which said, "Below is an extract from the first official broadcast made to the people of Japan by Rear Admiral Zacharias, in which he clarifies the recent statement by the new U.S. President Truman." Admiral

Zacharias was well known in Japan. He had been stationed in Tokyo and in 1931 accompanied the Japanese Prince and his wife on a two-month tour of the United States. Zacharias said, "I am specifically authorized to reiterate that unconditional surrender is a purely military term, meaning only the yielding of arms. It does not entail enslavement. It does not entail extermination of the Japanese people."[42] When a propagandist has to explain what the President meant, he is at real disadvantage, especially when the unfortunate wording forces a senior American official to clarify that the president does not want to enslave or exterminate the audience.

A study of our psychological warfare program against Japan was written in 1998 by Allison B. Gilmore, an assistant professor in the Department of History at the Ohio State University in Lima. According to Prof. Gilmore,

> Two policies were central to Allied psywar operations: to tell the truth and to refrain from criticizing the Japanese emperor. The strategy of truth was designed primarily to establish and maintain the credibility of information disseminated by the Allies. It enabled propagandists to establish trust between themselves and the Japanese troops they hoped to influence. It dictated that psywarriors induce despair within the enemy's ranks by distributing accurate information. It prohibited the use of the 'big lie,' which was so typical of the informational programs of both Nazi Germany and imperial Japan. In a number of instances the strategy of truth significantly limited what propagandists could say. It was very difficult, for example, for propagandists to adhere to the strategy of truth and at the same time design propaganda that would mitigate the Allied policy of unconditional surrender. In the final analysis, however, it was an effective cornerstone of the campaign. Allied propaganda remained credible because it conformed to the real-life experiences of Japanese soldiers.

The question of the Emperor was extensively discussed by the Allies leadership. As Prof. Gilmore pointed out, "The decision not to criticize the Japanese emperor was also astute. Rather than blaming the emperor for the devastating results of the war, which would have alienated the target audience, Allied propaganda portrayed the emperor as an unwitting victim of the militarists who controlled Japan, whose policies were leading Japan down the path to destruction. Like the strategy of truth, portraying the emperor as a victim made Allied propaganda more credible to Japanese soldiers, who revered the emperor to such an extent that they could not bring themselves to hold him responsible for the debacle that was the Pacific War." [43]

One carefully crafted leaflet was distributed on in honor of the Emperor's birthday. It said, "Today, 29 April 45, is the birthday of H. M. the Emperor. It is regrettable that you Japanese soldiers must greet this day of public festival defeated everywhere by overwhelming superiority of ground, air and naval forces, and that, faced with hopeless conditions, you have to seek a useless death. The military leaders who are responsible for this war are again unable to offer the Emperor a victory on his birthday. Rather, they are afraid of exposure of their own incompetence. How much longer can these military leaders continue to deceive the Emperor?"[44]

Eugene H. Dooman was chairman of the Far East Subcommittee of the State, War, and Navy Coordinating Committee in 1945. Testifying before the Senate Judiciary Committee in September 1951, Dooman explained that based on interrogating high level Japanese prisoners of war the U.S. believed in April 1945 that the Japanese were ready to surrender. However, as long as the Japanese believed that the Emperor would be tried as a war criminal and punished, and that the monarchy would be abolished, they would not surrender.[45]

Again we find internal saboteurs who deliberately twisted the American propaganda message against a wartime enemy. With the defeat of Germany, Russia was expected to come into the war against Japan. A prolonged war would benefit the Soviet Union as it would give Stalin time to get into the war. From the Soviet viewpoint, prolonging the war, despite the loss of American and Japanese lives, would serve Moscow's purpose.

On March 14, 1952, Owen Lattimore testified before the same Senate committee as Dooman. During the war Lattimore served as the director of Pacific Operations for the Office of War Information. He was asked by the Committee, if there had not been a directive that there would be no attacks on the Japanese Emperor in American propaganda. He agreed that there was such a ruling but claimed that he had never violated it. What he had done, he said, was broadcast a quotation from an article in a Chinese newspaper attacking the Japanese Emperor. Since this was not an attack by the United States, but only quoting the Chinese writer, Lattimore felt that it did not violate the directive.[46] Lattimore used the same excuse that Barnes, the GRU agent at the Office of War Information in New York, had used in the "moronic little king" incident. The subcommittee consisting of two Democrats and one Republican concluded unanimously that "Owen Lattimore was, from some time beginning in the 1930's, a conscious articulate instrument of the Soviet conspiracy."[47]

Chen Hansheng, a Communist International intelligence agent who had been part of the Richard Sorge spy ring in Shanghai and Tokyo, was sent from Moscow to New York in 1936 to assist Lattimore in editing the journal *Pacific Affairs*. Chen remained in that job until 1939.[48] The subcommittee was aware that Chen was a communist but until Chen's book *My Life During Four Eras* was published in 1988 in Beijing, many of the details of his work and connection with Lattimore were unknown.

Cold War, hot propaganda

The end of World War II brought us the Cold War. The concept was that a cold war was the alternative to a hot war. The Cold War was a war primarily of propaganda rather than shooting, at least as far as the Soviet-U.S. rivalry was concerned.

The first major military conflict of the Cold War began June 25, 1950 when North Korea invaded South Korea. The North Korean Communists seemed to be winning in the early days of the war. With United Nations support the United States sent troops to repulse the invasion. General Douglas MacArthur's landing at Inchon cut off most of the North Korean army, which disintegrated leaving a large number of North Korean soldiers in American and South Korean hands. In December 1950 China entered the war pushing the American and South Korean forces fifty miles south of Seoul by late January 1951.

An American and South Korean counter attack pushed the Chinese back to the 38th parallel north of Seoul. On June 23, 1951, Soviet U.N. Ambassador Jacob Malik called for truce talks. For over two years, the truce talks continued. One of the major stumbling blocks was that the United States, having learned the lesson of forced repatriation in World War II, refused to force Chinese and North Korean POWs to return home. The United States insisted that the POWs be given the free choice of returning home or remaining free in South Korea.

In November 1952, American planes dropped leaflets over North Korea telling the people about this issue. The leaflet said in part,

> People of North Korea! Here are the facts about the truce talks at Panmunjon. The U.N. called a recess on 8 October 1952, because the communists kept stalling on the question of prisoners, mainly, whether prisoners who did not want to return to communist territory would be sent back. ... But in April of 1952 the U.N. told the communists that a large number of prisoners asked by petition not to be sent back to communist-ruled areas. In fact, many said they would rather die than go back. This made the communists very angry, so angry, in fact, that the world began to believe the communists only wanted to punish their former soldiers for daring to choose to stay with the U.N. The U.N. has never changed its stand on prisoners, and

in October of 1952 General Clark, U.N. Commander in Chief, said
the U.N. would never force prisoners to go back to the communists.
The truce talks will remain in recess until the communists agree to
U.N. suggestions or suggest some plan the U.N. can agree to.[49]

The Chinese Communists and North Koreans demanded that the
POWs be sent to neutral countries where they would then have to be
returned to their own countries. In March 1953, the Chinese, using a
light plane, flew over the American and South Korean lines and
dropped leaflets to South Korean troops and near the Korean capital
Seoul. The leaflets contained a statement of Kim Il-Sung, the head of
North Korea demanding that "If the allied army truly desires peace, it
should accept our fair proposal without fail."[50] The writer was serving
with the United States Army in Korea at the time and found some of
the leaflets dropped on a nearby South Korean unit the next morning.

The POW problem was solved by South Korean President Syngman
Rhee. On June 8, without consulting the American commanders, he
released some twenty-seven thousand Chinese and North Korean
prisoners. They scattered to villages throughout South Korea and could
not be forced to return home. The POW issue being solved, the truce
talks continued and on July 27, 1953, the armistice was signed and the
war was over.

Anatomy of Soviet disinformation campaigns

The Korean War was the occasion for a major Soviet disinformation
campaign. Using the Chinese Communists and a network of
international Soviet fronts the Soviets accused the United States of
using germ warfare in Korea. The campaign began in March 1952 with
a press release by Frederic Joliot-Curie, the president of the World
Peace Council, (also called World Council of Peace) the largest and
most active of a network of international Soviet fronts. The network
consisted of fronts targeted at different segments of the international
population such as World Federation of Democratic Youth,
International Union of Students, Women's International Democratic
Federation, International Association of Democratic Lawyers,
International Organization of Journalists and the Christian Peace
Conference. The World Peace Council coordinated the propaganda
activities of these fronts under the direction of the International
Department of the Central Committee of the Communist Party of the
Soviet Union. By using the fronts, the Soviet Union could deny
responsibility for the gray propaganda. The network of international
Soviet fronts was listed at a 1983 meeting in Prague.

According to Joliot-Curie, he had received a message from the head of the Chinese World Peace Council committee, Kuo Mo-Jo reporting that "Between January 28 and February 17 U.S. military aircraft in Korea disseminated, at the front and in the rear, the microbes of plague, cholera, typhus and other frightful, contagious diseases."[51]

The various sections of the World Peace Council soon got into the act. Dr. James G. Endicott, head of the Canadian Peace Congress, the Canadian section of the WPC, visited China where he supposedly was given evidence of American germ warfare in China and Korea.[52] In December 1952, Endicott received the Stalin Peace Prize for his "leadership of the Canadian peace partisans and condemnation of the American use of germ warfare in China."[53]

The head of the Austrian Peace Council, Heinrich Brandweiner, organized a meeting in Graz, Austria, to protest the American germ warfare in Korea. At the meeting he distributed pictures of the supposed germs that the Americans were using.[54] Brandweiner had to wait for his reward until 1958. By that time the name of the Stalin Peace Prize had been changed to the Lenin Peace Prize and Brandweiner had to settle for that.[55]

Brandweiner had an interesting history. When the Nazis took over Austria in 1938, Brandweiner joined the Nazi Party and was issued membership book number 6 236 254. When the Red Army conquered Austria, Brandweiner became a communist.[56] Such a transformation is not unusual among political opportunists and adherents to totalitarianism, a trait that is not uncommon in present-day extremist movements.

In June 1952 a delegation of doctors organized by the international Soviet fronts arrived in Peking. They studied the question and came to the conclusion that the Americans were indeed using germ warfare. The World Peace Council published their report. It was then reprinted by the International Union of Students. Additional copies were printed and distributed by the official Chinese Communist New China News Agency.[57]

Another international Soviet front, the International Association of Democratic Lawyers, sent a separate delegation that issued a similar report claiming numerous atrocities by the American in Korea including germ warfare. Their report was printed by a number of communist fronts including the newspaper *Shanghai News* and by the newspaper *Korean Independence* in Los Angeles, California.[58]

An Australian journalist named Wilfred Burchett played major part in germ warfare campaign. Burchett's work appeared in a number of influential newspapers including the *Daily Telegraph*, *The Times*, and the *Daily Express* of London, and the *Christian Science Monitor*, a small but prestigious paper published out of Boston. Burchett was extremely active in trying to get other Western reporters to carry stories on the supposed American use of germ warfare in the Korean War. He played a similar role later during the Vietnam War. Burchett can be better understood from a document found in the Russian Presidential Archives by Vladimir Bukovsky. The document, dated July 1957, was a request by the KGB to the Council of Ministers of the USSR to authorize the payment of twenty thousand rubles and a monthly subsidy of three thousand rubles. The Council of Ministers agreed that KGB agent Burchett be given the money. According to a KGB document in the file, "By our instructions, Burchett was asked to penetrate the American and West European bourgeois press." At that time, Burchett was the Moscow correspondent of the left-wing newspaper *National Guardian*, in New York. According to the KGB, the *National Guardian* had little money and could not afford to pay Burchett, so the KGB had to provide a subsidy. Burchett was an agent under KGB control.

Highest-level counterpropaganda

The United States government answered the false germ warfare charges at the United Nations and through out the world. At the U.N. session on October 24, 1952, Secretary of State Dean Acheson said,

> I wish to call attention to the charges of the use of biological bacterial, and gas warfare which have been made against the United Nations Command... The Communists, particularly the Soviet Union, make these charges on every occasion. There has been a campaign of unparalleled violence directed to this subject. It is, of course, utterly, totally, and completely false. It has been denied over and over and over again. We have offered to give any impartial body – the Red Cross or any other – full access behind the lines in the south or anywhere else to discover whether there is any truth in these charges. We have urged that this investigation take place. And what do those who make these charges do? The Soviet Union has vetoed a Security Council resolution providing for an impartial investigation. Now what can we think of representatives of a government or a government itself which will make charges of this sort, continue to make them, fill the world with these falsehoods, and when they are asked to come before an impartial body and prove that what they say is true, they run from it. What do you think of people like that? It seems to me unspeakable.[59]

After Stalin's death, in 1953, the false germ warfare accusations seemed to peter out. We didn't learn until 1998 why that had happened. In 1998, documents were discovered in the archives of the former Soviet Union, which showed not only that the accusations had been false but that the Chinese and Koreans had ceased making them on instructions from the Soviet Union. On April 13, 1953, Glukhov, a former advisor to the North Korean Ministry of Public Security, wrote a note to Soviet Ministry of State Security (MGB) chief Lavrenty Beria, explaining how the service (which would shortly be renamed KGB) helped the North Koreans create "false areas of exposure." Glukhov explained that In June-July 1952 a delegation of specialists in bacteriology from the World Peace Council arrived in North Korea: "Two false areas of exposure were prepared. In connection with this, the Koreans insisted on obtaining cholera bacteria from corpses, which they would get from China. During the period of the work of the delegation, which included academician N. Zhukov, who was an agent of the MGB, an unworkable situation was created for them, with the help of our advisers, in order to frighten them and force them to leave."

On May 2, 1953 the Soviet government sent a secret message to the Chinese, falsely claiming that they had been misled by the Chinese. The message said, "The spread in the press of information about the use by the Americans of bacteriological weapons in Korea was based on false information. The accusations against the Americans were fictitious." The Soviets "recommended" the Chinese "To cease publication in the press of materials accusing the Americans of using bacteriological weapons in Korea and China."[60]

As we shall see, nearly a half-century later and long after the collapse of the Soviet Union, the North Korean and Chinese Communist governments resurfaced the false germ warfare story.

Countering hostile propaganda

In the 1950's and 60's the CIA was very concerned about Soviet disinformation. It circulated information to other government agencies and occasionally made significant information public. In 1961, Richard Helms, then CIA Assistant Director, and later Director of Central Intelligence, testified before the Senate Subcommittee on Internal Security. His theme was Communist forgeries, and the printed transcript of the hearing contained copies of numerous examples.[61]

In 1965, the CIA provided Congressman Melvin Price (D-IL) with a report on *The Soviet and Communist Bloc Defamation Campaign*. Price read it into the *Congressional Record*, September 28, 1965. The report covered Soviet disinformation against the CIA and other government agencies. This report was the first public surfacing of the Soviet term disinformation (*dezinformatsiya*). According to the CIA, "'dezinformatsiya,' in Soviet terminology is false, incomplete, or misleading information that is passed, fed, or confirmed to a targeted individual, group, or country."

One example given was an eighty-page pamphlet published in England in 1961 called *A Study of a Master Spy (Allen Dulles),* which attacked the then director of Central Intelligence. The author supposedly was Bob Edwards, a British Labour Member of Parliament, and a journalist named Kenneth Dunne. The actual author was KGB Col. Vassily Sitnikov, a senior disinformation officer.

By the late 1960's, CIA was under attack in the American press. The attacks culminated in the early 1970's with lengthy hearings by the Senate and House Intelligence Committees (Church and Pike Committees). The CIA spent much of its time defending itself against congressional and media allegations – many proven to be without merit, and did little to counteract Soviet disinformation during this period.

The situation changed in September 1980. On September 17 President Jimmy Carter's press spokesman Jody Powell announced that an unidentified group was distributing a forged Presidential Review Memorandum on Africa that purported to show that the United States supported the apartheid government of South Africa and was persecuting American blacks. A few days earlier an advance copy of the September 18, 1980 issue of the *Sun Reporter*, a black newspaper in San Francisco, was distributed to selected recipients. The newspaper carried the text of the forgery. The publisher of the *Sun Reporter* was Dr. Carlton Goodlett, a member of the Presidential Committee of the international Soviet front, World Peace Council.

The forgery was particularly disturbing to President Carter, who prided himself on the support he received from black Americans. As a result the White House showed interest in the subject of Soviet disinformation that was being re-developed in the Central Intelligence Agency.

In April 1978, as part of the Congressional attack on the CIA, the House Intelligence Committee conducted a hearing on the CIA and the media. The witness was then CIA Director Stansfield Turner. He revealed new regulations that prevented the CIA from using journalists or journalist cover in its operations.

Pressed by Congressman John Ashbrook (R-OH), Turner admitted "A U.S. media representative quite legally could work for the KGB, but under these regulations not for me." Ashbrook requested that the CIA prepare an unclassified report "on activities by hostile intelligence services using the media." As a result CIA prepared a report on KGB operations in the world media. Included in the report was a study of the international Soviet front organizations and their role in Soviet disinformation. The CIA report was published in the Committee hearing record.[62]

Ashbrook kept pressing the issue and in February 1980 the CIA was willing to participate in a hearing on *Soviet Covert Action (The Forgery Offensive)*. The hearing was held in closed session with its proceedings sanitized for public release. A CIA team headed by John McMahon, then deputy director of operations, made the presentation. The CIA identified and reproduced a number of Soviet forgeries. The role of the Soviet international front organizations and foreign Communist Parties in Soviet disinformation was now available to the public.

Congressman Les Aspin (D-WI), Chairman of the hearing, asked the CIA witnesses about Khrushchev's secret speech about Stalin at the 20th Congress of the Communist Party of the Soviet Union. Aspin wanted to know whether James Angleton, who had been a CIA official, had "added several paragraphs to Mr. Khrushchev's prose." One of the CIA officers answered "The version which was made public was in fact the original version as we had it. It was not doctored."[63] The leaked Khrushchev secret speech in 1956 had a deviating affect on the international Communist movement. It was more effective anti-Communist propaganda than anything that the United States could have produced. Aspin's question was based on what was then a common leftwing fantasy that the splits in the world communist movement were somehow the fault of the United States. In fact, the text of the secret speech that was released by the State Department June 4, 1956 was identical with the text officially released in the Soviet Union decades later, in 1989.[64]

The U.S. government actually had obtained two copies of the Khrushchev speech outlining Stalin's crimes. One had been sent to the Canadian Communist Party, and was then given to American Communist Party official Morris Childs. The Childs copy was read to a meeting of the National Committee of the Communist Party USA. An eyewitness to the meeting said many of the members broke into tears on hearing the true nature of the man that they had considered their god. Childs also made a copy available to the FBI. He had been working undercover for the FBI as the American Communist Party representative to the Soviet Communist leadership. The FBI, in sending the Childs copy to the CIA and State Department, advised that it was highly classified because the identity of the source had to be concealed. Israel's Mossad intelligence service obtained the second copy of the Khrushchev speech in Poland. The Israelis had a long close relationship with Angleton and provided a copy to him. It was the Mossad copy that the State Department made public.

During the hearing Congressman Ashbrook asked the CIA about Soviet operations within the United States. McMahon answered, "As to the degree of Soviet influence within the United States, I would have to defer to the Bureau on that."[65] The committee asked the Federal Bureau of Investigation for a briefing on Soviet active measurers in the United States. The FBI agreed to do so, but with some restrictions. Only members of Congress and a few staffers were permitted to attend. No transcript could be taken and the FBI insisted that the closed session remain highly classified. Two years later the FBI agreed to presenting an up-dated version of the same information at a closed Committee hearing but allowed it to be sanitized for publication.[66] In the interim the US government had developed a major campaign to counter Soviet anti-American lies and disinformation.

Establishing a government counterpropaganda system

Early in its first term the Reagan Administration established an inter-agency working group on Soviet active measures. Meetings of the working group were held at the State Department with Deputy Assistant Secretary of State Dennis Kux as the chairman. The CIA, FBI, Department of Defense and the United States Information Agency participated. Kux developed much of the methodology for countering Soviet active measures. The working group sent briefing teams abroad to inform friendly governments, the press, and the public. By taking some of the more bizarre Soviet disinformation stories, used in the Third World, to European audiences, the U.S. provided the opportunity to point out to the Europeans that if the Soviet Union lied in the Third World, how could they be believed in Europe. This was a particularly successful counterpropaganda technique.

The Active Measures Working Group produced a series of *Foreign Affairs Notes* refuting Soviet forgeries and exposing international Soviet fronts. Three major reports were published by State Department, two by USIA and one by the FBI on Soviet active measures in the United States. These information products were possible because there was high level support for the working group's mission and activities.

The data used by the working group was compiled from State Department reporting, CIA reporting, including overt collection through the Foreign Broadcast Information Service, and reports from USIA public affairs officers in embassies around the world. The information put together in the working group was disseminated through publications distributed by State and USIA, the Voice of

America, and press conferences in the United States and abroad. The USIA used its fledgling television operation to set up interactive television press conferences with journalists located at U.S. embassies around the world who were able to watch and ask questions. The role of USIA Director Charles Z. Wick was vital in many ways. The public affairs officers were a mixed bag ranging from very good and hardworking to bureaucratic seat warmers. Because of Wick's interest in the subject of Soviet disinformation, the better public affairs officers (PAOs) had the opportunity to collect and supply the information the working group needed. The classified information supplied to the working group by CIA and FBI put the overtly collected material in context.

Although there was a significant amount of disinformation against the United States during the Carter Administration, it increased dramatically after the election of President Reagan. The most vital of the Soviet disinformation stories was the false charge that AIDS had been developed by the United States as a biological weapon. This was totally false. The development of AIDS was a natural phenomenon.

The false story was initially floated in an anonymous letter supposedly from a "well-known American scientist and anthropologist" in the Indian newspaper *Patriot*. This newspaper was one of the usual sources for surfacing Soviet disinformation stories. According to the KGB defector Ilya Dzhirkvelov *Patriot* was set up by the KGB in 1962 as a vehicle for Soviet disinformation stories.

The story lay dormant for two years until it appeared again in the Soviet weekly *Literaturnaya Gazeta* of October 30, 1985. In 1986 the KGB began a major campaign around this disinformation story. Dr. Jacob Segal, an East German professor, presented a paper at the September 1986 eighth summit of the Nonaligned Movement in Harare, Zimbabwe. Segal's claim was that AIDS had been developed at a U.S. government laboratory at Ft. Detrick, Maryland. His proof was "The first appearance of AIDS exactly coincides with the opening of a P-4 laboratory at Fort Detrick – taking into account the incubation period. This is also indicated by the fact, that the spreading of AIDS to the world emanated from New York, a city in the neighbourhood of Fort Detrick. The assumtion (*sic*) that AIDS is a product of the preparation of biological warfare can therefore be quite plainly be expressed."[67]

This would only be logical if one did not know that Ft. Detrick was nearly 250 miles southwest of New York City. A number of large American cities, including Washington D.C. and Baltimore, Maryland, are only 50 miles from the laboratory. The KGB picked up the Segal claim and made it the basis of a major dissemination. The story appeared in every major language and practically every country, with USIA receiving near-daily reports from American embassies around the world of the disinformation appearing in local publications. Many of the stories could be traced back to KGB media placements between late-1986 and mid-1987.

In July 1987 the State Department published a fourteen page *Foreign Affairs Note* titled "The USSR's AIDS Disinformation Campaign." The report detailed the Soviet disinformation campaign and refuted the arguments. In the summer of 1988, the Soviet disinformation apparatus was using an alleged quotation from New York Democratic Congressman Ted Weiss. They claimed that Weiss had confirmed in 1983 that AIDS was produced as a biological weapon by the United States. As chief of the USIA Office to Counter Soviet Active Measures, I obtained a letter from Congressman Weiss repudiating the Soviet claim and presented the letter in Moscow at the U.S.-USSR Bilateral Information Talks in September 1988.

In 1988 U.S. Surgeon General C. Everett Koop advised the Soviet Union that the United States would no longer supply them with the scientific information to cope with the AIDS epidemic if they continued this disinformation campaign. The effect was as if a faucet had been turned off. Suddenly the stories practically disappeared. The aggressive campaign of the United States government helped put a stop to the Soviet disinformation campaign. To this day, however, naive people continue to believe the false story.

In March 1992 Yevgeniy Primakov, head of the Russian Foreign Intelligence Service (the re-named KGB First Chief Directorate), revealed at a public meeting that the KGB had indeed fabricated the AIDS disinformation story.[68] We learned more the same year when two former officers of the East German Intelligence Service, Stasi, wrote a book about their work in disinformation. They wrote, "The content of our disinformation operation consisted of the following assertions: The AIDS virus had been made in the high-security virus and gene laboratory of the Military-Science Research Institute at Fort Detrick in Maryland. Roughly in 1977, it was allegedly communicated to the public through test subjects in an entirely uncontrolled fashion and thus triggered this deadly catastrophe." The former Stasi officers wrote in their book that they used East Berlin Professor Jakob Segal to spread this story. Then, "Stefan Heym saw to it that the AIDS lie would spread all over Europe; journalists brought the story to Africa and to other regions that were heavily ravaged by the disease."[69]

Stasi agent Segal set in motion the major AIDS disinformation campaign. Heym, whom we met earlier as the U.S. Army propagandist who wrote the World War II leaflet that encouraged the Germans to fight harder and who defected to East Germany during the Korean War, helped carry the story around the world.

Opportunities-based propaganda – and 24/7 counterpropaganda

Some Soviet forgeries or disinformation seemed to be at random. The Soviets took advantage of an opportunity to undermine the image of the United States, one of its allies or a Western official. At times it was possible to see a deeper motivation for a Soviet disinformation operation. After the Soviet invasion of Afghanistan in 1979, President Carter cancelled American participation in the 1980 Olympics in Moscow. In 1984, when Los Angeles was to host the games, the Soviets paid the United States back. First they announced that they could not participate in the Olympics in the United States because Soviet athletes were concerned that harm would come to them from the American "ultra-right." The story had no credibility since there was no danger to the Soviet athletes and Moscow was simply repaying the US for not participating in the Moscow Olympics.

In the months before the games African and Asian Olympic Committees received copies, in plain white envelopes, of two leaflets supposedly by the Ku Klux Klan threatening the lives of non-white athletes with vile racist slogans. The Active Measures Working Group took up the issue. The FBI was able to advise the working group that it had information that KGB had prepared the racist leaflets. However, details of the FBI's information could not be publicly used for security reasons. But we could say that the matter was indeed a KGB exercise and that investigation revealed that the letterhead used for the leaflets was not a known Klan letterhead. In addition we pointed to grammatical mistakes that would be made not by the type of ignorant American in the Klan, but by someone with Russian as a first language.

The State Department issued a public statement accusing the KGB of producing the leaflets and contacted each affected Olympic committee to advise them that the leaflets were forgeries. As a result, not a single Olympic committee pulled out of the games. The Soviets and their satellite countries were the only athletes that missed the Los Angeles Olympics.

When a Soviet air force plane shot down a civilian Korean Airlines jetliner on September 1, 1983, the international outrage embarrassed the Soviet Union. The KAL plane had accidentally flown into Soviet air space. On a number of previous occasions innocent civilian aircraft had been fired on and sometimes shot down by the Soviets in similar situations. After first denying that they had shot down the airliner, the Soviets produced a disinformation story that the KAL plane was a "spy plane." A few years earlier the Soviets had shot down a KAL plane over Soviet air space. Most of the crew and passengers in that incident survived and the Soviets recovered the plane. The KGB examined the plane and knew that it carried no spy gear. The 1983 plane broke up when it crashed in the Sea of Japan, killing all passengers and crew.

On September 6, 1983, U.S. representative to the U.N. Jeane J. Kirkpatrick spoke at the General Assembly and accused the Soviets of shooting down an innocent civilian plane. Ambassador Kirkpatrick produced an audiotape of the Soviet pilot communicating with his ground control before and during the shoot down. She refuted all of the Soviet excuses for shooting down the plane.

The only thing left for the Soviet propagandists was to promote the false story that the civilian Korean airliner was a "spy plane" and therefore the United States was to blame for the loss of life rather than the Soviet Union. For the next few years the international Soviet fronts promoted the false story in their publications. Local affiliates of the fronts also promoted the Soviet disinformation story. The U.S. Peace Council, the American affiliate of the World Peace Council, issued an eight-page brochure promoting the Soviet line. The piece bore the byline of Conn Hallinan, a regular writer for the Communist Party USA newspaper *People's World*.[70]

In Japan, Akio Yamakawa, a journalist who had been identified as a Soviet agent by KGB defector Stanislav Levchenko, published articles and gave lectures promoting the disinformation story.[71] In 1984 Novosti Press Agency in Moscow published a book titled *The President's Crime*, by Akio Takahashi, which claimed that President Reagan was responsible for the loss of lives on the KAL airliner because he ordered that it be used as a "spy plane." An English language edition of the book was published in Tokyo in 1985. The author was unknown in Japan but his reasoning closely conformed to that of Akio Yamakawa, leading to the suspicion that since Yamakawa had been exposed as a KGB agent the Soviets simply varied the name.[72]

Despite the Soviet efforts the international community remained horrified by the Soviet shoot down of an innocent civilian airliner. Ambassador Kirkpatrick's rapid response to the incident was assisted by the intelligence community providing the tape of the Soviet pilot, which she used so effectively at the United Nations. The USIA provided the graphics she used with the tape on the floor of the General Assembly.

The KGB had a longstanding dislike for the effective American ambassador. Kirkpatrick had defeated them in many debates before the KAL incident, and the KGB had tried to discredit her earlier. On

November 5, 1982, the British magazine *New Statesman* carried an article claiming that Kirkpatrick had a close relationship with the apartheid government of South Africa and that she had even illegally accepted gifts from that government. The magazine printed a copy of a letter to Kirkpatrick from the South African embassy that supposedly proved their point. The author of the attack article was Claudia Wright, a *New Statesman* writer who had a reputation for being pro-radical Arab (she once wrote an article about Saddam Hussein, describing him as "dashing"). Wright later penned pamphlets with titles like, *Spy, Steal and Smuggle: Israel's Special Relationship with the United States* and *The Politics of Liquidation: The Reagan Administration Policy Toward the Arabs,* both published in 1986 by the Association of Arab-American University Graduates, Inc.

The U.S. government immediately responded that the article was false and that the letter was a forgery. The December 3 issue of the *New Statesman* claimed that it had received the document from "a source in the U.S. State Department." The magazine printed another copy of the forged letter that had completely different spacing than the one they had previously printed. This in itself was evidence that the letter was a forgery.

Wright was exposed as a KGB agent in 1994 when her KGB control officer, Yuri Shvets, wrote a book after his defection to the United States and identified a husband and wife team as KGB agents. He concealed the names in his book on instructions of his publisher, but the present writer was able to identify the couple as Claudia Wright and her husband John Helmer.[73] Shvets then verified the true names of the agents in a broadcast on CBS 60 Minutes (which Helmer denied in the same program). John Helmer worked in the Carter White House. He later assisted his wife in her writing anti-American propaganda. They wrote for *Ethnos,* a Greek newspaper funded by KGB, as well as other left wing Greek publications that carried KGB disinformation. Wright also reported for the *Financial Times,* the *Atlantic Monthly* and other influential, mainstream press; Helmer reported on Russian business issues for the *Asia Times, Journal of Commerce* and other publications. On September 3, 1989, Claudia Wright wrote an article for the Dublin, Ireland *Sunday Times* in which she repeated the Soviet disinformation theme that "the Korean Airlines jumbo jet, shot down by the Soviet Air Force six years ago today, was on a spy mission for the U.S." Wright died in 2005. As of this writing, Helmer lived in Moscow.

My favorite forgery

The Chernobyl nuclear disaster in the Soviet Union created the circumstances for my favorite forgery. The world press had carried stories indicating a large number of casualties in Chernobyl. Soviet Communist Party leader Mikhail Gorbachev issued a public statement attacking the United States for supposedly spreading these stories. The United States had carefully not commented on the issue, although ultimately there were many more casualties than the Soviet Union admitted.

In August 1986, I received a phone call from John Goshko, a *Washington Post* reporter. Goshko was a gruff old curmudgeon and a well-known experienced journalist. He said, "I just got a copy of a stupid letter signed by you. Did you write it?" I answered, "I've written a lot of stupid letters, but I'd like to see it before I answer you." I went over to the *Washington Post*, looked at the letter and told Goshko, it was a forgery. The letter appeared to be my instructions to Senator David Durenberger on how we could make the Chernobyl disaster into an effective propaganda campaign. Aside from the fact that a USIA employee could not be instructing a U.S. senator, we had no such campaign. When I looked at the letter I realized it had been created from a letter that I had made available to a Senate committee at a hearing about a different forgery. The text of my letter had been removed and a new one inserted, but the letterhead and the signature block had been retained. I had given a copy of my letter to a Czech diplomat at his request after my Senate testimony. When I confronted the Czech diplomat, he apologized and said that he had sent the letter to Prague and they must have sent it to Moscow. I did not tell him that we knew that the forgery had been created in the KGB *rezidentura* at their embassy in Washington and that we knew that the Czech diplomat was in fact an intelligence officer working for the Soviets.

The FBI reported on this incident in an unclassified publication on *Soviet Active Measures in the United States 1986-1987*:

> During August 1986, a fabricated letter, believed to be a Soviet forgery, was mailed anonymously to the *Washington Post* and *U.S. News and World Report*. This document purports to be a letter by United States Information Agency (USIA) official Herbert Romerstein to Senator David F. Durenberger, former Chairman of the Senate Select Committee on Intelligence. The letter, dated April 29, 1986, described an alleged USIA campaign to spread disinformation on the Chernobyl nuclear power plant disaster. The forgery was designed to discredit the U.S. Government and damage its relations with Western Europe.

On August 19, 1986, the *Washington Post* reported some of the details of the USIA forgery. The forged letter suggested that USIA would attempt, among other things, to spread reports that the Chernobyl disaster had claimed 2,000 to 3,000 victims. Only 29 persons are said to have died from acute radiation sickness due to the accident. Although such inflated death statistics did appear in subsequent news reports on Chernobyl, USIA officials stated 'the reports stemmed from the confusion and rumors that swept Europe in the days immediately after the disaster.' USIA officials insist that they made no effort to encourage or spread the rumors and that neither Mr. Romerstein nor anyone else at USIA advocated such an idea to Senator Durenberger or to anyone else. An employee of Senator Durenberger's office reported that according to the Senator's office records no such letter from USIA was ever received by the Senator.

Mr. Romerstein reported some additional details concerning this particular forgery which makes it an especially interesting example of Eastern-Bloc support of a Soviet active measures operation. The USIA letterhead and the signature block on the forgery were taken from a genuine letter Romerstein had previously written to Lt. General Robert Schweitzer concerning the analysis of another Soviet forgery allegedly written by Schweitzer. During September 1985, Romerstein testified before the Senate Foreign Relations Committee on Soviet forgeries and offered to provide them with a copy of his letter to Schweitzer for Congressional publication. Subsequently, the Press Attaché of the Czechoslovakian Embassy, Vaclav Zluva, requested a copy of Romerstein's unclassified letter to Schweitzer. Romerstein provided him with a copy, but uniquely marked the one copy he gave Zluva.

When the forgery bearing Romerstein's name surfaced in the United States, it was obvious because of the unique markings Romerstein had put on the Schweitzer letter that it had been used as the exemplar to fabricate the Chernobyl forgery. When Romerstein confronted Zluva with the forgery, Zluva denied being involved in its preparation but admitted sending a copy of the Schweitzer letter supplied by Romerstein to Prague. Romerstein, who is an expert on active measures operations, believes Prague officials sent the Schweitzer letter to Moscow where it was used as the exemplar for the Chernobyl forgery. This forgery technique of photocopying a genuine letterhead and signature onto a document that contains a bogus text is common among Soviet forgeries. It facilitates preparation of the forged document and generally makes the task of analysis more difficult.[74]

The FBI and other organizations in the Active Measures Working Group used the forgery as an example of KGB methods and we in fact got more mileage out of it than the Soviets ever could have.

President Reagan, Secretary of State George Shultz, and USIA Director Charles Wick pressed the Soviets on the disinformation issue. At a Moscow meeting between Soviet leader Mikhail Gorbachev and Shultz, Gorbachev waved a copy of one of the working group publications that we had distributed throughout the world. He complained that the report went against the spirit of glasnost – the Soviet propaganda campaign that heralded Gorbachev's "openness." Shultz responded that when the KGB stops lying about us, we would stop exposing them. But later that year, at the Washington summit, Gorbachev told USIA Director Wick that it was time for "no more lies, no more disinformation." The forgeries and disinformation stories continued.

In September 1988, bilateral talks took place in Moscow between the United States and the Soviet Union. The Soviet delegation was headed by Valentin Falin, then head of the Novosti Press Agency and later chief of the International Department of the Central Committee of the Communist Party of the Soviet Union. Wick led the American delegation. I was at the meeting as a USIA representative.

Falin suggested that such meetings were useful to dispel misunderstandings. I suggested that annual meetings at such a high level were useful, but that working level meetings should be held more frequently. Falin agreed and took me aside after the meeting to establish the mechanism for such frequent meetings. Igo Bulay, the press counselor of the Soviet Embassy in Washington and Sergei Ivanko, Minister Counselor for Information at the Embassy represented the Soviet government. Todd Leventhal and I represented the U.S. government at the working level meetings. When I retired, Leventhal replaced me as head of the Office to Counter Soviet Active Measures at USIA, but I continued to attend the meetings as a consultant to the U.S. government.

We frequently complained to our Soviet counterparts about specific KGB disinformation campaigns and forgeries. The Soviets in turn complained to us about stories they did like in the American press and even in works of fiction, such as movies. The United States government, of course, had no say about what appeared in the American press and certainly not in films. The Soviets never reported to us any forgeries or disinformation campaigns that they could attribute to CIA. This was consistent with my own experience form 1978 to 1983 as a professional staff member with the House Intelligence Committee, where one of my responsibilities was monitoring CIA covert actions. I never saw a deliberately false story in the unattributed propaganda that CIA disseminated.

As the Soviet Union moved closer to its final collapse, disinformation did decrease. With the fall of the Soviet Union and the end of the Cold War, the Active Measures Working Group ended. There was little thought to maintaining a unit that would counter anti-American propaganda or disinformation from sources other than the Soviet Union. In reality after the Soviet collapse, some entities that had been created by the Soviets in the past or had been used by KGB still existed. Groups that had been formerly "friends of the Soviet Union" became friends of the Islamic extremists who shared their hatred for the United States and the West.

Exposing enemy attack elements in the media

When the Soviet Union and the East German dictatorship still existed, one of the jobs of the KGB and the East German Stasi was defaming not only Western intelligence services but also individuals in the West who opposed the communist regimes.

In 1986, KGB Chairman Viktor Chebrikov met in East Berlin with Stasi chief Mielke. The two communist intelligence bosses signed an agreement of cooperation in the work against Western governments, organizations, and individuals that they believed were anti-Soviet. They agreed "To work on subversive and other operatively important centers and organizations of the enemy, as well as certain anti-socialist elements in the given area of operations." The agreement included a decision "To seek out and fight organizations and single individuals" including Radio Liberty and Radio Free Europe (RFE/RL) and private Western pro-democratic organizations as PEN, Amnesty International, and Resistance International. Also on the list were individuals such as Ludwig von Stauffenberg, a West German human rights activist, and Gerhard Loewenthal, a West German television commentator who protested human rights violations in the Soviet bloc.[75]

In 1985 a magazine was established in Cologne, Germany called *Geheim* (Secret), whose purpose was to defame CIA, MI6 and other Western intelligence services. *Geheim* was closely connected with CIA defector Philip Agee and frequently carried lists of names of supposed CIA officers. The editor was Michael Opperskalski. The active measurers working group frequently exposed disinformation stories that appeared in *Geheim* and its English language version *Top Secret*. While it was clear that the magazines were spreading Soviet-created disinformation, the United States government refrained from identifying them as KGB controlled. After the collapse of the East

German regime, *Geheim* complained about too much perestroika in the Soviet Union. After the summer of 1991 no further issues of either magazine appeared. The KGB was in disarray after the August, 1991 coup attempt, and the Soviet system unraveled through December, when the USSR collapsed. In June 1992 *Geheim* sent a letter to its subscribers explaining that a shortage of money prevented them from publishing.[76]

The German government's investigation of Stasi activities revealed more of the story in 1993. In an official indictment of some Stasi officers the German government listed the publisher of the Cologne political magazine *Geheim* with the code name "Abraham" as a Stasi agent.[77] In 1999 Hubertus Knabe, a leading German expert on Stasi activities, identified the publisher of *Geheim* with the code name "Abraham" as Michael Opperskalski.[78]

Strangely *Geheim* is back in business with articles supporting Fidel Castro, and attacks on the Iraqis who were involved in opposing Saddam Hussein. An article signed by Opperskalski in the October 2002 issue assailed President George W. Bush and supported the Palestine Liberation Organization and the "Al-Aqsa Intifada." In 2003, Opperskalski spoke at a Berlin conference alleging that the Bush administration was behind the September 11, 2001 terrorist attacks.

Old propaganda themes survive, uncountered

The USIA has been merged into the State Department and virtually disappeared. Without a Charles Wick instructing public affairs officers (PAOs) to collect anti-American disinformation and send it to headquarters, there is no coordinated effort to counter anti-American propaganda. A small unit within the State Department continues to work but without information and support from American embassies abroad, or interest from political leadership in the bureaucracy and administration, they are considerably hampered.

No inter-agency working group exists that would have been the equivalent of the successful Active Measures Working Group. The FBI and CIA could not share information on terrorism in the 1990's. They certainly could not share information on anti-American disinformation, if they even collected such data.

In 1999 a book came out reiterating the old Soviet disinformation story that the United States had used germ warfare in Korea. *The United States and Biological Warfare*, published by Indiana University Press, was authored by Stephen Endicott and Edward Hagerman. Endicott was the son of James Endicott who had received the Stalin Prize in 1952 for spreading the same disinformation story.

The purpose of the book became clear when the Chinese delegation to the U.N. distributed copies of it on behalf of the North Korean delegation to promote the theme that the North Koreans should not have to allow American inspection of their nuclear facilities, which they had agreed to with the Clinton Administration. The Clinton Administration did nothing to expose the disinformation story. It even appeared in the March 12, 1999 issue of *Pacific Stars and Stripes*, a newspaper distributed to American servicemen. Even when the falsehood was exposed in print, the U.S. did nothing to refute the disinformation.[79]

The following July, Endicott and Hagerman wrote an article for *Le Monde diplomatique*, a French publication that in the past had frequently carried Soviet disinformation themes. Within weeks of the September 11, 2001 attacks, *Le Monde diplomatique* promoted the theme that "what happened in New York was sad, but the U.S. deserved it."

Immediately after 9/11 demonstrations were organized around the world against the United States and against any possible retaliation for the terrorist attack. Their coordination was reminiscent of the Soviet era of international front organizations. In the U.S., two groups organized the demonstrations. The main group was the Workers World Party, a group of extremist political organizers that is ideologically and politically tied to the regime in North Korea. The demonstrations were organized by the International Action Center, a WWP front. The Committees of Correspondence, a splinter group from the old Soviet-directed Communist Party USA (named after the committees that networked the American Revolution in the 1770s), also helped organize demonstrations.

The Workers World Party in June 2001 organized a supposed International War Crimes Tribunal on U.S. Crimes in Korea. The main speaker was activist Ramsey Clark, who has been involved in the defense of anti-American war criminals from Saddam Hussein to Slobodan Milosevic. One of the speakers was Lennox Hinds, the permanent representative to the U.N. of the International Association of Democratic Lawyers (IADL), another Cold War-era Soviet front organization that outlived its founding sponsor. Hinds read from a supposed study that IADL made in 1952 promoting the false germ warfare allegations. IADL, during the Soviet days, was one of the network of international Soviet fronts. A message was read to the gathering from Stephen Endicott, the author of the most recent book repackaging the old disinformation story.

Without counterpropaganda, we've unilaterally disarmed

Running a strategic counterpropaganda effort to fight against anti-American propaganda in Europe, the Middle East and elsewhere would be remarkably cost-effective. Using some of the lessons of the 1980's the U.S. and its allies can expose and discredit the disseminators of hostile propaganda. One could raise questions, for example, about why Islamist extremists are collaborating with remnants of the old Soviet agitprop networks. They receive legal help from an old Communist front, the National Lawyers Guild (NLG), which defends captured terrorists, assists them with their legal appeals, litigates and agitates to weaken or overturn counterterrorism laws and practices, and runs propaganda campaigns to discredit the United States to the terrorists' advantage.

Counterpropaganda themes directed at the anti-U.S. international left might concentrate on why non-Muslim activists are providing support to Islamist extremists who mistreat women and homosexuals, and want to establish a society where non-Muslims would have no rights.

Immediately after 9/11, John Wheat Gibson, Texas-Oklahoma Region Co-Vice President of the NLG issued a statement titled "Who crashed the planes? A Statement from the National Lawyers Guild." He said in part "The FBI and Mossad, acting either together or separately, have the most to gain from the attacks: the abolition of civil liberties in the U.S., which make it possible for Americans to criticize U.S. government support for Zionism; and the generation of anti-Arab hysteria that will make it possible for Israel to massacre the still surviving Palestinians without the criticism from the U.S. government and media, about which Israeli supporters have been complaining lately. Furthermore whipping up a war is the most effective way American presidents know to reverse an economic recession. Indeed, only the U.S. regime and the government of Israel have anything at all to gain from the attacks."

Shortly after 9/11 the NLG's Post 9/11 Project published a handbook addressed to Arab and Muslim Americans. It advised them "You do not have to talk to the police, FBI, INS, or any other law enforcement agent or investigator." It went on to say "Talking to the FBI can be very dangerous. You can never tell how a seemingly harmless bit of information might be used to hurt you or someone else. The FBI is not just trying to find 'terrorist', but is gathering information on immigrants and activists who have done nothing wrong. And keep in mind that even though they are allowed to and do lie to you, lying to a federal agent is a crime. The safest things to say are 'I am going to remain silent', 'I want to speak to my lawyer', and 'I do not consent to a search.'" The NLG and allied groups produced and disseminated legal advice flyers in the main languages of the al Qaeda terrorists, including Dari, Pashto, Punjabi, Urdu, and of course, Arabic.

Of course the FBI needed the cooperation of Arab and Muslim Americans, the overwhelming number of whom are considered loyal Americans. The handbook was to prevent the FBI from getting information from within the Muslim community that the authorities might use to monitor extremist groups and stop future terrorist acts.

On September 20, 2001 the Communist Parties of Jordan, Iraq, Sudan, Syria, Lebanon, Egypt and the Palestine People's Party issued a joint statement. After the ritual expression of sorrow at the loss of life on 9/11, the communists said, "But condemnation does not mean refusing to view this terrorist act in its reality, as being in one main aspect a bitter outcome of American policy itself. On the other side, it is a consequence of the tremendous resentment and anger which have been escalating all over the world, against injustice, oppression, exploitation and recklessness towards human beings and people; as well as against growing poverty and misery throughout the world."

Knowledge, insight and leadership

The loss of USIA did considerable damage to America's ability to carry out counterpropaganda. But restoring USIA would not be enough. The country would need to have leadership like Ronald Reagan and Charles Z. Wick to establish strategic communication goals and convince the bureaucrats that they had to do the job. But to organize an effective counterpropaganda campaign requires both having an apparatus in place to do the work but also an understanding of the target audience.

When President George W. Bush in the early days of the war against terrorism innocently referred to the war as a "crusade," he inadvertently played into many Muslims' worst fears. In our world, "crusade" is a positive political word almost shorn of religious connotations. Among many Muslims it is not. When Secretary of State Colin Powell suggested that there would be gratitude in the Muslim world for American help to the victims of the tsunami disaster, he also didn't understand his audience. Not only was there little gratitude, but the government of Indonesia impeded the rescue efforts by pressuring the U.S. to withdraw its aircraft carrier, *USS Abraham Lincoln*, far offshore because the authorities did want the U.S. Navy flying training exercises in Indonesian air space, or be as visible as it was in the relief effort. The State Department did little to promote the Navy effort for

strategic influence purposes. Sometimes others got the credit. One
evening a television news channel reported that the Japanese military
was helping the disaster relief. According to the report it was an
important development because it showed that the Indonesians no
longer hated the Japanese who had occupied them during World War
II.[80]

Counterpropaganda is not easy. But, lessons we learned in World
War II and the Cold War need to be applied today, with all the
advantages that information technology has given us, to rebuild the
apparatus to refute anti-American disinformation and to discredit the
enemies that spread it.

Notes

---

[1] *Information Bulletin*, published by Peace and Socialism Publishers, Prague
(North American edition, printed in Canada), August 1983, p. 24.
[2] *Al-Hayah*, London, October 21, 1992, in FBIS-USR-93-001, January 4,
1993, p. 47.
[3] "Overview of the Agitation Activities of the Ministry for State Security,"
report to *Comrade Minister* (Erich Mielke) from the head of the Agitation
Department, July 18, 1969. In Der Bundesbeauftragte fuer die Unterlagen des
Staatssichenrheitsdienstes der ehemaligen Deutschen Demokratischen
Republik, Berlin Mfs-HA 11/6 No. 1416, (hereafter referred to as Stasi
Archives) p. 18.
[4] *Social Psychology and Propaganda* (Institute of Social Sciences by Progress
Publishers, 1985), pp. 240 and 260.
[5] *The Reply to English Propaganda* by Reich Minister Dr. Goebbels, 8 page
leaflet in English reprinted from Völkischer Beobachter (official Nazi Party
newspaper), July 14, 1939.
[6] *The German News Agency and the News*, unattributed and no date or place
shown but printed in early 1940 and *Hitler's Words and Hitler's Deeds*,
unattributed with no date but "printed in England" early 1940.
[7] *7,000,000 Deutschamerikaner Klagen an!* 2-page British leaflet, code 477,
air dropped on Germany from the 14th of March to the 9th of April.
[8] *Ein Deutsches Flugblatt, Manifest der MünchnerStudenten*, 2-page British
leaflet, code G39, air dropped on Germany from July 3rd to 25th 1943.
[9] *The Treatment of German Prisoners*, 4 page leaflet, code number G4a and
the redone version *The Treatment of German Prisoners*, 4 page leaflet, code
number G4b.
[10] *Peace – Freedom – Bread*, British 2 page black leaflet supposedly signed
by the Red Circle.

[11] *Safe Conduct*, 2 page leaflet air dropped (a smaller version was fired from a shell), code US/GB-ZG61-1944.

[12] *Dear Friends*, German leaflet air dropped on American and British troops.

[13] *My Name is Joe Jones*, 2 page American leaflet, code 12AG20.

[14] Stasi Archives, AP 36.797/92, pp. 71-77.

[15] *1945 Churchill On the Approaching Peace*, 2 page British leaflet dated January 18, 1945, dropped on the German troops, Code G32.

[16] Robert E. Sherwood, *Roosevelt and Hopkins* (Harper & Brothers, 1948), p. 695.

[17] Clayton D. Laurie, *The Propaganda Warriors, America's Crusade Against Nazi Germany* (Univeristy Press of Kansas, 1996), pp. 176 and 77.

[18] Herbert Romerstein and Eric Breindel, *The Venona Secrets: Exposing Soviet Espionage and America's Traitors* (Regnery Publishing, 2000), pp. 433-434.

[19] U.S. House of Representatives, Select Committee to Investigate the Federal Communications Commission Hearings, 1943, Government Printing Office, Washington, DC, Volume 1, p. 388.

[20] *Main-Echo*, Aschaffenburg, Germany, February 16, 1946.

[21] U.S. House of Representatives, Select Committee [on the] Katyn Forest Massacre, 1952, Government Printing Office, Washington, DC. Julius Epstein was an Austrian Jew who fled when the Nazis took over his country in 1938. He worked in the Office of War Information during World War II and became a correspondent for German and Austrian newspapers after the war. His experience with the Nazis made a strong anti-Communist out of Epstein who saw them as basically the same.

[22] German leaflets published by Skorpion East. (1) Greetings From Stalin, (2) In the Name of Democracy, and (3) Eastern Sunrise in Nemmersdorf!

[23] German leaflet published by Skorpion East *Come and See for Yourselves!* Code SK J 2012

[24] Frontpost, Nachrichten für Deutsche Soldaten, Herausgeber: Die Amerikanischen Truppen in Westeuropa, March (1945), No. 1, p. 3

[25] Feldpost, Herausgegeben von der Amerikanischen Armee in Westeuropa, No. 5 for January 1945

[26] U.S. Senate Internal Security Subcommittee, *Interlocking Subversion in Government Departments*, Part 30, pp 2639-640. Reprint of article from *United Nations World* by Fred Smith.

[27] For details on White's espionage career see Romerstein and Brundel, Chapter 2.

[28] Die Feinde der deutschen Nation, Eine historische Dokumentation über die Deutschlandpolitik der imperialistischen Westmächte von 1942-1949 (The Enemy of the German Nation, a Historical Documentation on the German Policy of the Imperialist Western Powers from 1942-1949) by Prof. Dr. Karl Bittel, Kongress-Verlag GMBH, Berlin, 1952, pp. 13 and 19-22.

[29] Soviet 2-page leaflet *Hitler is Not Germany*, Code No. 1352

[30] *Don't Be a Sucker in Germany!* Restricted 12 page pamphlet.

[31] Tactical 2-page leaflet in Russian to former Soviet soldiers serving with the German forces titled *Fighting Men!*

[32] James M. Erdmann, *Leaflet Operations in the Second World War* (privately printed, 1969), p. 491-492.

[33] 2 page Soviet leaflet in Ukrainian, air dropped in late 1944 signed Tarnopol regional headquarters of the Soviet partisans.

[34] American four page leaflet in thirteen languages titled *Instructions*, code VG1.

[35] Julius Epstein, Operation Keelhaul, The Story of Forced Repatriation (Devin-Adair Company, 1973).

[36] Soviet 2-page leaflet to Germans titled *Foreigners Take Your Place* including drawing of foreigner in bed with a German women., Code 1857.

[37] Soviet internal leaflet in German for propagandists For Field and Trench Transmissions, Theme "How are the Germans Living in the areas occupied by the Red Army?

[38] ISCOT 502, transmission from Moscow to Germany, June 29, 1944. ISCOT was the British code word for the intercepted transmissions from the Communist International radios broadcasting to communist underground groups behind the German lines. ISCOT was original top secret but has been declassified and is available at the NSA library at Fort Meade, Maryland.

[39] ISCOT 519, Germany to Moscow, July 7, 1944.

[40] ISCOT 528, Germany to Moscow, July 9, 1944.

[41] American leaflet in Japanese titled *American President Speaks!* Code 12-J-1

[42] American leaflet in Japanese titled, *Peace With Honor,* Code 123-J-1

[43] Allison B. Gilmore, You Can't Fight Tanks With Bayonets, Psychological Warfare against the Japanese Army in the Southwest Pacific, (University of Nebraska Press, 1998), pp. 5 and 6.

[44] American leaflet in Japanese titled, *Today is The Emperor's Birthday*, Code 122-J-1

[45] *Institute of Pacific Relations*, Hearings before the Subcommittee on Internal Security of the United States Senate Judiciary Committee, September 14, 1951, Part 3, pp. 727 and 728.

[46] IPR volume 10, pp. 3597-3598.

[47] IPR Report 1952, p. 224.

[48] Maochun Yu, *OSS In China, Prelude to Cold War* (Yale University Press, 1996), p. 280

[49] U.S. leaflet in Korean to North Korean civilians, November 10, 1952, Code #1240

[50] North Korean leaflet in Korean to South Korea, May 30, 1953, Code 03406

[51] The Bulletin of the World Council of Peace, March 25, 1952

[52] I Accuse!, Dr. James G. Endicott Describes Germ Warfare, (Canadian Peace Congress, 1952)

[53] *Daily Worker*, New York, December 22, 1952

[54] *Schwarzbudh über den Bakterienkrieg*, Herausgegeben vom Österreichischen Friedensrat, Vienna, June 1952

[55] Bulletin of the World Council of Peace, March 15, 1958

[56] Ehemalige Nationalsozialisten in Pankows Diensten (Former Nazis in the Service of Pankov [the district of Berlin where the communist leaders lived]), (Investigating Committee of Free Jurists, Berlin, 1959), p. 12.

[57] Report of the International Scientific commission for the Investigation of the Facts Concerning Bacterial Warfare in Korea and China, (World Council of Peace). Identical copy printed by Hsinhua (New China) News Agency, Prague Office and International Union of Students as a supplement to their magazine World Student News, all 1952.

[58] *Report on War Crimes in Korea* (The Commission of International Association of Democratic Lawyers, 1952).

[59] *The Problem of Peace in Korea*, delivered by Secretary of State Dean Acheson, the Department of State, October 24, 1952, pp. 21-22.

[60] *Cold War International History Project Bulletin*, Woodrow Wilson International Center for Scholars, Washington, DC, Winter 1998, No. 11, pp. 180-183.

[61] *Communist Forgeries*, Hearing before the Subcommittee on Internal Security of the Senate Judiciary Committee, June 2, 1961, Government Printing Office, Washington, DC, 1961.

[62] *The CIA and the Media*, Hearings before the House Permanent Select Committee on Intelligence, Government Printing Office, Washington, DC, 1978, pp. 304 and 305, and 531ff.

[63] *Soviet Covert Action (The Forgery Offensive)*, Hearing before the House Permanent Select Committee on Intelligence, Government Printing Office, Washington, DC, 1980, pp. 26.

[64] Izvestiya of the Central Committee of the Communist Party of the Soviet Union, March 1989.

[65] Soviet Covert Action, p. 23.

[66] *Soviet Active Measures,* Hearing before the House Permanent Select Committee on Intelligence, Government Printing Office, Washington, DC, 1982.

[67] *AIDS – its nature and origin* by Prof. Dr. Jakob Segal, Dr. Lilli Segal, Dr. Ronald Dehmlow, mimeographed, pp. 38.

[68] *Izvestiya*, March 19, 1992 (in Russian).

[69] Günter Bohnsack and Herbert Brehmer, *Auftrag: Irreführung, Wie die Stasi Politik im Westen machte* (Carlsen, 1992), pp. 219-220.

[70] *The Curious Flight of KAL 007,* by Dr. Conn Hallinan, published by US Peace Council, New York, 1984.

[71] *The Japan Times*, May 15, 1984, p 10 and Gunji Minron (People's Military Forum) June 1, 1984. (the later carried Yamakawa's article claiming that the KAL was an electronics warfare plane.

[72] Akio Takahashi, *President's Crime, Who ordered the espionage flight of KAL 007?* (Ningensha, 1985), reprint of Russian language edition published by Novosti, Moscow, 1984.

[73] See Yuri B. Shvets, Washington Station, My Life as a KGB Spy in America (Simon & Schuster, 1994).

[74] Soviet Active Measures in the United States, 1986-1987, Prepared by the Federal Bureau of Investigation, also printed in Congressional Record December 10, 1987.

[75] Stasi files, MfS-BdL/ No. 001861, pp. BSTU 2 and 3.

[76] *Soviet Active Measures in the "Post-Cold War" Era, 1988-1991*, United States Information Agency, Washington, DC, June 1992, pp 56-9. Editor's note: *Geheim's* financial woes paralleled those of Soviet international front organizations. In December, 1991, the editor was in Helsinki and visited the World Peace Council headquarters, discovering a dejected skeleton staff of three. They readily admitted, when pressed, that the Soviets had been funding the organization and that since the August putsch they had received almost nothing because the anti-Soviet government of Russian President Boris Yeltsin, which took over Soviet institutions, was not interested in promoting peace.

[77] Der Generalbundesanwalt beim Bundesgerichtshof, Anklage, gegen, Rolf Günter Wagenbreth, Wolfgang Albert Mutz, Rolf Otto Herbert Rabe, Bernd Werner Michels, pp. 69.

[78] *Die unterwanderte Republik, Stasi im Westen*, by Hubertus Knabe, Propyläen, Berlin, 1999, pp. 112.

[79] This writer wrote an article exposing the disinformation in the *Washington Times* of February 21, 1999, but there was no word on this issue from the Administration.

[80] The report only showed the lack of historical knowledge at Fox News, which reported the story. The present regime in Indonesia is the political and ideological heir of the first independent government of Sukarno. The Dutch had turned over the East Indies to him. Sukarno, like many of the rulers who were given power by the former colonial rulers of the area, had been a Japanese puppet. He had been the head of quisling government installed by the Japanese occupation army. See Peer de Mendelssohn, *Japan's Political Warfare* (George Allen & Unwin Ltd, 1944), pp. 113.

8

Recovering the Lost Art
of Counterpropaganda:
An assessment of the war of ideas in Iraq

ANDREW GARFIELD

Background: The challenge in Iraq

The defeat of the insurgency and terrorism in Iraq requires an approach that does not focus on the eradication of such threats through force of arms alone. Instead, as the successful experiment in Al-Anbar proved, a much more holistic approach is required that addresses the underlying causes of the insurgency and the perceptions of those who have embraced extremist ideas, or who have provided the insurgents with safe havens, recruits and resources.

To defeat these adversaries we must therefore adopt our own asymmetric approach that seeks to influence the Iraqi population. The approach must persuade Iraqis to reject extremism and violence through a combination of dialogue, inducements and the proportionate use of force. The main characteristic that distinguishes campaigns of insurgency from other forms of war is that they are *primarily* concerned with the struggle for men's minds.[1]

Success in Iraq requires effective engagement and dialogue with key segments of the Iraqi population, achieved in part through a comprehensive information campaign. This type of campaign has variously been described as information operations, propaganda, strategic communications, influence operations, psychological operations and perception management. While the terminology may vary, the intent is the same: to influence the hearts and minds of key target audiences through the effective use of information. This dialogue must uplift the legitimacy of the Iraqi government system and of the

Coalition, while repeatedly highlighting the vices of the insurgency. It must also effectively challenge the propaganda of the insurgency, an enemy that for a long time was far more effective than the Coalition has at engaging the local population. In some places, the enemy still is.

The overall aim of this information campaign is to win support for our actions or at least the acquiescence of the affected population. The campaign should bolster morale, which has been severely stressed by the shock effect of the years following the 2003 invasion; by unwelcome or unfamiliar change; and because of deprivation, loss, and intimidation. This campaign must also challenge the personal appeal, ideology and propaganda of the insurgents, who seek to promote their own agenda to encourage supporters or coerce the uncommitted and who attempt to portray every Iraqi government and Coalition action negatively or steal the credit for our rare successes – for example, by portraying political or economic improvements or a redress of grievances as resulting only from their violent campaigns.

The keys to a successful information campaign are to develop lines of persuasion and messages that will actually resonate with the target audiences, use culturally sensitive and relevant narratives, and exploit *all possible avenues* to reach hearts and minds. The counterinsurgents' information campaign must be timely, quickly exploiting all successes and rapidly challenging enemy propaganda before opportunities are lost and the lies and deceits of the insurgents gain credibility.

In an asymmetric conflict, we simply cannot allow an information vacuum to develop, because it will be filled with gossip and with the lies of the insurgents and extremists. This type of campaign will fail if it simply extols a government ideology and/or vague abstractions such as the benefits of democracy or a free-market economy. Instead, it must focus on what really matters to people – local and personal issues such safety, jobs and representation.

To achieve these objectives requires the coordination of a broad range of capabilities and expertise, little of which is found in sufficient numbers or quality within either the Iraqi government or the Coalition. These include the types of skills and experience found in the advertising, marketing, public relations, lobbying and political campaign industries, and within the broadcast, print and new media. And of course, this all has to be done in a foreign language to an audience that is culturally alien to the Coalition. The Coalition therefore faces a number of significant challenges in Iraq that it must overcome in order to win the war of ideas with the insurgents and extremists.

For the counterinsurgency side, not winning is losing

From firsthand experience in Iraq, I could only conclude prior to the 2007 surge that we were losing not simply the physical battle but perhaps even more importantly the psychological conflict. Many political observers in the U.S. and Europe had already declared the Coalition's defeat. The Coalition had failed to systematically counter enemy propaganda either by responding rapidly with effective counter messaging or more proactively by directly challenging the messages, methods and ideology that the insurgents and extremists promote and exploit. The Coalition's mostly uncoordinated and largely ineffectual strategic communications efforts to date have failed to gain any significant traction with key segments of the Iraqi population. Progress made with the Sunnis was offset by loss of influence among many Shi'ites.

In contrast, the insurgents quickly secured the initiative in the struggle for the hearts and minds of contested populations. Although the Coalition achieved some sustained success at the tactical level, most often by psychological operations (PSYOP) units, it was too little too late to counter the words and deeds of our asymmetric adversaries – adversaries who clearly understand that they are engaged in a psychological rather than physical conflict. The enemy's psychological conflict strategy is designed not to lead to the military defeat of the Coalition, but instead to the collapse of local Iraqi support for their government and the support of Coalition publics and political leaders at home for the war itself. Against both targets, one can only conclude that the insurgents had the upper hand across much of Iraq until the surge.

In the face of what can only be described as propaganda onslaught, we have demonstrated ourselves to be little more than dedicated amateurs in the war of ideas in Iraq, while our adversaries have shown themselves to be remarkably effective propagandists. This is nothing new for the western democracies in fighting insurgencies. More than four decades ago David Galula, a French army officer who served in China, Greece, Southeast Asia and Algeria, pointed out in his seminal work on counterinsurgency, "If there is a field in which we were definitely and infinitely more stupid than our opponents it was propaganda."[2]

In Iraq, the insurgents, extremists, and militia groups have shown themselves to be highly adept at releasing timely and effective messages that undermine support for the Iraqi government and Coalition and which bolster their own reputation and perceived potency. They are quick to exploit Coalition failures and excesses; they respond rapidly to defend their own actions, often by shifting blame to the authorities; and they are able to hijack Coalition successes and present them as proof that change only occurs as a result of their own violent campaign. They have taken a leaf out of the insurgent playbook written by the Brazilian anarchist Carlos Marighela, who wrote in his doctrine for urban guerrilla warfare the following advice:

> It would be necessary to turn political crises into armed conflicts by performing violent actions that will force those in power to transform a political situation into a military situation. That will alienate the mass who, from then on, will revolt against the army and police and thus blame them for the state of things.[3]

Adversary capabilities

How have our adversaries established their dominance in the information space? The answer is simple – through the effective use of words and deeds. Like numerous other asymmetric opponents before them, the insurgents and terrorists in Iraq have expertly utilized violence as the most effective of their propaganda tools. This is certainly not a new strategy. For example, the 19th Century revolutionary Johannes Most advocated the systematic use of terror by small groups of activists utilizing the most modern technology available in pursuit of what he termed the "propaganda of the deed." Our opponents have exploited the propaganda of numerous violent deeds to intimidate the uncommitted, to undermine confidence in the authorities, to bolster and expand their own support base, to demonstrate their potency, to provoke a disproportionate military response from the Iraqi authorities and the Coalition, and to sow the seeds and then fan the flames of sectarian conflict.

Recognizing that the use of violence is intended primarily to achieve psychological effects, the insurgents in Iraq adopted both an attritional and maneuverist approach to its application. They have conducted an effective attritional psychological campaign using improvised explosive devices (IED) and explosively formed projectiles (EFP), small scale attacks, marksmen, mortars and rockets to inflict a steady stream of casualties. These attacks, which had no significant impact on Coalition combat effectiveness, sapped the morale of Coalition publics and politicians. The insurgents also demonstrated their maneuverist tendencies by orchestrating attacks to coincide with key events such as U.S. elections in order to achieve a desired political impact in Washington.

To support their violent campaign and also as a line of operation in its own right, our adversaries in Iraq have utilized numerous multimedia channels to convey sophisticated messages to multiple audiences. They have manipulated journalists and media outlets to ensure that their messages and actions are conveyed to the widest possible audience. They have produced countless CDs and DVDs, which are distributed widely within contested communities. They have exploited the mosques in order to convey their messages to the faithful – messages enhanced with an apparent divine sanction, given by radical Imams. They have encouraged the spread of extremist graffiti which provides communities with a constant and intrusive reminder of the presence and potency of these groups and which serves as a defiant gesture towards the authorities. They have posted flyers, distributed leaflets, published newspapers and authored articles and editorials.

They have used SMS text messaging and Iraq's Coalition-built cellular telephone system to reach vulnerable individuals and even to target members of the Coalition. They have exploited the arts including paintings, poetry and songwriting. The insurgents are also expertly exploiting information technology and the Internet to great effect, thereby increasing their ability to reach mass audiences and to respond quickly and effectively to Iraqi government and Coalition messaging with their own counterarguments.

By contrast, the Coalition was and often remains largely precluded from cyberspace for fear of blowback to the domestic audiences at home – an ill-informed, knee jerk decision not to engage that all but handed key terrain in the war of ideas to our adversaries in the crucial first years of the fight.

Most worryingly of all, the insurgents, both Shia and Sunni, have used violence to silence their critics thereby creating an information vacuum that they then fill. They can do this far faster than the Coalition – deploying messages that really do resonate with the local populace and in real or near real time. Until the Coalition is able to counter this sustained, coordinated and effective enemy propaganda effort and seize the influence initiative permanently, these adversaries will continue to have an advantage in an area where they should have none. Coalition capabilities have improved in some areas, but at the initiative of warfighters and civilian contractors on the ground, not at the national strategic level.

Coalition information operations

To counter this threat, what was the Coalition doing before the surge and the implementation of the new counterinsurgency doctrine?

Certainly, the Coalition spent tens of millions of dollars on advertising in Iraq. Some individual efforts have been highly effective. Most of the successes are advertisements designed and produced by the Iraqis themselves and not by international advertising agencies. However, most Coalition advertisements, which saturated the airwaves, lacked resonance and relevance; for years they were near-useless. Some Coalition ads actually have done more harm than good, causing mostly anger, incomprehension and derision. For example, the use, at great expense, of Hollywood style *Matrix*-like stop action cinematography, sanitized to avoid any portrayal of the true bloody horrors of a suicide bombing, had little or no impact on ordinary Iraqis who live first hand with the realties of streets running with blood from countless such attacks. Or the ad was seen simply as yet another example of none too subtle American propaganda. Either way, opportunities were lost, audiences potentially alienated, and money and time clearly being wasted. This is not said in hindsight; some of us on the ground warned about it at the time.

Controversially, the Coalition has actively encouraged elements of the Iraq media to provide balanced reporting and commentaries. This was done partly through inducements – a necessity, given the media environment in Iraq – but it remains a contentious action nonetheless. It has distributed tens of millions of leaflets, displayed hundreds of billboards, and sent out hundreds of thousands of text messages. It has deployed loudspeakers throughout Iraq. It has established radio stations and even occasionally contested cyberspace. All of these efforts, however, have been unable to seize the information initiative from the insurgents.

In part this lack of success is due to factors beyond the control of the information operations (IO) practitioners in the military. The deteriorated security situation and the slower than desired progress to restore essential services and economic stability in Iraq, for example, severely undermined efforts to win support and took years to overcome. That said there remain serious operational shortcomings that have undermined the Coalition's IO effort. These shortcomings have included the following:

- No central coordinating authority;
- Lack of consistency in messages and products;
- Pedestrian and bureaucratic approval process;
- Fear of using information as a weapon;
- Focus on abstract concepts and rhetoric (e.g. democracy, anti Iraqi forces) that have little or no relevance for ordinary Iraqis;

- Lack of adequate target audience understanding;
- Lack of understanding of the nature of the threat;
- Failure to use all media including entertainment and new media;
- Development of products that resonate with the Coalition but too often not with Iraqis;
- Failure to respond in a timely manner to key events;
- Failure to co-opt and develop local spokespersons;
- Development of messages that are boring and turn audiences off;
- Failure to adequately monitor, pre-empt and counter enemy propaganda;
- Focus on measures of performance rather than effectiveness;
- Insufficient funds;
- Unclear, obsolete or timid policy and legal authority from civilian leadership, including Department of Defense General Counsel;
- Severe shortage of necessary skills and manpower;
- Failure to effectively use and manage private sector support.

All of these shortcomings are worthy of lengthy discussion, but for the sake of brevity this chapter will focus on seven. The first is the use of abstract concepts and meaningless rhetoric.

Abstract concepts

All too often, the lines of persuasion upon which the Coalition's IO campaign is built relate to abstract concepts such as the promotion of democracy, citizenship, or the legitimacy of the Iraqi Security Forces. Those issues have little or no relevance to the majority of Iraqis or are simply not recognizable to them. Such issues are important to strategic development but often at the expense of immediate-term military needs where lives are at stake. As a result, Coalition information products and campaigns do not resonate with most of their intended audiences and are as such unlikely to change attitudes, let alone behavior. Most Iraqis care far more about real-life issues such as personal security, jobs, and utilities; are heavily influenced by the political positions of their ethnic group, tribe or clan; or are polarized by the real world actions or inactions of their security services and government. All too often in Iraq the Coalition has developed campaigns that promote a utopian vision for the country that bears little resemblance to the realities of a bitterly divided nation on the verge of collapse and civil war.

Similarly, the Coalition continually uses meaningless rhetoric and politically correct terms to describe groups and events in Iraq, the subtleties of which are lost on Iraqis. The rhetoric and wording are the subjects of derision. They delude our own troops. Worst of all they hand propaganda victories to the enemy. For example, insurgents of all hues are now routinely described as "anti-Iraqi forces." What does that mean? Coalition personnel are probably the only people in the country that think that the insurgents are anti-Iraq. Indeed many consider the Coalition itself to be anti-Iraq. Such terms do not reflect how the insurgents portray themselves or how they are perceived by the various communities in Iraq. Instead they describe our adversaries the way we see them – through a lens that is frankly irrelevant in Iraq. The descriptions are another example of how the Coalition sees Iraq as we would like it to be rather than as it is.

Early in the war, Iraqi men were commonly referred to as MAMs or military-age males. This was a dehumanizing and simplistic term that provoked anger among average Iraqis and desensitized Coalition troops to the fact that not all young Iraqi men are insurgents. Coalition officials and the troops a large also refer to the insurgents as jihadists, hajjis or the Muj – all terms of honor in the local culture that bestow a dignity and divine legitimacy on the same adversaries we are also trying to denigrate and delegitimize. The Coalition's information campaigns therefore need to do a far better job of linking Coalition objectives to the issues that matter to Iraqis, exploiting narratives that actually resonate with the people, and use terms that accurately describe our adversaries without promoting their agenda.

Generic audience

The next shortcoming is the fact that too many Coalition campaigns are aimed at a generic Iraqi audience that simply does not exist. There still seems to be a general assumption that all Iraqis are broadly similar and therefore the same messages and emotional appeals will resonate with them all. In reality, Iraq is a highly complex ethnically and ideologically diverse – one could even say divided – country. Therefore overarching, national-level campaigns are rarely going to appeal to the majority except in the case of a few "national" issues such as a general election. Even much more specific campaigns aimed at each of the three main ethnic groups are not going to resonate with everyone within a given group. This is because there are also significant intragroup differences mainly along tribal and ideological lines that necessitate much more focused and nuanced campaigning. For example, the difference between the supporters of the key Shi'a groups are profound, and Coalition messages need to take due account of this in order to achieve the desired effect. Indeed, a positive message for one community may actually be received negatively by another.

The challenge of developing such focused campaigns is compounded by the fact that the primary means of reaching many key audiences is television and the preponderance of national and international satellite stations makes it very difficult to develop focused broadcast media products aimed precisely at the right audience. Developing the right types of programming also places a premium on cultural knowledge to include audience preferences. This knowledge is only derived from extensive social science and attitudinal research and this type and depth of research has not always been available to Coalition planners, a situation that required quick rectification.

Approval process

Another problem undermining the Coalition's ability to deploy timely and effective arguments is its own approval process. Even excellent products developed by Iraqi authors for their own ethnic group, containing messages that will assuredly resonate with that audience, can take days and even weeks to be staffed through what can only be described as a byzantine U.S. or Coalition approval process. Even simple newspaper reports and advertisements aimed at the readers of a paper with a circulation of less than 50,000 have to be sanctioned by an approval chain that includes numerous IO and PSYOP staffs, lawyers, and senior officers up to the rank of three-star general. For example, imagery of critical events filmed by Coalition assets and sent to Coalition HQs in near real time, which could be used to highlight the atrocities being committed by the insurgents far more effectively than Hollywood commercials, can still take days to clear the approval process. By the time approval is granted, the message has become overtaken by further propaganda events.

It has to be acknowledged that in part, the approval process has become so convoluted and requires the involvement of the lawyers because of past problems with the content of the messages that were developed and the means used to deploy them. Some of those problems include the lack of cultural sensitivity, the use of inappropriate messages and themes, and the payment of Iraqi journalists. However, unless the approval process is radically overhauled so that the time taken to secure release approval can be reduced to only a few minutes, the Coalition will continue to struggle to prevail in the battle for the hearts and minds of Iraqis. The insurgents most assuredly are not encumbering themselves in the same way and it shows.

Lack of essential skills

Another shortcoming concerns the competency of the operators tasked to execute the Coalition's IO campaign and the resources allocated to them. While a minority of personnel does have some of the necessary skills, for example PSYOP operators, some IO personnel and Public Affairs Officers (PAO), most are seconded from other branches of service and have at best only a short IO course to prepare them for what is an extraordinarily complex undertaking. They are of course dedicated and resourceful but they are not experts. In reality this type of operation requires the government to have access to an extensive combination of skills and experience encompassing existing IO, PSYOP, and PAO professionals as well private sector expertise from the strategic communications, marketing, advertising, public relations, lobbying, political campaigning, journalism, and multimedia production and broadcasting industries.

This combination of public and private sector expertise must also be underpinned by experts from the key social sciences to ensure cultural understanding and from the attitudinal research industry to assess attitudes and campaign effectiveness. Most importantly, senior leaders themselves need expert advice to enable them to exploit IO to maximum effect and to fully consider the influence implications of all other operations. Even after more than three years of occupation in Iraq, this full array of skills and experience is still missing. This shortcoming is compounded by the rotation of key PSYOP and IO personnel who have gained the necessary skills and experience through on-the-job training, but who are then replaced by the next batch of committed but nonetheless inexperienced personnel who arrive with only limited training and who must then start the learning process all over again.

Failure of the private sector

The next shortcoming is the Coalition's failure to properly utilize the private sector contractors who are supposed to provide the Coalition with those skills and experience that are not available in the public sector. In the first instance, the government has generally been a poor client, which has allowed some contractors to provide inadequate services. Requests for proposals (RFP) are all too often poorly written and reflect a lack of understanding of the actual operational requirements of commanders, of the complexities of IO mission and of the strengths and weaknesses of the private sector. Thereafter the contractor selection process is undertaken by personnel who are either placed under draconian time constraints or who simply lack the technical knowledge and business experience needed to determine if a contractor's proposal is achievable and to ensure that prospective contractors' claims regarding capabilities are genuine.

This lack of due diligence in the selection process is a primary reason why some contractors have failed to deliver the level of service that was required and promised. No commercial organization would award a contract worth tens of millions of dollars to a supplier without first undertaking a comprehensive due diligence process to determine the capabilities, viability and integrity of that company, and yet this has been done with alarming regularity in Iraq. After a contract has been let, some Coalition personnel also lack the technical skills needed to assess contractor performance properly, and are unable to effectively demand an improvement in service when standards slide as they sometimes do.

More recently these shortcomings have been compounded by a government switch to a lowest bid selection process. This cost cutting measure has encouraged some companies to significantly underbid their more competent but more expensive rivals to secure contracts they have neither the resources nor competencies to execute properly. These shortcomings ensure a perverse cycle of failure where too much is often asked of companies in the RFP process, the lowest priced and often least able companies win contracts, there is an inadequate due diligence and too little is demanded from these contractors after a contract is awarded.

The typical IO operator is therefore placed in a catch-22 situation. He knows that he lacks the full range of the skills needed and he knows that the private sector can provide them. He does not, however, have the wherewithal or know how to secure the type of support he really needs from the right contractors – those who actually do possess the necessary skills and who care as much if not more about the mission than they do about profits.

Contractor shortcomings can include the failure to provide the full extent of services promised in the winning proposal, usually because of an inability to deploy sufficient numbers of suitably qualified staff. This situation in large part results from the fact that some contractors, in order to secure an IO contract, regularly include in their proposals the resumes of individuals who cannot or will not deploy to Iraq. The hope is that the right personnel can be recruited after the fact, which is often not the case.

Other shortcomings can include the failure to provide effective (and costly to the company) in-country management to ensure that standards and discipline are maintained. In a time of war one of the worst crimes of a small number of companies is the attempt to secure as much profit as possible from each contract, over and above the margin declared in a proposal, rather than commit all funds to the successful execution of a contract. Making a profit is acceptable even in a time of war. Gouging is not. Overall it is assessed that some IO contractors have failed to deliver an adequate service to the government, their performance has been inferior; and worse, that poor performance and leaks from disaffected staff have undermined public confidence in the IO mission.

Measures of effectiveness

Critical to the success of any IO campaign is a comprehensive, independent and impartial review of all such operations. Unfortunately the Coalition has typically shown a preference for measures of performance over effectiveness. For example, the main anchor of the information campaigns at the national level has been television advertising undertaken by large international firms that have made countless expensive ad spots of 30 or 60 second duration. From the limited amount of research that has been done, it seems likely that these campaigns have had little long term positive impact on the attitudes of most Iraqis let alone on their behavior. These same firms and other Coalition assets have also undertaken more localized advertising using, for example, billboards and newspaper advertisements, but the producers have used the same abstract concepts drawn from the Coalition's lines of persuasion that simply do resonate adequately with most Iraqis. The success of these expensive campaigns is not generally measured on the basis of their impact but all too often simply on quantitative performance. How many ads were made? How quickly were they released? How often they were aired? How many people were watching?

The reality is that performance based indicators only confirm that a message has been seen or heard, not what impact they had. Coalition officials perpetuated this failure by regularly describing the success of the IO effort on the basis of the number of commercials shown and the amount of money spent, not on what immediate or lasting positive impact had been achieved.

Some success has been achieved for sure, most often at the battalion level and by PSYOP subunits. These units have undertaken grassroots campaigns using loudspeakers, meetings, leaflets, billboards, comics, and newspaper placements promoting issues that matter to the people in their areas of operation. However even at this level insufficient resources are subordinated to units to conduct a proper measure of effectiveness.

The case for IO

The final and perhaps most important failure in this war of ideas is our failure to win domestic public and political support for the use of information as a weapon. As the press controversy in late 2005 over the payment of Iraqi journalists has demonstrated, a compelling case for the need to engage in counterpropaganda in Iraq and elsewhere has not yet been made. As a result, it sometimes appears that the American press and politicians are far more comfortable advocating the use of violence rather than reasoned arguments and inducements to defeat this adversary. And yet in the end, this adversary can only be defeated, stability restored, and reconstruction completed if the influence war is won. This must include an effective and timely information and counter propaganda campaign.

Whenever a limited public debate does occur on this topic, opponents often deploy the word "propaganda" to denigrate our use of information as a weapon, and yet the only alternative to dialogue is the employment of increasing levels of violence and intimidation. The U.S. government therefore has to make a compelling case to the American public to justify the necessity for this type of operation and to gain political and public acceptance of the tools that must be deployed. Whether the public agrees or disagrees with the Iraq War, winning the hearts and minds of the Iraqi public is vital in order to bring peace to that country and this necessitates securing domestic public and political support for the various tools of an influence based campaign. As one IO officer noted, "If we cannot win this argument, how on earth are we going to succeed in stabilizing and reconstructing Iraq?"

The key to success: Effective counterpropaganda

In order to seize the information initiative in Iraq or anywhere else where we engage in a struggle for the hearts and minds of contest audiences, it is essential that we develop a properly coordinated counterpropaganda capability. This capability must be able to not only counter enemy propaganda (both words and deeds) it must also be able to seize the information initiative. Outlined below are some of the requirements for and components of a successful counterpropaganda campaign.

In the first instance our leaders have to recognize that we are engaged in an influence war. This is a war in which we need to deploy all of the soft and hard levers of power we have at our disposal in order to secure the support or at least the cooperation of key communities. These levers of state power include the proper use of coercive force and a combined military and civilian effort to restore stability and essential services. It must include the regeneration of failing or shattered economies leading to a perceptible rise in standards of living. It also involves the development of effective and representative governance. All of these measures are essential to win hearts and minds and will likely have far greater overall effect than any information campaign that we could deliver. That said, victory in the information space is still critical. If properly organized and resourced, our strategic communications and counterpropaganda effort can be used to explain our motives and actions, set expectations and when necessary to apologize for missteps and mishaps. It can be used to restore morale, hope and pride. And most importantly, it must be used to denigrate our adversaries and to counter their words and deeds.

The keys to success in this struggle are simple. In the first instance we must undertake a comprehensive propaganda monitoring and collection effort that captures examples of all types of enemy propaganda. Simple media and website monitoring efforts using the Internet and the most obvious hard copy news sources are an important first step but are also only the tip of the iceberg. It is also essential to collect CDs and DVDs, leaflets and posters, capture the content of graffiti, and secure transcripts of sermons, speeches and even gossip. Any and every source of enemy propaganda must be captured.   This material then needs to be properly analyzed by experts who actually understand what they are looking for.   Those experts must include experts from the intelligence and PSYOP communities and also professionals from all relevant social sciences: psychologists, historians, political scientists, theologians, cultural anthropologists and economists; and from the attitudinal and market research communities. Questions about counterpropaganda that must be asked and answered include:

- Who is the intended audience?
- What effects do the propagandists desire?
- What effects have they achieved?
- Which other audiences have heard or seen this message?
- What do these messages indicate about an adversary's perceptions, capabilities, vulnerabilities, and intent?
- What are the intentional or unintentional inaccuracies, inconsistencies, or deceits in the messages that we can exploit?
- What counter arguments can we deploy, to whom, and how?

It is vital that all insurgent and terrorist attacks, the so-called "propaganda of the deed" are also assessed through this prism to determine what the insurgents' desired psychological effects of these atrocities were. Who are these attacks really aimed at? What impact or response is desired? What success has been achieved? This analysis is vital because the target of attack is not always the real target. For example, the attack on the Samarra mosque was not aimed at the building or the worshippers who use it. Rather the attack was intended to divide the Shia and Sunni communities and spark a sectarian conflict.

Armed with this knowledge it is then possible to begin the complex process of developing an effective counter propaganda campaign. Such a campaign requires the development of lines of persuasion and message themes that will actually resonate with the target audience. It must utilize culturally sensitive and relevant narratives, which can convey our messages in ways that our audiences can understand and except. We must be able to develop, test, and deploy a comprehensive range of multimedia products and acquire the capabilities, connections and resources needed to exploit all possible avenues to reach critical audiences. This campaign must then be subjected to a systematic and objective assessment process that considers both performance and effectiveness. This campaign also has to be timely, quickly exploiting all successes and rapidly challenging enemy propaganda before opportunities are lost and the lies and deceits of the enemy gain credibility. This necessitates a rapid approvals process.

We do not yet have anywhere near all of the capabilities, skills and resources needed to execute such a campaign. We do not have sufficient political and public approval to do so. And we still do not have the full support of all senior officials and commanders. While we struggle to overcome these critical challenges our enemies continue to win the hearts and minds of countless vulnerable populations in Iraq and globally. The information war in Iraq may already be lost. We cannot afford to replicate that mistake elsewhere. We must therefore develop a comprehensive strategic communications strategy now and acquire all of the capabilities needed to undertake effective counterpropaganda.

In conflict the enemy always gets a vote. Winning the influence war ensures that its vote does not count.

Notes

---

[1] Frank Kittson, Low Intensity Operations: Subversion, Insurgency and Peacekeeping (Stackpole, 1971), pp. 290.
[2] David Galula, Counterinsurgency Warfare: Theory and Practice (Praeger, 1964, 2006).
[3] Carlos Marighela, *Minimanual of the Urban Guerrilla* (Erban Gorila, pamphlet, 1960, 1971). In author's collection.

9

The Interagency
Active Measures Working Group:
Successful template for strategic influence

HERBERT ROMERSTEIN

The United States government did not regularly combat Soviet disinformation and active measures until 1982, after congressional committees forced the issue into the public. U.S. leaders then recognized the importance of combating Soviet propaganda directly and at a high level. The Reagan administration established an ad hoc body, the Interagency Active Measures Working Group, coordinated from the White House to implement a strategic response.

Disinformation had been a Soviet technique since shortly after the Russian Revolution. In the early days of the Cold War, the CIA tracked Soviet disinformation and forgeries and periodically attempted to expose them. During the mid-1970's the CIA, severely damaged by the Senate (Church Committee) and House (Pike Committee) Intelligence Committees, turned inward. The Agency did little to respond to anti-American disinformation.

On April 20, 1978 the CIA director, Stansfield Turner, testified before the House Intelligence Committee. He reported new regulations to prevent the CIA from using American media. Congressman John Ashbrook (R-OH) asked him "Do the Soviet bloc intelligence services use newsmen from non-Communist countries as sources, witting or unwitting, agents of information, disinformation, or agents of influence?" Turner answered: "We certainly suspect that highly. I am not sure that I have concrete evidence." Congressman Ashbrook asked that CIA prepare an unclassified report on this subject.

The report was prepared by CIA and published as an appendix to the hearing on *The CIA and The Media*.[1] Congressman Ashbrook kept pressing the CIA to take a more pro-active role in exposing KGB anti-American disinformation. In October 1979 the CIA had a stroke of luck. Stanislav Levchenko made contact with American officials and asked for political asylum in the United States. Major Levchenko was the head of the Active Measures Line of the KGB Rezidentura in Tokyo. Each KGB station (*rezidentura*) was divided into units called Lines. Active Measures was a Soviet term for influence operations that included disinformation, forgeries and agents of influence.

Levchenko explained to the CIA the workings of the Soviet apparatus and how it was carried out, under his direction, in Japan. Based on his information, and that of Ladislav Bittman who had been the deputy head of the Czechoslovakian Intelligence Service's Disinformation Department, the CIA understood many of the operations that were being carried out against the United States and reported to policy makers and Congress on these activities.

In February 1980 the House Intelligence Committee published a hearing on Soviet *Covert Action (The Forgery Offensive)*. It contained a lengthy CIA report and the testimony of John McMahon, the CIA's Deputy Director, accompanied by four undercover CIA officers. The CIA cleared the testimony for public release. Two weeks later the Committee heard the testimony of Ladislav Bittman. The published hearing record provided a lengthy unclassified insight into the KGB activities in this area.[2]

On September 17, 1980 the press spokesman for the Carter White House, Jody Powell, called a press conference to denounce a forged Presidential Review Memorandum on Africa that suggested a racist policy on the part of the United States.[3] Congressman Ashbrook instructed me to investigate the forgery. It first appeared in an African-American newspaper in San Francisco called the *Sun Reporter* in its edition dated September 18, 1980, but distributed a few days earlier. The *Sun Reporter*'s political editor, Edith Austin, claimed in that issue of the paper to have received the document from the "African official on her recent visit on the continent." Edith Austin had been affiliated with the *Sun Reporter* for many years, and has a long record of radical activities in the San Francisco area. The publisher of the *Sun Reporter* was Dr. Carlton Goodlett. Dr. Goodlett was a long-time supporter of communist causes. At that time, Goodlett served as a member of the Presidential Committee of the World Peace Council, which had been exposed in the 1978 report as the major international Soviet front organization. As we studied Soviet forgeries, we found that a number of them were surfaced through the international Soviet fronts particularly the World Peace Council.

During the 1980 hearing, Congressman Ashbrook responded to the CIA testimony that the Soviet Union was subsidizing the foreign Communist Parties. He asked, "How much of that do you trace back to the United States?" Deputy CIA Director McMahon responded that there was no CIA interest in the Communist Party of the United States "since the Communist Party functions openly in the United States...I am sure it can receive funds from anybody as long as they duly report it, by law." Ashbrook answered, "I hope that you do not accept the idea that the Communist Party is a legitimate party." McMahon responded that, "talking to the Bureau [FBI] on this point is the proper place to direct that question. We just cannot respond to it."[4]

The House Intelligence Committee at the request of Congressman Ashbrook asked for a FBI briefing on Soviet active measures. The FBI agreed but insisted that only limited staff could attend the briefing and that no transcript be taken. Some Senate staffers asked to attend but the FBI refused their request. The briefing was an eye opening account of Soviet operations in the United States, but not until almost two years later would the FBI make this information available to the American people.

When the Reagan Administration came into office, the atmosphere changed. Now, the United States would directly challenge Soviet disinformation and active measures. In 1981 an Interagency Active Measures Working Group was established at the State Department. Deputy Assistant Secretary of State Dennis Kux, a career Foreign Service Officer, was the chairman. Representatives of the CIA, the FBI, Department of Defense, and the United States Information Agency were among the government agencies that served in the group. Kux was not only the chairman but developed some of the ways to raise the cost to the Soviets for their anti-American disinformation activities. CIA and FBI provided information on a regular basis.

In 1981, while a Professional Staff member of the House Intelligence Committee, I was brought in to brief the Working Group on the subject. In 1983, I left the House Intelligence Committee and went to the United States Information Agency where I was head of the new Office to Counter Soviet Disinformation. In that capacity I became a member of the Interagency Working Group. I was soon joined by USIA staffer Pete Copp, an experienced journalist. After Copp's retirement, Todd Leventhal, who had come to USIA from Voice of America, joined me at the Working Group.

Under Dennis Kux' leadership the Working Group organized briefing trips to various countries. We briefed not only the governments but the press and academics. It was Kux' idea to collect Soviet disinformation that had been used in Third World countries and provided to audiences in Western Europe. Our theme was "These Soviet stories are obviously lies – so how can you believe what the Soviets tell you." This created problems for the Soviet propagandists in Europe who were sometimes careful to use "gentle" themes in trying to appeal to the public.

My previous experience as a Professional Staff member for the House Intelligence Committee came in handy when we would get questions such as "Doesn't everybody do this?" or "Doesn't the CIA do disinformation?" My answer was "No." I pointed out that during the six years doing oversight on CIA covert actions, there was not a single time that they used political propaganda forgeries. I would say "I have seen forgeries signed President Reagan, President Carter and other U.S. government officials. I have never seen a forgery signed Brezhnev, Andropov, Gorbachev, or any other Soviet official."

In July 1982 both the CIA and FBI agreed to participate in a hearing on "Soviet Active Measures" before the House Intelligence Committee. This was the first time that the FBI agreed to allow public use of its information on this subject. The CIA's Deputy Director, John McMahon was again a witness. Edward J. O'Malley, Assistant Director for Intelligence of the Federal Bureau of Investigation testified on the following day.

The Committee also heard the testimony of Stanislav Levchenko. The release by the Committee of the testimony was the first public appearance of the former KGB major. On the instructions of the Committee I then organized two press conferences for Levchenko, one with the American press and one with the foreign press. I also organized a meeting for Levchenko with a delegation of members of the Japanese Diet. This meeting, hosted by Congressmen C. W. "Bill" Young (R-FL), was in response to a request of the Japanese lawmkers to hear from Levchenko a detailed account of his operations in Japan as head of the KGB Active Measures Line.

After I became a member of the Interagency Working Group, I frequently had the opportunity to consult with Levchenko. He explained Soviet operations and on a few occasions briefed journalists and academics with me. On October 20, 1986, the USIA held a press conference at its Foreign Press Center. The occasion was the surfacing of a KGB forgery signed with my name. We immediately exposed the forgery and an article appeared in the *Washington Post* describing Soviet forgeries rather than one attacking the United States as the KGB intended.

The Interagency Working Group was able to combine the information from USIA posts around the world, CIA reporting, and FBI investigations. USIA was an important part of the information gathering process. With USIA posts, called USIS abroad, reporting to headquarters on disinformation and forgeries, they were a front line unit for American defense. As with all government agencies, the USIA's Public Affairs Officers (PAO) were a mixed bag. There were many that were hardworking valuable government officials. This was particularly true in India and in some African countries, where the PAOs used local employees to carefully read the press, watching for anti-American disinformation and forgeries. A few PAOs were of little use to us, interested only in distributing press releases and the daily "Wireless File" which reprinted articles from the American press.

The hardworking PAOs were inspired by the leadership of USIA Director, Charles Z. Wick, who periodically sent them "Z-grams" urging them to pay attention to Soviet anti-American disinformation. It was clear from our experience with the Active Measures Working Group that bureaucrats needed high level encouragement to carry out the sometimes-difficult assignments. Not all of them appreciated the guidance. The Working Group itself was encouraged by the interest of William Casey, Director of the CIA, high level State Department support, and the input of John Lenczowski who represented the National Security Council and actually attended some of the meetings. High-level State Department support was shown, for example, when Lawrence S. Eagleburger, Under Secretary of State for Political Affairs, wrote an article for "NATO review" in April 1983, titled "Unacceptable Intervention, Soviet Active Measures." The article showed a picture of Levchenko briefing on Soviet disinformation.

The Working Group issued a series of State Department Foreign Affairs Notes that USIA distributed to journalists, academics, and other interested persons abroad by the United States Information Agency. One of the publications distributed by the Working Group was the House Intelligence Committee hearing on Soviet Active Measures. It was important to show foreign audiences that there was congressional support for exposing Soviet disinformation.

In June 1985 the State Department and CIA cosponsored a conference on Contemporary Soviet Propaganda and Disinformation. The members of the Active Measurers Working Group, including CIA, State Department and USIA officers took part in the conference. Among the active participants were Stan Levchenko, Ladislav Bittman, Peter Deriabin and Ilya Dzhirkvelov, two former KGB officers. Michael Voslensky, a distinguished scholar who had left the Soviet Union also participated, as did John Lenczowski, representing the

National Security Council.[5] The proceedings were published by the Government Printing Office and distributed abroad by USIA.

In 1985 the Congress passed a law requiring that the Interagency Working Group publish a series of reports on Soviet active measures. In response to this, the State Department published three reports in 1986, 1987 and 1989. Significantly, the FBI provided reports printed in these publications on Soviet active measures in the United States. This was particularly useful when we briefed foreign governments to encourage them to share with us examples of Soviet operations in their countries.[6]

In 1987 the House Appropriations Committee instructed USIA to prepare reports on Soviet active measures in the era of glasnost. In March 1988, Charles Wick presented the first of such reports to the Congress. He said, "In 1987, the House Appropriations Committee requested that the USIA prepare a report on Soviet active measures in the era of glasnost. Soviet active measures, which include forgeries and disinformation, have been a significant problem in U.S.-Soviet relations. I presented the report to the House committee on March 8, 1988. It was prepared by USIA's Office to Counter Soviet Active Measures, which is headed by Herbert Romerstein. Todd Leventhal, the Policy Officer on Soviet Disinformation and Active Measures, works in that office and had the major responsibility of compiling the report." In 1992 Leventhal wrote the last of the reports required by the House Committee on Appropriations.[7] The USIA distributed these reports through its posts around the world.

The 1989 State Department report explained what the U.S. government was doing to counter Soviet disinformation particularly the Soviet lie that AIDS was deliberately created in U.S. government laboratories. According to the State Department, "U.S. policy has been to respond vigorously to Soviet disinformation, on both diplomatic and public levels. The State Department's Bureau of European and Canadian Affairs and Bureau of Public Affairs, the USIA, American Embassies and U.S. Information Service centers abroad, and the VOA have been actively engaged in unmasking and combating the Moscow product at home and around the world. Via the VOA in particular, millions of Soviet listeners during the past year learned that their government was still vigorously practicing information deception abroad – a policy that could hardly bode well for hopes of real *glasnost* at home.

"Along with these coordinated information efforts, the United States made clear at several government-to-government levels that there could be no cooperation with the Soviet Union on the cure and treatment of AIDS while the Soviets continued to disseminate the lie that U.S.

scientists had deliberately created and spread the disease. At an April 1987 session of the U.S.-U.S.S.R. Joint Health Committee, Health and Human Services (HHS) Assistant Secretary Robert Windom and Surgeon General C. Everett Koop directly expressed to Soviet opposite numbers their 'strong displeasure' at Moscow's attempts to 'use a grave international public health problem for base propaganda purposes.'"[8]

The Soviets stopped using the AIDS disinformation story. It became clear, as Dennis Kux had predicted, that they would back off when the cost of their lies became too much for them.

During a Reagan-Gorbachev summit meeting, USIA Director Charles Wick confronted Gorbachev personally about Soviet disinformation. Gorbachev responded, "no more lies, no more disinformation." This became grist for our mill. As new disinformation stories appeared, we pressured the Soviets on their failure to carry out Gorbachev's promise.

In 1987 and 1988, the USIA director had a series of meetings with Valentin Falin, then head of Novosti Press Agency and later the head of the International Department of the Central Committee of the Communist Party of the Soviet Union. The International Department was the coordinating body for Soviet disinformation and active measures. The black (covert) disinformation was carried out by KGB. The white (overt) disinformation was carried out by the Central Committee Propaganda Department. The International Department, not only coordinated the other two, but carried out gray (not very well concealed) disinformation and propaganda through the foreign Communist Parties and the international Soviet fronts.

When Wick met with Falin, he knew he was dealing with a major Soviet propagandist. He pressed Falin on the issue of Soviet disinformation. We later learned more about Falin's role. In September 1991, the Moscow publication *Kuranty* carried a story saying, "the head of the American information service, USIA, lodged a personal protest to then APN (Novosti) Chairman V. Falin. The addressee was selected extremely well. Shortly before the sensational 'discovery,' a special group of staff and not only staff, 'undercover' APN employees was created by Falin's personal order under the direction of Colonel M., newly invited to join the agency. It is said that Falin had met the disinformation professional while serving as an ambassador to [then] West Germany." According to the article, the Colonel's unit was disbanded due to "forceful pressure" from the U.S.

In September 1988, the USIA sent a delegation to the Soviet Union to meet with Falin and his associates. Wick again pressed the issue of disinformation. Early in the discussion, Wick emphasized that Soviet disinformation continued to be a major problem impeding better relations between the United States and the Soviet Union. I then raised the question about the AIDS disinformation story and pointed out that Novosti had distributed it around the world. One aspect of the story was a false quotation from the late Congressman Ted Weiss (D-NY) who was supposed to have said that AIDS was created in U.S. government laboratories. I said that the quotation came not from the U.S. "mass media" which Falin had claimed but from a monthly homosexual newspaper with a circulation so small that USIA had difficulty even locating a copy. What we did however was have a letter addressed to me by Congressman Weiss denying that he had made such a statement. I presented the letter to Falin.

Falin suggested that it would be useful to have regular meetings between Americans and Soviets on the issue of disinformation. I responded that this would be good to do on a working level. Falin agreed and he and I met separately to organize the meetings. As a result, Todd Leventhal and I met regularly with officials of the Soviet embassy where we had the opportunity to answer the disinformation stories. We reported on these meetings to the Interagency Active Measures Working Group. The inability of our Soviet counterparts to authenticate the disinformation stories was valuable to the Working Group as we worked out ways of pressuring them.

Notes

[1] *The CIA and The Media*, Hearings Before the Subcommittee on Oversight of the Permanent Select Committee on Intelligence, House of Representatives, US Government Printing Office, Washington, DC, 1978, pp. 304 and 531ff. A reprint of the appendix, titled *The KGB and the Media*, was published by Crossbow Press in 2006.
[2] *Soviet Covert Action (The Forgery Offensive)*, Hearings Before the Subcommittee on Oversight of the Permanent Select Committee on Intelligence, House of Representatives; U.S. Government Printing Office; Washington, DC, 1980.
[3] *New York Times*, September 18, 1980.
[4] Soviet Covert Action, p. 27.
[5] *Contemporary Soviet Propaganda and Disinformation, A Conference Report, Airlie, Virginia*, June 25-27, 1985, Sponsored by The United States Department of State and The Central Intelligence Agency; Department of State Publications; Washington, DC; March 1987.

[6] Active Measures: A Report on the Substance and Process of Anti-U.S. Disinformation and Propaganda Campaigns, published by U.S. Department of State; Washington, DC; August 1986; Soviet Influence Activities: A Report on Active Measures and propaganda, 1986-87, published by U.S. Department of State; Washington, DC; August 1987; and Soviet Influence Activities: A Report on Active Measures and Propaganda, 1987-1988, published by U.S. Department of State; Washington, DC, August 1989.

[7] *Soviet Active Measures in the Era of Glasnost*, published by United States Information Agency; Washington, DC; July 1988; and *Soviet Active Measures in the 'Post-Cold War' Era, 1988-1991*; published by United States Information Agency; Washington, DC, June 1992.

[8] Soviet Influence Activities, August 1989, p. 2.

10

Political Warfare:
A set of means for achieving political ends

ANGELO CODEVILLA

"Political warfare" is the art of heartening friends and disheartening enemies, of gaining help for one's cause and causing the abandonment of the enemies' through words and deeds. The concept is sometimes misunderstood as the preposterous proposition that political, meaning non-violent, means can substitute for the violent measures of war. Sometimes, the term is thought meaningless because all of warfare aims at political results.

All warfare is indeed political. But political stratagems are weapons of war among others. Just as shooting usually occurs in a political context, seldom is violence or the prospect thereof absent from political stratagems. Far from substituting for reality on the battlefield and other fields of strife, psychological operations are effective insofar as they reflect it, even as effective diplomacy is the verbal representation of coercive reality. Seldom do people strengthen, weaken, or shift allegiances on the basis of "tricks," nor are effective political allegiances merely reflections of opinion polls. People redouble their support for leaders and causes, or abandon them, on the basis of the evidence before them about what people and events mean for them – which persons or causes are to be feared or despised. Words are powerful to the extent that they refer to powerful realities. Political warfare is about reflecting or changing those realities. It is a fundamental element of any strategy worthy of the name.

Any and all means that produce such changes – coercive diplomacy, economic coercion, propaganda, agents of influence, sabotage, coups de main, and support for insurgents – are acts of war in the same sense that armies crashing across borders or airplanes dropping bombs are acts of war because their results can be as intrusive or conclusive as the results of armies and bombs. In public as well as in private affairs words have bloody consequences. Whether any act, regardless of the admixture of violence it may contain, is an act of war depends on the seriousness of the actor's commitment, and on how reasonably the action is calculated as part of a plan to produce victory – to bend the enemy's will or to remove him as an obstacle to the peace one seeks. Not used seriously, political stratagems are bloody foolishness, just as are politically unserious or incompetent feats of arms.

Political warfare

"Political warfare" is a term that covers a set of means for achieving political ends. That set is distinguished from another set of instruments for achieving those same ends, which we might call "military warfare" and from others yet on which we would pin labels such as "economic warfare" or "information warfare." Anyone who would list the tools or techniques in all of these sets would find himself placing in any one set, items that he had already placed in others. Deception, for example, is as important in military affairs as it is in political or economic stratagems.

Nevertheless the sets are somewhat distinct. In taxonomic language, "political warfare" is akin to a genus, while the set of means that we group under it, such as coercive diplomacy, public diplomacy, propaganda of various colors, bribery, subversion, deception, paramilitary pressure, etc. are akin to species. Case studies of subversion, for example, would be studied as individual exemplars of one or more of these tools or techniques.

Before delving into the genus of political warfare however we take note of the environment in which all conflict takes place – namely the underlying dispositions of the peoples involved. Only in recent years has that environment been given the name by which it is now known, "soft power." Just as sailors must take into account the strength and direction of the prevailing wind, warriors must deal with the disposition of the peoples involved in the conflict.

Political warfare and soft power

Two things must be kept in mind about soft power, just as they must be about the weather: By itself, it determines nothing. And it presents challenges and opportunities to all sides in the conflict. Visiting his native Poland in 1979, Pope John Paul II struck what turned out to be a mortal blow to its Communist regime, to the Soviet Empire, and ultimately to Communism. We do not know whether the Pope intended this political result directly, indirectly, or whether he thought of what he was doing in any political terms at all. Poland's Communist leaders however thought of it in no other terms. They used all their power to show a true fact: the Pope's Polishness did not alter their capacity to distribute the goods of society, to promote, demote, and punish. They hoped that the Pope's abiding by the rules they set would show the Polish people that they too must abide by those rules. And if the Pope dared to stir up riots here and there, they would crush them while blaming the suffering on him. They had all they needed to win the political struggle.

The Pope won that struggle by transcending politics. His was what Joseph Nye calls "soft power" – the power of attraction and repulsion. He began with an enormous advantage, and exploited it to the utmost: He headed the one institution that stood for the polar opposite of the Communist way of life that the Polish people hated. He was a Pole, but beyond the regime's reach. By identifying with him, Poles would have the chance to cleanse themselves of the compromises they had to make to live under the regime. And so they came to him by the millions. They listened. He told them to be good, not to compromise themselves, to stick by one another, to be fearless, and that God is the only source of goodness, the only standard of conduct. "Be not afraid," he said. Millions shouted in response, "We want God! We want God! We want God!" The regime cowered. Had the Pope chosen to turn his soft power into the hard variety, the regime might have been drowned in blood. Instead, the Pope simply led the Polish people to desert their rulers by affirming solidarity with one another. The Communists managed to hold on as despots a decade longer. But as political leaders, they were finished.

Note well that by 1979 the Polish regime was waging its war under certain self imposed restrictions. Stalin would not have given his enemies the chance to gather under one leader, and if millions had shouted, "We want God!" he would have expedited their departure to the Pearly Gates. Even as the Polish regime was collapsing in 1989, events in China confirmed that, at least in the short run and against a determined enemy, soft power is no match for the hard kind. People who try to stop tanks by standing in front of them with flowers can be run over at the touch of a gas pedal.

Yet even in the face of the hardest military facts, one can see the power of politics. Chinese tanks would not have rolled over the 1989 political movement in Beijing's Tiananmen square had the last unit called upon to do so refused, just as previous ones had. The 1989 movement almost succeeded politically in depriving the regime of the option to disregard soft power.

In 2004 the Ukrainian opposition succeeded where the Chinese had failed. To TV viewers around the world the sight of some half million Ukrainians blocking government buildings in their capital's central square to protest a fraudulent election backed by Russia looked like the triumph of pure soft power over hard. Yet the signs were unmistakable that the opposition's political victory involved much more than spontaneous demonstrations of adolescents in the streets. The Ukrainian Interior Ministry's troops, though ready, willing, and able to roll over the bodies in the square, did not move. Any observer could guess why: high officials of the country's intelligence service had told the crowd that they – and presumably their comrades, and hence presumably the army they well-nigh controlled – stood with the people and for legality. And in fact, the highest officials of the army and the intelligence service had been in league with the opposition for months, for a variety of reasons.

The Interior Ministry's troops would have had a fight on their hands, at the very least. Moreover, the people's invasion of the central square had been organized long in advance – with some help from pro-democracy activists indirectly financed in part by the U.S. government through the National Endowment for Democracy. In short, Ukraine's turn westward rather than eastward in 2004 resulted from a variety of hard political maneuvers that empowered the Ukrainian people's soft preferences.

Another, often overlooked essential aspect of soft power, is that different parts of populations are attracted or repelled by different things, ideas, images, or prospects. Moreover, the power to affect events is spread very unevenly among and within nations. Hence to note that one sector of a population, though it be the majority, entertains a certain set of sympathies and antipathies, that its "hearts and minds" are disposed thus and so, says little about how any given political struggle will turn out.

How important the dispositions of any set of persons may be depends on what role those persons turn out to play in the conflict. The disposition of one set of "hearts and minds" matters little if the persons in whom they reside are irrelevant to the conflict.

There is no better example than the Vietnam War. Today as during that war American elites insisted that it was a struggle for the hearts and minds of the people of South Viet Nam. Nonsense. If ever that had been the case, the people of South Viet Nam rendered their judgment unambiguously and invariably by fleeing from Communist controlled areas – never toward them – and by taking to the seas in all manner of craft to escape the Communist victory. Their hearts and minds did not matter. The hearts and minds whose changing dispositions determined the course of the war resided in Washington, D.C., New York, Los Angeles, and faculty lounges in countless American universities. The decisive battles of the Vietnam War were political, and were fought in carpeted rooms, not jungles. The winners were the Communist powers, who were astute enough to realize that the winds of elite opinion in America were blowing their way. And their political – military maneuvers made use of those winds. While American elites were sacrificing their underlings in a largely irrelevant, superfluous effort to win hearts and minds in Southeast Asia, their own hearts and minds were tacking into a kind of cultural – political war against the majority of their countrymen.

Still, even if we consider the "soft power" of public sentiment to be a kind of wind, and the craft of political warriors akin to that of skillful sailors, we must recognize that regimes well supplied with the hard power of well controlled armies and police forces are like walls and rocks against which wind-driven ships smash. Thus for nearly a half-century Cuba's Fidel Castro has stood against his people's unremitting preference for nearby America, thwarted foreign political maneuvers, and preempted any and all from within the regime who might have wanted to take advantage of the people's preferences. His tools have been from the ancient kit bag of tyrants: nip opposition in the bud, rotate subordinates, break the ones which become popular, and load on them the responsibility for harm that the regime inflicts on the people.

No lines demarcate the practice of political warfare from that of vigorous politics on one side, and from subversion, counter-subversion, and war on the other. Such names describe concepts by which we distinguish phenomena that, in reality, exist intermingled with one another.

The elements of political warfare

Each individual is beset by private urges, hopes, and fears. He wants to know what is right, as well as what will affect him and those dear to him, with whom he will have to deal tomorrow. When deciding towards which side in a conflict he should lean, he wants to know which way the wind is blowing. Each side's prospects in the struggle do more to attract or repel, encourage or dis-spirit, than do love or hate.

Contempt for the enemy is more encouraging than hate for the enemy. But contempt for the enemy must be based on faith in the success of one's own cause, and that must be based on the people who embody that cause. Causes live in persons just as much as in words. Hence, each combatant side must convince all that the causes and people against which it is fighting have no future – and that anyone who stands with them will suffer. Each side must show that it is capable of winning, committed to winning, that it has a plan for winning, and that it is in fact winning.

The audience must know that it is facing people who will not waver, who, like Hernan Cortes upon landing in Mexico, burned his ships behind him or who, like the signers of the American Declaration of Independence, had committed not just their fortunes and honor to the cause, but their very lives as well. In 2004 Ukrainians trusted Viktor Yushchenko in part because his body bore the obvious scars of the government's attempt to assassinate him. Such people will not betray you because they will not betray themselves. Seriousness is politically potent.

No mere commitment of resources conveys politically potent commitment. Much less do declarations of policy. Between 1991 and 2003 U.S. leaders of both parties vied with one another in using "strong language" to denounce Iraq's Saddam Hussein. The U.S. Congress voted resolutions that he be overthrown, and (oxymoronically) publicly approved money for covert actions to do it. President Clinton and his successor George W. Bush ordered air strikes against Iraqi air defenses. Clinton even ordered cruise missiles to destroy the headquarters of Iraq's intelligence service – at night, killing only cleaning ladies. No surprise then that these dozen years' ill conceived "political war" proved counter-productive, bolstering Saddam's claim to be the Arab, and even the Muslim, world's leader against an impotent America.

The acme of this principle was President Jimmy Carter's dispatch of a squadron of F-15 fighters to Saudi Arabia in 1979, to reassure the Saudis against Iran. But Carter did not want to appear threatening to anyone. So he announced that the F-15s would be unarmed. But airplanes deliberately stripped of their armaments conjured up the exact opposite of the image of a powerful ally ready, willing, and able to come to the rescue.

Even the commitment of resources to actual operations is politically ineffective unless these are part of a success-oriented plan. From 1981 to 1988 President Ronald Reagan spoke eloquently about the evils of Nicaragua's Sandinista regime and of the dangers it posed to the United States. He also asked for money to support the armed resistance to that regime. But since Reagan also claimed that the United States planned to get along with the Sandinistas in the long run, they concluded, logically, that they needed fear no more than some harassment. And in fact though the Sandinistas suffered a setback as the Soviet empire fell, they never had to fear for their lives and, two decades later, retained more power, wealth, and privilege in Nicaragua than any other group.

The bottom line in war, and hence in political warfare, is whose enemies die or fear for their lives, and who gets to live confidently. This was illustrated as well as it ever has been by the assassination of Egyptian President Anwar Sadat in 1981. Sadat had inherited a country deeply en-meshed politically and financially with the Soviet Union and taken up by war with Israel. He expelled the Soviets from Egypt, ceased paying for Soviet arms, and became the annual recipient of some $2 billion of American aid. This made him public enemy number one of the Soviet Union and of its sympathizers. In 1979, after the Shah of Iran, a longtime ally of the United States, had been overthrown by Islamists allied with the Palestine Liberation Organization, one of the Soviet Union's allies in the region, "progressive" propaganda blared that Sadat's end was near and began referring to him as "Shah-dat." No sooner did Sadat die in a hail of bullets in October 1981, than anyone who turned the dial of a shortwave radio could hear in a variety of languages from the four corners of the world that the same would happen to anyone else who dared to stand with the Americans in the great worldwide struggle. Who's next?

The tools of political warfare

Most political warfare works by sowing dissention in the enemy camp. However, two of Thucydides' better known accounts illustrate how diplomacy can turn neutrals into allies even without pitting foe against foe. The Spartan General Brasidas moved his army deep into Athenian territory by convincing neutral cities to open their gates to him by professing friendship for them, and eagerness to treat them as allies, while surrounding them and making it clear that he had the power to destroy them. But he requested little of them as proof of friendship – just that they facilitate his passage. That was all he needed from them. The cities, impressed by the small price they had to pay for safety from so grave a threat, gave in. In short, Brasidas offered the whole city a deal it could not refuse.

A similar deal emerged from the confrontation between Athenian and Syracusan diplomats in the Sicilian city of Camarina. The Athenians promised the Camarineans that, if they would help Athens defeat Syracuse, they would be out from under any imperial power. Athens, they said, was too far away to play the oppressive role that Syracuse was then playing in Sicily. The Syracusans drew attention to the fact that they would continue to live close by no matter what, and added that they would never forgive the Camarineans were they to side with Athens. The Camarineans found Athens' offer attractive. They hated Syracuse. But they were most impressed by Syracuse's ability to do them harm in the long run. Again, the point is that coercive reality is a potent political tool, and that mere diplomacy can be enough to wield it.

The standard approach is simply to state that if the people would just upset the existing balance of power amongst themselves, there would be no need to fight foreigners. The point is to divide the target country's population, or at least to split the population from its government. The statement can be made diplomatically, or by various kinds of propaganda. But it is usually driven home by policies consistent with the statement, as well as by a variety of political tools that we ordinarily think of as subversive. Overt policy forcefully backed by reality is the most powerful tool of political warfare. This is not to deny the occasional usefulness of minor currents of policy that run secretly against the mainstream. These can target different audiences simultaneously with messages tailored for them. But any undercurrent always carries the danger of self-contradiction.

The most politically damning self-contradictions however stem from actions. The Anglo-American bombing of German cities discredited Allied propaganda's insistence that the Allies were only fighting Nazis and meant no harm to the German people. This and insistence on unconditional surrender confirmed Goebbels' propaganda and weakened the cause of the anti-Hitler opposition in Germany.

The U.S. government's conduct of its Iraqi wars in 1991 and 2003 was another polar opposite of political warfare. In 1991 the U.S. aimed its guns and its words at the invasion of Kuwait, for which effectively it held all of Iraq responsible. This gave neither Saddam Hussein nor the Ba'athist regime any reason to fear, nor the Iraqi people any cause for hope. In 2003 the U.S. made the opposite mistake by aiming its guns and words at Saddam and his closest collaborators alone. So, unwittingly, instead of warning Iraq's Sunni minority to distance itself from the Ba'ath or die with it, the U.S. did its best to reassure the Sunnis. This convinced the bulk of the Ba'ath that it could shield itself within the Sunni community as it fought to retain its privileges. Effectively, U.S. policy pushed together the Ba'athist regime and its natural Sunni constituency. Bad politics.

Even more self-contradictory were the U.S. government's policies toward the Soviet Union in the 1980's. On the one hand President Reagan rhetorically practiced classic political warfare, telling the world that the Soviet regime was illegitimate, doomed, and that the U.S. considered those who lived under it to be captives. On the other hand, the U.S. government was extending concessionary, untied loans to the regime, practicing what it called "exemplary compliance" with treaties that it was accusing the Soviets of violating, and treating its members most ceremoniously. Days before Ukraine, the Kremlin's major captive, seceded from the Soviet empire and killed it, President George Bush told Ukrainians not to do it. Political warfare requires, as all warfare does, serious coordination between ends and means.

Domestic support and gray propaganda abroad

Domestic support strengthens a government's hand in political warfare. A government's policies appear more politically potent to the extent that they are supported by a variety of unofficial as well as official sources at home. When a government calls forth such sources it is said to be practicing gray propaganda (in contrast to white propaganda of an overt nature, and black propaganda, whose source is completely camouflaged). In the late 1940's Europeans who were wondering how deep was America's official commitment to fighting communism saw that commitment confirmed through U.S. newspapers, labor unions, chambers of commerce, and letter writing campaigns by private citizens. These sources had been partly inspired and sometimes paid for by the U.S. government.

Gray propaganda can also allow a government to disclaim responsibility for the events and pressures it is fostering. Thus in our time acceptance of the fiction that the television station al Jazeera is independent - though it is owned jointly by Qatar's ruling family and by the government the family runs - has allowed the Qatari regime to be perhaps the Middle East's major purveyor of anti-Americanism while retaining good relations with this country. Information (true or false) that appears to come from a source other than the one from which it actually originated, known as black propaganda, enjoys the further appeal of appearing to come from a disinterested source when in fact it does not.

But, speaking while avoiding responsibility for what they say tempts governments to say things that they do not really mean, or have not really thought through. For example, in the 1950's the U.S. semiofficial Radio Free Europe and Radio Liberty gave East Europeans the impression that were they to revolt against Soviet rule the United States would come to their aid. But U.S. policy makers had spoken, thoughtlessly perhaps, though unofficially. So, when Soviet tanks crushed the East German and Hungarian rebellions of 1953 and 1956 with impunity, it turned out that the U.S. government had really subverted itself and the political forces in the Soviet empire which it favored. Thereafter, embarrassed U.S. policymakers pointed out that the radios were not the voice of official U.S. policy. But they had never claimed to be. Nor had they specifically promised that U.S. troops would come to the aid of Eastern Europe, any more than had U.S. officials. But both sets of people had used euphemisms that a reasonable audience would interpret as in fact they were interpreted. The transcripts of the broadcasts and the official statements of U.S. policy makers differed in vehemence – not substance. This was no mistake. The euphemisms' ambiguities reflected unresolved differences within the U.S. government. Some officials at the State Department and CIA fully expected to support the uprising actively. Countless heartbreaking requests for action flowed up these bureaucracies' chain of command. In the case of the East German revolt, the decision not to act was taken by John Bross, who was substituting for his vacationing boss who would have decided otherwise. Three years later, when the Hungarians revolted, the U.S. decision not to help so surprised CIA's Frank Wisner that it broke his spirit and his health. The point here is that words, especially unofficial ones, are so cheap as to be tempting.

Agents of influence and spies

Subversion through various kinds of agents is a potent tool of political warfare. Agents of influence are people whom the enemy mistakenly believes are on his side. Good ones cannot be bought. Their work can be far more valuable, subtle, and dangerous than that of a mere spy. Thus in the final stages of World War II Alger Hiss, a major Soviet agent who was also a minor spy, helped shape U.S. foreign policy toward the Soviet Union. When he was exposed, he enjoyed the support of most of the Democratic Party's elites. He went to jail only because he had lied under oath about illegally passing documents to Soviet intelligence. By contrast Harry Hopkins, President Franklin Roosevelt's alter ego, fully identified his agenda with Stalin's but never went to jail. He exercised more power over U.S. foreign policy than anyone other than President Franklin Roosevelt. But he never did anything illegal, and his pro-Soviet attitude was widely shared within the Democratic Party, as Vice President Henry Wallace (1941-45) showed.

The point here is that these agents were effective because they were part of a friendly faction within the enemy camp. The most valuable agents are potent in their own right. They are not puppets, but allies with their own agendas. In most cases it is futile to try steering them against those agendas. Josef Stalin became the incomparable master of agent management by extending to his foreign networks the deadly rigid discipline he instilled in the Soviet communist party. But not even Stalin's carnage combined with faith in Communism kept the network intact as the twists of his foreign policy forced agents into conflicts with their own personal commitments. Some prominent Soviet agents simply turned into anti-Stalinists, and then anti-communists. The very great successes of Soviet subversion – which continued until the very end of the Soviet state – came from the work not of "controlled agents" but of persons the Soviets called "fellow travelers" – whose agendas paralleled the Soviets' and who needed little if any coordination. Agents are allies. Allies are problematic. But when governments try to control their agents tightly, to get them to do things that they really do not want to do, the result is often that they lose potent agents and retain only impotent ones.

'Useful idiots'

Much has been written about the art of marshaling support in the enemy camp through what Comintern founder Willi Münzenberg called "innocents' clubs" or "useful idiots," and are best described by the Stalinist title "popular fronts." The term applies both to individuals and to governments. The craft consists of a few outright witting agents of a foreign power gathering many unwitting persons around an ostensible common cause, say the promotion of peace or the uplift of the poor, and then making sure that the group's activities actually support the foreign power's policies – or simply sow dissension. The essence of the craft however, is to tap into sectors of the target country's population whose enmity for their own country is great enough to dim their understanding of what in fact they are doing.

Dangers of agents

Governments less expert than Stalin's have scarcely a prayer of making worthy agents follow instructions that run against their agendas. Hence, for example, though the intelligence services of all Arab countries infiltrate the terrorist groups in their own and in other countries with people they consider their own, and through them entice and prod these groups to support their agendas, they seldom can manage more than simply to direct them towards the targets they prefer. When these countries want to pull off a specific assassination at a particular time and place, they rely on their own "intelligence" services.

Even when individuals or groups used as tools of political warfare hit their designated targets, their inherent independence makes them dangerous to their masters. Thus during World War I, German political-warfare strategists transported V. I. Lenin back from Switzerland to St. Petersburg in a sealed train to aggravate an already grave revolutionary crisis and get Russia out of the war in 1917. The Bolsheviks seized power, sued for peace and granted Germany a peace at Brest-Litovsk that was fabulously advantageous. But Lenin's Communist comrades, heartened by the Bolshevik revolution, helped to bring the fall of Imperial Germany, and came close to seizing power in Central Europe. Worse, Lenin's Soviet Union became so powerful that it ended up occupying Germany's Eastern third, including its capital, for half a century.

Recruitment

No agents worth having join losing causes or merely enlist as paid pawns. Recruiting allies requires at least pretending to be committed to victory. True, foreign factions are often used as pawns, and using them as such requires much deception. But doing this leads to the discrediting, isolation, and defeat of whoever does it. For example, in 1975 and again in 1991 the U.S. encouraged Iraq's Kurds and Shi'ites to fight Saddam Hussein, only to abandon them to his tender mercies. Hence in 2003 as U.S. armed forces invaded Iraq there was no reason for Americans to wonder why Kurds and Shi'ites did not respond to America's invitation to rise. They waited to see what America's intervention would mean for them.

Subversion

Subversion is the proximate end of most political warfare, whether it is affected by agents, propaganda, or policy. Deception is so essential to subversion that the two words describe almost the same phenomenon. The paramount fact essential to understanding deception is that it requires cooperation between the deceiver and the deceived. Just as no one has ever been seduced or subverted against his will, seldom is anyone convinced that something is true that he does not wish were true. Hence the craft of deception and subversion lies mostly in discovering what the target wants to hear and to do. The essence of execution lies in providing just enough excuse for the target to deceive and subvert itself.

Tactical deception

Tactical deception, such as the Western Allies' effort to convince Hitler that their 1944 invasion of Europe would take place at Calais instead of Normandy, functions by the same mechanism – accentuating self deception – as does strategic, political deception. But the latter is actually much easier, since it aims at and uses judgments with which enemy politicians have identified themselves more fully than they ever could with tactical judgments. The best illustration may well be the Soviet Union's generation-long deception of U.S. officials that arms control – especially the banishment of anti-missile defense – was an enterprise for mutual benefit. Not once since 1961, when the Soviet Union broke a mutual moratorium on nuclear testing did U.S. officials see any evidence that the Soviets were restraining their strategic weapons programs in any way.

Until 1968 Soviet leaders and diplomats actually told their U.S. counterparts that it was immoral for any nation to eschew missile defense. But so much did U.S. officials want to believe that the Soviets thought of arms control just as they did, that no facts or arguments could prevent them from deceiving themselves. Many Americans made faith in arms control a test of social acceptability for other Americans. The Soviet Union's political war against U.S. strategic forces hardly needed the agents and propaganda that Soviet leaders put into it. Americans were subverting themselves quite well.

Now consider the Spanish Civil War of 1936 – 39. Like most civil wars, it invited the intervention of foreign powers that used the war to fight each other politically. To do that, Germany and Italy on one side and the Soviet Union on the other had to bend the Spanish sides who sided with them to their own purposes. The story of the Spanish Civil War, in a nutshell, is the story of how the Soviet Union seduced, subverted, used, and abandoned the people and the cause of Republican Spain, while at the same time Spain's nationalists used the massive help they received from Italy and Germany while avoiding subversion. The nationalists were not subverted because they, and especially their chief, Francisco Franco, focused tightly on their objectives for Spain. Unlike the Republicans, the Nationalists were hardly tempted to become part of whatever larger enterprises their foreign allies represented. In short, the Republicans subverted themselves by erasing distinctions between themselves and communists, who lived not for Spain but for Stalin. The Republicans' bitterest enemies, from day to day, would be the Trotskyites and whoever else were Stalin's enemies du jour. Stalin's political warfare in Spain was easy and fruitful, while Hitler's was hard and gained him nothing.

Special operations

Special operations are often misunderstood as consisting of physically demanding acts. In fact, their special quality comes much less from the character of the troops than because they are specially crafted to have a bearing on war's political issue out of proportion to the small forces they employ. Such operations can hold or gain allies, influence neutrals to stay neutral or stray from neutrality, help resistance movements in enemy-occupied territory, and introduce sabotage and dissension into the enemy country.

In September 1943 King Vittorio Emmanuele III of Italy constitutionally cashiered his prime minister, Benito Mussolini, and appointed a new one who promptly imprisoned his predecessor in a mountain fortress. Overnight, Germany faced the prospect of enemies on its undefended southern borders. But Major Otto Skorzeny's commandos landed under Mussolini's prison by glider. Within hours, Il Duce was organizing an Italian collaborationist counter-government that made it possible for Germany's General Kesselring to conduct a brilliant elastic defense in Italy until the end of the war.

Special operations can be used to establish relationships with foreign forces, to coordinate actions with them, and to gather information from them. Of course, during such operations troops can take and interrogate prisoners and, if they can slip in and out unnoticed, emplace and maintain networks of remote sensors. Whether they are helping resistance forces, sowing dissension among the enemy, or influencing third countries, special troops must be political leaders. They must organize people who have their own priorities and idiosyncrasies. Hence a well-stocked special operations department must have officers of widely different backgrounds and widely different personal, religious, and political preferences.

Paramilitary

Affecting the enemy's polity through paramilitary means differs from open, across-the-border warfare only in its pretense that something other than war is happening. Just as the effectiveness of deception depends more on the deceived than on the deceiver, so the effectiveness of paramilitary operations depends less on the quality of those operations than on whether the target country chooses to deal with them as if the paramilitaries themselves were the enemy, as if it did not know whence they come, or whether it chooses to make war directly on the paramilitaries' sources and causes.

Paramilitary operations are a form of indirect warfare, the essence of which is the (inherently thin) pretense that the country whose cause the paramilitaries serve is somehow not responsible for them. The reason why the pretense ever works at all is that the target county's official eyes may not see what real ones do. The body politic as a whole may lack courage, or a significant part of it may sympathize with the enemy's cause, or so dislike its fellow citizens as to inhibit the common defense.

When paramilitary operations target innocents, they are properly described as terrorism. But regardless of whom they shoot or bomb, the political purpose of paramilitary operations is to discredit the target government. A government that proves powerless to stop armed attacks on its citizens or territory is useless. If it is afraid to confront the sources of its troubles it earns contempt. Because of this, small military operations can win definitive political victories without ever scoring any militarily significant ones. All that paramilitary forces have to do is to survive. The target governments may make their devastating political points for them. The political success of paramilitary operations – often simply terrorism – comes about as, and is signified by, the target government's acceptance of claims of innocence it knows are not true. Hitler's conquests in Europe between 1933 and 1939 were political triumphs of will over victims wanting in conviction, resolve, and courage. Hitler's whiff of violence, the pro forma pretense that Nazi violence across Europe was independent of the Reich, combined with protestations of peace, broke the will of those who might have resisted him. His "table talk" records his view that political operations would break the enemy's will to resist, much as artillery prepares the way for the success of infantry. Hitler was neither the first nor the last to think this way about the political effect of physical fear and moral discredit.

In our time, the successes of Arab countries in cowing Europeans and Americans, and even Israelis, comes from the Westerners' acceptance of the proposition that the terrorists who come from Arab countries, Iran and elsewhere, and who fight for those countries' causes are somehow private individuals for whom the countries are not responsible. So eager have Western governments been to find some authorities to which they can confer benefits in exchange someone for a cessation of terrorist attacks on themselves that they imagine it possible that Arab governments, and even the largest terrorist groups, are both not responsible for terrorism and have the power to put a stop to it. They imagine it though they know perfectly well that it is not true.

Perhaps the prototypical illustration of this point came from an Associated Press report concerning the long running struggle of the British and Irish governments to end the Irish Republican Army's terrorism by making some deal with the ostensibly non-violent representative of the IRA'a political causes, Sinn Fein:

IRISH OFFICIAL SAYS SINN FEIN COMMANDS IRA.
Government weary of assertion groups are separate.

In an unprecedented confrontation the Irish government yesterday publicly identified three of Sinn Fein's top figures – including party leader Gerry Adams – as members of the Irish Republican Army's command.

The government's blunt declaration indicated it no longer would tolerate Adams' protestations that his party should not be held accountable for IRA actions... Over the past decade of Northern Ireland peacemaking, leaders of successive Irish and British governments have privately considered Adams and Martin McGuinness, Sinn Fein's deputy leader, to be members of the seven-member IRA command... To maintain good relations with Sinn Fein neither government has confronted them in public...

The Irish minister of justice condemned the Sinn Fein's leaders' "deep, deep, dishonesty." But of course he had proved his own, his government's and the British government's equally deep dishonesty by confirming that they had dealt with a negotiating partner on the basis of a claim of innocence it knew very well to be a lie. Thus do governments discredit and defeat themselves in political war.

Using the tools

In our time, the past master in the techniques of political warfare may well have been Iraq's Saddam Hussein. Between 1991 and 2003 politics was Saddam's "weapon of mass destruction." With it he reversed the results of his military defeat of 1991, became the most important personage in the region, forced support from states like Saudi Arabia that feared him, hampered the Americans' will to deal with him, destroyed what respect the Americans had earned in the Arab world in 1991, used the United Nations' economic sanctions against him to corrupt officials from Paris to New York, gather billions of dollars for his terrorist regime, turned some of America's European allies against it, put himself at the head of the cause of Islam in the world despite his bloody anti-Islamic record, and quite simply ended up driving the world's agenda. In the end however he wound up facing the gallows because his political virtuosity was not backed by military power.

Better than his American enemies, Saddam understood that since they had declared victory in the Gulf War without having overthrown him, any attempt they might now make to do it would be a self-indictment of their previous judgment. So he calibrated his challenges to a level high enough to embarrass the Americans but just below what would make it necessary for them to come get him. Twice he moved troops a few miles toward Kuwait, then as American forces were mobilized and at sea, he played yo-yo with them, pulling them back a bit and leading the world in laughter as the Americans went back to the other side of the globe. By the time the Americans got wise, they had become objects of contempt in the Arab world and Saddam a hero.

The Arab world's masses were looking for a symbol of revenge, a savior of their pride. Saddam presented himself as just that. As early as the autumn of 1991, crowds of hundreds of thousands filled the capitals of the Arab world shouting pro-Saddam slogans. Even (indeed especially) the Muslim leaders who had sent military contingents to the U.S. side in the Gulf War hurried to speak of "brother Iraq" (Morocco's King Hassan) and to look forward to working with Saddam (Egypt's President Hosni Mubarak). The Saudi royal family began treating Saddam as someone who its subjects revered more than their rulers and the Americans as more trouble than they were worth. Because of Saddam, the Arab world feared the Americans less and hated them more. By the turn of the 21st century his activities earned greater attention on Arab television than those of any other Arab leader.

Saddam saw that the U.S.-sponsored United Nations rules that empowered a host of officials to administer his sales of oil were his chance to funnel millions of dollars both to those very officials and to persons in Europe who would become his advocates and would help turn European opinion against America. He caused shortages of food and medicine among his domestic enemies, then publicized their suffering and blamed the Americans for them. Clandestinely, his intelligence service trained and sent forth anti-American terrorists. Publicly, he became a cheerleader and financier of suicide bombing against Israel. His cheerleading for anti-American violence was even louder than that for anti-Israeli violence.

Debate in America has only just begun on the role that Saddam's intelligence service played in the 1993 bombing of the World Trade Center, on the meaning of the overlap between the organizers of the 1993 attack and the 2001 attack, and on connections with al Qaeda. But there is no doubt that his intelligence services had infiltrated the region's terrorist groups at least as deeply as had the services of other Arab countries. Nor is there doubt that of the existence in Iraq of training programs for non-Iraqi terrorists. The Iraqi services stand accused credibly of having attempted the assassination of the first President Bush. There is no explanation for the fact that the commander of the 1993 attack, Ramzi Youssef, carried Kuwaiti identity papers falsified during Iraq's occupation of Kuwait other than that Iraq's services falsified them. In short, there can be little argument with the proposition that if Saddam did not sponsor any given terrorist act against America, it was not for want of trying.

Saddam understood his opponents' political vulnerabilities better than they understood his, and used all the tools of political warfare as well as they might be used. He ended up driving the world's agenda. Then his well calibrated political war was overcome by military force majeure, and he ended up facing the gallows. Even then, he turned his trial into another propaganda theater against the United States and the legitimacy of the new Iraqi government. Saddam taught an important lesson by showing both the strength and the weakness of political warfare.

11

Getting Psyched:
Putting psychology to work to shorten
conflicts and save lives

MICHAEL COHN

Introduction

This chapter will examine the use of psychology as a means of shortening conflicts, preventing conflicts, and saving lives. The United States must be able to define, decipher, and ultimately manage and dominate the psychological battlespace of any international situation, dispute or conflict. Americans do this in politics, law, business, entertainment, education and culture. They do not excel in it in the realm of diplomacy, military doctrine and national security strategy. Yet the field is not difficult to study or master; to gain the necessary grasp of sensory, cognitive and social psychology, one need go no further than basic college psychology textbooks and apply them to a strategic influence strategy.

Power can be wielded in physical *and* psychological forms. Every expression of national action or inaction, every word, tone, or connotation, every image has a psychological effect. If these effects are not anticipated and managed, not only do we forfeit a potent weapon in the national arsenal, the consequences can be devastating. This is not to suggest that statesmen become psychiatrists, but they must develop a deeper understanding of basic psychology if they are to wield it effectively in the international arena. Every facet of American statecraft should be analyzed through a psychological prism to ensure it will not have unanticipated and detrimental consequences. Any successful marketer or campaign strategist will find this to be second nature.

Most work on the use of psychology for political ends does not address the actual psychological mechanisms, but instead focuses predominantly on the intentions, techniques, or organization of influence operations. This chapter attempts to close the gap. The first step is to delineate and define the principle psychological mechanisms along with the larger process of which they are a part. We can then discuss how they operate and how they can be managed or manipulated. Throughout, we will explore the different types of psychological research that may be practical and applicable for securing the national interest.

Psychological statecraft can be strategic or tactical and have long-term or short-term goals, but it should always be coordinated with long-term national objectives. Too frequently, the United States opts to use force to secure its interests without exhausting the political and psychological arsenal. In the war of ideas, the battlespace is the mind. While physical combat tends to be localized, psychological combat spills outside the immediate battlespace spreading through print, electronic media, and social, political, and cultural networks. To both policymakers and citizens alike, the threat of manufactured information finding its way into the mainstream media at home and abroad, makes them uncomfortable. It leads to cries of propaganda and manipulation. The truth is, however, that psychological techniques are being used against the United States by its enemies on a daily basis and with great effect. As such, it is vital that American policymakers, diplomats, intelligence collectors, and others within the foreign policy establishment, begin to better understand psychology as a tool of statecraft not only to improve our own policies but to defend against the asymmetrical attacks of our enemies.

Psychological first things in the art of persuasion

Internal vs external

In a diverse world, the design and execution of psychological influence requires a sophisticated understanding of the target culture. Differences in traditions, spiritual beliefs, language, political systems, economic strength, defensive capabilities, and even the environment lead to profound differences in how an individual processes information. As such, a given operation may have very different results on individuals from different cultures. Effective psychological strategy, thus, requires effective cultural intelligence, and since vital details change from region to region and even tribe to tribe, local insight and assistance is often essential.

Influencing the mind(s) of a given audience requires the identification of their psychological touch points or vulnerabilities. To succeed, one must distinguish between the internal and external causes of psychological motivations. Internal causes include perception, cognition, attitudes, beliefs, and personality. External causes include such factors as familial structure, societal incentives and disincentives, and role requirements. At the same time, however, the line between internal and external can be vague. For example, personality, which is internal, is heavily influenced by both internal (biological) and external (societal) forces. Moreover, identity, which is at the heart of politics, is the product of personality reacting to a given cultural environment. Although deeply personal, identity is only given expression when an individual becomes part of a group. The strategic communicator must understand the nature of, and distinction between, these psychological variables. Only then can the process of influence be grasped and the art of persuasion mastered.

In sensation and perception psychology, the term 'threshold of excitation' is often used to describe the point at which an individual reacts to a particular stimulus. It is significant because it reveals the level of intensity needed for a given stimulus to trigger a desired reaction in an individual. Stimuli with an intensity below that threshold can still affect the psyche, however, and if repeated or combined with other stimuli, can still provoke the desired response. As such, the strategic communicator needs to be sensitive not to over or under-excite the target audience. A reaction can be stimulated overtly or covertly, and stimuli are not by definition negative or harmful. On the contrary, effective stimuli can often be appealing and even beneficial.

Environmental stimuli

The senses are the fastest connections to the brain. It is helpful to think of them as extensions of our nervous system in contact with the external environment. The senses are often so strong as to be able to override our ability to think critically. Known as environmental variables, temperature, humidity, precipitation, scenery, scent and noise level represent very effective stimuli when attempting to influence the perceptions and emotions of a given audience.

Color is a significant environmental variable. It can be differentiated according to shade, intensity, and hue. Darkness can induce anxiety or discomfort. Intense brightness can disorient and unsettle; Color can affect mood, which in turn can affect perception and behavior. Red, for instance, is the color that draws the most attention. It is the warmest and most energetic color in the spectrum and is associated with love, danger, desire, speed, strength, violence, anger, and emergency. Red can even evoke a fight-or-flight response or raise blood pressure. Blue is one of the most popular colors. It causes the opposite reaction as red. Peaceful and tranquil, blue causes the body to produce calming chemicals, so it is often used in bedrooms. Blue can also be cold and depressing. Whatever the hue, color is a powerful psychological agent.

Sound is another important variable. The use of sound has been part of psychological warfare for millennia. Harold Lasswell wrote that, "the idea is found in the oldest manuals of military strategy."[1] "In night fighting," Sun Tzu noted, "beacons and drums are largely used... and the enemy's... ears are confounded."[2] Bagpipes had the dual effect of being great motivators for Scottish warriors before and during battle while also intimidating the enemy. American Indian war cries made so profound an impression that the Confederate Army adapted them for use against the North in the American Civil War. Rock music was famously used during the capture of Manuel Noriega's in Panama. The discomfort and disorientation caused by continuous high decibel audio levels played a key role in Noriega's eventual surrender. More recently, similar uses of loud rock music have proved effective in Iraq and Afghanistan.

The last century has brought technological innovations that allow for the use of every imaginable sound for psychological purposes. Rock music has also been used to tighten troop morale on the one hand, and to break the will of prisoners to resist interrogation on the other. The sonic boom of a low altitude fly-over can be an intimidating psychological symbol. Weapons capable of directing hypersonic and sub-sonic sound waves can stimulate intense physical reactions including panic, nausea and extreme nervousness, and can disperse entire crowds without the use of lethal force.[3] Research in social, emotional and personality psychology shows that pre-existing moods influence judgment. As moods can be manipulated through sound, peoples' emotional and physical reactions are consequently susceptible to modification through the use of sound.[4] A common example is the use of music in filmmaking to enhance the dramatic appeal of critical moments in an unfolding plot.

One who is able to understand and predict the way in which intended audiences will react to images and sound has gained a valuable tool in the war of ideas.[5] The skillful combination of images and sound, as with other environmental stimuli, is highly effective at manipulating emotions. In the commercial realm this has led to an increasingly sophisticated set of emotional measurements and predictions.[6] Unfortunately, however, this lesson has not yet been applied to American information operations, public diplomacy, and public affairs.

Perception and cognition

From the senses we move to perception. Perception is defined as the attachment of meaning to environmental stimuli received through the five senses. Perception is limited to what the mind is capable of processing at any one time, and so the mind has evolved mechanisms for efficiently prioritizing the information to allow the individual to act quickly in a given environment. These mechanisms are instinctive and not deliberate. In fact, the cognitive process is most often reflexive or automatic in nature and absent of reason. To fully understand the importance of perception, we must learn more about this process

Psychology distinguishes between two processes of cognition – the *central route* and the *peripheral route*. It is helpful to think of them as the two avenues through which the individual is persuaded. The central route is characterized by logic. It involves conscious deliberation and rational argument. Traditional and public diplomacy in strategic communication rely on the central route to deliver messages through traditional media. By stimulating logical analysis, one increases the persuasiveness of strong messages and diminishes that of weak ones. The peripheral route, on the other hand, is stimulated by perceptual and physical triggers which precipitate automatic associations. Often the peripheral route to persuasion is appealed to in conjunction with, or in support of the central route. With peripheral cues, the arguments are generally not as persuasive as the thoughts and images they evoke in the recipient's mind. These cues can be sensual, i.e. intensity of light or sound as described before, or they can be symbolic – most often there is a combination of the two.

Understanding the distinction between the central route and the peripheral gives the strategic communicator an advantage when it comes to persuasion. Deeper thinking is generally associated with the central route. Superficial thinking is usually connected to the peripheral. In deep thinking, any changed viewpoint will be more likely to persist and be resistant to attack where as peripheral route persuasion is often more temporary. That said, a peripheral argument can be designed to bypass the central route and trigger very deep feelings or beliefs. In order to do so, one would likely need to have intimate knowledge of the psychological vulnerabilities of the target. If one was aware, for instance, of a traumatic accident that deeply affected the target, an image or sound slipped into an otherwise innocuous scenario might yield powerful results. In such situations, the peripheral route can be more efficient than the central route.[7]

Advertisers, for instance, have traditionally used visual images as peripheral cues, and the last quarter century has seen them become an increasingly important tool of the politician. At the beginning of the Democratic Party's 2007 primary season, for instance, an advertisement appeared on the internet which adapted Apple Computers' famous 1984 introduction commercial into anti-Hillary Clinton propaganda. Widely hailed as brilliant, it depicted Hillary as a Nazi-type authoritarian. Its real effectiveness, however, was much more subtle. The commercial ended with the famous multicolored apple logo adapted into the letter O for Obama. With this simple image, the creator made sure the connection with Apple was driven home for those who may not have been aware of the original commercial. The commercial demonized Clinton for alleged dictatorial tendencies, and connected Barack Obama with the culturally popular Apple computers, iPods and other devices in the minds of the viewers. The parody commercial is an excellent example of bypassing the central route using subtle manipulation of associations and meanings in order to trigger the peripheral processes.

Distraction is another effective means of using peripheral cognitive processes to persuade while hindering any resistance to a message. Distraction is especially effective when the message is simple – other background factors from the sensual to symbolic can stimulate more of the conscious and unconscious energy of the audience. Surprise attacks, unanticipated information, as well as when an idea comes from an unlikely source – are all forms of distraction and can increase the prospects for persuasion through the peripheral route.[8]

Perception results from a process of inference, and not just from direct observation. As with other forms of inference, perception is thus subject to systemic biases. As cognitive mechanisms are designed to efficiently process information, the brain will not incorporate every detail. The brain organizes information based on experience and familiarity, creating patterns to use as reference for interpreting new information. Both central and peripheral routes are rife with perceptual biases designed to streamline the interpretive process. These biases are at the root of stereotypes; they form the basis for attitudes, and are central to an individual's self image. Biases also determine how individuals develop expectations and preconceptions and organize new information.

Perceptual expectations vary according to circumstances. Both mass marketing appeals and military PSYOP exploit this fact by controlling the circumstances by which perception takes place, i.e. by controlling the presentation of stimuli.[9]   For example, television cameras indirectly influence the viewers' perceptions according to the design of the director, i.e. the camera shot manipulates perception to support the director's objectives.

Nearly every filmmaking school studies the techniques of German cinematographer Leni Riefenstahl, whose pro-Nazi film *Triumph of the Will* was central to building Hitler's cult of personality and the ideology of National Socialism. Riefenstahl's use of telephoto lenses to create a distorted perspective, moving cameras, aerial photography, and her novel approach to music and cinematography were revolutionary at the time. For instance, the technique of filming a character from ground or waist level with a telephoto lens was first used in *Triumph of the Will.* It would become the standard technique to impart power and authority. Such was her genius that the evil purpose has not kept the film from being recognized as one the greatest movies of all time, with Hollywood embracing and refining its techniques to capture viewer sentiments and emotions.

Harold Wallbot, an early twentieth century experimental psychologist, conducted an experiment in which he controlled people's perception of emotions by manipulating the setting in which a face was viewed. Filmmakers call this phenomenon the Kulechov Effect after a Russian film director who was famous for skillfully guiding viewers' inferences by manipulating their assumptions.   Lev Kulechov demonstrated the phenomenon by creating three short films that presented the face of an actor with a neutral expression after viewers had been shown an image of a dead woman, a dish of soup, or a girl playing – making the expressionless actor seem sad, thoughtful or happy. This finding is supported by the visual, and perhaps biological, phenomenon whereby individuals automatically experience the emotion of a person simply by seeing the person's facial expression.[10]

Peripheral cues can often have a dramatic reflexive affect. When shown geometric figures for less than 0.01 seconds each, people will deny having seen anything more than a flash of light. Yet they will later express a preference for the forms they saw. Likewise, flashed words can prime our response to later questions. If a word is flashed too briefly to recognize, one may then detect a flashed related word more easily than an unrelated word. Filmmakers and advertisers occasionally use this subliminal technique, though the method usually backfires once it is uncovered. In all of these situations a set of conditions controlling the presentation of stimuli is able to direct the perception of the information by the audience and therefore set them up to process information in a particular way. This process of 'setting-up' is often referred to as priming.

Priming

Priming is the introduction of stimuli which are designed to manipulate the future processing of other associated stimuli by activating particular associations in memory. Jacques Ellul referred to this process as "pre-propaganda."[11]

Sometimes the target is aware of the priming stimuli, sometimes it is unconscious. Not only does such priming allow one to "prep" the audience's disposition before one delivers a message, but it allows one to exploit another tendency called the misinformation effect. Also called the "Oliver Stone effect," it is the process by which one introduces false information into an audience's memory of an event. Experiments have repeatedly demonstrated that when participants unknowingly incorporate inaccurate information into their memories, they later interpret the falsehoods as fact.

"We hear and apprehend only what we already half know," wrote Henry David Thoreau. Priming creates prejudices and these prejudices color subsequent perceptions and interpretations. As with other psychological weapons, priming can take the form of sensual stimuli or symbols and ideas and can act as internal or external cues. Moreover, priming works in the reverse as well. As before-the-fact judgments bias our perceptions and interpretations of future events, after-the-fact prejudices can bias our memory of past events.[12] Understanding the misinformation effect is essential in the battle for hearts and minds. Without it, effective countermeasures to hostile misinformation and disinformation that do great damage to the interests of the United States and its allies will continue to elude US policymakers.

When an experiment or psychiatric therapist manipulates people's recollection about their past, a sizeable percentage of individuals will construct false memories. In its search for truth, the mind sometimes constructs a falsehood to fit its presumptions. In an experiment where participants are asked about a fictitious childhood story, one in four will recall the tale as if it were true.[13]

Furthermore, when stimuli are ambiguous, we, nevertheless, tend to formulate a specific hypothesis about what we are experiencing. The longer one is exposed to ambiguous data or images, the greater confidence one develops in the initial and perhaps erroneous impression. Repeated or sustained, ambiguous initial impressions can have great impact on the target's subsequent perceptions.[14]

Seeing lights in the sky or distant objects on the surface of water are good examples of what is meant by ambiguous stimuli. People are often quick to perceive these stimuli as evidence of UFOS or lurking sea creatures. The conclusions are often important for the individual in closing the gap in perception caused by the ambiguity of the stimuli. Furthermore, this attachment of meaning, truthful or erroneous, to stimuli in the perceptive process in order to make sense of the world is a fundamental priority for the individual.

Biases are very important for understanding how one can become convinced of the truth of a seemingly obvious falsehood. A biased view will construct biased memories, thus reinforcing the warped perception until the falsehood becomes a deep-seated "fact." This also relates to what researchers call the confirmation bias: a tendency to search for information that confirms one's perceptions, even if that information is demonstrably inaccurate or false. As such, current viewpoints tend to govern our recollections, even if one's view was quite different in the past. We revise the past to suit our present views.[15] The result can be a self-reinforced circle of falsehoods.

The more ambiguous the information, the greater the tendency to assimilate it into pre-existing viewpoints. Cognitive biases allow individuals to form perceptions of a relationship where none exists, or perception of a stronger relationship than actually exists. Abundant experiments and research findings prove that people easily misperceive random events as confirming their beliefs.[16] There is clear evidence to support the idea that cognitive mechanisms designed to process information efficiently are not entirely rational and can often lead an individual to interpret false information as true. Biases, prejudices and deeply held beliefs are of vital importance in determining how an individual mind will interpret new stimuli. It also seems evident there is a clear need of the human psyche to attach meaning to information in the interpretive process – this need can be so strong as to be the reason why an individual can convince him/herself of falsehoods.

This is very important in understanding how false beliefs about the United States spread rapidly around the world. This knowledge might also translate into an offensive weapon against America's enemies in a wartime environment – the ability to control certain aspects of the information environment and a sophisticated sense of how to exploit local prejudices and biases may prove quite effective in weakening enemy morale and cohesion as well as their ability to make effective decisions based upon sound information. As such, the ability to manipulate these pre-determinants is, therefore, an essential skill for the strategic communicator.

Beliefs, attitudes, and attitude-change

As we have seen, perceptions exert significant influence on attitudes and opinions. Thus, we often view reality through the lens of our beliefs and values. For example, once an individual perceives a country or movement as hostile, he is likely to interpret its ambiguous and even its innocuous actions as hostile. As was noted above, our preconceptions strongly influence how we interpret and remember events. Conventional wisdom is supported by experimental psychology on this point: the stronger a target's assumptions (especially if one is committed to them), the more the target will ignore or twist information inconsistent with them.[17] We see this especially evident in relations among nations that have a past marred by conflict. Often words and deeds are interpreted by the respected sides as confirming suspicions, continuously perceived as disingenuous or even down-right hostile. Especially in these cases, when the circumstances are ambiguous, where information and meaning are not clear, assumptions about the other's intent tend to guide how new information is processed.

Therefore, it is generally easier to reinforce an individual's beliefs than it is to try and change them. Attempts to isolate methods that are effective in altering strongly held beliefs have shown that the key was the amount and timing of contradictory information rather than its quality. Large quantities of information delivered in a short period of time had the greatest effect.[18] For the most part, however, historical and experimental examples that successfully played on a audiences predispositions are much more numerous than those that reversed a target's expectations.[19] A number of America's enemies exploited the September 11, 2001 attacks to spread rumors that the American Government was in some way responsible for the attacks. Capitalizing on the utter shock and surprise the attacks caused as well as the ambiguity in the initial aftermath of who was responsible, many ideological communities with political positions suspicious of the United States were quick to believe and spread such a rumor. Their susceptibility to the rumor as well as their willingness to transmit it was directly related to their pre-formed opinions and attitudes about the United States Government.

An attitude is an evaluative reaction toward something or someone, i.e. environmental stimuli, which is informed by one's beliefs, opinions, or feelings. As such, they add another variable to the cognitive process. To learn how attitudes can be altered, one must understand their affective and cognitive components.[20] Affective is a term used to describe an individual's level of attachment toward an attitude. Cognitive, as mentioned earlier, refers to reflexive and reflective processes of perception, such as automatic/unconscious mechanisms and thoughtful/logical processes, i.e. peripheral and central route processes, respectively. The important point for our purposes, is that the affective and cognitive components of an attitude are, at almost any given point in the evolution of that attitude,[21] congruent with each other. In other words, the level of attachment an individual has for an attitude will always be relative to how the individual perceives the "facts" related to that attitude. If the two are not in agreement, tension and anxiety will result and the individual will search for ways, rational or irrational, to 'fix' the inconsistency. This eventuality is referred to as dissonance and is a motivating factor in the individual's need to organize meaning and perception into an understandable whole, mentioned in the earlier sections.

When the affective and cognitive components of an attitude are in balance, the attitude is in a stable state. When they are out of balance, the attitude will change until the affective and cognitive components are back in line.[22] Unstable and inconsistent components of an attitude are either altered to achieve consistency or they are omitted from conscious awareness. Communicators can create dissonance by designing messages which target either component.

Attitude change is another area where intensity is vital. Studies show that mild attacks on attitudes can be counter-productive.[23] When committed people are attacked strongly enough to cause them to react, but not so strongly as to overwhelm them, they became more committed to their positions. Indeed, they are often driven to even more extreme behaviors in defense of their previous commitment.[24]

The above suggests an all-or-nothing approach, but successful attitude change does not necessarily require an all out attack. There are ways to prepare an audience to be more open to a message – the priming or "pre-propaganda" as Ellul described it.[25] One way is to send messages that are agreeable to the audience. Another is to offer a two-sided appeal if the audience is less uniform in their positions. Surprise attacks on attitudes can be especially effective with people who are strongly attached to their beliefs; if given several minutes forewarning, these people will prepare psychological defenses.

On the other hand, people whose attitudes do undergo change often insist, later on, that they have always felt that way.[26] The reason for this is based on the individual's primary need for psychological consistency. This need is as the basis of the formation of individual identity.

The self: Personality meets the social world

Many psychologists and sociologists refer to the concept of identity as the self. The self, or identity, is formed in the interaction between individual personality and the social world. Although identity is constructed from symbolic meaning and attachments derived from the social environment, the experience of identity is intensely personal – even at times active only at the unconscious level.

Our sense of self is probably the main factor affecting the processing of information. When information is relevant to our self-conceptions, we process it quickly and, unless it is subsequently disproven, incorporate it permanently. The more closely an attitude is related to one's self-conception, the greater will be one's resistance to changing it. In order for the American strategic communicator to achieve a desired psychological effect, they must consider the prevailing particular needs, frustrations, and anxieties of the individuals in a targeted group. The closer a psychological message comes to meeting one's predispositions or fulfilling one's needs, perceived or unconscious, the more effective the message.

As long as humans can establish survival and security for themselves, they, as individuals, are perpetually obsessed with their own individual social standing – a condition that causes them to engage in constant impression management to bolster their image in the eyes of others. Coupled to this is an individual's sense of responsibility to family and societal role requirements. This dynamic forces individuals to constantly assess their competence, verify their self-conceptions, and seek ways to enhance their self-image. We are all prone to making social comparisons, evaluating and comparing our own and others' successes and failures others. This is true regardless of whether the culture is oriented toward the individual or the collective, as identifications with groups only enhances the projective range of the self.

Human consciousness is thus overwhelmingly self-preoccupied. The more self-conscious we are, the more we believe the "illusion of transparency," in which we perceive that our inner thoughts and emotions are explicit to others around us.[27] This illusion can be targeted to induce general unease and even paranoia, panic, neurosis, and, potentially, eventual madness. Self-consciousness is thus a variable that is ripe for manipulation; it can be either increased or decreased making it respectively more or less sensitive to such things as ridicule or lionization. Individuals can also be mobilized, distracted, disoriented or made more apt to misjudgments if given an inflated sense of self-confidence. Political leaders are very often individuals with a heighten sense of self-consciousness making them vulnerable to attacks as well as appeals.

The pliability of self-consciousness is also an important point in relation to morale and the mobilization of political will. At a fundamental psychological level, the confidence of an individual or group rests on the level of control they have over particular circumstances. If we want to increase confidence in our own or allied troops then we must create conditions in which we can enhance their sense of control over their situation, even at the micro level, like increasing the choices for meals in a mess hall. If we want to demoralize enemy troops, political leaders, or populations, than we should seek to reduce their sense of control, creating a sense of hopelessness. We can do this by attacking their command and control structure, issue false documents or announcements, and/or manipulate and discredit leaders in order to confuse and disorient their followers, thereby affecting the enemy's overall ability to make effective decisions or carry them out. This decrease in effectiveness translates into a loss for the enemy's sense of locus of control – this sense of weakness can lead to despair and can be the breaking point of an enemy's will to fight.

There is a tremendous amount of literature on the self – insights about the subtle nuances of individuals perpetually constructing assumptions about themselves and constantly engaging the environment in order to confirm those assumptions can be found in psychoanalysis and other studies on personality development, psychiatry and abnormal psychology, sociology as well as in fiction, like works by Jane Austen or Lawrence Stern's *Tristram Shandy*. Impression management and the maintenance of self is a primary motivating factor in an individual's behavior as well as how he/she perceives the world. But the self does not develop in a vacuum – for no man is an island. The 'stuff', i.e. the environmental stimuli by which the individual draws from to construct the self is dependent upon interaction with a social world.

Social psychology

We now turn to the sub-field of social psychology. Social psychology is the study of the effect of other human beings on the individual. A person's opinions and attitudes, indeed his/her sense of self and personality, develop within a social setting, namely through membership in groups such as a family, clan, neighborhood, gang, club, school, religious faith or congregation, linguistic group, nation, culture or ideology. Particular power dynamics within and amongst these groups can be exploited. An individual's viewpoint, his frame of reference, his value system, and his philosophy of life all reflect mores that he has developed in these groups. Moreover, as mentioned before, the social roles one must perform in these groups will exert a significant influence on attitude and belief formation and will be reflected in other group affiliations and behavioral patterns.[28]

The social group exerts tremendous effect on the individual. The larger a group, the greater the tendency to conformity to collective values, principles, beliefs and attitudes – and not just numerically, but also in terms of percentage. People tend to conform to certain norms more when they must respond publicly in front of others rather than privately. On the other hand, when observing someone else's dissent – even when it is wrong – an individual is more likely to garner their own sense of independence and be influential in subsequent behavior.

A minority opinion from someone outside the group is less likely to sway opinion than the same minority opinion from someone within the group.[29] As a general rule, people will respond better to a message that comes from someone in their group. The perceived nationality of the message maker is a vital factor in the success of a message. An American diplomat lecturing Shiitte Iraqis on the merits of an independent judiciary will be a nonstarter, but if the same message came from Moqtada Al-Sadr it could be very effective. When the choice concerns matters of personal value, taste, or way of life, communicators who are similar to their audiences have the most influence. But on individual judgments of fact, confirmation of belief by a foreigner can sometimes do more to boost one's self-confidence more than does confirmation coming from within the group. A foreigner, or better yet an unbiased expert, provides the appearance of more independent judgment and thus more legitimacy to the individual's confirmation of their assumptions about themselves.

Similarity and attractiveness are often just as important as substance. Persuasion is often more potent when conditions of direct contact with other people, especially those that are well-known and/or good looking, is the principle channel of communication. More life-like and personalized media, such as the Internet and video, are the most persuasive where direct human-to-human contact is not possible. The marketing industry is a good example of the deployment of this understanding. Marketers and advertisers often approach the propagation of their brand or product as a process of humanization. This is a technique, whereby the attempt is made to build emotional relationships and positive associations between the consumer and the company or product. This allows the consumer to interact with the company or product as if it were human, creating attachments, positive associations and influencing the construction of identity.[30] However, although this process works, it should be noted that the likelihood of further persuasion on the part of the advertisers decreases as the significance and familiarity of the brand or product for the target increases.[31] This last point is also important because it highlights another example where intensity matters – the strategic communicator, even a grand-strategist must know at what point the audience becomes bored or oversaturated with the presence of the U.S. or how it communicates a particular message.

Symbols

It should be evident that the dynamics of a group exerts significant influence upon the formation of the individual and his/her attitudes and beliefs. Now, the formation of groups is predicated upon a shared system of communication. Symbols are the basic building blocks of social exchange and are therefore the foundation that makes communication possible. The vehicle by which an individual participates in the thought and action of the group is the symbol. A symbol is also a cognitive tool, often serving as a simplified idea or object that helps to organize information, provide meaning and can act as the principal mode of identification and association for the individual.

Effective psychological manipulation uses multiple symbols linked in such a way that some evoke known images and appeal to emotions, while others can create tension and dissonance by expressing paradox, inconsistency or multiple appeals to conflicting ideas. Political use of symbols can be used to divide groups or mobilize diverse peoples – in either case symbols help to focus and consolidate the various energies of a group. Because they are representations and abstractions symbols are often open to reinterpretation. This creates a descent amount of room for maneuver – a point that is as important from a defensive standpoint as it is from an offensive.

Cognitive psychology defines 'symbol' as a form of knowledge representation. Symbolic representation is a mental representation arbitrarily chosen to stand for something through the use of analogy and metaphor. As the capacity for analogy is, according to the definition, arbitrary, there is left considerable range for the use and relation of symbols. A symbol may be defined as a repository of value or meaning bestowed upon it by those who use it. The meaning or value of a symbol is in no instance derived from or determined by properties intrinsic in its form, but by those who use the symbol. Symbols "have their signification" to use John Locke's phrase, "from the arbitrary imposition of men."

The American strategic communicator would be well advised to acquaint themselves with the fluid and dynamic nature of symbols and their meanings. They should be weary of their power as well as capable of harnessing it for strategic or tactical advantage. Since the symbol is the cognitive foundation by which language and communication are possible, they are the first principle of persuasion. They are a critical tool of statecraft because they are easy to create, to communicate, to understand and to retain. Their use in tactical and strategic considerations is seemingly boundless. As such, a comprehensive understanding of the power of symbols to mobilize groups should be required for any strategic communicator.

Manipulating the environment

The preceding sections have shown there are many ways to manipulate the assumptions and expectations of others by exploiting cognitive processes and biases, factors related to the development of personality, and forces inherent in group dynamics. We began this discussion with the essential building blocks of the nervous system, the senses, and we have seemingly progressed from that starting point further and further from the biological aspects of psychology, i.e. internal causes into the outside environment, the most external of causes. In this section we consider the environment as a variable to manipulate. With this we have a further option for the American strategic communicator to consider, albeit a difficult one to implement. It is important to consider how one might shape or manipulate the environment where expectations originate. How might the environment be changed as to make an audience more conducive to accepting a message or policy?

Most of a person's everyday life is determined, not by his conscious intentions and deliberate choices, but by unconscious mental processes that are reactions to changes in the environment. Events may alter our associations without our realizing it. Indeed, how easily one can change a target's mind seems dependent in part on environmental pressures on decision-making. The marketing and advertising industries create such environmental pressures, and similar methodologies may be applied abroad for national defense purposes.

One of the giants of modern propaganda, Edward Bernays, mastered the manipulation of social setting to induce desired behavior or attitudes in his commercial clients' target markets. He defined the practice of propaganda as the "consistent, enduring effort to create and shape events to influence" attitudes and behavior.[33] Bernays used peripheral cues in the environment to trigger associations and feelings that would prime the target audiences into thought or behavior patterns, which in turn would lead in the direction he wanted them to go. The idea, as well as its success, remains striking. In the same vein, another forefather of contemporary advertising, Walter Scott Dill, sought "to create the motives that will affect the sale of the producer's wares."[34] The psychological point they were attempting to exploit was that "incentives to action are found in the stimuli of varied everyday environments."[35]

Everyday environments are defined by both social and physical structures. In the first case, the public diplomat, information operations practitioner and political warrior might look to shape social and political environments. Political, economic, legal, and cultural structures give form to action and guide behavior and psychological development through a predetermined set of possibilities. These social structures are obviously variable and inherently changeable. Laws, economic and tax policies, institutional norms and expectations as well as the overall societal system of incentives all predetermine a set of behavioral limitations and organize or redirect action in a desired direction. Changing these limitations can result in different expressions of behavior. Over time these changes may influence larger social circumstances or influence individual decision-making. In the second case, physical variables can be exploited but are not as easy to change – such factors can be climatological like temperature and weather, geographic factors like time of day, urban layout and city infrastructure – some of the effects of light and temperature were discussed earlier in the section on the senses – others factors like space and organizational flow can also have affect. All exert a level of influence on the individual but this influence is most often fixed.

Because these factors are fixed, it does not mean we cannot take advantage of the influence they exert. Future urban development and city planning may provide opportunities to influence new commercial and housing development policy offers one possibility of exerting a degree of control over the environment, the ability to guide action and the potential to manage impressions. Other, more extra-ordinary possibilities might include the manipulation of weather or the manufacture of a staged provocative event. Often, however, the more practical course involves capitalizing on conditions rather than creating them. Capitalizing on advantageous weather conditions, attacking at night or releasing potentially damaging information during holidays when most people are not paying attention are just a few of the ways one can make the external causes of the environment useful to managing psychological impressions and achieving particular policy objectives.

Social and physical aspects of the environment are indeed variables vulnerable to manipulation and can serve as factors of psychological influence which pose different advantages at different times and in different situations. If these external causes are manipulated or exploited in a systematic way, the possibilities are there to influence a host of psychological processes and behavior toward a desired response. As a program or in support of other initiatives, affecting the social and physical environment of a target audience might prove to be a striking weapon of subtlety in the attempts to win over hearts and minds.

Conclusion

> *"It's a game of momentum, it's a game of ebb and flows...*
> *It's a game... of rhythm."*
> White Sox announcer on telecast, July 16, 2006

Although the Chicago White Sox announcer was describing the game of baseball, he could have been describing the dynamic inherent in the competition for psychological power. But because these are only general clues, developing a scientific approach to strategic communication, unlike the game of baseball, has remained problematic. Although a firm grasp of fundamentals can increase the likelihood of success, as in baseball, the success of any strategic communication program ultimately depends on the skill of the practitioner and his/her intuitive 'feel' for the game.

Political power depends, in part, upon favorable perceptions and impressions, and the psychological process which governs the organization of information is often subject to biases, misperceptions, self-fulfilling prophecies, cycles of reinforcement and even willful ignorance. The American strategic communicator must compete in an atmosphere that is riddled with misinformation, misconceptions and misunderstandings, which can cause unsustainable damage to the political capital of the United States. The key to success lies in practicing the fundamentals while always being ready to capitalize on an opportunity. Keep in mind that opportunities can often arise from setbacks as well. The strategic communicator must take the pulse of his audience, recognize and exploit momentum, and know when to strike. Innovation is also a precious commodity in psychological statecraft as the field is largely uncharted territory. Some situations will call for subtlety, others complexity, others still simplicity. But however daunting the path, it must be traveled or the United States will continue to pay a heavy price.

One of the points of this chapter has been to suggest that the rules of the psychological game have not yet been established. It is the cutting edge of statecraft and is played at the national and individual levels, and across the spectrum of war and peace. Psychology adds a mother lode of dynamics, variables, and ultimately, vulnerabilities to be exploited – and to be protected against. Its effective use challenges us to find ever-more creative ways of using it, along with developing a strong set of morals and doctrines about when, if and how to do what to whom, and why.

The art of effective strategic communication is the art of influence; it is an art of affect. The preceding survey of commonly accepted sensual, cognitive and social psychology was meant to begin a badly needed conversation. There is much work to be done in the application of psychology to strategic communication. There are endless questions in need of answers that will help explain how psychology can be wielded in support and defense of U.S. policy. In the end, the art will be defined by first knowing when to initiate a psychological influence program and then choosing the right format from the daunting array of available variables.

Notes

[1] Harold D. Lasswell, "Propaganda and Mass Insecurity," in Alfred H. Stanton and Stewart E. Perry, eds., *Personality and Political Crisis: New Perspectives from Social Science and Psychiatry for the Study of War and Politics* (The Free Press, 1951), pp. 15-20.

[2] Sun Tzu. *The Art of War*. Translated by Ralph D. Sawyer (Westview Press. 1994), p. 198.

[3] Jürgen Altmann, "Acoustic Weapons? Sources, Propagation and Effects of Strong Sound," paper presented to the Acoustical Society of America, March 1999, accessed November 2006 at:
http://trauma.cofa.unsw.edu.au/Infrasound/acousticweapons.pdf.

[4] Daniel Vastfjall and Mendel Kleiner, "Emotion in Product Sound Design," *Proceedings of Journees Design Sonore* (Paris), March 20-21, 2002.

[5] David Huron, "Sound, Music and Emotion: An Introduction to the Experimental Research," paper delivered at the Society for Music Perception and Cognition Conference, 1997.

[6] Ibid.

[7] Ibid.

[8] Ibid.

[9] Alfred H. Paddock, Jr., "U.S. Military Psychological Operations: Past, Present and Future," in Janos Radvanyi, ed., *Psychological Operations and Political Warfare in Long-Term Strategic Planning* (Praeger, 1990).

[10] Walter Scott Dill, "The Psychology of Advertising," *Atlantic Monthly*, Vol. 93, No. 555, 1904.

[11] Jacques Ellul, *Propaganda : The Formation of Men's Attitudes* (Alfred A. Knopf, Inc. 1966), p. 15.

[12] David G. Myers. *Social Psychology*, 7th ed. (McGraw Hill, 2002), pp. 103-104.

[13] Ibid.

[14] Ibid.

[15] Ibid.

[16] Ibid., pp. 113-114.

[17] Richard M. Ryckman, ed., *Strategic Military Deception* (Wadsworth Publishing, 2000), p. 21.

[18] Myers, p. 103.

[19] Donald C. Daniel and Katherine L. Herbig, eds., *Strategic Military Deception* (Pergamon Policy Studies Press. 1982), p. 42.

[20] Milton J. Rosenberg, Cognitive Reorganization in Response to the Hypnotic Reversal of Attitudinal Effect (Yale University Press, 1959).

[21] Attitudes are referred to here as having "histories" because we can consider attitudes to be more a process than a finite object. Attitudes are processes in themselves, in a constant state of development. An exception to the point in the history of an attitude is when the attitude is in the process of "changing."

[22] Rosenberg.

[23] Daniel and Herbig, eds., p. 49.

[24] Myers, p. 275.

[25] One of the best examples of this was the radio broadcast of *Der Chef* in central Europe, during World War II, especially Germany. *Der Chef* was an Englishmen posing as a German. He was well received, very popular, and most effective as an instrument of black propaganda throughout the war years because he was ruthless to all sides. Fundamentally, of course, he was with the Allies, but his pre-propaganda of skewering everyone prepared his audiences to be receptive to his ultimate pro-Allies message.

[26] Myers, p. 275.

[27] Ibid., p. 42.

[28] Ibid., p .137.

[29] Ibid., pp. 224-5.

[30] Dill, pp. 29-36.

[31] Myers, p. 267.

[33] Edward Bernays. *Propaganda*. With an Introduction by Mark Crispin Miller (IG Publishing, 1928 and 2005).

[34] See Dill.

[35] Paul M. A. Linebarger, *Psychological Warfare* (Washington Infantry Press, 1948), pp. 110-130.

12

Political War vs. Political Terror:
Case study of an American success story

JOHN J. TIERNEY

Years after having invaded Iraq and toppled Saddam Hussein, the United States was still searching for the right combination of civil-military strategies to close the book on what President Bush once practically proclaimed as "mission accomplished." The administration discovered an ancient truth: that the swift conventional victory over opposition armies can be extremely deceptive if insurgents, guerrillas and terrorists remain concealed and active within the remote terrain of an occupied population. It is not necessary that the population be overwhelmingly hostile to the occupiers; only a segment of opposition is needed to spark rebellion.

The first public indication that something had gone wrong, that the swift battle triumph in Iraq did not end the war, came just two months after the U.S.-led invasion, on July 16, 2003, when the American military commander in Iraq, General John P. Abizaid, declared that the enemy was engaging "a classical guerrilla-type" campaign against over 130,000 Coalition occupation forces. This revelation abruptly changed the dynamics of the entire operation. As attacks and casualties mounted during the ensuing months and into 2004, he Bush Administration scrambled for new answers to a problem as old as warfare itself: the clash between "irregular" and "regular" conceptions of conflict. By mid-October 2003 Secretary of Defense Donald Rumsfeld was challenging his staff, in the famous leaked memo, to "think through new ways to organize, train, equip and focus to deal with the global war on terror... [that] we lack metrics to know if we are losing." He admitted that the struggle in Iraq "will be a long, hard slog."[1]

Such a reality check was long overdue, but the reappraisal did not hide the fact that the administration found itself blindsided by the emergence of an insurrection opposed to the presence of American-led armies inside Iraq. The United States had, in fact, become a "foreign troop," and even the most cursory reading of history should have been sufficient to warn against the potential problems derived from this basic reality. Instead, the administration deceived itself that the initial glow of a brilliant military triumph had effectively ended the war. As we now know, it only brought the war to another level, increased violence in Iraq and created confusion and partisan accusation at home. Such is nearly the universal by-product of unplanned counterinsurgency.

The word "guerrilla" and the companion term "insurgency" recall the early stages of the Vietnam War more than forty years ago. But the deeper history of the word, and the U.S. engagement against guerrillas, is part of an American past which remains largely obscure to the public and, apparently, to its leaders as well. If the ghosts of past insurrections have returned to haunt us in Iraq, we have no one to blame but ourselves for the ignorance of our own history or for the presumptions that brought us to these dilemmas in the first place.[2]

But we are far from the first to discover this problem. It goes back millennia. The current American scenario in Iraq has hundreds of precedents throughout history. An example is the effort waged by the British in arresting the rebellion in Malaya during the 1950's. As Professor James E. Doughtery of the University of Pennsylvania once wrote, even the British Army, with centuries of experience in colonial warfare, was forced (as the U.S. has been today) to devise new tactics, almost from scratch:

> During the first two years of the war, the British relied almost exclusively on conventional military measures to put down the rebellion. But they gradually realized that the orthodox modes of warfare taught at Sandhurst were not applicable against an elusive jungle foe who was bent on protracting the conflict as long as possible... By early 1950, the British had recognized the fact that they were making little or no headway against the MRLA [guerillas]. They began to devise new approaches, which required a fuller strategic perspective of the situation.[3]

This problem has afflicted American armies as well. *Without exception,* not a single case from U.S. history can demonstrate where an infantry, either by doctrine, equipment, or tactics, was prepared against insurrection when faced with such a challenge. In each case surprise turned into shock and anger and tactics had to be improvised through frustrating trial and error. The current imbroglio in Iraq, seen from this perspective, has a deep and logical historical pedigree, available but ignored. "There is nothing new under the sun," we are told in *Ecclesiastes*, but, often, the light blinds the observer.

This chapter will bring to life the long history of U.S. engagements in similar situations throughout history, and the importance of the psychopolitical tool in counterinsurgent warfare. Although a number of case studies and scenarios can be developed, the case of the Philippines can be seen as the most illustrative and comparable from a number of perspectives.

In each perspective, the proper combination of civil-military actions, highlighting what is now called "political warfare," was central to the eventual resolution of the issue. The Philippine Islands remain vital to U.S. history, not merely as the only significant American "colony" to achieve independence but as a classic theatre of not one, but two, major insurrections. Both instances, in which the end was eminently successful from the U.S. point of view, remain today as powerful lessons of the timeless importance of political action as adjacent – and often superior – to standard military solutions.

The Philippine Insurrection

The Philippine archipelago had been a Spanish province for over four centuries when the Treaty of Paris was signed in 1898, ending the Spanish-American War. After Admiral Dewey's victory over the Spanish fleet in Manila Bay, the United States dispatched 12,000 soldiers (the Eighth Corps), led by General Wesley Merritt, in order to remove the Spaniards from their stronghold in the city itself. After mounting only token resistance, the Spanish army surrendered and U.S. troops began occupying Manila and its surroundings. By then, a native independence movement had already been organized around Emilio Aguinaldo, a twenty-nine year old revolutionary from the Cavite province. Ironically, the Spanish had sent Aguinaldo into exile, and U.S. authorities returned him in the naive hope that he would prove useful in the occupation. This was only the first of many mistakes the North American newcomers made.

Aguinaldo had been the acknowledged leader of the Philippine nationalist movement against Spanish rule, having won that position through his personal charisma and the military leadership he displayed in the earlier Philippine attacks against Spanish troops. He and his top commander, General Antonio Luna, had already assembled an army of about 80,000 insurgents and had established a shadow government, which included Aguinaldo's own Central Revolutionary Committee and a Filipino Congress. But, as U.S. actions came more and more to resemble those of an occupying power rather than a liberator, the two sides began preparations for a possible showdown. Aguinaldo's troops were facing the American army in defensive positions in the suburbs around Manila. As the treaty negotiations stretched out through the autumn of 1898 the two armies continued to glare at each other nervously. Filipino hopes for a peaceful transition to independence were dashed when the terms of the Treaty granting American sovereignty were announced. By early 1899 Aguinaldo had already laid plans to forcibly evict the Americans.

The war began as an orthodox combat, but that phase was to last for less than a day. The battle of Manila began on February 4, 1899, when Aguinaldo declared war on the United States and his Filipino forces charged the entrenched American positions. When it was over the next day, the Filipinos were scattered into retreat north of the city, having lost nearly 5,000 dead, compared to only 59 for the U.S. This battle, later termed by one historian as "the bloodiest conflict in Philippine history, including World War II,"[4] impressed Aguinaldo with the impossibility of defeating the American army with regular infantry tactics. His conversion to guerrilla war had begun. By the end of March the Filipinos had been pushed away from Manila and their capital at Malolos, twenty miles to the northwest, had fallen to forces under General Arthur MacArthur.

After the Philippine disaster in Manila, Major General Elwell S. Otis, who was in command of the 30,000 U.S. troops in the country, confidently believed that no more men would be required to quell the nascent rebellion. After the Battle of Manila he reported back that:

> the demoralization of the insurgents which the rough handling they had received from the American mode of conducting warfare hitherto unknown in these islands, and pronounced by them to be new and unsoldierly, continued for two or three days, the leaders confessing that their men were over-matched by our troops, contended that they could overcome by numbers what was lacking in individual characteristics.[5]

Obsolete military thinking and misperception

Throughout 1899 Otis continued to judge the situation in West Point terms, despite growing evidence that a guerrilla insurrection was brewing. Instead of sending small, mobile columns into the territories vacated by the retreating Filipinos, he sent large columns in two or three directions at once. Rather than occupying territory, he ordered his men back to base, while Aguinaldo was permitted to regroup and to reoccupy the areas he had just vacated. The Filipinos were beginning to harass U.S. outposts and consolidate political support at a time when the American army could have been deployed throughout the archipelago.

General MacArthur, who understood irregular warfare much better than Otis, described Aguinaldo's new battle tactics as:

> a modified Fabian policy [Roman General Q. Fabius Maximus' policy of slow attrition of the enemy], which was based upon the idea of occupying a series of strong defensive positions and there from presenting just enough resistance to force the American army to a never-ending repetition of tactical deployments. This policy was carried out with considerable skill and was for a time partially successful, as the native army was thus enabled to hover within easy distance of the American camps and at the same time avoid close combat.[6]

It was not until late in 1899, however, that an American force ventured beyond sixty miles of the capital. During the spring and summer of 1899 Aguinaldo and his force remained just outside the reach of American strength. Beginning in April they launched a series of minor raids against railroads and U.S. installations, killing American troops in the process. Otis sent a division under Major General Henry Lawton to destroy them, but after taking twenty-seven days to march through jungle terrain, they had advanced only fifty-eight miles. Although Lawton had occupied the town of San Isidro, he remained confused both to his mission and to the nature of the enemy. Cabling back to Otis, he wrote:

> The delays in my movements disturb me very much. The rice fields are now in places covered with water and twenty-four hours rain will render travel with transportation impossible. The weather is now favorable and every day lost may cost us dearly. I am possibly mistaken, but the enemy has not impressed me as being in very great force or as showing much pertinacity.[7]

At the same time, Americans were beginning to understand the non-military hazards of conducting operations in the tropical denseness of the Philippine jungle canopy. Out of 515 casualties in Lawton's division, only nine killed and thirty-five wounded came from insurgents' bullets. The rest came from dysentery, diarrhea, malaria, heat exhaustion and other forms of jungle illness. MacArthur's own force, which had been on the move since February, suffered in a similar way. By May, of the 4,800 troops in his division, 2,160 (45 percent) were on sick report, one regiment alone having 70 percent in the hospital. The great strain imposed on the troops, with the constant patrolling against a nearly invisible enemy, was magnified by these geographic and medical difficulties. Volunteers who had enlisted only for the war with Spain clamored to go home. With the rainy season due for the summer, Otis postponed operations temporarily until weather and fresh troops would permit destruction of an enemy which he had faced only once in battle and which, to his way of thinking, was already defeated.

By the autumn of 1899 the inconclusive war had already lasted longer than the great victory over Spain. Yet against a seemingly ragtag collection of backward and illiterate peasants the American troops found only disease and frustration. General Otis still harbored the orthodox notion that pursuit of the opponent's armed forces was the only strategy to follow in wartime. Yet, his persistent underestimation of the irregulars, plus severe climactic conditions, produced an extremely cautious policy even within his own illusions. The characteristic American impatience with the lack of visible success in battle, however, was beginning to affect opinions in Washington. In August, the office of Secretary of War Elihu Root sent the following telegram to Otis:

> Secretary of War desires to know what, with all the light you now have, you consider an undoubtedly adequate force for complete suppression of insurrection during the coming dry season. In view of the impatience of the public, which may affect legislative provision for conduct of war, rapid and thorough action is important. The Secretary would rather err on the safe side in sending too many troops than too few.[8]

Impatient public opinion began to pressure Congress to de-fund the war effort in that hot summer of 1899. By September, Otis had over 45,000 troops, with more promised. He resolved to end the war then and there by sweeping all of northern Luzon with three columns, hoping to capture Aguinaldo in the process. Up to this point, the central province of Luzon had been the theater of war for all the American operations.

The United States was basing its military activity on the assumptions that sufficient engagements against the enemy would result in a quick end to the war and that, once the Americans established enough contact with the local populace, mutual good feeling would inevitably result. After that, it was reasoned, whatever threat there might be to U.S. occupation would exist in the form of sporadic "ladronism" (banditry) that had been a historic problem in the more remote regions of the archipelago.

Otis' October offensive was beset with torrential downpours and an irritating lack of supplies. Although Lawton's column was hot on the heels of Aguinaldo, all they were able to do was affect the capture of his mother and sister. The insurgent leader and his main force escaped to the wild mountains of the north where they began preparations for a more elaborate and systematic adoption of full-scale guerrilla warfare. Although a number of minor engagements occurred, the offensive was simply one of hide and seek. The effect on the American troops, as described by William Sexton, was miserable:

> Many of the men's clothes had not been dry for two weeks. Constant wetness had rotted leather and stitching in shoes, and many of the men were barefoot. The majority were suffering from malarial fever and chills. Many faces were pale and emaciated, the indication of dysentery. Nearly everyone had dhobie itch in one form or another. Everyone was hungry.[9]

The fact that the rebels had been forced underground gave the impression to the American commanders that the war was over. U.S. leaders were formally schooled in the art of regular war. When the enemy left the field, conventional war theory assumed, the war was over. Nowhere in their schooling and training was the opposite suggested, but in the tradition of guerrilla war the conflict didn't really begin until the rebels had been swept away by the regular troops. This was precisely what was occurring when MacArthur cabled the following wire of November 23, 1899 to Otis: "The so-called Filipino Republic is destroyed. The Congress has dissolved. The President of the so-called Republic is a fugitive as are all his cabinet officers, except one who is in our hands."[10]

News like this received a naturally sympathetic hearing from General Otis. Doctrinaire in his understanding of war, he had long since closed his mind to any interpretation beyond the usual one. In a national periodical of the time, Leslie's Weekly, he informed the American people, "The war in the Philippines is already over ... all we have to do now is protect Filipinos against themselves... There will be no more real fighting..."[11] During the month of December he cabled Washington on four occasions that the war was over.

But in a very real sense it had only begun. Aguinaldo's full conversion to guerrilla war took place in November 1899; for nearly three years thereafter his men engaged a rotated total of 125,000 U.S. troops in a protracted political-military campaign that challenged more than just the concept of warfare that had grown up in American society. Before it was over, the Philippine insurrection against American rule brought out issues that touched the very core of American society and values. Largely forgotten amidst the more important conflicts with the world's great powers, this war dragged on intermittently without visible end in sight – and without any resounding military victories – until President Theodore Roosevelt formally declared it over on July 4, 1902. Like most guerrilla insurrections that fail, this one didn't simply end, it just simmered down to a tolerable level until it faded away. Left in its wake were over 220,000 dead Filipinos, 4,234 American soldiers killed in action (almost an equal number later died of service-connected diseases) and a U.S. war bill of $170 million.

The important military events of the conventional war with Spain occurred in a span of weeks, if not days. It took the United States three and a half years, however, to arrest the rebellion in the Philippines, a time period slightly less than that of the Civil War and about the same length as American participation in the Second World War. Additionally, the United States won this war primarily because of the political and administrative control it came to exercise over Philippine life, rather than its military prowess... From the beginning, the very nature of this conflict presented the U.S. authorities with a challenge to their conception of war – and their corresponding code of operations – that had not been experienced since the early days of irregular operations against North American Indians.

U.S. leaders only gradually realized the change in the situation from Fabian attrition tactics to guerrilla insurrection. With American garrisons occupying all of the northern part of the principal island, Luzon, the U.S. took up expeditions through southern Luzon in early 1900. At the same time, the U.S. began to penetrate the central islands and the Moslem haven, Mindanao. Little opposition was encountered at first, but military authorities on the ground soon perceived a subtle change in the atmosphere. Only later did this perception reach Manila or, even later, Washington and the American public. When it did, the political roar at home reached a crescendo against a conflict that seemed both unlikely and unreal, a war that the United States at first, according to one authority, "was rather blindly waging.[12]

The insurgents' second front:
American public opinion

By the time of the 1900 election, a full-scale anti-war protest movement, the Anti-Imperialist League, had disrupted the electorate and had captured the Democratic Party and its presidential candidate,

William Jennings Bryan. Indeed, President William McKinley had to fight a two-front campaign: the political war against domestic protest groups and the Democrats as well as the insurgency in the Philippines. The incumbents eventually succeeded on both fronts, thanks largely to the political warfare waged by the incumbent Republicans.

By May 1900, the Americans fortified virtually every island of consequence in the archipelago. Military operations were monotonously similar to those of the year before: the insurgents were so wary of American power that a U.S. advance served almost as a signal for a rebel retreat. Upon their dispersal, the insurgents would invariably harass the flanks and rear of U.S. columns, occasionally preying upon isolated Americans and, at times, inflicting serious casualties and taking prisoners. As U.S. authorities slowly realized, occupation in guerrilla war was one thing, pacification quite another.

Pursuing a policy of attraction

Despite U.S. military occupation of all the major islands of the Philippines, engagements with hostile forces multiplied. Rather than toning down the situation as American officials expected it would, the presence of foreign soldiers had the opposite result. During the first ten months of conflict – the "regular" phase of the war – the United States averaged 44 contacts per month.

Between December 1, 1899 and June 30, 1900 – the first seven months of guerrilla insurrection – the monthly figure more than doubled to 106, despite the extension of U.S. authority over the archipelago and despite the collapse of any Philippine pretensions to civil or governmental legitimacy. Between May 1900 and June 1901 the U.S. Army noted 1,026 contacts with guerrillas in a chronological listing that totaled 734 pages.

The same essential dilemma confronted the American army beyond Luzon, where Aguinaldo had his headquarters, and throughout the archipelago: Panay, Negroes, Leyte, Samar, and to a lesser degree in the islands of Cebu, Bohol and in northern Mindanao. To end the irregular stalemate, General MacArthur and the new leadership began to turn to more conciliatory measures: policies of attraction to supplement military sweep-and-destroy tactics. An amnesty program gave insurgents both money and security as incentives. MacArthur secured $1 million for a project to construct better roads through the provinces and obtained authority for the organization of a local constabulary recruited among the natives. This force, named the "Scouts," received official authorization in February 1901, but never exceeded more than 12,000 men during the insurrection. The U.S. also inaugurated an extensive land reform program, providing landless peasants with properties once owned by oligarchs. All such projects were intended as long-term solutions, and they reflected a sober reconsideration of the guerrilla problem on the part of most U.S. officials. The course of the war had finally affected American leaders' own evaluation of its real nature and of the appropriate countermeasures.

General MacArthur had earlier demonstrated an unusual appreciation of the extent of Aguinaldo's support. In 1899 he told an American correspondent, "When I first started against these rebels, I believed that Aguinaldo's troops represented only a fraction. I did not believe that the whole population of Luzon was opposed to us; but I have been reluctantly compelled to believe that the Filipinos are loyal to Aguinaldo and the government which he represents."[13] During the middle of 1900 he further diagnosed the same problem as it extended throughout the Philippines. Noting their "almost complete unity of action," he reported that:

> wherever throughout the archipelago there is a group of the insurgent army, it is a fact beyond dispute that all the contiguous towns contribute to its maintenance... Intimidation has undoubtedly contributed much to this end; but fear as the only motive is hardly sufficient to account for the united and apparently spontaneous action of several millions of people.[14]

With such a large backing, it became clear to the United States that military measures alone simply could not end the insurgency. After almost two years of near-constant fighting U.S. officials conceded that the situation was much worse than before, and that there was no indication of victory in sight. U.S. military officials and administrators were fast gaining an education in the trials and tribulations of irregular warfare. For the first time in their recent memories, military force pushed to its logical conclusion was inappropriate for any meaningful victory. Other measures would have to be found and, in fact, it was precisely this political and administrative course of events – both in the Philippines and at home – that eventually turned the tables on Aguinaldo and the insurrection.

When it became obvious to him that to defeat the United States militarily was out of the question, Aguinaldo decided on guerrilla war and, in effect, turned the insurrection from a military to a political affair. He drew moral support from the antiwar movement in the United States and the presidential electoral campaign. Thereafter, the sole rationale for his continued resistance was to exhaust American patience until a Democratic victory in the 1900 presidential elections would hopefully undercut domestic support for the inconclusive war and affect an American withdrawal. The duel between Aguinaldo and MacArthur with their respective forces and strategies came to represent a classic illustration of guerrilla insurgent versus regular counter-insurgent. Once both contestants understood each other the conflict was to be settled by a competition between the very fiber and support of their respective societies. In effect, they both waged the war for the other's population. Before it was over, the Philippine Insurrection was more than just a war: it was a test of the determination, persistence and strength of the two peoples: political warfare writ large.

Aguinaldo and his lieutenants mastered techniques of political and psychological warfare. They succeeded in enrolling critical segments of the archipelago into their cause. Starting almost from scratch, without even the rudimentary weapons or wherewithal for large-scale warfare, they helped oust the Spanish and later tied down the United States for a total of three and a half years of exasperating conflict. While fear and terrorism certainly played an important role, the nationalistic basis which underpinned the whole movement undeniably made the difference.

Even General MacArthur was forced to concede that "the adhesive principle comes from ethnological homogeneity which induces men to respond for a time to the appeals of consanguineous leadership..."[15] Not only were the Filipino leaders tenacious and dedicated in purpose, but they also knew how to communicate their cause to the great mass of the people. Their propaganda depicted the Americans as ponderous and awkward agents of empire, intent on robbing the archipelago of its natural right of independence. The twin themes of courage in the face of U.S. strength and political liberty for Filipinos were time and again used against the occupying power. The following excerpt from *La Independencia* was typical of how the Filipino insurgents propagandized irregular warfare:

> Our enemies will be able – why should they not? – to wheel their heavy wagons of war over our fields. They will leave the imprints of their vandal heels in our villages. But at every turning in their path, behind every bush, at every corner, they will meet resistance – a handful of men, who will check their course, who will disturb their triumphant passage, who will be the little rock to spring the wheel of their vehicle off its axle, the boghole in which their gun-carriage will mire, and who will make them see most clearly that in vain do they juggle with the rights of a people that desires to be united, free, and sovereign.[16]

Although the United States was able to control the surface aspects of the war, the guerrillas were the real masters of the country in spite of the fact that they held very little real estate. Aguinaldo was a supreme manipulator of the psychology of the Philippine nation; he was their spokesman and hero and personified their aspirations. He was also just as personally ruthless against his own rivals inside the system as he was against those who violated its mandates. In effect, he was a Filipino Stalinist. He connived in the murder of his best general, Antonio Luna, and helped remove his chief political rival, Apolinario Mabini, from office.

His Achilles' heel, however, lay in the fact that he depended too much on his ability to indirectly influence political events inside the United States. He probably could have continued the insurrection indefinitely, but he realized the futility of a system that offered no hope whatever of military victory. His only chance lay in the exhaustion of the American electorate's patience against an inconclusive and politically divisive war. He pinned his hopes, therefore, on the electoral victory of William Jennings Bryan and the Democrats who, at the time, were riding the crest of an increasingly vitriolic "anti-imperialist" crusade against the Philippine Insurrection.[17]   While no evidence suggests that Aguinaldo worked directly to manipulate American press coverage of the war as later insurgents would do, he certainly relied on his power of influence, which fueled the "anti-imperialist" movement and, in turn, aided Bryan's campaign.

The Democrats carried the offensive against President McKinley, but without sufficient vigor and consistency to win. McKinley was certainly vulnerable on a number of war-related issues, but the country's general prosperity in conjunction with the hesitation of many anti-war Republicans to bolt the party undoubtedly hurt the Democratic cause. In addition to the other charges against it, the administration was also vulnerable to what Vietnam-era critics would later call the "credibility gap." The well-publicized and overly-optimistic statements by General Otis and other leaders did not sit well against a military expedition that was nearly into its third year without evident progress, despite more than double the original number of U.S. soldiers then in the islands.

The military's censorship of news from Manila, furthermore, ran against the grain of the strong American tradition of freedom of the press. From the beginning, many American journalists challenged the official U.S. view of the war. Their perspective, based upon personal observation, detected a massive political revolt, and not simply the marauding bands of robbers General Otis often referred to as the primary source of the fighting. The journalists stressed the small number of rifles that the U.S. had been able to take from the enemy, plus the fact that most of the insurgent leaders were still at large as evidence of a continuing war, rather than a sporadic series of flare-ups. Furthermore, they wrote back home, there existed a paramilitary underground organization, headed by Aguinaldo, which had united almost the entire archipelago against the United States. Otis slapped a heavy censorship on news dispatches, but many got through. Eleven of them, for example, mailed the following dispatch from Hong Kong reported,

> We believe that, owing to official dispatches from Manila made public in Washington, the people in the United States have not received a correct impression of the situation in the Philippines, but that these dispatches have presented an ultra-optimistic view that is not shared by the general officers in the field... We believe the dispatches err in the declaration that the 'situation is well in hand,' and in the assumption that the insurrection can be speedily ended without a greatly increased force. We think the tenacity of the Filipino purpose has been underestimated, and that the statements are un-founded that volunteers are willing to engage in further service.[18]

Despite the anti-war movement, American voters re-elected McKinley by a plurality of 7,219,530, compared to Bryan's 6,351,071. Bryan's political defeat effectively crippled the anti-imperialist movement and allowed the U.S. a much greater degree of freedom in its overall war policies. In the Philippines, the Republican victory was a bigger blow to the insurrection than all the previous military defeats combined. Since his initial adoption of guerrilla war, Aguinaldo had determined that his only hope lay in the protracted erosion of the American willpower to remain in the archipelago. The split in U.S. domestic ranks inspired the insurgents, who naively came to believe their own propaganda. Without any real appreciation of the U.S. political system, the Philippine insurgents looked forward to November 1900 when, as Aguinaldo put it, "the great Democratic party of the United States will win the next fall election... imperialism will fail in its mad attempts to subjugate us by force of arms."[19]

American election has effect on insurgency

With McKinley reaffirmed in the White House, and public protest confined, the insurrection cause rapidly disintegrated. Almost immediately after the results were in, the administration, released from the pressures of having to defend its policy for an election, adopted much harsher methods against the guerrillas. With over 70,000 fresh troops, MacArthur imposed martial law over the entire archipelago. Mass arrests and imprisonments followed, and thirty-two Filipino leaders were rounded up and deported to Guam. Seventy-nine important captives were convicted of war crimes and all were executed. The press was muzzled, and those Filipino papers that refused to publish U.S. handouts were immediately suppressed. In his December 1900 announcement of martial law, MacArthur stated that, henceforth, any insurgent captured was guilty of violating the recognized "laws of war" and would be subject, therefore, to either death or imprisonment. At the same time, the institution of the Federal Party, composed of wealthy and conservative Filipinos favorable to American rule, offered the country an alternative to Aguinaldo's lingering movement.

The results of MacArthur's more systematic and militant policy showed in the battle statistics. During September and October 1900, at the height of the election campaign, there were 241 clashes, 52 of these labeled as "aggressive" on the part of the insurgents. During November and December, however, the number of clashes was reduced to 198, and only 27 of these were classified as aggressive. During September and October only 54 guerrillas surrendered; in the months of November and December 2,534 came in. In February 1901, moreover, the enlistment of natives from the Maccabee tribe (the same tribe that had earlier helped the Spanish) began the auxiliary "Scout" troops that aided the U.S. considerably in intelligence and reconnaissance functions.

It was a troop of Scouts, in fact, that a month later abetted the United States in what undoubtedly was its greatest single "maneuver" of the entire war: the capture of Aguinaldo. More than any other event, this ruse de guerre broke the guerrilla resistance and, coming as it did in the wake of McKinley's victory and General MacArthur's new toughness, sealed for good the fate of the Philippine Republic. U.S. Brigadier General Frederick Funston discovered through a captured insurgent that Aguinaldo, still directing the war from his hideout in northeastern Luzon, needed 400 more guerrillas immediately.

Exploiting this rare piece of intelligence, Funston used 81 Maccabee Scouts as guerrilla replacements, with himself and four other American officers disguised as prisoners. After a strenuous march of over 100 miles this extraordinary group penetrated Aguinaldo's heretofore unknown retreat, took him prisoner and returned triumphant to American territory.

Soon afterward, the ex-rebel chieftain swore allegiance to the American flag and delivered an appeal for surrender. Funston emerged as probably the only legitimate hero from this nasty and increasingly vicious guerrilla war. He was subsequently given a commission as a

Brigadier General in the regular army, in addition to the Congressional Medal of Honor. With plaudits coming from all corners of the nation, there was even talk of running him for the presidency in 1904. Aguinaldo dropped from public life for good.

With the leader of the insurrection out of the picture, the fighting in the main area of Luzon subsided considerably. In the rest of the islands, ambushes, raids and covert resistance to U.S. authority went on but, increasingly, the rebellion began to resemble the writhing death throes of a headless body. Between June and September of 1901 scores of officers and over 4,000 formerly active insurgents had surrendered. By June of the same year the number of U.S. troops in the Philippines had been reduced to 42,000, and over 23,000 insurgent rifles had already been collected.

President McKinley was assassinated on September 14, 1901. At about this time, the political phase of the U.S. strategy moved into high gear. It was reinforced by the iron political will of the new President, Theodore Roosevelt, that the American cause in the Philippines was irreversible. As one U.S. general put it, "We have got to live among these people, we have got to govern them. Government by force alone cannot be satisfactory to Americans."[20]

Political action began in the capital, Manila, where insurgents had cut the water supply and where near-anarchy prevailed. U.S. administrators cleaned up the filth off the streets and provided free medical care to the near half-million residents, including the vaccination of thousands in a massive campaign against spreading diseases. As the Americans fanned out beyond the capital they distributed food, sanitized cities and towns, and released thousands of political prisoners. Hundreds of schools were built or rebuilt, often with soldiers as instructors.

Washington then gradually began transferring administrative authority from military officers to civil authorities. In 1900 a Philippine Commission, headed by the Ohio judge and future President William Howard Taft, was dispatched to the Philippines with authority to supervise all phases of the intervention, including, eventually, even the military. Beginning in September, all legislative power of the government was exercised by this commission. During the first few months in which it exercised legislative powers, Taft's group passed 157 acts dealing with almost every conceivable phase of administrative life: civil service, education, war relief, sanitation, mining, forestry, the administration of justice, tax collection, the regulation of commerce, etc. In effect, the Taft Commission supervised all the essential, non-military policies of the Philippine islands.

In the provinces that were not deemed sufficiently pacified for the full inauguration of civilian rule, the military still exercised authority. As fast as pacified provinces could be organized and civilian rule established, they were removed from military jurisdiction and placed under Taft's supervision. By the middle of 1901, civil government had begun in 22 of the archipelago's 77 provinces, but these constituted about half the full population of the country (approximately seven out of fourteen million). In the remaining provinces in which military rule still prevailed, resistance to U.S. authority continued, but it was not as intense or as systematic as before. These areas were relatively wild and sparsely settled and some of them had not even been occupied by the Spanish. But by September 1901, 13 more provinces were placed under civil authorities, with the insurrection clearly on its last legs.

For the most part, American counterguerrilla policies against the Philippine insurgents employed the use of force judiciously. There was (of course) no airpower, no sustained artillery, no massive campaigns of excessive firepower and little, if any "collateral damage." Yet, there were occasions of individual severity and prisoner abuse. The use of the infamous "water cure" against POW's brought out a nationwide domestic protest, which curtailed its use. The brutal campaign of destruction and burning waged by U.S. General Jacob ("Howling Jake") Smith in Samar likewise resulted in political backlash and a court martial. Yet, the victory in the Philippines was a result of effective political warfare, what General Edward Lansdale would in a later generation label as a campaign where the U.S. "out-revolutionized" the revolutionaries.

Compared to the Taft Commission and the Republican Party that governed the islands, Aguinaldo was a social conservative. This remarkable transformation and political irony was also extended to Mindanao province, where the majority Muslim population had always resisted the authority of Catholic Manila. Here, the sensitivities of the Muslims, known as Moros, were recognized by General John J. Pershing, who spent many years there in effective political warfare against fanatic religious terrorists. Because of the Moros the U.S. had to develop the .45 caliber pistol, the standard .38 being too small to stop a charging Moro tribesman.

Pershing and his staff applied this effective firepower with a divide and rule policy, which combined with local civic action to eventually erode Muslim resistance. Divide and rule kept the Moros from uniting while economic development projects, local "trade fairs" and other civic improvements attracted them to the occupation. This was new to Mindanao, quite the opposite from four centuries of Spanish repression, and proved sufficient to placate much of the extreme (and often drugged) behavior of these aborigine terrorists.

Hukbalahaps:
Defeating the insurgents with political warfare

William Howard Taft was a product of the Ohio Republican political machine, which had originally elected President McKinley, who once admitted that he couldn't identify the Philippines on a map within 2,000 miles. Taft, who had a similar background, was thus a most unlikely candidate for intuitive and creative political warfare in distant, hostile climes.

Yet, by the time he had ascended to the presidency in 1909, the political warfare policies developed by his commission in the Philippines had helped overturn centuries of Spanish rule and had effectively ended guerrilla and terrorist resistance by the disciplined and American-hating insurgents. These insurgents had a nationalist base and widespread support, but the Americans won the war, stayed for the long haul and, in retrospect, waged *political warfare* years before the term even entered the vocabulary.

Still, in 1901 the notion of a policy of attraction was way ahead of its time. The image of the 350-pound Taft, who danced into the night with tiny Filipino women and embraced the men as America's "little brown brothers," never appealed to the military. A popular barracks ballad of the time expressed the soldier's disdain for political warfare: "He may be a brother of Big Bill Taft, But he ain't no brother of mine."

Let us now fast forward nearly a half-century, to the post-World War II political arena, amidst a burgeoning Cold War, which saw a fast-rising Communist insurrection infecting nearly every island of the newly-independent Philippines. The counter-guerrilla war against the Communist Hukbalahap ("Huks" or "People's Army"), and their leader Luis Taruc, had certain similarities with the original insurrection, except that American foreign policy, preoccupied with Europe, was unable to support the Philippine government with ground forces. If this war was to be won, it would be (almost) entirely up to the Filipinos themselves.

U.S. support was consisted of aid and advice, in particular the assistance brokered by Air Force General Edward G. Lansdale. The ultimate eventual defeat of the Huk insurrection in 1953 was largely the work of one of the greatest political-military combinations in modern history: the American, Lansdale, and the brilliant Philippine Defense Minister, Ramon Magsaysay. These two were instrumental in the tactical and technical devices which turned a losing and frustrating counterinsurgency, led by infantry and firepower, into a high-powered political warfare machine which turned the tables on Taruc and the Philippine Communists.

Huk resistance in the remote areas of the Philippines began against the Japanese during World War II and was quickly converted into an anti-government, Communist-dominated effort by 1946. Initially, the Manila government reacted with standard operating principles learned from the American occupation forces. Typically, however, successful resistance to the Huks occurred only after the initial period of trial and error using conventional tactics had failed to produce results. Worse, the ponderous military sweeps conducted by Philippine armor, aircraft and artillery – backed by U.S. aid – initially helped recruit more peasant sympathizers to the Communist cause, and its land-reformist propaganda. Estimates of active peasant support of the Huks hovered around 10% of the population, with 10% opposed, leaving the vast middle 80% as fertile ground for either side. Peasant dissatisfaction with the government's incapacity to implement land reform initiatives was seized upon by Huk activists as proof of official complacency and incompetence.

Active, large-scale military measures in peasant areas only made matters worse. Unable to obtain reliable intelligence from disaffected peasants, the government began the time-honored conventional tactic of isolating the insurgency through the type of "cordons" the U.S. used in the Caribbean or the British "blockhouse" tactic employed in South Africa. In the Philippines they were called *zonas,* whereby targeted villages would be screened off from the outside by troops, the intention being to "isolate" the guerrilla "fish" from the "sea" of his support. These methods, awkward as they may have been, worked in other circumstances, but failed in the Philippines, principally since they reminded peasants of identical policies used by Japan in the late war. Large-scale search and destroy operations, another favored army tactic, also backfired. As related by Huk guerrilla chief Luis Taruc, these operations rarely found sufficient numbers of Huks to justify their effort:

> If we knew it was going to be a light attack, we took it easy. If it might give us more trouble than we could handle, we slipped out quietly in the darkest hours of the night, abandoning the area of operation altogether... it could be both amusing and saddening to watch the Philippine Air Force busily bombing and strafing, or to see thousands of government troops and civil guards cordoning our campsite and saturating, with every type of gunfire, the unfortunate trees and vegetation. Or we would watch them, worn and weary,

scaling the whole height and width of a mountain, with not a single Huk in the area.[21]

After six years of such army, Taruc estimated that exactly 12 guerrillas had been killed.

Other army methods also played into the hands of the irregulars. These included notorious "open area" firing techniques, whereby troops were instructed to shoot at anything that moved within certain field zones, road checkpoints, which allowed soldiers to rob peasants at will and the "Nenita" units, which consisted of gangs of ruthless killers who murdered peasants indiscriminately, often without proof of Huk allegiance.

By 1950, Huk resistance, aided by clever "agitprop" political warfare tactics throughout central Luzon, had produced a steady growth of peasant support. With an active insurgent force of about 12,000, Huk strength in Luzon relied upon approximately 150,000 peasant villagers within a population of nearly two million people. But the tide of Huk power began to wane after 1950, when internal dissension and tactical confusions, including the lack of a sustained geographic sanctuary and poor overall coordination led to a decline in Communist appeal and effectiveness.

The insurgents' own heavy-handed terror also helped turn the course of the war against them. Most important in this regard, however, was not so much a loss of Huk resolve, but, rather, a remarkable surge in the popular approval and tactical sophistication of governmental counter-measures. Under the leadership of newly-installed Defense Minister Magsaysay in 1950, the Philippines had finally found strategic solutions to the insurgency riddle.

By then, both the U.S. team and the Philippine government were ready to wage authentic counter-guerrilla war. After four years of trial and error the government had begun to discover that light infantry units, armed civilians and special scout squads operated best against insurgents. Two of the Philippine governments' best military leaders, N.D. Valeriano and C.T. Bohannan, described how a variety of small patrol tactics were able to keep the Huk guerrillas on the run:

> [there were] regular patrols which passed through specified areas almost on a schedule, following roads or trails. There were unscheduled, unexpected patrols, sometimes following an expected one by fifteen minutes. There were patrols following eccentric routes, eccentric schedules, moving cross-country at right angles to normal travel patterns, which often unexpectedly intercepted scheduled patrols.[22]

With Magsaysay installed as defense minister, and with Lansdale constantly at his side, important political reforms emerged. Lansdale arrived in the Philippines in September 1950; the Huk rebellion would be over within two years. After surveying the wreckage that the military had left in its wake, Lansdale concluded that "the most urgent need was to construct a political base for supporting the fight. Without it, the Philippine armed forces would be model examples of applied military doctrine, but would go on losing."[23] Once a viable political base had been established, he believed, it would be able "to mount a bold, imaginative and popular campaign against the Huk guerrillas."[24] Political warfare had become the counterinsurgency norm.

A key element of the new political offensive engineered by Lansdale was the psychological dimension. Noting that, "at the time I arrived in the Philippines, the Huks clearly outmatched the government in this weapon," he immediately set out to change this imbalance.[25] The Huks followed the Communist tradition by using slogans as an approach to the peasantry. Posters proclaiming, "Land for the Landless" and "Ballots not Bullets" recalled Lenin's earlier appeals to Russian masses for "Peace, Land and Bread." Such slogans may seem simplistic to post-industrialized suburbia but that very simplicity was, in fact, their inner appeal to the target audience. The slogans told a story and offered hope with a few words, something now off-handedly called a "soundbite" in sophisticated American newsrooms, but is in reality much more powerful.

The Huks had an organizational structure for their psychological operations. Each military unit contained a political officer in charge of propaganda, morale-boosting, self-criticism and agitprop. These latter operated in secrecy throughout the population, producing propaganda leaflets, gossip and other "whispering" campaigns.

Lansdale and his team began their own campaign to "out-revolutionize the revolutionaries." He created a Civil Affairs Office, (dubbed "cow") to train personnel and soldiers to undertake "peoples war." Each Battalion Combat Team (BCT) was assigned a CAO section trained to instruct troops in the proper behavior toward the civilian population, as Lansdale put it, "to make the soldiers behave as the brothers and protectors of the people... replacing the arrogance of the military" which had plagued civil-military relations to a low point.[26] Lansdale invented the term "civic action," which has since become the universally accepted term for such activity.

In the Philippines this new kind of warfare began with a transformation of attitude and behavior. The government and army began assisting farmers in land courts, care of civilian casualties in hospitals was improved, soldiers undertook cheap labor in peasant areas and a widespread program of agrarian credit converted the rural peasantry from bitterly opposing the government to actively assisting it against the Huks. The soldiers were instructed to talk with the population and attend local events. The result was a transformation of "raw take" tactical intelligence on Huk movements, often in less than a week's time.

Defense Minister Magsaysay and Lansdale personally toured affected provinces, overseeing projects of civic action, including the construction of "Liberty Wells" for pure water. Propaganda teams attended local fairs and parties, distributing pro-government leaflets and announcing civic action programs through bullhorns that Lansdale personally brought in from the U.S. With the cooperation of the Roman Catholic Church, Lansdale and Magsaysay arranged to infiltrate Huk areas with government sympathizers, who conducted on-ground "whispering" campaigns against the Communists and their anti-Catholic messages and methods. Propaganda via the airwaves was introduced by establishing radio stations in barrios and distributing receiving sets throughout the population.

"Dirty tricks" were also part of civic action. The Huks had been buying weapons and ammunition from corrupt government suppliers. Lansdale discovered the chain of supply and Magsaysay gave them an "offer they couldn't refuse." Rather than being prosecuted it was arranged that faulty and contaminated material be sent to Huk guerrillas. Grenades and rifles began exploding prematurely in Huk hands and weapons refused to fire at all. Within weeks of this operation, illicit sale to the Huks ground to a halt.

Lansdale also played on local superstitions and cultures as a means of political warfare. In Philippine cultural lore an *asuang*, or vampire, haunted interior regions at night. Regular troops in many of these areas had been unable to move against Huk strongholds until a combat psywar team began planting stories that an *asuang* was living in Huk-infested hills. The psywar squad killed a Huk insurgent and punctured his neck with two holes, vampire-fashion, then held the body up by the heels and drained it of blood, and finally put the corpse back on the trail. The following day there were no Huk guerrillas within miles of the area.

Human intelligence was also a mainstay of the political counter-revolution. With the Huks trying hard to recruit manpower, Lansdale arranged for a large number of volunteer agents to infiltrate Huk units. Many of them not only provided critical intelligence to the army but rose rapidly in the Huk command structure. Aware that many of their own men might secretly be government agents, many Huk irregulars converted and turned themselves in.

The concept of civic action by the military was introduced and the Army was instructed to improve troop behavior toward civilians. Corruption was cut down and discipline in both the Army and government improved. Magsaysay was running a tight ship. He eliminated "free fire" areas, which killed innocent civilians but had been a primary tactic of conventional troops. Interrogation techniques were made more civilized and soldiers went into local "barrios" armed with food, clothing and medical supplies. Magsaysay was beating the enemy on his own terms, offering hope of a better future and eliminating the source of Filipino grievances against the government. He also came to realize that local armies recruited from within the population, especially those with personal reasons to enlist, provided the best anti-guerrilla personnel. Additionally, the fact that Americans were *not* involved as ground troops helped the cause immeasurably. As a Philippine lieutenant colonel wrote at the time:

> Foreign troops are certain to be less welcome among the people than are the regular armed forces of their own government. Local populations will shelter their own people against operations of foreign troops, even though those they shelter may be outlaws. For this reason, native troops would be more effective than foreign forces in operations against native communist conspirators. It would be rare, indeed, if the use of foreign troops would not in itself doom to failure an anti-guerrilla campaign.[27]

Gradually, the civilian populace came over as Huk support eroded fast. An imaginative propaganda campaign complete with loudspeakers, leaflets and other popular devices, gained even more adherents. The institution of a system of rewards for information about suspected Huks helped turn the insurgents to the defensive. The government instituted land reforms and a generous amnesty program convinced thousands of Huks to abandon the war. In effect, the Magsaysay-Lansdale team usurped the Communist call for land reform by making that issue the lead item in the government's 1951 political campaign. The politicians were mastering counterinsurgency in areas where soldiers never dreamed of going.

The November 1951 elections were fair and free. Philippine troops guarded public meetings to prevent Huk coercion and high school students and ROTC cadets guarded polling places. In a turnout of more than four million (where five million were registered) the army transferred and guarded ballot boxes in full view of both the local public and American press and observers. The result was a definitive victory for democracy and a crushing defeat for the Huk insurrection.

As a final blow against the communist guerrillas, the election allowed Lansdale an opportunity to "pay them back in their own psychological coin. And I took it."[28]

Lansdale had used authentic Huk ID material and, via agitprop cells, succeeded in planting "Boycott the Election" instructions into Huk propaganda channels. The ruse succeeded beyond imagination and within days the entire Huk apparatus was defiantly urging a boycott on voters. As Lansdale himself related, this psywar deception felled the Huk movement for good:

> Then came election day and its shockers for their side: the huge turnout of voters and the clear evidence of honest ballots. The government forces, the press, and the citizen volunteers ... publicly called to the attention of the Huks and their sympathizers how wrong had been their predictions about the election. Ballots, not bullets, were what counted! If the Huk leaders could be so wrong this time, then in how many other things had they been wrong all along? Why should anyone follow them anymore? The Huk rank and file starting echoing these sentiments, and Huk morale skidded. Groups of Huks began to come into army camps, voluntarily surrendering and commenting bitterly that they had been misled by their leaders. Well, it was true enough. They had.[29]

Within eighteen months of taking office, Magsaysay, with help from his U.S. advisors, had stopped the Communist insurgency in its tracks and had employed a variety of political measures as front line strategies. In retrospect, the Huk insurgency in the Philippines was a true popular rebellion, which had originated during the war to harass the Japanese occupation. Magsaysay and his team ended the war by employing even more popular measures, combined with police-style battle tactics. The example of the Philippine government's victory and the role of Lansdale and the other American advisors had considerable influence among counterinsurgency specialists in the years immediately prior to American intervention in Vietnam. This model succeeded spectacularly in 1980's El Salvador, and represents to this day, classic examples of the superiority of policies of attraction versus policies of suppression.

The Philippine experience against the Huks, however, went generally unheeded within the U.S. military hierarchy. Most U.S. military leaders instinctively preferred conventional tactics and weapons, regardless of circumstances. The post-World War II U.S. Army *Field Service Regulations*, for example, had only eight paragraphs on guerrilla war.

While the vast experience of Americans in the Philippines, twice within a half-century, was able to produce outstanding results, neither experience was incorporated into official strategic doctrine nor were either of these cases appreciated by the general public. They are seen even today as isolated instances, brought up episodically rather than as ingrained strategic guidelines or as tactical models. The net legacy still treats insurrection and guerrilla/terrorism as *aberrations*, rather than recurrent challenges consistent with the timeless tactics of those insurgents in the world who lack the regular means and tactics to challenge nation-states and their military machines.

Conclusion

In some ways insurrection in the Philippines has never ended. Ramon Magsaysay translated his popularity into electoral power and won the presidency in 1953 and began a series of long-overdue social reforms. These came to an abrupt halt with his tragic demise in an airplane crash four years later. The subsequent dictatorship of Ferdinand Marcos, from 1972 – 1986, ran parallel with another surge in the historic Muslim uprisings in remote Mindanao.

The guerrilla/terrorist army of the Moro National Liberation Front (MNLF) plus another Communist resurgence by the Maoist National Democratic Front and its military wing, the New People's Army (NPA), have terrorized peasant areas of the Philippines in an insurrection now into its fifth decade with no end in sight. These areas are now critical theatres for the Global War on Terrorism, but it remains to be seen whether the lessons gained by the U.S. in the twentieth century will be applied in the twenty-first. The evidence is inconclusive, but one fact remains clear: this mission is far from accomplished.

Should the United States opt for a conventional solution against these Islamists, as it has in Iraq, the results will be still another quagmire. Should the U.S., on the other hand, apply a creative political and psychological warfare strategy, as it did against the Huks, it will have a good chance for a positive outcome.

Notes

[1] Donald Rumsfeld, memorandum dated October 16, 2003, cited in *USA Today*, October 22, 2003.

[2] Editor's note: For greater treatment of this subject, see the author's book on insurgency, John J. Tierney, *Chasing Ghosts: Unconventional Warfare in American History* (Potomac Books, 2006).

[3] James E. Dougherty, "The Guerrilla War in Malaya," *U.S. Naval Institute Proceedings*, September 1958.

[4] Leon Wolff, *Little Brown Brother* (Doubleday, 1961), p. 221.

[5] William T. Sexton, *Soldiers in the Sun* (Books for Libraries Press, 1939), p. 97.

[6] Robert N. Ginsburgh, "Damn the Insurrectors," *Military Review*, January 1964, p. 62.

[7] Sexton, p. 136.

[8] James E. LeRoy, *The Americans in the Philippines* (Houghton-Mifflin Co., 1914), Vol. II, p. 54.

[9] Sexton, pp. 184-185.

[10] Ibid., p. 198.

[11] Wolff, p. 289.

[12] LeRoy, p. 162.

[13] Wolff, p. 311.

[14] Ibid.

[15] Ibid.

[16] LeRoy, p. 245.

[17] See, for example, Daniel B. Schirmer, *Republic or Empire: American Resistance to the Philippine War* (Schenkmen Publishing Co., 1972).

[18] Wolfe, p. 262.

[19] Ibid, p. 252.

[20] Anthony J. Joes, *America and Guerrilla Warfare* (Lexington: University of Kentucky Press, 2000), p. 114.

[21] Luis Taruc, *He Who Rides the Tiger* (Praeger's, 1967), p. 42.

[22] N.D. Valeriano and C.T. Bohannan, *Counterguerrila Operations - The Philippine Experience* (Praeger's, 1962), p. 130.

[23] Joint Army-Air Force Low Intensity Project, p. 160.

[24] Ibid.

[25] Edward G. Lansdale, *In the Midst of Wars.* (Fordham University Press, 1991), p. 69.

[26] Lansdale, p. 70.

[27] Joint Army-Air Force Low Intensity Project, op. cit.

[28] Lansdale, p. 92.

[29] Ibid., p. 93.

13

The Importance of Words
In Message-Making

J. MICHAEL WALLER

Introduction

Words and images are the most powerful weapons in a war of ideas. Used skillfully, they can serve the cause well. Used carelessly, they cause collateral damage and the equivalent of death by friendly fire. Effective messages require understanding, development, and deployment of the proper words – not only as Americans understand them in English, but as the rest of the world understands them in many cultural contexts. Message-making requires sophisticated understanding of both friend and enemy. It requires confident self-knowledge. It requires instinct about how information works today. Most of all, successful message-making requires personal courage against critics abroad and at home. Inexpert use of words undermines the mission and inadvertently aids the enemy every bit as much as the careless dropping of bombs or the military indiscipline that made Abu Ghraib a metaphor for America's presence in Iraq.

In this chapter, we:

- study how words are used as instruments of conflict and weapons of warfare;
- look at how the meanings of words differ among languages and cultures, and often within the same language and culture;
- examine how the nation's adversaries and enemies have used our own understandings of words against us, and how we accepted those hostile definitions as our own; and

- discuss how we can take the language back from the enemy and make it work for the wartime and long-term interests of civilized society.

Words as weapons

The human mind is the battlespace of the war of ideas. Words and images create, define and elaborate ideas, and are used to popularize or destroy their appeal. They require relentless repetition. Words are not static objects. The written and spoken word, as George Orwell said, can be used "as an instrument which we shape for our own purposes." In his famous essay "Politics and the English Language," Orwell explained the relationship between language and thought: "if thought corrupts language, language can also corrupt thought. A bad usage can spread by tradition and imitation, even among people who should and do know better."[1]

Deliberate and unwitting corruption of language and thought applies as much to law, literature, love, marketing and politics as it does to diplomacy and warfare. Like iron, words can be forged from plowshares into swords and back again. Men have been using words to fight wars since the beginning of recorded history. Thucydides, in his monumental history of the Peloponnesian Wars, noted how the upturning of society during the Corcycrean civil war of 427 B.C. was paralleled by distortion of language on the part of the combatants:

> To fit in with the change of events, words, too, had to change their usual meanings. What used to be described as a thoughtless act of aggression was now regarded as the courage one would expect to find in a party member; to think of the future and wait was merely another way of saying one was a coward; any idea of moderation was just an attempt to disguise one's unmanly character; ability to understand a question from all sides meant that one was totally unfitted for action. Fanatical enthusiasm was the mark of a real man...[2]

Terms of moral judgment were used to describe actions and events wholly alien to their true meanings, so that men could better justify deeds that would have been deemed reprehensible in times of peace. The chaos that resulted from the devious political manipulation of words did much to exacerbate the conflict and serves an early example of the power of rhetoric in conflict.

Niccolò Machiavelli, the 15th century Florentine political philosopher and strategist, revolutionized statecraft in the western Christian world with his cynical, often amoral guidebook *The Prince*.

His plays on words, invented definitions and purposeful distortions of language were part of his craft, yet most translators of his works, according to Angelo Codevilla of Boston University, attempted to fix what they saw as Machiavelli's errors of syntax and usage, and inadvertently denied readers of English an accurate understanding of the use of words as weapons. Codevilla translated *The Prince* with as faithful a preservation possible of Machiavelli's word games, making heavy annotations throughout. The result was a richer if less smooth-sounding translation that offered a deeper understanding of Machiavelli's devious mind.[3]

The idealistic architects of American independence two-and-a-half centuries after Machiavelli saw word meanings change with their own ideas. They viewed themselves as patriotic Englishmen living in America, loyal to king and empire. Their grievance was that in America, the crown was denying them their rights as Englishmen.

By 1769, Samuel Adams in Boston began successfully changing public opinion so that the loyal English patriot in America seeking his just rights was now an American patriot. One by one, over the years, other colonial leaders underwent the same transformation. Words and political organization were Adams' sole weapons, and the incendiary political strategist used them well. More than most, Adams recognized and worried about the enemy's distortion of language: "How strangely will the Tools of a Tyrant pervert the plain Meaning of Words!"[4]

Free people must safeguard their languages. They must jealously protect the true meanings of words. Czechoslovakian President Vaclav Havel, just as the Soviet bloc was collapsing in 1989, warned the Western democracies about words and their double-edged power to corrode and demoralize the good. "Alongside words that electrify society with their freedom and truthfulness, we have words that mesmerize, deceive, inflame, madden, beguile, words that are harmful – lethal even," Havel said. Giving example after example, the former political prisoner-playwright-turned-president noted, "The same word can, at one moment, radiate great hope; at another, it can emit lethal rays. The same word can be true at one moment and false the next, at one moment illuminating, at another deceptive."

Havel's strongest example was the word *peace*: "For forty years, an allergy to that beautiful word has been engendered in me, as it has in every one of my fellow citizens, because I know what the word has meant here for all those forty years: ever mightier armies ostensibly to defend peace."[5]

Semantics and rhetoric

Semantics, derived from the Greek *semantikos*, for "significant" or "significant meaning," is "the branch of linguistics and logic concerned with meaning," according to the Oxford dictionary. Webster gives semantics a more operational definition: "the language used (as in advertising or political propaganda) to achieve a desired effect on an audience especially through the use of words with novel or dual meanings." The first cousin of semantics is rhetoric, the ancient art of using expression and language effectively in order to persuade.

Even Aristotle, who produced the first systematic treatment of rhetoric and invented the idea of logic, saw the dark side of the art as well as the bright. To Aristotle, rhetoric consisted of three "proofs" of persuasion: *logos* (words), *ethos* (character of the speaker), and *pathos* (the psychological element).[6] A competent rhetorician could argue through use of words in a logical form to move popular passion, explain complicated ideas simply, whip up emotions and calm down hatred and fear. Aristotle discussed how rhetoric fits in a democratic society. He seemed torn by his own idea. Among his concerns about the use of rhetoric was the danger that in the hands of the wrong people, the art could be a destructive weapon. We can conclude from Aristotle that, like any weapon, rhetoric is a danger when used by the enemy and when used carelessly, by ourselves. Democratic forces must not be unilaterally disarmed. They must be thoroughly trained, enculturated and mobilized to be as adept with words as they are with precision arms.

Americans in government have lost the art of rhetoric as an instrument of statecraft, though many of the Founding Fathers, including Samuel Adams, were devoted students of Aristotle. Sixty years ago Orwell saw a sharp decline in the skillful use of language among English-speaking politicians and journalists. He warned after World War II that if the trend continued, the societies and leaders of the English-speaking world would find that poor use of language would corrupt their thought processes and alter their perceptions of their own civilizations. Critics of today's "political correctness" movement would agree.

Twenty-first century Americans have demonstrated little inclination or ability to use language effectively in the war of ideas abroad, showing much greater facility and ease with destroying fellow human beings physically as a first option, instead of trying to "destroy" the pernicious ideologies that fuel their hostile will. Yet they use semantics and rhetoric instinctively and skillfully in fighting political wars against one another at home, with politicians of all stripes routinely using

military jargon in their civil discourse and action.[7] One can see how the
political lines are drawn about any one issue by picking out the
wording that a faction consciously or unconsciously uses. Each side
employs idealistic or distorted language to promote one's own views
while demonizing or otherwise delegitimizing the positions of the
other.[8]

Complications of culture

Cross-linguistic and cross-cultural factors complicate semantics and
rhetoric, especially where there is no Webster to standardize
definitions, and where meaning is in the beholder's mind. To
demonstrate how even some of the most successful communicators can
fail by misunderstanding semantics, many marketing and business texts
and seminars point to a disastrous mistake that General Motors is said
to have made in the 1960's when it sold one of its most successful U.S.
models, the Chevrolet Nova, in Latin America. To a Spanish-speaker,
some textbooks say, the English word Nova sounds similar to the
Spanish expression *no va*, which means "won't go." Understandably,
despite a reversed syllabic order, the unintended slogan "Chevy won't
go" helped explain the car's poor regional sales and why GM changed
the name for Spanish-speaking markets.

Or so the storytellers said. The tale is an urban legend. The Chevy
Nova, in fact, sold well in Latin America as the Nova. In trying to show
how ignorant the world's largest automaker could be despite its army of
Spanish-speaking marketers and dealers, the legend's purveyors and
believers display their own lack of cultural awareness. They presume
that English words and phrases have exactly the same meaning when
translated literally to or from other languages. The Nova/*no va* blunder
simply does not translate. Cars might "go" in English, but not in
Spanish. Depending on regional word usage and the age of the speaker,
automobiles "walk" (*caminar*), "march" (*marchar*), "function"
(*funcionar*) or "serve" (*servir*). Cars that "go" and "run" sound as
absurd to the Spanish speaker's ear as cars that walk and march sound
to the ear of the native speaker of English.

The entirety of the Nova myth, from the false story itself to its
almost unquestioned repetition, illustrates how misunderstanding of
even the most familiar foreign languages and cultures can affect our
perceptions of the rest of the world, both as we see other peoples and as
we attempt to deliver messages to change perceptions, attitudes and
behavior abroad.[9] Our main sources of public information, political
leaders and journalists, use foreign words and expressions in their own
daily written and verbal communication, and inject them into public

discourse. Satisfied with popular usage or Webster's American English definition, many fail to double-check with linguists or scholars about the precise or varied meanings, and many occasionally repeat "new" words, readily accepting them at face value without regard to the source, and pass them and the distortions of their meanings to the public and decisionmakers.

Those distortions, a form of shorthand that becomes unverifiable "known facts," affect the new users' perceptions and can adversely influence policy. Unquestioned acceptance or repetition of the distorted words can cause fundamental misunderstandings, and not only at home. By their cumulative repetition in the press and in public statements they can be politically or diplomatically damaging abroad as well. Our adversaries can and do exploit this weakness with relative ease and without our awareness.

Defensive mechanism

We in the United States have no institutional defense against our own misinterpretations of true meanings, or against the conscious efforts of adversaries to induce or reinforce our own misunderstandings. Concerned about the problem during the heated years of the Cold War, the U.S. Advisory Commission on Public Diplomacy reported,

> We believe that the times require a conscious effort to improve the accuracy and political impact of words and terms used by our leaders in speaking to the world. By so doing, they can help disclose the hypocrisy and distortions of hostile propaganda. This is not a problem that will go away, and we must be prepared to deal with it on a systematic and continuing basis.

The commissioners recommended:

> that a task force be created, under the National Security Council and including representatives of the Departments of State and Defense and USIA [US Information Agency], to assess the problem and propose an institutionalized means to respond to inaccurate or misleading terminology in international political discourse.[10]

The recommendation was not to form a task force to counter disinformation; the White House National Security Council already had an interagency working group and USIA had established a new office for that purpose.[11] Nor would the task force craft positive messages about the United States, which was one of the decades-long public diplomacy missions of the USIA as a whole. The commissioners were referring specifically to a task force devoted words and terms that, through misuse or abuse, had the unintended consequence of aiding the enemy.

Semantic infiltration

A war of ideas is well-fought when a skilled or persistent semanticist can persuade an opponent to accept his terms of debate, especially when the words are those that form the ideas that motivate the will. The opponent thus unwittingly, even willingly, adopts the semanticist's usage of words and by extension, the ideas, perceptions and policies that accompany them. Fred Charles Iklé, in a 1970's Rand Corporation study on the difficulties the United States faced in negotiating with Communist regimes, called the phenomenon "semantic infiltration." According to Iklé,

> Paradoxically, despite the fact that the State Department and other government agencies bestow so much care on the vast verbal output of Communist governments, we have been careless in adopting the language of our opponents and their definitions of conflict issues in many cases where this is clearly to our disadvantage.
>
> Or perhaps this is not so paradoxical. It might be precisely because our officials spend so much time on the opponents' rhetoric that they eventually use his words – first in quotation marks, later without.[12]

Commenting on Iklé's paper, the late Senator Daniel Patrick Moynihan called semantic infiltration "the systematic distortion of the meaning of certain words to confuse or mislead." Semantic infiltration, said Moynihan,

> is the process whereby we come to adopt the language of our adversaries in describing political reality. The most brutal totalitarian regimes in the world call themselves 'liberation movements.' It is perfectly predictable that they should misuse words to conceal their real nature. But must we aid them in that effort by repeating those words? Worse, do we begin to influence our own perceptions by using them?[13]

By adopting communist labels, the senator and former U.N. ambassador argued, the State Department bought into the enemy's rhetoric and adversely affected U.S. attitudes toward a particular conflict. In Moynihan's words,

Even though the State Department proclaimed its neutrality in the conflict there, its very choice of words – its use of the vocabulary of groups opposed to our values – undermined the legitimacy of the pro-Western political forces in the area. We pay for small concessions at the level of language with large setbacks at the level of practical politics.[14]

That "totalitarians will seek to seize control of the language of politics is obvious; that our own foreign affairs establishment should remain blind to what is happening is dangerous," Moynihan said. Soft-line foreign service officers weren't the only culprits. Even some of the staunchest hard-liners proved susceptible in Moynihan's time, as they can today, to semantic infiltration.

The worst totalitarians of Moynihan's era, the Soviets, mastered the use of semantics in political warfare, corrupting positive words like "democratic," "fraternal," "liberation," "progressive," "people" and, as Havel noted later, "peace," and applying them to totalitarian and terrorist regimes and movements.[15] It was as if the West had stopped believing in its own values. American officials often shied away from using those words in defense of U.S. policy. Worse, they sometimes applied them in ways that benefited Soviet propaganda. They even were reluctant to turn Soviet jargon against Moscow, shying from calling the USSR a dictatorship or empire and deriding those who did. "Soviet imperialism" was almost never a term of U.S. public diplomacy; the State Department ceded the words – and thus the ideas – to the Politburo to dominate.

For example, many in the American media and politics referred to Soviet-backed insurgent groups as "liberation movements," idealistic and selfless manifestations of oppressed people's democratic aspirations for social justice. Radical protests in Europe against the U.S. and NATO were led by "peace activists," when in reality they were always anti-American and never anti-Soviet, never truly pro-peace. They were, indeed, under the influence or control of the KGB and Soviet-controlled fronts.[16] Some Americans denounced their government's efforts to halt Soviet expansionism as "American imperialism," a made-in-Moscow epithet that has long outlived the USSR. Few in the mainstream ever referred to Soviet expansionism in an imperialistic light until after the Soviet collapse in 1991.[17] Meanwhile, the Soviets raged against American "imperialism" while U.S. officials cringed and sneered at calling the USSR an empire, even after their president did. Though few really believed that the Soviets were committed to "peace," these critics considered the U.S. and

NATO the more clear and present dangers. Most of the world completely accepted and unwittingly helped to spread misleading communist jargon like "German Democratic Republic" and "People's Republic of China," validating totalitarian propaganda that suggested these regimes were republics of, for, and by the people.

Indeed, during the Cold War, Soviet use of peace propaganda had made many in the West so cynical that those who understood the Soviet danger best, from the center-left Havel to Reaganite conservatives, had difficulty using the word "peace" constructively or even with a straight face. Such was the noxiousness of Soviet political warfare: civilized society lost control of the ideas that peace animated, and the Soviets hijacked naïve western hopes and fears by infiltrating, funding and manipulating the peace movements in the democracies.

Those who saw through the propaganda were usually ideologically hostile to the Soviets and communism. However, they generally responded not by taking back the word but by allowing the Soviets to redirect their propaganda victory, and declaring the "peace" movement to be nothing more than a sham of dupes and fools, hippies, sellouts, and often traitors. Some proudly proclaimed their militancy against the Soviet threat with statements and actions that reasonable but ill-informed people could perceive as being truly anti-peace. Until a communicator like Reagan arrived to lead, and even long afterwards, many anti-Soviet intellectuals used rhetoric and policies that alarmed the soft middle-of-the-roaders who found the KGB line so soothing. They ended up playing into the hands of Soviet propagandists.

Havel noted the difference: "The same word can be humble at one moment and arrogant the next. And a humble word can be transformed easily and imperceptibly into an arrogant one, whereas it is a difficult and protracted process to transform an arrogant word into one that is humble."

Welcome others' definition – and lose the language

We willingly embrace terminology that others applied to us with calculated and hostile intent. Most Americans like, or at least fully accept, the idea that their nation is a superpower. However, the word was not invented as a compliment. The late Chinese communist leader Chou Enlai coined the term "superpower," pejoratively against both the USSR and the United States. He did so in a 1970 interview with French journalists, as part of an effort to show developing nations a third way between America and the Soviet bloc. The name stuck.[18] Both the Soviets and the Americans identified with the term and applied it proudly to themselves, though the idea helped crystallize fear and resentment around the world – sentiments that remain against the United States and complicate the current war effort. The term also helped solidify a global attitude of moral equivalence between the U.S. and the USSR.[19]

This easy, unchallenged acceptance of the adversaries' terms of debate showed a lack of national confidence and conviction, almost an admission that we thought we were on the losing side of history. It appeared to show an abandonment in some quarters of the exceptionalism that had given the U.S. its moral standing in the world. Many Americans – shapers of opinion and policy among them – actually believed it, resigning the world to permanent "peaceful coexistence," at best, with the USSR, and rejecting as dangerous the idea that the U.S. could nudge the decayed and overextended Soviet system to collapse from within.[20] The peaceful coexistence and détente advocates made it all the more difficult to resist or combat the infiltration of the adversaries' semantics into the American lexicon.

Some recognized the problem and tried to change it. Early in his presidency, Ronald Reagan issued a directive to: "prevent the Soviet propaganda machine from seizing the semantic high-ground in the battle of ideas through the appropriation of such terms as 'peace.'"[21]

For three years in a row, the Advisory Commission on Public Diplomacy under Edwin Feulner repeated its recommendation to institutionalize a means to challenge inaccurate or misleading terminology. The government ignored it. Then came the Soviet collapse. The United States entered into a period of drift and withdrawal in the early 1990's. It abolished the highly successful U.S. Information Agency, folding USIA's remains into the State Department where the agency lost its independent culture and mission, and degrading the nation's public diplomacy capabilities. When faced with a new enemy, U.S. leaders found themselves groping for the right words in the new war of ideas, wondering why it was so difficult to get the world to support or understand our cause.

"The costs of inattention seem to escape even those among us who pride ourselves on their 'hardheadedness' in matters of geopolitics and military strategy," Moynihan wrote in 1979. Neither political party was immune: "This is not a phenomenon of one administration, but almost, I think, of our political culture."[22] The words could have been written today. The more receptive the United States and the world become to enemy terminology, as the enemy defined and used it, Moynihan warned, "the more will the nations of the world begin to accommodate themselves" to the adversary's strategic aspirations.[23]

This maxim was so during the height of the Cold War when a Soviet collapse was furthest from the minds of almost everyone, except those few who believed it could and must happen – and who took action to make it reality. And it is true today in the "Global War on Terror," not only among Americans or in the West, but in the *ummah* of Islam itself.

Conclusion

Knowing and dominating the definitions of words is key to winning the international war of ideas. Public diplomacy, public affairs, information operations, psychological operations, political warfare, and other aspects of strategic communication will be effective only if their practitioners fearlessly exploit the wealth of words that culture offers to define ideas and shape understanding of them. That means taking two basic approaches:

- Stop using words and terms as the enemy defines them, and take the words back to undermine the enemy narrative; and
- Take the enemy's own words and use them against it, to expose its hypocrisy and inconsistencies, and to condemn it with its own terminology and ideas. Prosecutors do this every day in the courtroom.

Those practitioners must lead: not only at the presidential or cabinet level, but at every level in the bureaucracy of every government agency involved with communication. They need not wait for bureaucratic reorganizations, legal reviews and congressional appropriations cycles. Fundamental shifts require a policy decision that can begin with a single speech and skillful, persistent follow-up work. Successful shifts require leadership and relentless repetition at all levels. But the war of ideas will continue to suffer setbacks as long as those at the top continue to misunderstand or abuse words without regard for their best meanings, and cede the semantic war to the enemy.

Notes

[1] George Orwell, "Politics and the English Language," in Sonia Orwell and Ian Angus, eds., *George Orwell: In Front of Your Nose, 1946-1950*, Vol. 4 (Nonpareil Books, 2002), pp. 127-140.
[2] Thucydides, *History of the Peloponnesian War*, 3.82[.4], trans. Rex Warner (Penguin, 1954, 1972). Richard Crowley translates 3.82.4 as, "Words had to change their ordinary meaning and to take that which was now given them."

[3] Niccolò Machiavelli, *The Prince*, trans. Angelo Codevilla (Yale University Press, 1997).

[4] Alexander, p. 74; Samuel Adams, letter to John Pitts, January 21, 1776, in Harry Alonzo Cushing, ed., *The Writings of Samuel Adams*, Vol. III (G. P. Putnam's Sons, 1904-1908; Gutenberg Project eText 2093, 1999). For more on the propaganda of the American Revolution, see "The American Way of Propaganda: Lessons from the Founding Fathers," *Public Diplomacy White Paper* No. 1, Institute of World Politics, January 2006.

[5] Vaclav Havel, "A Word About Words," in absentia speech, Frankfurt, Germany, October 15, 1989, trans. A. G. Brain, published in the *New York Review of Books*, January 18, 1990.

[6] Aristotle, *On Rhetoric*, trans. George A. Kennedy (Oxford University Press, 1991); and Aristotle, *The Art of Rhetoric*, trans. H. C. Lawson-Tancred (New York: Penguin Books, 1991). Also see Aristotle, *The Politics*, trans. Carnes Lord (University of Chicago Press, 1984).

[7] See John J. Pitney, Jr., *The Art of Political Warfare* (University of Oklahoma Press/Red River, 2000).

[8] Depending on one's political or philosophical views today, a controversial public program is paid either with "government funding" or "taxpayer dollars," i.e., money that is either property of the government (and therefore nobly "invested" on the public's behalf), or the fruits of the work of the people (a waste of people's own hard-earned money). Congress either "taxes the rich" (good, according to some) or "penalizes the most successful" (bad for those who work hard). The abortion debate is loaded with the labels "pro-choice" or "pro-abortion" on one side, depending on who is doing the labeling, and "pro-life," "anti-abortion," or "anti-choice" on the other. Each side views the subject through completely unrelated frames of reference. Other examples in current usage: Illegal aliens (bad) or undocumented immigrants (good); liberal (bad) or progressive (good); right-wing (bad) or conservative (good).

[9] What passes for proficiency in foreign languages in the U.S. government shows that we are unlikely to understand the cultures with which we hope to communicate.

[10] Edwin J. Feulner, Jr., Chairman, United States Advisory Commission on Public Diplomacy, *The Role of USIA and Public Diplomacy*, January 1984.

[11] For a firsthand account of how that task force operated, see Herbert Romerstein's Chapter 9 of this volume. The USIA unit was the two-man Office to Counter Soviet Disinformation and Active Measures, which existed from 1983 to 1989. Under Romerstein's direction, it authored the "Counterpropaganda" chapter in this book.

[12] Daniel Patrick Moynihan, "Further Thoughts on Words and Foreign Policy," *Policy Review*, Spring 1979.

[13] Ibid., p. 53.

[14] Ibid.

[15] See Georgi Arbatov, *The War of Ideas in Contemporary International Relations* (Moscow, USSR: Progress Publishers, 1973); and Graham D.

Vernon, ed., *Soviet Perceptions of War and Peace* (National Defense University Press, 1981).

[16] Vladimir Bukovsky, "The Peace Movement and the Soviet Union," *Commentary*, May 1982; and U.S. Information Agency, *Soviet Active Measures in the 'Post-Cold War Era,' 1988-1991* (Report for the Committee on Appropriations of the U.S. House of Representatives, June 1992);

[17] Not that some didn't try. Hugh Seton-Watson's *The New Imperialism* (Dufor Editions, 1961) is an example. The bitter controversy surrounding President Ronald Reagan's 1983 denunciation of the Soviet Union as an "evil empire" shows how unacceptable such truth-telling was even in the Cold War's final years.

[18] Daniel Patrick Moynihan, "Further Thoughts on Words and Foreign Policy," *Policy Review*, Spring 1979, p. 57.

[19] At home, seeking convenient labels as shorthand to explain foreign issues to a domestic audience, the prestige press routinely and inaccurately referred to the KGB as the Russian "equivalent" to the FBI at home and CIA abroad, as if it was a legitimate law enforcement and intelligence service. And so on.

[20] The Reagan administration laid out the strategy to bring down the Soviet Union, as one of the architects, Norman Bailey, describes in his monograph. Norman A. Bailey, *The Strategic Plan that Won the Cold War – National Security Decision Directive 75* (Potomac Foundation, 1998).

[21] Ronald Reagan, "U.S. Relations with the USSR," National Security Decision Directive No. 75, January 17, 1983.

[22] Ibid., pp. 58-59.

[23] Ibid., p. 55.

14

Hearts and Minds Online:
Internetting the message in the infosphere

HAMPTON STEPHENS

The war of ideas that Islamist totalitarians have been waging against the United States for more than two decades involves mastery of methods and means of communicating cross-cultural political ideology. Historians of propaganda and political warfare know that communication in war has always been important – especially in conflicts that are in essence ideological. However, the disciplines of political warfare and propaganda are critical factors in the present conflict for reasons beyond ideology.

This war is occurring during the most profound communications revolution in human history. The revolution is based on a signal instrument, the Internet, which enables human communication to occur with a depth, breadth, speed and ease that far surpasses any previous information and communication technology.

In the fifteenth century, Gutenberg's printing press marked the first great step in the democratization of communication, bringing an end to an age when propaganda was a "royal attribute."[1] By speeding the spread of Martin Luther's theology, the printing press helped spark the Protestant Reformation and the political upheaval that followed. The next great revolution in communication technology began in the nineteenth century with the telegraph, and continued with industrialization of newspapers, and the invention of the telephone, film, radio and television.

But the effects of these latter technologies on the political communication of common men were not nearly as profound as the effects of the simple printing press. The telegraph, no doubt, brought previously unimagined speed to the dissemination of news and information. And the sounds and sights of radio and television broadcasts introduced mass communications of unprecedented psychological power.

Franklin Roosevelt revolutionized presidential communication with his radio fireside chats, but control and use of new communication technologies remained beyond most citizens. In free societies, the use of radio and television for political purposes was limited by expense, and in authoritarian countries such tools were the provenance of the state. Thus, even in the age of mass communication the printing press remained the preferred tool of dissidents and of grassroots activists, as Soviet-era *samizdat* illustrates.

The Internet, then, is not just the latest advance in communications, but a technology that has redefined the nature of communications and how human beings and nations interact. In fact, what we call the Internet is not really a technology at all, but a way of communicating that is enabled by numerous technological advances, such as complex silicon chips and integrated circuits, packet switching, fiber optics and wireless technologies. The essence of this new communications paradigm is the network, in which every member is connected to every other member and each can communicate as narrowly or broadly as they choose.

The World Wide Web and other Internet applications allow anyone with online access, and with the knowledge necessary to use a small number of software tools, simultaneously to receive and send communications, to be both a producer and consumer of increasingly sophisticated content. Internet access also is inexpensive. At Internet cafés around the world, an hour of Internet use can be bought for scarcely the cost of a cup of coffee, and the software tools necessary to view and publish Web pages, send and receive e-mail, post audio and video, and perform other kinds of communications are largely free.

While much has been made of an international "digital gap" between developed and developing countries, Internet use cannot easily be measured simply by counting computers and connections. In the economically troubled Middle East for example, "Internet cafes, some containing only a few computers, are in evidence from the refugee camps of Gaza to the suburbs of Tehran, each with their teeming mass of young men hunched over computer screens, downloading the latest music MP3, playing video games, chatting with unseen others, or, when no one is looking, surfing porn."[2]

Cell phone technology brings instant communication even to rural peasants and tribesmen who have no access to computers. In Iraq today, more people have cell phones than land lines, and Iraqis use text-messaging widely.

Social networking sites such as Facebook and MySpace have gone global, numbering into the hundreds of millions of members; Iran, which long banned the social networking media, has embraced Facebook as a means of promoting its foreign policy. President Ahmadinejad has his own blog in various languages, and surprises his critics by posting and responding to their comments.

Practically free Internet access provides endless opportunities for the U.S. to reach almost any connected audience it wishes, from the broadest all the way to the most narrow interest groups, with customized messages for each.

The Internet as a terrorist weapon

Unfortunately, however, an active minority in the Middle East and across the Islamic *ummah* uses the Internet for more than just civil communication and entertainment.. For committed Islamist extremists as well as the merely politically curious, the Internet is a potent tool for spreading the mix of fundamentalist theology, totalitarian politics, anti-Americanism and angry militancy that make up Islamist extremist thought. From any point on Earth with a connection, the Internet provides a resource base of actual manuals for bomb-making, command-and-control, and countersurveillance, and databases of commercial airline flights, architectural diagrams, satellite imagery, and personal information on public officials, plus instant and customizable news aggregation that can make a single user a one-man intelligence service. Terrorist groups like al Qaeda figured this out long before their enemies in Western governments did.

As early as 1993, RAND Corp. analysts John Arquilla and David Ronfeldt pointed out that terrorist organizations are particularly suited to waging "netwar" using information technology because they themselves are organized as networks. The information revolution "is favoring and strengthening network forms of organization, often giving them an advantage over hierarchical forms," Arquilla and Ronfeldt wrote. "The rise of networks means that power is migrating to nonstate actors, because they are able to organize into sprawling multiorganizational networks (especially 'all-channel' networks, in which every node is connected to every other node) more readily than can traditional, hierarchical, state actors."[3]

Terrorist organizations use the Internet to recruit followers, train these recruits in terrorist tactics and, above all, to distribute propaganda that dehumanizes their enemies, justifies their extremism, and glorifies their victories. Islamist mastery of the Internet took place long before many in the West were watching, and enabled small groups of individuals with few resources to collect intelligence from around the world, run surveillance in target areas, indoctrinate and recruit cadre without even meeting them, raise funds, transfer cash, plan attacks, and organize political and legal support to intimidate and frustrate foreign security and law enforcement services.[4]

For example, Al Qaeda broadcasts a weekly video news broadcast over the Internet and publishes its own Internet journal, *Sawt Al-Jihad.*[5] When the late Abu Musab Al Zarqawi wanted to tell Sunni Muslims to make war against "infidel" Shi'ites, he did it in an audio recording posted on an Islamist Internet site.[6] A Toronto terrorist ring that was broken up in June 2006 is a clear example of the increasingly important role the Internet plays in international terrorism. The investigation by U.S. and Canadian authorities revealed that several young Toronto Islamists and another group in Atlanta – all of whom reportedly were previously unconnected to terrorist groups – were encouraged to commit terrorist acts by a London-based Islamic militant, Younis Tsouli. Better known by his screen name "Irhabi 007," (Irhabi meaning "terrorist") Tsouli communicated with the North American cells through Islamist Web sites and chat rooms, using PowerPoint presentations to teach his pupils how to make bombs.[7]

Constructing the logic of extremism

Most extreme Islamist propaganda found on the Web does not directly advocate violence or seek recruits for carrying out specific terrorist operations. Rather, most is aimed at bolstering the ideological base of Islamism. In political tracts, Koranic analyses and impassioned apologia, Islamist sympathizers construct the logic of extremism. In chat rooms and discussion boards they trade grievances and provide a welcoming home for young converts seeking a repository for their anger and a place to nurture their misguided zeal. Insurgents in Iraq, for example, can use these sites as a valuable means of recruitment to their cause. Although the vast majority of such sites are in Arabic, there are a number of English language sites as well. For example, on IslamicAwakening.com, one can read "scholarly" essays on "the obligation of re-establishing the Caliphate" and "the Islamic ruling with regards to killing women, children and elderly in a situation of war" (it's permissible when necessary, of course), among other sophistry.[8]

This kind of propaganda poses a particular problem for law enforcement and counterterrorism authorities. The U.S. Federal Bureau of Investigation was able to pursue the Toronto case because it involved direct incitement to terrorist attacks upon the United States. However, short of direct incitement to violence or raising money for terrorist groups, even the most vile online Islamist propaganda is protected in the U.S. by the First Amendment. Thus, while the U.S. military can attempt to shut down Web sites that foreign terrorists in Iraq use to foment opposition to American forces there, domestic law enforcement authorities can do little about Islamist propaganda sites that are being accessed by potential terrorists living in U.S. cities – even when such sites reside on computers inside the United States. In fact, the majority of Islamist Web sites are hosted by U.S.-based hosting companies, using satellites and root servers controlled by the American military.[9]

Even if authorities could shut down Islamist Web sites, it is not clear this would be preferable. Internet sites make it easier to track trends in Islamist ideology, which benefits those who want to understand their thinking. Author Stephen Schwartz says the vast majority of the research for his book, in *The Two Faces of Islam: Saudi Fundamentalism and Its Role in Terrorism*, came from the Internet. "I want to know what the enemy is thinking and the only way I can know that without spending all my time in a Muslim country... is to read these Web sites," Schwartz says.[10] In his role as director of the Center for Islamic Pluralism, Schwartz, a convert to Shia Islam, uses the information he learns on such cites to actively counter extreme Islamism and promote moderation among Muslims.

The public diplomacy role

But private citizens should not be alone in waging the battle ideas against Islamism during time of war. Beyond law enforcement and military action, the U.S. government and its allies must play a role in this war as well. In order to do so effectively however, the government must be prepared to change the way it conducts public diplomacy and wages the war of ideas. U.S. public diplomacy has not changed much since it contributed to the collapse of the Soviet empire, even as communications technology has advanced dramatically. The Internet is the fastest growing medium for spreading political ideas, but government-funded broadcasting has not progressed much beyond the old media of radio and television.

Current U.S. government public diplomacy websites are weak in style, content and functionality. If adherents of a medieval ideology like militant Islam can adopt modern technology, then the United States government – which, after all, sponsored the invention of the Internet and owns global infrastructure equities, should be able to use it effectively and expertly to promote values like liberty and democracy, and to attack enemy disinformation, propaganda and ideology. Some progress is being made in Internet-based public diplomacy, with a new Web strategy announced in 2007, but that progress is little, slow and late.

Until five years after the September 11, 2001 attacks, an Internet strategy was disturbingly absent from U.S. public diplomacy programs. The United States launched two Arabic broadcasting services, Radio Sawa and Alhurra television, but government broadcasters seemed to ignore the promise of the Internet as a tool of public diplomacy. Comparing the Internet presences of Al Jazeera, the most popular television network in the Muslim world, and Alhurra, the American-funded network designed to compete with it, illustrates this point. Al Jazeera built an attractive, dynamic, interesting, interactive and personalized Web site comparable or even superior in quality to MSNBC's excellent news site. In 2002, in only its second year of operation, Al Jazeera's Web site received more than 161 million visits, according to the network.[11]

But Alhurra broadcasters have not taken advantage of the synergy of the Internet and television. The State Department and the Broadcasting Board of Governors (BBG), the quasi-independent entity that runs U.S. government broadcasting which runs the outlets, showed no understanding of how the Internet works.[12] The Voice of America (VOA), with a content-rich site in English and some other languages, eliminated its Arabic-language Website, and with it, shut off Arab editors who had been pulling the well-written stories from the Web and printing them in their own newspapers. For 18 months after the network's founding in February 2004, Alhurra's Web site was not merely less sophisticated than Al Jazeera's site; it could scarcely be called a Web site at all. It was an embarrassment: alhurra.com consisted of a single, static white page containing the station's logo, a basic schedule for the network's television programming, directions for tuning into its broadcast signal and a few words describing the network's mission. The site contained no outside links or even its own news feed. While Al Jazeera delivered its online content directly to people's computers, cell phones and PDAs, Alhurra and the BBG did nothing.

Alhurra's new Web site, launched in August 2005, was a significant improvement, featuring text news stories as well as streaming audio and video feeds of Alhurra programs. Though the site looked more like that of a real news organization, qualitatively it still lagged behind its competitor. Its quality has been uneven and unprofessional. At the time In early 2008, Alhurra's homepage consisted of fresh, clean graphics and a broadcast schedule, but contained little visible content. It hosted almost nothing to interest anyone to come and visit, absorb information and take part in discussions. A year later the site had improved, with richer content and functionality, but still lagged.

Radio Sawa, the Arabic-language popular music and news station, has a Web site containing short print articles and audio clips of Sawa programming, and provides live audio streaming, but it is not nearly as comprehensive as Al Jazeera's site or, for that matter, as good as the Web sites of the vast majority of comparable professional news operations. Radio Sawa's Farsi-language cousin, Radio Farda, is better; it runs a Web site with lively and dynamic written news and graphics, and live audio streaming.

Other U.S. public diplomacy online

Secretary of State Condoleezza Rice and Under Secretary of State for Public Diplomacy Karen Hughes both vowed soon after taking office to expand the role of technology in U.S. public diplomacy. In September 2005, in one of her first speeches to State Department employees, Hughes announced a technology initiative to use the Internet, web chats, digital video and text messaging to communicate American ideals to foreign publics.[13] Following this lead, the BBG said it planned to expand the scope of audio and video streaming across all its Web sites and make better use of new Internet technologies like Real Simple Syndication. The board made the Web site of Radio Sawa the focal point of its Arabic-language Internet news operations.[14] The speed and frequency with which the site's news stories are updated now compares more favorably with the sophisticated Voice of America News Web sites, and is the only major civilian U.S.-sponsored Arabic-language site on the Internet. The BBG is also continually working on ways to get around access restrictions that governments like China and Iran put on its Web sites.

The State Department's Bureau of International Information Programs has also made some initial efforts to use the Internet to communicate and spread American ideals. The most prominent example, a program called Democracy Dialogues, was launched in January 2006. Democracy Dialogues is a multilingual Web site that aims to educate people outside the United States about democratic principles. The site translates important democratic documents like the Declaration of Independence, the U.S. Constitution and the Emancipation Proclamation into Spanish, French, Russian, Chinese, Arabic and Persian. International democratic treatises, from the Magna Carta to the Helsinki Final Act, are also featured. For those Muslims who believe Islam is incompatible with liberalism, the sites publish the 1990 Cairo Declaration on Human Rights in Islam. Every two months, the site highlights a new democratic principle. So far, freedom of speech and women's rights have been featured topics, with "independent courts, free and fair elections, freedom of worship, and minority rights" planned for the future.[15] Periodic Web chats with experts, discussion boards, and educational materials for foreign schools support each theme.

Did it work? In April 2006, State Department officials said the site received about 40,000 visitors in the first four months after its launch. That is not many. The department said, nearly five years after 9/11 and three years after the invasion of Iraq, that it had yet to market the site aggressively. State Department officials said in early 2006 that the Chinese and Arabic sites were proving to be most popular and that the most foreign visitors were coming from China, Egypt and Iran.[16] But more popular than what? Forty thousand visitors in four months is only 10,000 a month, an average of 333 a day, or fourteen people an hour, out of a global population of 6.4 billion. Third-rate bloggers, operating in their pajamas at the kitchen table with no budget, have better numbers than that.

These first steps might show promise, but there are significant obstacles that must be overcome if the United States government is ever to compete with its enemies in using technology for propaganda. One problem is resources. As American servicemen died in combat by the thousands, the State Department was slow to make technology-driven public diplomacy a priority. Of the $591 million the BBG spent on international broadcasting in fiscal year 2005, just $6.9 million, or about 1 percent, went toward Internet services.[17] As of May 2006, just two State Department employees were devoting "a majority of their time" to Democracy Dialogues.[18] The Meanwhile, the Pentagon has forged ahead with a huge online information presence through defenselink.mil and scores of other sites.

But resources could be the least of the problems. As the terrorists show, one can do much with little or no money. The real obstacles are lack of vision and will from the political leadership and trepidation from the bureaucracy where innovation is seldom rewarded. Few in the government are able to use the Internet as it must be used: a 24/7 battlespace of words and images, where a committed and persistent few, with the barest of resources, can wield a disproportionately large influence on news, information, perceptions, opinion, and behavior.

Networking public diplomacy

With a few specialized exceptions, government bureaucracies are ill-suited to operating in the world of new media. Using the Internet for public diplomacy requires quickly adapting to new technologies and new habits of communication. To do so, the State Department needs creative, technology-savvy employees with responsibility and authority to implement their ideas like the military and CIA. An effective Internet public diplomacy strategy would involve much more than building sparsely-visited and poorly promoted informational Web sites: It would take advantage of the Internet's dynamic strengths in networking and interactivity, using blogs and social networking applications, for example, to elevate sympathetic voices online, build moderate Muslim virtual communities, and discredit the enemy. Meanwhile the military and intelligence services would handle the black operations to take down the enemy online.

By most accounts, the department is very slow to develop and implement new approaches to its public diplomacy mission, and the BBG specifically exempts itself from an official public diplomacy role. For example, in early 2006 it was clear that Democracy Dialogues needed, among other things, a better online marketing program and more creative and interesting subject matter to attract significant numbers of visitors. But State Department officials said their plans for promoting the site consisted mostly in face-to-face efforts by U.S. embassy personnel and partnerships with a small number of NGOs. When asked about several obvious Internet marketing strategies, such as simply placing a link to Democracy Dialogues on the Arabic-language RadioSawa.com site (which averages 7 million page views per month)[19], State Department officials said they had not considered such an approach. Neither had they considered solutions such as enlisting established pro-Western bloggers in the Middle East to link to Democracy Dialogues.[20] Months after the officials heard such ideas, the Democracy Dialogues page remained as before.

Even when some employees in a bureaucracy embrace new ways of doing business, they often find it difficult to sell their ideas to risk-averse higher-ups, who usually hold the purse strings. Indeed, if terrorist networks, with their flattened, horizontal organizational structures and decentralized decision-making, are tailor-made for operating on the Internet, hierarchical government bureaucracies find decentralization and greater operational freedom to be anathema.

John Burgess, a 25-year public diplomacy veteran, said he decided to retire from the State Department in 2005 after running into intense opposition from superiors to an idea to use technology for public diplomacy. At a time when news coverage of the war in Iraq was overwhelmingly negative, and positive news was not getting out, Burgess proposed a group blog written by State Department officers to explain "what was actually going on there, day-to-day, across the country." This idea was killed not because it would have been ineffective, but because senior department officers feared losing control. "You can be fairly confident that the majority of officers assigned to the smaller town in Iraq were junior officers. Senior officers could not abide the thought that these people would be broadcasting to the world at large without the message being massaged and okayed at multiple levels," Burgess said. "Rather defeats the purpose of a blog, no?"[21]

The State Department improved its blogging capabilities a year or two later, retaining a small number of full-time bloggers in Farsi and other languages to post overt, official comments on websites and blogs around the world. These posts are surprisingly well received.

Bureaucratic resistance is less of a problem in the military and the intelligence community which are better organized to act quickly and decisively in crises. The military's information operations components have funded propaganda operations in Iraq. In 2005, for example, numerous press reports revealed that the Lincoln Group, a Defense Department subcontractor, was leading a program to influence the Iraqi public's opinion of coalition forces by ghost writing articles and op-ed pieces and paying Iraqi newspapers to run them.[22] Although the program was controversial, the incident illustrates the U.S. military has greater flexibility to experiment with new approaches to public diplomacy. Private outfits have begun to explore ways to use technology to influence public opinion, and the employees of such firms – whose culture more closely resembles a dot-com startup than a government bureaucracy – are better equipped to develop innovative public diplomacy solutions using technology. However, the Department of Defense has been slow to embrace them. Furthermore, intelligence agencies' technological know-how, as well as their ability to operate covertly, make them well-suited for overcoming popular ambivalence about the use of propaganda to defeat the enemy.

Non-wartime situations

Public diplomacy and the other elements of strategic influence must also function in peacetime. The new communications paradigm created by the Internet and other networked information technologies, in which the negative perceptions of a few can overnight become significant political problems, makes persistent public diplomacy more important than ever. In this new world, cartoons published in Danish newspapers can be exploited to spark violence around the world, or a single news report about the handling of a Koran by a U.S. soldier can further degrade the reputation of the United States among Muslims. Outside the *ummah*, public diplomacy is just as important. Traditional state-to-state conflict will have a growing propaganda component in the Internet world.

The Chinese government, for example, has perfected the art of using the Internet as a tool of regime propaganda. Xinhua, the Chinese state-owned "news" organization, has a massive Internet presence in English, and it manages to pass itself off as a legitimate news organization to gullible Western news consumers despite being an obvious organ of Chinese Communist Party propaganda. China uses the open policies of popular American aggregators like Yahoo and Google News, which regularly pick up Xinhua propaganda reports as straight stories.[23] Besides using the Internet to bolster its reputation abroad, the Chinese Communist Party also seeks to keep political communications over the Internet from hurting its legitimacy at home. Of all the governments in the world, China's has had the most success in controlling the use of the Internet within its borders.[24]

Other authoritarian regimes, such as the one in Iran, where the use of the Internet is growing quickly, and in Russia, where Internet use is widespread, are following the Chinese example. Government efforts to censor the Internet will probably fail eventually because the resources needed to do so will be unavailable as Internet use continues to grow around the world.[25] But eventually could be a long time, and in the interim, undemocratic states are likely to use the Internet to sow enmity toward the United States and its Western allies among their populations, using American news organizations and communications technology to do so.

While terrorist organizations are well-suited to using the latest information and communication technology because of their agile and decentralized structure, super-bureaucratic governments like China can effectively use the Internet with the necessary speed. The Chinese regime decided by fiat to build the most complex Internet censorship and filtering system in the world, and it is motivated to do so because free discourse poses a grave danger to its survival. A lone terrorist or activist needs no one's permission to post propaganda on a Web site, and he is motivated to do so by his ideological zeal. A democratic government like the United States, meanwhile, finds itself in a battle of ideas against both kinds of enemies but is ill-suited to the playing field. Apathetic or timid rather than zealous about the effect of ideas on its power and interests, encumbered by the slow-moving machinery of government and simultaneously limited by its democratic character in its ability to fully leverage government's power and reach, the United States seems to be at a disadvantage of it own making.

Conclusion

And yet, in a war of ideas the United States has the advantage of having the best ideas on its side. Ideals like freedom and democracy hold more appeal for the greatest part of humanity than the brands of tyranny – theocratic or otherwise – espoused by the enemies of the United States. But even if one believes that the best ideas win out in the end, history demonstrates that millions can suffer and die in even the brief interregnums when parts of humanity fall under the spell of men like Lenin, Mao or bin Laden. To keep men from falling for such false prophets they must be shown a better way while the false prophets are exposed. The United States and its allies around the world have an unprecedented opportunity, a chance made greater by the fact that Americans started this revolution and still lead the world in technological knowledge. But if this opportunity is not to be missed, the United States government must find a way to overcome the bureaucratic inertia and lack of political will that so far at have been holding it back.

Notes

[1] Harold D. Lasswell, Daniel Lerner and Hans Speier, eds., *Proganda and Communications in World History: Volume I, The Symbolic instrument in Early Times* (University of Hawaii, 1979), p. 575.

[2] Rafal Rohozinski, "Secret Agents and Undercover Brothers: The Hidden Information Revolution in the Arab World," Cambridge Security Programme, March 2004, accessed in July, 2006 at http://www.ssrc.org/programs/itic/publications/ITST_materials/rohozinskibrief 3_4.pdf.

[3] John Arquilla and David Ronfeldt eds., *Networks and Netwars* (RAND, 2001), pp. 1.

[4] The SITE Institute is one of the premier non-governmental organizations monitoring extremist Websites, at siteinstitute.org.

[5] Middle East Media Research Institute's Jihad and Terrorism Studies Project. Dispatch Nos. 993 and 804. http://memri.org/jihad.html.

[6] Zarqawi Urges Iraqi Sunnis to Shun Shi'ites: Web," *Reuters*, June 1, 2006.

[7] Robert Block and Jay Solomon, "London Case Led to Terrorist Arrests in Canada," *The Wall Street Journal*, June 6, 2006.

[8] IslamicAwakening.com

[9] Hampton Stephens, "Hosting Terror," *Foreign Policy*, July/August 2006, pp. 93

[10] Stephen Schwartz (director, Center for Islamic Pluralism), in interview with the author, May 2006.

[11] Web statistics provided by AlJazeera.net chief editor Abdulaziz Al-Mahmoud.

[12] By contrast, the Pentagon invested in online media, at least for the purposes of communicating with the American public and the English-speaking world. It modernized Defenselink.mil and set up a constellation of other websites and online services – much to the dismay of some in the public diplomacy community, where purists saw the military overstepping its bounds.

[13] Karen Hughes, "Remarks at Town Hall for Public Diplomacy" (State Department's Loy Auditorium, Washington, DC, September 8, 2005). http://www.state.gov/secretary/rm/2005/52748.htm.

[14] Bert Kleinman (then-president, Middle East Broadcasting Networks), in interview with the author, September 7, 2005.

[15] Judith Siegel (International Information Program deputy coordinator), in written responses to questions, March 30, 2006.

[16] May 4, 2006 author interview with State Department officials who did not wish to be identified.

[17] BBG spokesman.

[18] Ibid.

[19] Bert Kleinman (then-president, Middle East Broadcasting Networks), in interview with the author, September 7, 2005.

[20] May 4, 2006 author interview with State Department officials who did not wish to be identified.

[21] John Burgess (former Bureau of International Information Programs official), in an e-mail to the author, August 24, 2005.

[22] "Washington in Brief," *Washington Post*, January 27, 2006, pp. 11.

[23] Reporters Without Borders, "Xinhua: The World's Biggest Propaganda Agency," Sept. 30, 2005, http://www.rsf.org/IMG/pdf/Report_Xinhua_Eng.pdf

[24] OpenNet Initiative, "Internet Filtering in China 2004-2005: A Country Study," pp. 1, http://www.opennetinitiative.net/studies/china

[25] Hampton Stephens, "Digital Walls, Digital Holes," *TCS Daily*, April 19, 2006. http://www.tcsdaily.com/article.aspx?id=041906F

15

Toward a Theory of Low Intensity Propaganda

STEVEN C. BAKER

Introduction

How might the U.S. adopt an effective strategic communications approach that fully supports diplomatic and military objectives, yet retains the flexibility, foresight and quick response time needed to inflict crippling psychological defeats on an adversary? American military doctrine envisions and practices crushing, overwhelming destruction of an enemy force that breaks the enemy's ability and will to resist, ensuring a swift victory at the lowest possible human cost.

That approach worked well in the Serbia/Kosovo conflict of the 1990's, the invasion of Afghanistan in 2001 and the invasion of Iraq in 2003. But as insurgency and counterinsurgency increasingly define the conflict in Iraq and elsewhere, strategic communication and its public diplomacy and political warfare elements must enhance proven counterinsurgency approaches. Those approaches apply not only to a counterinsurgency as in Iraq, but in any drawn-out ideological conflict that tests long-term American will. The nation's adversaries continue to make greater use of television, video and the Internet as their delivery systems of choice in their propaganda wars of attrition.

A protracted counterpropaganda doctrine and capability, in both a shooting war and even in situations with little or no explicit political violence, will become increasingly important if the United States expects to prevail in conflicts currently and in the future. The 2006 counterinsurgency doctrine of General David Petraeus has taken important steps to address this issue. This chapter is intended as a contribution toward developing the doctrine and the practice.

LIC meets LIP

Low Intensity Conflict (LIC) is familiar to warfighters as guerrilla warfare or counterinsurgency. The U.S. military defines LIC as:

> political-military confrontation between contending states or groups below conventional war and above the routine, peaceful competition among states. It frequently involves protracted struggles of competing principles and ideologies. Low intensity conflict ranges from subversion to the use of armed force. It is waged by a combination of means, employing political, economic, informational, and military instruments. Low intensity conflicts are often localized, generally in the Third World, but contain certain regional and global security implications.[1]

The U.S. is advancing its LIC capabilities in the area of counterinsurgency, but has very far to go in terms of understanding and countering the component that we will call Low Intensity Propaganda (LIP).[2] LIP presents a combination of technologically unsophisticated ideational tools that have complemented and served to prolong the strategically significant LIC of terrorist attacks, roadside bombings and other insurgency operations. A clearer understanding of the relationship between LIP and LIC, in the early stages of this conflict, and the former's *strategic* rather than tactical implications, could have benefited U.S. policymakers and led to strategies aimed at countering propaganda (the messages and the mechanisms) before the 2003 ground war began in Iraq.[3]

The word "propaganda," though loaded with political and emotional baggage, is a neutral term of communications art. Edward Bernays, the self-described American propagandist of the early 20th century who is more popularly known as the "father of public relations," tried without success to revive use of the term after World War I. In his 1928 book, Bernays called propaganda the "consistent, enduring effort to create or shape events to influence the relations of the public to an enterprise, idea or group."[4] LIP is therefore a distinct genus of propaganda.

Unlike American concepts such as public affairs, public diplomacy or other traditional, largely overt means of influencing foreign audiences, LIP under other names was used most often as a covert tool – its originator being unknown to the public – and did not seem to be designed primarily to affect foreign attitudes or influence American or Western audiences. Instead, LIP was used by hostile low-intensity actors to influence domestic constituencies that were actual or potential allies of the hostile force, or passive fence-sitters at best. More simply,

LIP is a low-level psychological component that buttresses and sustains the early stages of an insurgency when the political and ideological environment either lacks, or does not require, modern technological means to disseminate propaganda.

Measured study of these various forms of low intensity propaganda, and the knowledge of the strategic and operational significance that terrorists and others assign to them, may help U.S. policymakers design more comprehensive strategies to use political and ideological means not only to persuade the ambivalent of soft opposition, but to compel an opponent to do one's bidding or accept one's will.[5] Such a strategy, properly designed in advance at the national strategic level, could have helped stem an incipient insurgency in the initial stages and increased the odds of an earlier Coalition success in Iraq and in other theaters.

This chapter makes several observations about the use of LIP in Iraq and the intimate and essential relationship with the world of terrorism. Specifically, it focuses on the conflict in Iraq and how LIP reinforced existing political and ideological beliefs in order to 1) incite or prolong violence against Coalition forces, 2) recruit followers, 3) redirect blame for Muslim-on-Muslim violence, and 4) later justify Muslim-on-Muslim violence. Furthermore, it seeks to explain how LIP was utilized broadly to influence, to inform, to shape, and ultimately to wage a strategic political and ideological warfare campaign vis-à-vis selected audiences engaged in, or peripheral to, the low intensity conflict in Iraq. Finally, this chapter proposes novel ways of combating LIP's influence in concert with other, and more accepted, public diplomacy and information operations practices.

Low intensity propaganda and the war of ideas

Current U.S. political-ideological strategies (using radios, satellite television, internet, public affairs, public diplomacy, or information operations) toward Arab and Muslim audiences are based on strategic Cold War models that came into being during a period of bipolarity and within an intellectual environment dominated by theories of containment. That obsolete approach presumes that the United States' intended audiences are starved for American information and are eager to receive U.S. messages. That presumption is wrong.

Yet the new approach to warfare rejects containment theory as a guiding philosophy for combating global terrorists and the states that sponsor them. The doctrine of pre-emption, known as the Bush Doctrine, assumes that time and asymmetry favor the terrorists and their allies. Therefore, as a matter of policy, the United States will act *before* the terrorists do.[6] However, the pre-emption doctrine has failed so far to influence the manner in which the U.S. government designs and executes its political and ideological warfare at the strategic level.

Moreover, now that "transformation" is a leitmotif around Washington, and plans are moving forward to restructure the military to give policymakers and warfighters the flexibility to anticipate and respond to an increasing number of low intensity conflicts around the globe, one must pay renewed attention to those who place a premium on influencing over killing. This is not to say that the conflict-averse State Department should have the primary role. If the U.S. military and intelligence services still accept ancient Chinese strategist Sun Tzu's well-worn aphorism that "to subdue the enemy without fighting is the acme of skill," they should recognize that they have much to master. And if the public diplomats and soft power theorists truly seek to win by influencing, they must transform their ways of thinking and acting to accept, and indeed welcome, a new government-wide emphasis on influence over brute force, and empower the military accordingly.

The United States has the capability *par excellence* to locate and terminate terrorists anywhere in the world but has no comparable "soft" weaponry. As long as official Washington refuses to acknowledge, discuss and resolve this glaring deficiency, "war of ideas" is just a mindless slogan.

Some policymakers have recognized that the ultimate defeat of insurgents and terrorists depends more on how the United States fares in the war of ideas against radical Islamists than on the success of its military operations. By this, it is meant that the United States cannot tolerate a situation whereby individuals enter the "terrorist world" (through political and/or ideological indoctrination) at a rate "equal to or faster than" the ability of the United States "to capture and kill them."[7]   The bottom line, as then-Secretary of Defense Donald Rumsfeld noted, is that, "We need to find ways to make sure we're winning the battle of ideas and that we're reducing the number of terrorists... that are being taught to go out and murder and kill innocent men, women and children."[8] While little more than a vision years after they were spoken, Rumsfeld's words represent forward thinking appropriate for the global mission; but judging from some post-9/11 strategic efforts to win the "hearts and minds" of our potential enemies – be it through tactical PSYOP in Iraq and Afghanistan, information operations, or public diplomacy and "strategic communication" – it is not likely that the war of ideas will be successful in the short-term.

Public diplomacy, public affairs, radio and TV broadcasting, and other "traditional" (read: Cold War-inspired) tools that utilize Information Age means of information dissemination are appropriate implements for a *long-term* strategy. But the institutional and theoretical reluctance to confront LIP as a separate *strategic* threat – requiring the *strategic* use of what are considered, from a U.S. perspective, to be traditional, tactical PSYOP or information operations[9] – leaves policymakers vulnerable to the political-ideological warfare operations (read: LIP) carried out by low intensity actors.

LIP in Iraq

If Iraq is indeed the "central front in the War on Terror,"[10] then the "battle of ideas" must take center stage there. But apart from meeting operational military needs, it appears that the U.S. has done little to study how particular forms of LIP were affecting the perceptions of Iraqis and the impact that these perceptions have had on U.S. operations.

In order to illustrate the importance of studying LIP, it is easiest to begin with an examination of the situation in Iraq after the fall of Saddam Hussein's regime on April 9, 2003. At that point, Iraq was experiencing a serious information vacuum where rumors and myths became the main source of information. A military analyst described it in these terms:

> I do believe there has to be some... wave of uncertainty going through Baghdad right now because if there was anyone in control, there would be some evidence of that to the people in that city. And with no TV, with no media at all, with nothing – nothing alive in that city except rumor and myth, and the image of Saddam as a ghost, I think that right now, there's this huge sense of uncertainty.[11]

Similarly, CNN reported only a few days later that "With little access to hard information and used to a regular diet of propaganda from the former government's radio and television services, people here appear to be filling their information vacuum now with fears, rather than facts."[12] Rumors circulating Baghdad included: "Americans want our oil;" "Americans want the chaos... so the Iraqis can't govern... and they can justify their occupation;" and "Americans want to destroy Iraq."[13] Some rumors reflected the conspiratorial mind of Iraqi and Arab cultures in general: "I saw it with my own eyes... Americans opened the doors of the bank to let the thieves go in;" "It's all a game to destroy the Arabs to benefit Israel," and even "Saddam Hussein is in Washington with Bush."[14]

Shortly after arriving in Baghdad to head up the reconstruction effort at the time, General Jay Garner had to downplay "rumors he's come [to Iraq] to rule the country."[15]   His response: "I don't rule anything. I'm the coalition facilitator to establish a different environment where these people can pull things together themselves."[16] His response was rational, from a Western perspective, but one that was not likely to resonate with average Iraqis who are accustomed to strong-man rule.

The U.S. did not quickly establish its credibility among Iraqis as a guarantor against Saddam coming back to power. On April 27, 2003, Agence France Presse observed that, "the feeling of dread has still not completely left Baghdad. The capital is full of the most unlikely rumors about Saddam's return. According to one urban myth, Saddam has been waiting for his birthday to re-emerge and dole out punishment for all who dared to challenge him."[17]   Uncertainty was cited most often as the reason for the decision many Iraqis made to refrain from openly supporting the American presence. There was a general fear that Saddam Hussein was not dead and that his brutal regime could reemerge.   As a result, American troops had to operate in an unnecessarily hostile environment.

Two days later, when a firefight erupted in Fallujah between American soldiers and Iraqis, leaving more than one dozen Iraqis dead, CNN speculated that Iraq's "rumor mill" would complicate and amplify the gravity of this event.   When asked by CNN's Anderson Cooper whether "word of what happened in Fallujah had reached Baghdad," the correspondent replied:

> Yes, the rumor has reached Baghdad. It's difficult at this stage to
> judge exactly what the mood is as a result of that. As you say, most
> people at this stage in Iraq, within Iraq, are getting their information
> from rumors. Those rumors, as you can imagine, are expanded and
> run like wildfire. [18]

One month after the invasion, on May 10, the Associated Press reported that the streets of Baghdad were full of talk because there were "few newspapers, little electricity for radios or TVs, no authorities to give definitive answers and enough desperation and fear to excite an already overactive rumor mill." [19] It went on to report that, "with little law enforcement, gasoline or electricity in Baghdad, most commercial establishments are closed.   That leads…to a lot of free time for trafficking in rumors in a part of the world where conspiracy theories flourish."[20]

These few examples illustrate the scope of the rumor problem in Iraq following the liberation of Baghdad (the result of an information vacuum that Coalition forces left unfulfilled and which various inimical actors subsequently dominated). It was only a matter of time before experienced low intensity actors seized the opportunity to fill the information and political action void with low intensity propaganda in an effort to influence and manipulate the opinions as well as actions of particular audiences.

It is easy for Westerners unaccustomed to Arab culture to dismiss the content of these rumors (and other forms of LIP) as harmless gossip or strange phenomena, but the fact is that rumors and conspiracy theories play a very significant role in Iraqi society and help shape the perceptions and actions of average citizens. Left alone, rumors proved to be a very inexpensive but effective motivator and precursor to violence.

Beyond gossip

Apart from these seemingly harmless rumors and the gossip that permeated the public discourse in Iraq are examples of orchestrated terrorist efforts to influence, for better or worse, the hearts and minds of the people in the first months and years of the occupation.

Al Qaeda's leader in Iraq, the late Abu Musab al-Zarqawi, wrote a letter that Coalition forces captured and made public in February, 2004. Zarqawi outlined an ideological and operational plan for resisting and fighting Coalition forces and their Iraqi allies. The letter highlights al Qaeda's recognition of the relationship between LIP and LIC: "We are seriously preparing media material that will reveal the facts, call forth firm intentions, arouse determination, and be[come] an arena of jihad *in which the pen and the sword complement each other*"[21] (emphasis added).

This is a remarkable statement because it identifies the equal and symbiotic relationship between terror tactics (the sword) and propaganda (the pen). This relationship is apparent in the March 2004 attacks that killed over 100 Shi'ite Muslims during Ashoura festivities, the April 2004 attacks in Fallujah and Ramadi and the coordinated June 2004 attacks in five Iraqi cities, and in subsequent and more spectacularly deadly attacks. Like most acts of terrorism, the attacks were "propaganda by deed," that is, actions taken mainly for their political and psychological value.

For example, according to a news report at the time, the March 2004 bombings in Karbala and at the Kazimiya shrine in Baghdad, linked to Zarqawi, "sparked a wave of Shi'ite outrage – much of it directed at U.S. troops."[22] It appears that the timely use of LIP helped to re-direct the resultant confusion and anger toward the American forces in the area. According the one report, loudspeakers outside one mosque blared: "The Jews and the occupation troops are behind these blasts." [23] And the head of U.S. Central Command, General John Abizaid, confirmed during a news conference that followed the attacks that LIP played a significant role in these attacks: "It was clear that the people that planned this outrage also planned to blame it on the United States. And there is some indication that they planted leaflets very shortly after the explosions in Baghdad that claimed that the United States had mortared the worshipers."[24]

LIP also played a role in the violent April 2004 anti-Coalition attacks attributed to radical Shi'ite cleric Muqtada al-Sadr in the Fallujah and Ramadi areas.   The Associated Press reported that "portraits of al-Sadr were posted on government buildings, schools and mosques, along with graffiti praising him for his 'heroic deeds' and 'valiant uprising against the occupier.'"[25] According to the *Washington Post*, the attacks in Fallujah were "urged on by leaflets, sermons and freshly sprayed graffiti calling for jihad, [and] young men are leaving Baghdad *to join a fight* that residents say has less to do with battlefield success than with a cause infused with righteousness and sacrifice"[26] (emphasis added). The *Post* went on to note:

> Fresh graffiti sprayed in sweeping Arabic letters is turning up across the city. On one wall in the southern Baghdad neighborhood of Jihad, the messages were spaced 10 yards apart: "Long live Fallujah's heroes." "Down with America and long live the Mahdi Army," a Shi'ite militia. Then: "Long live the resistance in Fallujah." And finally, "Long live the resistance." [27]

In this particular case, LIP played a signal role that both inspired these low intensity actors and prolonged the conflict. Supporters and sympathizers with al Qaeda and other anti-U.S. forces supported the LIP operations globally online.

Finally, LIP emerged during the June 2004 coordinated "sabotage" attacks – aimed at bloodying the handover of sovereignty to the Iraqi people – in the Iraqi cities of Baquba, Fallujah, Ramadi, Mosul and Baghdad. These attacks were propagandistic deeds designed to inform local Iraqi police and government officials who cooperate with Americans that they would be marked for death. According to Reuters, "scores of black-clad gunmen, some claiming loyalty to Jordanian militant Abu Musab al-Zarqawi, attacked a police station and other government buildings in Baquba."[28] In order to ensure that the meaning of these attacks was clear, the terrorists concurrently handed out "leaflets warning Iraqis not to 'collaborate' with Americans."[29] These leaflets proclaimed barbarically: "The flesh of collaborators is tastier than that of Americans."[30]

Even the crudest forms of low intensity propaganda can be effective. In Iraq, they fill people with fear and prevent them from cooperating with friendly forces. Some of the results are an impaired counterinsurgency effort and the increased likelihood that constant, protracted, low-level terror tactics televised to provide a daily diet of defeatism, could achieve the terrorists' strategic ends of forcing a premature Coalition withdrawal and destabilization of the fragile new institutions in Iraq. Thus the insurgents appear to have learned from the North Vietnamese model of how to fight the United States and win.

Rumors as weapons

As the theory of LIC matured in the 1980's, someone forgot to develop a parallel theory for low intensity political-ideological warfare. The soft side of low intensity conflict was under-rated despite its recognized value.[31] More than two decades before, in his seminal book *Propaganda: The Formation of Men's Attitudes*, French sociologist Jacques Ellul acknowledged the power of what we call LIP shortly after the end of major combat operations. He described situations similar to those subsequently found in Iraq:

> Given the ease of releasing [simple, elementary sentiments], the material and psychological means employed can be simple: the pamphlet, the speech, the poster, the rumor. In order to make propaganda of agitation, it is not necessary to have the mass media of communication at one's disposal, for such propaganda feeds on itself, and each person seized by it becomes in turn a propagandist. Just because it does not need a large technical apparatus, it is extremely useful as subversive propaganda... Any statement whatever, no matter how stupid, any 'tall tale' will be believed once it enters into the passionate current of hatred. [32]

Ernesto "Che" Guevara, who failed in all of his guerrilla campaigns but inspired scores of other insurgencies, attested to the importance of propaganda in irregular warfare. In his manual titled *Guerrilla Warfare* he wrote: "The revolutionary idea should be diffused by means of appropriate media to the greatest depth possible... the most effective propaganda is that which is prepared within the guerrilla zone."[33] One of the great proving grounds of LIC and counter-LIC, El Salvador in the 1980's, is also a case study of a formidable low-tech integrated LIP strategy. The Soviet-backed Farabundo Martí National Liberation Front (FMLN) guerrillas waged a brilliant, if lost, LIP campaign as a fundamental part of its paramilitary strategy and its ultimate political survival after the war. The FMLN's LIP was in many ways superior to that of the entire U.S. government; the Salvadoran military enjoyed the full might of U.S. weapons, intelligence and training but, with generous American advice and development aid, focused disproportionately on the traditional military front. Some observers estimate that the U.S. and Salvadoran side fought the FMLN with inverse proportionality: whereas the FMLN's weapons were notionally 90 percent psychological-political, the counterinsurgency was 90 percent force.[34] It took a disproportionately large U.S.-led effort to promote the desired level of political and economic reform, and to compete with and dismiss the narrative put forth by the FMLN. Guerrilla warfare or terrorist tactics are both asymmetrical endeavors designed to match strength against weakness. However, the U.S. tends to fights the guerrilla or terrorist on his military weakness not his political or psychological strength, even though it can afford to do both.

The historical use of rumors

Evidence from the past appears to support the thesis that rumors can be useful, as a legitimate form of propaganda, to influence and shape the perceptions of target audiences. This is especially true where media are restricted, censored, not trusted, or nonexistent. A careful study of their application prior to Operation Iraqi Freedom could have informed policymakers about the deadly challenges that this form of LIP would pose for Coalition forces. Roy Godson of the National Strategy Information Center wrote of black propaganda, that is, messages whose true source is hidden:

> Black propaganda is probably as old and widespread as civilization. The ancient kingdoms of Mesopotamia circulated false rumors to influence enemy troops. Shamshi-Adad, ruler of Shubat Enlil, used fifth columnists to help capture the city of Zalmaqum by encouraging its citizens to revolt against their rulers as he advanced into the region. He often used such 'men of rumors' to spread tales of an advancing Assyrian army, persuading the enemy to abandon its positions without a fight. Millennia later, the founder of China's Ming Dynasty used deep-cover agents to spread false rumors that led to the disbanding of a large army set to oppose him.[35]

It would appear that as a means of disseminating propaganda, in the context of primitive technological conditions, rumors were an appropriate tool. During World War II, the Office of Strategic Services (OSS) maintained guidelines regarding the use of rumors.[36] The OSS advised: "tell the story casually, and if especially hot, confidentially. Never speak the rumor more than once in the same place, and never disclose a source that a skeptic could easily discredit."[37] The United States used a rumor successfully during World War II to hide the whereabouts of one Herr Gisevius who was implicated in the plot to assassinate Adolf Hitler.[38] The OSS "spread the rumor that Gisevius had succeeded in escaping from Berlin (where he was actually in hiding) to Switzerland, with the result that the Gestapo hunted him in Switzerland thereby allowing him to escape from Berlin."[39] During and after World War II, Harvard University psychology professors, among others, studied the use of rumors in wartime.[40] Rumor-mongering has ample precedent as a legitimate military tool.

The British were equally interested in the use of rumors during World War II and were prepared methodologically to use them. Nigel West, writing about the British Security Coordination (BSC), noted that the British maintained "direct contacts" with the Japanese Embassy in Washington, D.C. and its consulates in New York and San Francisco. These contacts permitted the British to "both gauge official Japanese reaction to specific operations and to use official Japanese communications as 'rumour' channels."[41] According to West, the BSC's Far Eastern Political Warfare unit not only tried to "destroy the German-Japanese Alliance," but also intended to harden resistance in the U.S. and the Far East to Japanese aggression.[42] This strategy was executed in part by sponsoring the "publication and distribution of pamphlets, and the planting of rumours in enemy and neutral missions."[43] The British developed a separate unit, the Political Warfare Executive (PWE), to carry out psychological warfare against the Nazis.[44]

The BSC apparently felt that rumors were of such import that it 1941 it created "an organization for spreading rumours."[45] Like its American cousin, the Office of Strategic Services, the BSC established ground rules for its rumor organization:

- A good rumour should never be traceable to its source...
- A rumour should be of the kind, which is likely to gain in the telling...
- Particular rumours should be designed to appeal to particular groups...
- A particular rumour should have a specific purpose...

- Rumours are most effective if they can be originated in several different places simultaneously and in such a way that they shuttle back and forth, with each new report apparently confirming previous ones. [46]

306   STRATEGIC INFLUENCE

These rules illustrate the importance given to the use of rumors as political and psychological warfare instruments. BSC rumor activities included "whispering campaigns among dock workers, seamen and employees of plants and factories." [47]   The British spread rumors in Latin America by "word of mouth" and targeted "different social levels through the contacts which agents maintained with governmental, diplomatic, professional, social, commercial and working-class circles as well as with various minority groups..."[48] Consistent with rule three, the BSC "planted high-level rumours... with traveling diplomats, and simpler rumours with crews and third-class passengers."[49] The ultimate effect of these campaigns is not known exactly, but West reports that rumors initiated on ships were often "repeated to their originators as gospel truth before the ship had sailed."[50]

The Germans also utilized rumors as a propaganda technique during World War II. One of the major functions of the black Axis radio station Debunk reportedly was to disseminate rumors. [51] Germans also were reported to have used, albeit unsuccessfully, "deliberate whispering campaigns, started by word-of-mouth rumor agents, early in the war and just before Pearl Harbor."[52]

In one remarkable case of strategic deception prior to Operation Barbarossa, as described by Christopher Andrew and the late Vasili Mitrokhin: "the Abwehr, German military intelligence, spread reports that rumors of an impending German attack were part of a British disinformation campaign..."[53] They noted that this tactic exploited Stalin's paranoia toward Churchill; namely, the belief held by Stalin that Churchill "designed to continue the long-standing British plot to embroil [Stalin] with Hitler."[54] In addition, Andrew and Mitrokhin wrote:

> As it became ever more difficult to conceal German troop movements, the Abwehr spread rumors that Hitler was preparing to issue an ultimatum, backed by some display of military might, demanding new concessions from the Soviet Union. It was this illusory threat of an ultimatum, rather than the real threat of German invasion, which increasingly worried Stalin during the few weeks and days before Barbarossa... A succession of foreign statesmen and journalists were also taken in by the planted rumors of a German ultimatum. [55]

Discussion of rumors would not be complete without greater reference to Soviet propaganda. Former Czechoslovakian disinformation officer Ladislav Bittman argued in his book *The KGB and Soviet Disinformation: An Insider's View* that the Soviets scored a "major victory" over the United States by preventing Iran from remaining an American ally after the overthrow of the Shah.[56] Soviet covert action "in the form of forged evidence, rumors, and manipulation of leftist organizations contributed directly to the general confusion and anti-American hysteria" after the seizing of the U.S. embassy.[57] Specifically, Bittman pointed out, the Soviets disseminated rumors in May 1980 that were designed to confuse exiled Ayatollah Ruhollah Khomeini and the Iranian public and to create the impression that the events surrounding the Iranian revolution were directed by the CIA. [58] Bittman cited one Soviet rumor in particular that is as bizarre as those that circulated Iraq a generation later. "Widely circulated rumors," he wrote, "claimed that President Carter had tried to mail a poisonous snake to kill the American hostages so that he could use their deaths as a pretext for military invasion."[59] As ludicrous as the story sounds to the Western ear, the theme may have been appropriate for the target audiences.

Finally, Soviet oral disinformation, including a KGB black radio station in Baku, played into the general anti-American sentiment and distrust felt by many Arabs and Muslims when Moscow spread the rumor that the United States was behind the seizure of the Grand Mosque of Mecca in 1979.[60]

These historical examples are retold for the purpose of illustrating the serious nature of rumors as a form of propaganda. In societies where objective information is strictly limited, or where psychological/cultural conditions permit them, rumors can be dangerous weapons with which to shape perceptions and influence the behavior of individuals.[61]

The relationship between rumors and official state-sponsored propaganda

The stock market is perhaps the best illustration of the effectiveness of rumors. Prices of stocks and other equities fluctuate with unconfirmed reports, release or leakage of unconfirmed or unreliable data, news or fears of a diplomatic crisis or otherwise insignificant military action, the parsing of words of a foreign leader or the Federal Reserve chief, careless journalism, and even speculating about made-up stories.[62]

In the Middle East, what often passes for "news" and general information is often patently false, misleading, and incitive. An example is a 2004 Iraq case where Army Gen. John Abizaid denounced Arabic-language media outlets Al Jazeera and Al-Arabiya for "broadcasting what he said were false reports of American troops deliberately targeting civilians in Fallujah."[63] Steady reportage of such falsehoods has a tangible cumulative effect. Throughout the region, government controlled media spew forth bizarre, recycled, vitriolic messages, the gravity and long term consequences of which much of the West has been unwilling to comprehend or confront.

The facility and ease with which individuals believe outlandish information begs an obvious set of questions: Why do people of all mental and intellectual capacities come to accept nonsense as truth and truth as nonsense? What can explain this cognitive behavior? And how can the United States come to terms with its influence in order to avoid a repeat of what happened in Iraq relating to the use of low intensity propaganda?

George Orwell left us a good place to begin. He was referring to Stalinism, but his words apply to new forms of militant statism and fanaticism that seek to change or enforce what people think and believe:

> Totalitarianism has abolished freedom of thought to an extent unheard of in any previous age. And it is important to realize that its control of thought is not only negative, but positive. It not only forbids you to express – even to *think* – certain thoughts but it dictates what you *shall* think, it creates an ideology for you, it tries to govern your emotional life as well as setting up a code of conduct. And as far as possible it isolates you from the outside world, it shuts you up in an artificial universe in which you have no standards of comparison. The totalitarian state tries, at any rate, to control the thoughts and emotions of its subjects at least as completely as it controls their actions.[64]

In that broadcast Orwell explored the effect that totalitarianism and the totalitarian state would have on literature writ large (poems, critical essays). But it also provides an apt description of how a totalitarian state functions as a propaganda state; the latter being necessary to ensure the continuation of the former, and vice-versa. It is this mix of totalitarianism and propaganda that characterizes Islamism and other extremist movements, such as Venezuelan Bolivarianism, in the world today, even in societies not fully totalitarian. State controlled media spout and repeat virulent anti-Western ideas that belie the true source of the oppression and degradation that characterize these parts of the world and provide the ideational basis for the beliefs that support or justify acts of terror. The messages are not only from the state, but from extremist-run mosques and non-governmental organizations and movements. They are spread abroad through migration, television, internet, proselytism, and political action.

It is easy to see the extent to which many Arab and Muslim leaders and state-controlled media misinform, disinform, and misguide their listeners, viewers, and readers, and propagate pernicious ideas that make the concomitant rumors appear reasonable. The Middle East Media Research Center (MEMRI) and other groups that publish reliable translations of extremist messages, allowing speakers of English who do not read Arabic, Farsi and certain other languages to view firsthand the intellectual and political climate that consumes normal societies.[65] For instance, the Saudi government daily *Al-Riyadh* published an item that made international headlines. Columnist Umayma al-Jalahma of King Faisal University wrote: "I chose to [speak] about the Jewish holiday of Purim... For this holiday, the Jewish people must obtain human blood so that their clerics can prepare the holiday pastries. In other words, the practice cannot be carried out as required if human blood is not spilled... the blood of Christian and Muslim children under the age of 10 must be used..."[66] This example, extreme but not atypical, is indicative of a pattern of behavior that illustrates the destructiveness that even governments closely allied with the United States have tolerated and promoted.

Swimming in a seemingly unending torrent of propaganda from regional media outlets in countries traditionally considered pro-Western, it is no wonder that low intensity propaganda, as a tool in the hands of individuals engaged in a low intensity conflict against U.S. and allied forces in Iraq and elsewhere, had a demonstrable effect. LIP simply reinforced political, ideological and cultural ideas, norms suspicions, myths, and beliefs that were introduced or repeated to the public via "mainstream news" outlets and the internet. Reciprocally it received reinforcement, and a large degree of legitimization, even from governments, organizations and societies that oppose and even fear the extremists. Little counterpropaganda existed to neutralize the radicals or provide cover for the civilized.

How rumors affect perceptions in Iraq

After the fall of the Ba'athist regime, powerful anti-Coalition rumors flourished due to the psychological/cultural conditions that existed within the mind of Iraqis. Saddam Hussein's study and manipulation of rumors exacerbated the mindset.

The deposed Iraqi dictator "institutionalized the study and use of rumors. Saddam clearly viewed them as a tool of power. His security services monitored and collected them. His intelligence services fabricated and spread them," a journalist reported from Baghdad three months into the invasion. The correspondent interviewed Maan Izzat, a former editor in the Ministry of Information, who admitted that "Every day without fail... Saddam would receive a report with details of the most prevalent rumors, as well as political jokes. That was his way of keeping his finger on the pulse of the people, and of knowing when to get tough." The interviewer also noted that, "while Saddam's intelligence services were spreading rumors, his security service, which was a separate agency, was collecting them. Agents around Baghdad wrote daily reports that attempted to gauge the public mood by identifying rumors."[67] Ba'ath party propaganda hid Saddam behind "a screen of deliberate myth, deception, misinformation and cultivated rumors."[68] An Iraqi working for the Coalition Provisional Authority (CPA) as a media analyst summed up the challenges that faced this governing body: "Saddam Hussein propagated thousands of lies over three decades, maybe people find it hard to trust the CPA."[69]

No evidence suggests that the United States was prepared strategically to fill the information vacuum that existed during and after Operation Iraqi Freedom. No baseline for truth was established during the formative period when the Coalition was creating uncertainties and the Iraqis were searching for answers. In a country where, according to the editor of *Al Sabah*, a new Iraqi daily, "people had to depend on rumors because they could not trust the media,"[70] it is no wonder that Saddam loyalists or other terrorists could supplement their terror tactics with low intensity propaganda to manipulate and mobilize sympathetic individuals, or to terrify ordinary Iraqis. In truth, we find in retrospect that the U.S. hardly tried.

Here are a few examples of enemy LIP in the months following the fall of Baghdad:

- The bloody and destabilizing November 2003 "Ramadan attacks" can be traced back to "leaflets" and "rumored warnings" which called for a "day of resistance" beginning Saturday, November 1. The leaflets which spawned the rumors were "attributed to the ousted Ba'athists," according to the Associated Press.[71]

- The deadly incident in Fallujah discussed above came about in part as a result of "rumors spread that U.S. soldiers were using their night vision goggles to spy on Muslim women...and other stories of soldiers handing pornography to children."[72] One Iraqi, a local baker, admitted that, "these rumors affect the people in a negative way... They push people to use their weapons against Americans."[73]

- As reported by the *Chicago Tribune*, "red" mosques, "led by imams hotly opposed to U.S. troops in Iraq," act as one source for bitter accusations and lies that often become rumors. [74] According to the *New York Times* "banners calling for jihad, or holy war, against American troops" were placed around many "important" Sunni mosques. [75]

- On 9 June 2003 the Associated Press ran a story about Islamic author Alaa el-din al-Mudaris and "Iraq's first homegrown book about the war." The AP described his 124-page book, written and published in *two weeks*, as a "hodgepodge of anti-American tirades and wartime rumors" which "feeds the web of myths" and repeats some of the rumors that were prevalent under Saddam Hussein's rule. The AP reported that the book was published locally by the Al-Rageem publishing house in Baghdad (only two months after the fall of Baghdad), and was "funded by the author."[76]

- In the Iraqi city of Mosul, extremists used loudspeakers to carry the messages of angry, anti-American imams into the streets and into the rumor mills. At the Haibat Khatoun mosque, the imam delivered a "fiery sermon" which reportedly accused American troops of "insulting" the Koran and "trampling the honor of women."[77] Other mosques in Mosul reportedly became "channels for anti-American rhetoric" which taps into the "perceptions of Western dominance" and painted the "occupation as a religious struggle." [78] This included the al-Shaheed Bashar Qalander mosque whose leader, Sheik Safo, admitted calling for "armed jihad... 'in public, without hesitation.'" [79]

- Even propaganda as makeshift as graffiti can lead to dangerous rumors. [80] Messages scrawled on bridges read: "Long live the leader Saddam Hussein" and "We swear to God... that we will chop all the hands that wave to American soldiers whose hands are stained by the blood of our great martyrs." [81] These were powerful messages that played upon the fear inspired by Saddam Hussein and his henchmen and they delivered an instantly recognizable warning to those who might have welcomed the liberators. They showed the powerlessness of the Coalition to control information in a society accustomed to strict controls.

- Short term, tactical efforts to dispel rumors and to instill confidence in the Iraqis have been met with mixed success. *Al Sabah* was reportedly asked to debunk some of the rumors after they had become "so numerous."[82] Authorities in Iraq also reportedly increased their presence on Arab television and took to the streets "with evidence designed to defuse gossip."[83] Other materials such as "well-designed posters" urging Iraqis to trade in their arms for cash were practically ignored, according to a report. [84] (Editor's note: See the Andrew Garfield chapter on information operation.)

- One would think that only the uneducated could believe nonsensical rumors (such as one that spoke of "X-ray vision" sunglasses worn by U.S. troops).[85] But even an engineering student, someone trained to reason with quantifiable data, commented that, "with those glasses, he can definitely see through women's clothes."[86]

Without a political-ideological blueprint comparable to its overwhelming military strategy, Coalition forces had to play catch up. More than five months after the fall of Baghdad, the *Washington Times* reported:

> The Coalition Provisional Authority is still struggling to get its message to the Iraqi people. Meanwhile, Al-Jazeera, Iranian state-sponsored broadcasting and others are filling the information vacuum with a bias that is harmful to our mission in Iraq.[87]

And two months later, in December 2003, the *Washington Post* observed:

> the coalition's own attempts to broadcast news and information [in Iraq] have been woefully deficient. Although it controls Iraq's main broadcast channel, two domestic radio stations and a major newspaper, the authority and its American contractors have failed to capture the Iraqi audience – news programs, in particular, smack of sanitization. The problem is made all the more serious by the fact that Arab satellite broadcasters are at once more skilled in production, more credible with many Iraqis and wildly biased against the U.S. mission.[88]

The Pentagon scotched a plan to support an independent, high-quality Baghdad newspaper, run by Iraqis for Iraqis, with news, commentary and features that the local people actually would want to read. Proponents argued that, with the right Iraqi editors, the U.S. would not need to control the newspaper, but would enable the creation of an Arabic-language paper that would not necessarily toe a U.S. policy line, but would serve U.S. interests by its general editorial approach and its independence. The Pentagon ultimately rejected the idea, creating instead a military-sponsored giveaway paper that few Iraqis found interesting or relevant, and even fewer chose to read.[89]

The problem is not unique to the Bush administration or Iraq, but reflects a human tendency throughout history. In a 1950's essay titled "The Use of Rumor in Psychological Warfare," John P. Kishler and Kenneth W. Yarnold, et al. noted an all too common problem that persists even to this day:

> During wartime, officials concerned with propaganda had to respond to immediate needs using the best information or the most insightful guesses of which they were capable at that time. They were much more concerned with operations than with scientific research likely to be useful in a future war. [90]

Rumorfare

The United States government is wedded predominantly to passive, overt information dissemination techniques and it seems reluctant to meet the enemy in his own intellectual or psychological territory other than in a tactical manner. The meager sums (relative to the overall defense budget) that are spent on political-ideological warfare operations are appropriated for media services like the Voice of America or new endeavors such as Radio Sawa or the Alhurra Middle East Television Network.[91] While those outlets have their own merits, the point here is not to question or debate them, but to show that these traditional means of reaching desired audiences in the Middle East are the progeny of Cold War models that were based on containment theories and a "Long War" paradigm. In contrast, the "Global War on Terror" is a pre-emptive endeavor (a hot war in which time works against us) that rejects the containment approach, at least rhetorically, and to which the containment model often does not apply. Therefore, political-ideological warfare operations need to be synchronized with the prevailing doctrines that are currently guiding national security policy around the world.

It was a luxury, relatively speaking, during the Cold War to have an apposite amount of time to expose Soviet active measures. But in a n information age low intensity conflict, defensive measures are restricted by the brief time it takes for various forms of hostile low intensity propaganda to incite resistance to and violence against U.S. soldiers and allies. As Herbert Romerstein notes in his chapter on counterpropaganda in this volume, the side who has to explain or defend himself is likely to find himself the loser. That reality begs for a proactive, even pre-emptive doctrine that can fulfill the political-ideological warfare requirements that any potential battlefield – political, diplomatic or military – demands. The adversary or enemy should not be allowed to dictate the terms of this engagement. Done well, the engagement will need minimal military force – or none at all.

In the case of Iraq, the appropriate strategy could have focused its attention on "the rumor" and the other forms of low intensity propaganda (leaflets, banners, graffiti, "red mosques") that help to create and maintain still more rumors that are responsible for serious violence and acts of terrorism against U.S. and Allied forces. A well designed rumorfare campaign could have exposed, countered, and *pre-empted* the spread of inimical rumors as well as attenuate their influence in the post-Hussein environment. Like any political, diplomatic, or military, the rumor will occasionally have unintended consequences and even prove counterproductive at times. This should not preclude use of the tool, however. The most carefully crafted and benignly worded press releases, diplomatic communiqués and leaflets can occasionally backfire.[92] Procedures to inoculate U.S. intelligence collectors and analysts from inadvertently picking up U.S.-made rumors, and other safeguards, must be an integral part of rumor deployment. Journalists, as paid employees of private media corporations, should professionalize and improve their standards so as not to pick up rumors and report their contents as fact. But that is a not a job for the American government.

Why rumors?

In Iraq, rumorfare is likely to be more successful than any direct attempt to challenge more material forms of LIP such as banners, graffiti and leaflets. Truthful rumors can be designed and spread covertly to foretell and complement policies, actions, and decisions that are disseminated in more mainstream channels or even to support covertly disseminated materials in support of the mission or strategy.

One rumor that circulated Iraq in September 2003 might have been received more favorably had the United States integrated a strategic LIP program with other overt strategic information operations and public affairs. Iraqis, as well as interested audiences in the region, were unprepared socially for the rumors that spoke of U.S. plans to "privatize" the Iraqi economy. CNN reported the following on September 23, 2003:

> One of the principal concerns [among Iraqis] – and I asked about this morning – is the rumor that the United States is going to try to privatize the economy here. Now, under Saddam Hussein, Iraqis got very cheap electricity, privatization means that they are going to be paying more, and they are going to be paying more when many of them don't have jobs to pay for the current low prices on electricity. More alarming is, of course, the issue of health insurance here, or rather healthcare, if, indeed the rumors are true, which are sweeping Baghdad today, that the United States is going to try to privatize healthcare here. That means many Iraqis fear they won't be able to afford it, because they paid only a nominal cost for healthcare under Saddam Hussein, and this, too, leaves them more than a little anxious.[93]

If Iraqis had been informed prior to Operation Iraqi Freedom that the privatization of Iraqi industries would lead to economic prosperity for the country and increase individual wealth, then these rumors might not have caused further anxiety among an already anxious people. At the same time, it is dangerous to have rumors, like official public affairs packages, that over-promise and unfairly raise the people's hopes.

Put simply, rumors, like it or not, are more likely to resonate in the minds of people of many cultures than official news and public affairs statements sponsored overtly by the United States government or U.S. authorities. As Kishler and Yarnold noted a half-century ago:

> Rumor is potentially useful in psychological warfare since its source is not obvious and does not depend on a formal communication system for its dissemination. Typically its dissemination occurs in a friendly face-to-face situation of mutual trust. For this reason, rumor tends to be more credible than conventional means of propaganda. It is particularly suitable for use in primitive communities where formal communications are ill-developed, uncontrolled and uncentralized.[94]

Since those communications help define the battlespace, one finds a sound basis for adopting a low intensity propaganda campaign that focuses on rumors designed to counter those being propagated by adversaries using similar means.

How to proceed

The United States government never developed a permanent set of political-ideological warfare instruments that it could wield strategically to pursue its interests and promote its values in any context apart from the Cold War.

The largest impediment to the creation of a strategic political-ideological warfare apparatus comes from the belief that the United States government should not disseminate "propaganda," a word, which carries with it a negative connotation. Edward Bernays acknowledged this stigma in his 1928 monograph *Propaganda* but also challenged the pejorative use of the word: "I am aware that the word *propaganda* carries to many minds an unpleasant connotation. Yet whether … propaganda is good or bad depends upon the merit of the cause urged, and the correctness of the information published."[95]

Harold Lasswell's definition of propaganda is also useful. It captures the essence of the word and makes clear why the United States should not fear its use in officialdom, especially if it intends to win the proverbial "battle of ideas." Lasswell wrote succinctly in *Propaganda Technique in World War I* that, "propaganda is the war of ideas on ideas."[96] Propaganda, he said,

> refers solely to the control of opinion by significant symbols, or, to speak more concretely and less accurately, by stories, rumors, reports, pictures and other forms of social communication. Propaganda is concerned with the management of opinions and attitudes by the direct manipulation of social suggestion rather than by altering other conditions in the environment or in the organism.[97]

Because of the contaminated reputation of the word, there are propagandistic reasons for avoiding the term "propaganda," just as the public relations profession chose a different name from what its father Bernays had advocated. Propaganda, as popularly misunderstood, is bad public relations. However, the concept is sound, be it called public diplomacy, counterpropaganda, political warfare, public relations, public affairs, or some other term, and its mission here is to attack and counter the propaganda of our adversaries.

Coalition forces in Iraq understand from their operational standpoint the gravity of unanswered rumors. Many months into the campaign, the forces set up a "daily intelligence document that chronicles the latest street talk in the Iraqi capital, however ill-founded, bizarre or malevolent" after "American military leaders realized rumors themselves had become a security problem."[98] The daily, known as

The Baghdad Mosquito, is a "collection of rumor, gossip and chatter called, 'What's the Word on the Streets of Baghdad?'" According to a news report, "The *Mosquito*'s reports helped...fine-tune advertisements, posters and billboards that focus on new Iraqi security forces."[99] Overall, however, policymakers seem wedded to the notion that overt and traditional political-ideological warfare techniques *by themselves* (VOA, Radio Sawa, the Middle East Television Network/Alhurra, billboards) are sufficient strategic tools with which to address the issues of terrorism or, more broadly, to fight and win the "battle of ideas" vis-à-vis Islamic radicals.

Novel initiatives like Radio Sawa or Alhurra are important and increasingly successful on certain levels, but they *cannot* be the *principal* means by which the United States government wages political-ideological warfare. Their missions, staffing and institutional ethos preclude it. They depend on transparency and building relations of trust with their audiences and with the public and Congress back home. They are already stigmatized by their relationship to the United States and could very well fail in the long-term if listeners and viewers come to believe (thanks to hostile propaganda) that these initiatives are mere tools of the "Great Satan" or the "Zionists." More immediately, these tools (as they are currently structured) are outmatched and inapplicable in a low intensity conflict scenario (as in Iraq).

If low intensity propaganda can be understood strategically in relation to low intensity conflict, then it may be possible to deny in advance the political-ideological warfare means used by terrorists. The low-tech nature of LIP can be amplified regionally and globally through integration with electronic communications. Information technologies present an excellent opportunity to use LIP strategically outside the territory of Iraq in order to influence audiences within Iraq. For instance, the May 2000 *Report of the Defense Science Board Task Force on the Creation and Dissemination of All Forms of Information in Support of Psychological Operations (PSYOP) in Time of Military Conflict* observed that, "A leaflet handed out in Bosnia is just as likely to be shown by a reporter on the nightly news in the United States or Europe as it is to be read in Sarajevo."[100] Unfortunately, this same report noted two pages later that U.S. "handbills" are "typical tactical PSYOP actions," an analysis that assigns strategic value to enemy leaflets, but tactical value to the American version. The Defense Science Board's 2004 report on strategic communications was a much better product, taking a more comprehensive and integrated approach, but it still failed to integrate strategic information operations, public diplomacy and other forms of communication with the accelerant of political warfare.

The United States and its allies could lose in Iraq and elsewhere if they do not 1) come to understand the strategic role of low intensity propaganda within the context of strategically significant low intensity conflicts; 2) develop strategic, rather than tactical, solutions to counter the various forms of low intensity propaganda; and 3) establish a permanent, strategic-level apparatus that can carry out the missions in the first two points prior to and during U.S. involvement in future low intensity conflicts.

Conclusion

In closing, there are some concerns that need to be addressed in reference to the idea of using LIP to counter other forms of LIP. For one, rumors can be unpredictable and may lead to unintended consequences that could hurt U.S. interests rather than advance them; leaflets can be ignored or destroyed; graffiti can be white-washed; banners can be torn down; and rumors perceived to be untruthful and attributed to the United States will tarnish U.S. credibility.

The idea is not to rely solely on LIP to promote American interests or to counter the LIP of America's enemies. Rather, the U.S. should use LIP as a *complement* to other forms of strategic political-ideological warfare after it is studied seriously and comprehended extensively by professional political-ideological warriors in and out of uniform. The hope is that low intensity conflicts may be shortened by neutralizing or muting the ideational inspiration that often accompanies them. If the United States can succeed at this endeavor, then it will be that much closer to winning its battle of ideas.

Traditional public diplomacy and public affairs efforts by the United States government will meet with limited success unless they take into account the severity of the messages that they are attempting to challenge, counter and ultimately defeat. Early in the war, U.S. public diplomacy efforts were likened to the marketing of Uncle Ben's rice. Selling rice to an American or world audience under the brand of a warm and friendly old uncle, however, would have been impossible if potential consumers had been instructed for generations that rice was poisonous, cancerous, or evil. Therefore, an appropriate mechanism needs to be developed that will permit the United States to wage a "battle" or "war" of ideas on terms familiar with the mindset of individuals whose cognitive processes have been groomed to suspect or even reject all that is perceived to be American.

But this battle cannot be fought, nor the war won, without first comprehending the function that state-sponsored propaganda, and even the propaganda of non-governmental groups, around the world has served over the years. In sum, it has made natural the outgrowth of low intensity propaganda as the appropriate adjunct to any low intensity conflict – with or without an Internet.

Notes

[1] *Department of Defense Dictionary of Military and Associated Terms*, Joint Pubs 1-02, March 1994. The intensity of the conflict is a matter of perspective. For people on the ground, both military and civilian, the intensity may be quite high, but from a national strategic level, the intensity is low in comparison to all-out warfare as conventionally conceived.

[2] This author introduced the term "low intensity propaganda" in November 2003 to describe the various forms of propaganda that were prevalent in Iraq during the months immediately following the fall of Baghdad and which became significant political-ideological weapons utilized by anti-Coalition forces. See Steven C. Baker, "Iraqi Lies, American Blood," FrontPageMagazine.com, November 11, 2003, source: Internet, http://www.frontpagemag.com/Articles/ReadArticle.asp?ID=10746.

[3] For instance, a rumor can be a means to disseminate information, it can refer to the content contained therein, or it can be both. Example: 1) Jane used rumors to destroy Bob's untarnished reputation; 2) The rumors about Bob' adulterous liaisons were true; 3) Jane repeated rumors about Bob's adulterous liaisons in order to destroy his polished image.

[4] Edward Bernays, *Propaganda* (Ig Publishing, 2005; reprint of 1928 edition), p. 52.

[5] See Paul A. Smith, Jr., *On Political War* (National Defense University, 1989).

[6] According to the White House's National Security Strategy published in September 2002, the United States "will disrupt and destroy terrorist organizations by... defending the United States, the American people, and our interests at home and abroad by identifying and destroying the threat before it reaches our borders. While the United States will constantly strive to enlist the support of the international community, we will not hesitate to act alone, if necessary, to exercise our right of self-defense by acting preemptively against such terrorists, to prevent them from doing harm against our people and our country." United States, Office of the President, National Security Strategy (September 2002), p. 6.

[7] "Secretary of Defense Donald H. Rumsfeld regional media interviews; interviewed by Katarina Bandini, WHDH, Boston," Defenselink.mil, October 27, 2003, http://www.defenselink.mil/transcripts/2003/tr20031027-secdef0822.html.

[8] Walter Pincus, "Creation of terrorists must be stopped, Rumsfeld says," *Washington Post*, November 3, 2003.

[9] According to the Defense Science Board, "Military tactical PSYOP are taken in a local area with focused impact. Loudspeaker operations, handbills, local radio broadcasts, and television programming are typical tactical PSYOP actions." United States, Department of Defense, Report of the Defense Science Board Task Force on The Creation and Dissemination of All Forms of Information in Support of Psychological Operations (PSYOP) in Time of Military Conflict (Office of the Under Secretary of Defense for Acquisition, Technology, and Logistics, 2000), p. 13.

[10] "Address of the President to the Nation," Office of the Press Secretary, September 7, 2003, source: Internet, http://www.whitehouse.gov/news/releases/2003/09/20030907-1.html.

[11] "Live report from Baghdad," Fox on the Record with Greta Van Susteren, Fox News Network, April 9, 2003.

[12] "FBI to aid in recovery of stolen Iraqi antiquities," News Night with Aaron Brown, CNN International, 17 April 2003.

[13] Ibid.

[14] Ibid.

[15] "Garner: Restoring Water, Power Top Priorities," News Night with Aaron Brown, CNN, April 21, 2003.

[16] "Live from the headlines: Does U.S. plan to keep bases on Iraqi soil?" CNN Live with Paula Zahn, CNN, April 21, 2003.

[17] Sonia Bakaric, "Candles already blown out on Saddam's 66th birthday bash," Agence France Presse, April 27, 2003.

[18] "Three dead in Tel Aviv suicide bombing; New Palestinian Prime Minister pledges fight against terror," News Night with Aaron Brown, CNN International, April 29, 2003.

[19] Niko Price, "In Baghdad, rumors abound: Saddam is in the United States; no wait, he's dead," Associated Press, May 10, 2003.

[20] Ibid.

[21] The Zarqawi letter was posted on the Coalition Provisional Authority website at http://www.cpa.gov/transcripts/20040212_zarqawi_full.html, but the U.S. government deleted the links (instead of redirecting them) when the Coalition Provisional Authority was abolished.

[22] Tarek al-Issawi and Hamza Hendawi, "Blasts kill 125 at Iraq Shi'ite Shrines," Associated Press, March 2, 2004.

[23] Ibid.

[24] Vicki Allen, "U.S. General: Evidence links Zarqawi to Iraq attacks," Reuters, March 3, 2004.

[25] Bassem Mroue, "U.S. hits Fallujah mosque; 40 said killed," Associated Press, April 7, 2004.

[26] Karl Vick and Anthony Shadid, "Fallujah gains mythic air," *The Washington Post*, April 13, 2004.

[27] Ibid.

[28] Alistair Lyon, "Rebel attacks in five Iraq cities kill 75," Reuters, June 24, 2004.

[29] Ibid.

[30] Ibid.

[31] Editor's note: The National Defense University is a notable exception. It sponsored a conference on the issue and published the proceedings in 1989. See Frank Barnett and Carnes Lord, eds., *Political Warfare and Psychological Operations: Rethinking the U.S. Approach* (National Defense University, 1989).

[32] Jacques Ellul, *Propaganda: The Formation of Men's Attitudes* (Vintage Books, 1965), p. 74.

[33] Che Guevara, *Guerrilla Warfare* (Monthly Review Press, 1961), p. 97-98.

[34] See, for example, Jose Manuel Moroni Bracamonte and David E. Spencer, Strategy and Tactics of the Salvadoran FMLN Guerrillas: Last Battle of the Cold War, Blueprint for Future Conflicts (Praeger, 1995); and J. Michael Waller, The Third Current of Revolution: The North American Front of El Salvador's Guerrilla War (University Press of America, 1991).

[35] Roy Godson, *Dirty Tricks or Trump Cards* (Transaction Publishers, 2001), pp. 154-155.

[36] John J. Pitney, Jr., *The Art of Political Warfare* (University of Oklahoma Press, 2000), p. 108.

[37] Ibid.

[38] John P. Kishler and Kenneth W. Yarnold, et al., "The Use of Rumor in Psychological Warfare," in Willian E. Daugherty and Morris Janowitz, eds., *A Psychological Warfare Casebook*, (The Johns Hopkins Press, 1958), p. 666.

[39] Ibid.

[40] See Gordon W. Allport and Leo Postman, *The Psychology of Rumor* (Henry Holt and Company, 1947).

[41] Nigel West, ed., *British Security Coordination* (1998), p. 93.

[42] Ibid, 98.

[43] Ibid.

[44] See David Garnett, The Secret History of PWE: The Political Warfare Executive, 1939-1945 (St. Ermin's Press, 2002).

[45] West, pp. 109-110.

[46] Ibid, pp. 111.

[47] Ibid, pp. 110.

[48] Ibid.

[49] Ibid, pp. 111.

[50] Ibid.

[51] John P. Kishler and Kenneth W. Yarnold, et al., "The Use of Rumor in Psychological Warfare," in William E. Daugherty and Morris Janowitz, eds., *A Psychological Warfare Casebook*, (The Johns Hopkins Press, 1958), p. 661.

[52] Ibid, p. 663.

[53] Christopher Andrew and Vasili Mitrokhin, The Sword and the Shield: The Mitrokhin Archive and the Secret History of the KGB (Basic Books, 1999), p. 93-94.

[54] Ibid.

[55] Ibid.

[56] Ladislav Bittman, *The KGB and Soviet Disinformation: An Insider's View* (Pergamon-Brassey's, 1985), p. 125.

[57] Ibid, p. 125.

[58] Ibid, p. 123.

[59] Ibid.

[60] Western Goals Endowment Fund, *Soviet Active Measures against the United States* (Western Goals Endowment Fund, 1984), p. 95.

[61] It should be emphasized that this paper focuses only on the effectiveness of LIP – particularly rumors – and does not examine the intentions of those who have used LIP in the past to propagate information.

[62] National Public Radio reported in March 2003 shortly before the commencement of Operation Iraqi Freedom that Wall Street experienced a sharp rally after a "rumor" spread that Iraqi generals were considering plans to surrender to the United States before the war started. "Wall Street rally yesterday shows how susceptible the markets are to rumors," Morning Edition, National Public Radio, March 14, 2003.

[63] "U.S. General denounces Arab TV stations," Associated Press, April 13, 2004.

[64] George Orwell, "Literature and Totalitarianism," broadcast typescript, May 21, 1941 from George Orwell, *Essays*, Ed. John Carey, (Knopf, 2002), p. 362.

[65] See www.memri.org. Palestinian Media Watch monitors radical Palestinian movements, at www.pmw.org.il/new/.

[66] "Saudi government daily: Jews use teenagers' blood for 'Purim' pastries," Translated by The Middle East Media Research Institute, Special Dispatch Series – No. 354, March 13, 2002, source: Internet, http://www.memri.org/bin/opener.cgi?Page=archives&ID=SP35402.

[67] Michael Slackman, "A tale of two cities: In Fallujah, things are not going so well for U.S. forces," *Los Angeles Times*, June 14, 2003, p. F1.

[68] Lance Gay, "Using fear and terror, Saddam firmly in power," *Scripps Howard News Service*, October 17, 2002.

[69] Thanassis Cambanis, "Rebuilding Iraq/U.S. message; Iraqis turn a deaf ear to effort to win trust," *The Boston Globe*, August 23, 2003, p. A8.

[70] John Tierney, "After the war: The rumor mill; G.I.'s have X-ray vision. Of course," *The New York Times*, August 7, 2003, p. A10.

[71] Sameer N. Yacoub, "Iraqi rioters battle U.S. troops," Associated Press, October 31, 2003.

[72] Michael Slackman, "A tale of two cities: In Fallujah, things are not going so well for U.S. forces," *Los Angeles Times*, June 14, 2003, p. F1.

[73] Ibid.

[74] Laurie Goering, "Rumor mill grinds up truth in Iraq; Gossip of U.S. 'misdeeds' spreads fast," *Chicago Tribune,* July 11, 2003, p. 1, Zone C.

[75] Alex Berenson and Susan Sachs, "U.S. forces battle Iraqi guerrillas in intense firefight," *New York Times*, October 31, 2003.

[76] Hamza Hendawi, "Iraq's first book on war a mix of myth, rumors," Associated Press, June 9, 2003.

[77] Mariam Fam, "Mosques on front line of battle with U.S.," Associated Press, November 10, 2003.

[78] Ibid.

[79] Ibid.

[80] Niko Price, "In Baghdad, rumors abound: Saddam is in the United States; no wait, he's dead," Associated Press, May 10, 2003.

[81] Ibid.

[82] Ibid.

[83] Laurie Goering, "Rumor mill grinds up truth in Iraq; Gossip of U.S. 'misdeeds' spreads fast," *Chicago Tribune*, July 11, 2003, p. 1, Zone C.

[84] Thanassis Cambanis, "Rebuilding Iraq/U.S. message; Iraqis turn a deaf ear to effort to win trust," *Boston Globe*, August 23, 2003, p. A8.

[85] John Tierney, "After the war: The rumor mill; G.I.'s have X-ray vision. Of course," *New York Times,* August 7, 2003, p. A10.

[86] Ibid.

[87] Jeff Kojac, "Disinformation on Iraq; U.S. must answer hostile foreign press," *Washington Times*, September 30, 2003, p. A21.

[88] "Losing the Media War," *Washington Post*, December 1, 2003, Editorial, A22, source: Internet, http://www.washingtonpost.com/wp-dyn/articles/A24132-2003Nov30.html.

[89] Information provided by a U.S. official involved with strategic information efforts and who had firsthand knowledge of the Baghdad newspaper proposal.

[90] John P. Kishler and Kenneth W. Yarnold, et al., "The Use of Rumor in Psychological Warfare," in William E. Daugherty and Morris Janowitz, eds., *A Psychological Warfare Casebook*, (The Johns Hopkins Press, 1958), pp. 657-658.

[91] Harold C. Pachios, "Televising balanced, fair news: New Arabic network will provide America a voice in the Middle East," *Los Angeles Daily Journal*, March 28, 2003, source: Internet, http://www.state.gov/r/adcompd/rls/19557.htm.

[92] For a documented example on a local level in Iraq, a Reuters correspondent reported, "Thousands of leaflets urging Najaf's residents to hand in their weapons litter the street near a U.S. tank parked by the governor's office. Almost all of them have been ripped up. 'People read the leaflet and get annoyed and then deliberately tear it,' said Ahmed Mussawi, a tea boy standing opposite the fortified offices, where flyers not caught on the razor wire flutter in the air." Suleiman al-Khalidi, "Anti-American sentiment grows in Iraq holy city," Reuters, May 31, 2004

[93] "View From Iraq," CNN Live Event/Special with Aaron Brown, September 23, 2003.

[94] John P. Kishler and Kenneth W. Yarnold, et al., "The Use of Rumor in Psychological Warfare," in William E. Daugherty and Morris Janowitz, eds., *A Psychological Warfare Casebook,* (The Johns Hopkins Press, 1958), pp. 657-658.

[95] Edward Bernays, *Propaganda* (Ig Publishing, 2005), p. 48.

[96] Harold D. Lasswell, *Propaganda Technique in the World War* (Kegan Paul, Trench, Trubner & Co., Ltd.. 1927), reprinted as *Propaganda Technique in World War I* (The M.I.T. Press, 1971), p. 12.

[97] Ibid, p. 9.

[98] Thom Shanker, "U.S. team in Baghdad fights a persistent enemy: rumors," *New York Times*, 23 March 2004. [Editor's note: This author originally suggested that rumors were a significant security problem in Iraq in an article, "Iraqi Lies, American Blood," FrontPageMagazine.com, November 11, 2003. http://www.frontpagemag.com/readArticle.aspx?ARTID=15525.]

[99] Ibid.

[100] United States, Department of Defense, Report of the Defense Science Board Task Force on The Creation and Dissemination of All Forms of Information in Support of Psychological Operations (PSYOP) in Time of Military Conflict, (Office of the Under Secretary of Defense for Acquisition, Technology, and Logistics, 2000), p. 11.

16

Red Teaming Strategic Communication and Political Warfare

DAVID SPENCER

Definition

To measure the effectiveness of its doctrine, organization, weapons, strategies and tactics, and to stay ahead of any possible enemy, the U.S. military invests heavily in war gaming. The State Department and other diplomatic entities have preferred to leave such matters to the Pentagon, seldom gaming out diplomatic strategy to determine its usefulness in protecting and advancing the national interest. As such, gaming is almost exclusively the domain of the armed forces, unwanted by the diplomats and unappreciated by the public communicators. We can see the results today: Superior military strategy and tactics over any foe, but grossly inadequate public diplomacy, political warfare, information strategy, and PSYOP at a time when warfare more than ever depends on communication.

In general, war games are conceived as simulations of conflicts between at least two sides: friendly forces, which in United States lexicon are always Blue, and enemy forces, which are always Red.[1] In this chapter we will focus on "red teaming," which is the endeavor to portray or play adversarial forces in war games or simulations. Political warfare is the employment of politics as an instrument of war and nonviolent conflict. Generally, but not always, the elements of political warfare are non-military. These include the war of ideas, information war, psychological operations, economic and social policies, and diplomacy. All of these elements can and are used to ostracize, surround and strangle adversaries, laying them open to military action. If done masterfully, the use of military force may be minimal or even unnecessary. Therefore, red teaming strategic communication and political warfare is the playing or portrayal of these elements in a game or simulation. Red teaming political warfare is a relatively recent phenomenon. However, it will become increasingly important as the United States is challenged the dominant world superpower and the conflicts around the world become increasingly complex and asymmetric and hence require more non-military responses. The reality is that the United States is woefully unprepared to face these emerging challenges.

Why war game?

War gaming is a very popular pursuit, both within and outside of government. Within the military it is not something done for entertainment purposes. It is a very serious business and millions of dollars are spent every year by the U.S. military on related activities. War gaming is taken so seriously because experience has demonstrated that it can enhance performance in the event of war. The overwhelming victory of 1991 to repulse Iraqi forces from Kuwait can be attributed in part to excellent war gaming at all levels of warfare for exactly the type of challenge presented by Saddam Hussein. The U.S. has no equivalent for its training of diplomats and public diplomacy practitioners, or for the civilians who control the military.

A brief history of the development of war gaming

Modern war gaming has its origins, as do many elements of today's military structure, in the development of the Prussian General Staff during the 19th century. The Prussian General Staff was created as a countermeasure to the genius of Napoleon. Napoleon was a methodical and thorough planner who had a reputation for considering every aspect of a battle to include numerous possible variants or contingencies. His constant preparations for these contingencies made his French Army virtually unbeatable. The Prussians reasoned that while they had no single individual who could match Napoleon, they could counter him with a well-trained group of officers organized into a staff that divided up the tasks of planning and organization. Their adaptation succeeded. The new Prussian General Staff made a significant contribution to Napoleon's defeat between 1813 and 1815. However, a major problem that had plagued the armies of Napoleon's opponents persisted. This was their inability to systematically test and evaluate their military capabilities against the French before they reached the battlefield. One of the reasons that Napoleon was successful for so long was his opponents' inability to learn lessons from the defeats he had inflicted on others, and to incorporate these lessons systematically into their own planning to avoid the same mistakes.[2]

In the post-Napoleonic era the Prussian General Staff recognized the need for a way to test their ability to lead and manage the increasingly large and complex European armies before doing battle. To address this need, the General Staff developed *Kriegspiel* (War Play). *Kriegspiel* originated in an evolution of variations of chess, popular at the time, that a young Prussian officer figured out how to transfer from a board to a map. He converted the pieces into military units that adequately simulated combat capabilities. The Prussian military immediately recognized the value of *Kriegspiel* as a training tool for the staff, giving them an analytical tool for systematically evaluating the validity of military concepts and plans. Most importantly it gave the General Staff the ability to test their military plans before they went to battle. Since the 1820's, *Kriegspiel* evolved, allowing more sophisticated and realistic play, and thus an increasingly more useful analytical tool to evaluate plans and concepts. The Prussians developed and employed war gaming to provide training at the different levels of conducting military operations: tactical, operational and strategic.

The ultimate form of war gaming were the annual maneuvers. In the Prussian army war gaming was so serious that careers were made, accelerated, or broken by war game performance.[3] The overwhelming victories of 1864 against Denmark, 1866 against Austria and 1870-71 against France – foes that enjoyed tactical superiority, but strategic and operational incompetence – can be attributed to the superior training of the German General Staff which involved intensive and repeated war gaming.

The stunning victory over France in 1870 caused the world to pay attention, and by the end of the century, all of the world's major armies had established General Staffs and Staff Colleges of their own. An important component of the education system copied from the Prussians was war gaming and maneuvers.

Red teaming conventional enemies

Despite war gaming and maneuvers the concept of red teaming – the art of playing the role of the adversary – was still fairly elementary. However, war gaming was developed by conventional armies to fight conventional foes. Thus *Kriegspiel* generally assumed battles between equals. The enemy was essentially a mirror image of one's own forces. Up through mid-20th century Europe this was basically valid. The French military and the Prussian/German military looked very similar in terms of numbers, weapons and equipment. The arms races of the late 19th and early 20th centuries guaranteed that both France and Germany stayed abreast of each other in terms of military technology. Other European countries attempted to keep up with both powers to avoid falling behind. To make up for numerical differences due to differences in territorial and population sizes, the nations of Europe formed alliances to establish a balance of power. Thus throughout Europe there was rough military parity during this time period. This guaranteed that head to head, force on force encounters would essentially result in a draw. The challenge for war gaming was not, then, in applying force but rather in how to out-maneuver the opposition. The Germans used war gaming extensively to test their concepts of maneuver, acquiring superiority over their traditional enemies. Their superiority over the French in war gaming was manifest in the three major Franco-German wars: 1870, 1914, and 1940. Decisive defeats were inflicted on the French in 1870 and 1940 (and nearly in 1914, too, had there not been for on Moltke's blunder in moving troops to Alsace Lorraine, against the prescription of the von Schlieffen Plan). All three times, the Germans were able to outthink and outmaneuver the French who were marginally superior in numbers and technology.

The 1940 campaign was exemplary. It is popularly believed that the German victory was due to the superior technology and numbers of their armored forces. In reality, the Germans had fewer tanks than the French, armed with smaller guns and protected with weaker armor. Despite somewhat inferior numbers and technology the Germans easily outmaneuvered the French. The German concept of employment and maneuver was far superior, conceived and perfected through war gaming.

Another characteristic of war gaming during this era was that it generally did not involve political or diplomatic elements. It was basically assumed that all diplomatic and political maneuvering were separate activities and had been exhausted when hostilities commenced. It was then time for the generals to take over and continue politics by other means. War gaming did not integrate politics into the play.

Cold War shift

The post-World War II era changed this. With the development of the atomic bomb, maneuver of forces in conventional war became less relevant. Well-placed nuclear weapons could kill tens of thousands if not hundreds of thousands of combatants (and non-combatants). Initially both the United States and the Soviets tried to devise doctrines for attacking and defending with nuclear weapons. However, with the development of the hydrogen bomb, the intercontinental ballistic missile, and the ability to strike back even if struck first, created the doctrine of Mutually Assured Destruction, making superpower nuclear warfare impractical. Conventional war between nuclear powers became nearly obsolete because even if both sides agreed that a nuclear exchange was suicidal; if one side began to lose the conventional battle, the temptation to prevent conventional war defeat by escalating the conflict to nuclear war would almost be too great.

The 1962 Cuban Missile Crisis was sobering because it demonstrated that events in a seemingly insignificant country could push the world to the brink of nuclear war. Subsequently, both the Soviets and the United States tried to learn how to prevent such an incident from happening again. A substantial portion of the effort to learn the lessons of nuclear brinksmanship in the United States involved war gaming that involved possible contingency scenarios. Substantial political play became an element of these games.

To prevent a nuclear war the United States had to know how the Soviet leadership thought and what would push them overt he brink. Conversely, the other sides' uncertainty of the threat of nuclear war could be a very useful tool to coerce the other side into modifying behavior. This was high stakes poker, and knowing how far this card could be pushed without having the bluff called was vital. Simulation became necessary for working out all the possible variations. Red teaming became more sophisticated because war gaming nuclear brinksmanship required getting into the mind of the adversary more than playing mirror image forces.

This required an understanding of the adversaries', political system, history, and culture because it forced players to attempt to think outside of their own culture and frame of reference. It required focus on messages and perception, because cataclysmic decisions would be made on the basis of these two factors as much as others: actions had to be interpreted within a context, and messages and perception would be key to interpreting actions. We had to think like the enemy.

Nuclear brinksmanship war gaming was the simulation of the unthinkable to prevent Armageddon. In the end it contributed to preventing the United States and the Soviet Union from destroying each other and the world via nuclear war over miscalculations and misunderstandings. In the 1980's, calculated political and economic warfare against the USSR exploited the vulnerabilities and inefficiencies in the Soviet system to hasten its internal collapse.

Indirect warfare

The threat of nuclear destruction, of course, did not end warfare altogether. Since major conventional force-on-force clashes relying on grand maneuver were too perilous, the U.S. adopted an indirect approach of warfare. The indirect approach was a very old solution in the history of conflict, one that the Soviets had already been employing through their international networks of loyal Communist parties, front organizations, and "fraternal" anti-colonial movements.

In medieval times, the way to defend one's territory from an enemy attack was to build a castle. The strength of the fortification could defeat a conventional force-on-force assault. Finding himself at a disadvantage, (i.e. too weak to take the castle through direct assault), the aggressor would lay siege to the fortress. The concept of the siege was to prey on the castle's vulnerabilities rather than directly confronting its strengths, and take the bastion over time. If done right, an aggressor might not even have to assault the castle at all. The greatest vulnerability of a castle was the very people defending it. People needed food, water, sanitation, rest, and hope on a regular basis or they would not hold out the siege. Due to the very nature of castles, and their finite boundaries, the elements to sustain life were in limited supply, so if an aggressor could cut the castle off and maintain the pressure for a sufficiently prolonged period of time, the castle would inevitably fall. Military operations consisted of actions designed to erode the defender's will to resist, not necessarily destroy its forces. On the tactical level, the purpose of military operations was to harass defenders psychologically, contain them within the fortification and prevent them from breaking the siege.

Like the medieval armies, both the United States and the Soviets employed the indirect approach to countering each other. On the grand strategy level, this involved important elements of political warfare. The United States attempted to hem the Soviets in and prevent the spread of Communism by creating numerous defense treaty organizations. In Latin America there was the Rio Treaty. In Europe the Americans created NATO. In Asia they created SEATO, and in the Middle East they set up the short-lived Baghdad Pact; the Australia-New Zealand-U.S. (ANZUS) alliance completed the global network. The Soviets responded by creating the Warsaw Pact and, more importantly, by offering support to (or co-opting) nationalist and "national liberation" causes to break up the treaty organizations and turn the tables on the United States. This approach was successful in fracturing the Baghdad Pact over the United States' support for Israel (notwithstanding Stalin's backing of Israel's creation). The Soviets saw an opportunity and supported Arab nationalism, and successfully developed relationships with many Arab nations through the mid 1970's.

Nor did the United States stand still. Wherever the Soviets or their surrogates appeared, the United States countered. The superpower support for and against nationalist and "national liberation" causes and the danger of nuclear war through direct confrontation produced an intense era of comparatively small wars. Through these small wars, which never pitted U.S. and Soviet forces directly against one another, the Soviets were able to break out of the siege and gain allies in Southeast Asia, Africa and Latin America. However, the United States successfully assisted the prevention of pro-Soviet regimes from taking power in other nations in the same regions, and in defeating Soviet-backed movements.

War gaming and red teaming in this kind of grand strategy of political world domination and containment was fairly straightforward. Kids growing up played such popular games as Risk™; international relations and political science students were often required to play Diplomacy™. When they entered government service they had already received a basic training of sorts because war gaming this kind of grand strategy involved essentially much more sophisticated versions of the board games. This type of war gaming was fairly easy as it involved gaming traditional European style diplomacy and political warfare of nation states, something that was instinctively familiar. War gaming the small wars, however, was much more difficult.

Small wars

Small wars were certainly not a new phenomenon. The United States and most of Europe had fought or participated in numerous small wars throughout the 19th Century, although it is not clear that they ever war gamed them. Despite extensive experience with small wars, the Great Powers had never fought or supported small wars in the context of a bipolar world and nuclear umbrella. This framework meant that few small wars were isolated since the opposing sides of the Cold War left few states outside the purview of both superpowers.

Soviet sponsorship of anti-colonial movements and regimes led the U.S. to become more involved globally to keep Soviet expansionism in check. Outcomes of small wars had not only local, but also strategic implications. This meant that even wars in remote parts of Africa, Asia or Latin America received far more scrutiny than before. Because overt support by one side was quickly countered by support from another, a lot of great power involvement remained clandestine.

Clandestine support or involvement in a conflict meant that overt support by the other side became problematic as well. Clandestine support was particularly suited to a method of indirect warfare called insurgency. Insurgency, a particularly difficult form of small war, because of the intertwining of political and military actions, spread across the globe. As such, insurgency has been difficult to game.

Insurgency, a virulent form of small war

The most advanced insurgent warfare theory followed the basic approach of the medieval siege. Instead of being a physical structure however, the castle was the target political system. The vulnerability was the people, but instead of the people's physical needs such as food and water, it was specifically the people's willingness to sustain the system. The battle was then for the people's minds in the physical area of the nation, rather than for the physical space itself.

Thus insurgent warfare presented a new challenge to the military for a number of reasons. Political and military elements were intermingled, with the political moving to the fore and the military moving into the supporting role. Unlike the European wars of the 19th and early 20th Centuries, there was no clear dividing line between political actions and military actions. Second, the success or failure of a military action was far more dependent on perception of the operation than the objective outcome of the action. The victory was in people's minds, not in the body count. The Tet Offensive of 1968 is a precise example. Although U.S. and South Vietnamese forces virtually destroyed most of the Viet Cong National Liberation Forces (NLF), theirs became a pyrrhic victory because the political will in the United States to continue support for the war was severely weakened due to the perceptions of a North Vietnamese/NLF ascendance. Third, winning the military battle didn't guarantee winning the war. In fact, one could win all the battles and still lose the war, as the United States did in Vietnam. The latter lesson was learned through bitter experience. War gaming and exercises did a good job of teaching the military how to battle guerrillas, but not how to win wars. Much of the problem lay in the lack of understanding of the insurgent strategic framework and the psychopolitical nature of insurgent warfare.

The Maoist insurgency framework: Three tasks

Mao Tse-tung developed the most advanced and sophisticated theory of insurgency, which is relevant today despite shifts away from Marxist ideology and towards ideologies involving ethnicity or religion. The basic principles of the Maoist framework apply to insurgencies, terrorism and most forms of asymmetric warfare and they continue to befuddle and challenge United States national power. They currently present a significant red teaming challenge. Captured al Qaeda manuals show careful study of Mao and the incorporation of Mao's psychological approach to warfare into Islamist terrorist strategy.

Mao's challenge was to find a way to defeat the Japanese who invaded China in the 1930's as well as advance the Communist takeover of China. Mao understood that although he was at war, ultimately the struggle was political. He wrote that "war is politics with bloodshed," and "politics is war without bloodshed."[4] In other words, war and politics were different modes of the same struggle. Indeed, to Mao the term "political warfare" would have been redundant. This is a sharp difference from Western nations where political and military issues are carried out in different departments that often fail to communicate with each other.

Mao identified three essential tasks that the Chinese revolutionaries needed to achieve to attain victory. These were: the mobilization of the Chinese people into a united front against Japanese invaders, the formation of an international anti-Japanese united front, and the development of a people's revolutionary movement within Japan to destroy Japan's will to continue the fight. Sometimes these three tasks are referred to as "currents," and they formed Mao's grand strategy.[5] What is striking is that none of the three principal tasks of the revolutionary war mentions anything that is explicitly military. This did not mean that military tasks were irrelevant or unimportant, but rather that they were subordinated to political objectives. Everything the insurgents did had to support one of these political tasks.

The first current

The most important of the tasks was the mobilization of the Chinese people.[6] Mao fills most of his pages with discussion of this issue. He was well aware that the Japanese were militarily much more advanced, organized and disciplined than the Chinese. How then could China hope to defeat Japan? Mao came to the conclusion that the basic principle had to be to "do the utmost to preserve one's own strength and destroy that of the enemy."[7] While this may seem so obvious as to not be worthy of mention, as a guiding principle for the Chinese, it meant finding a different way of fighting war other than principally conventional war. The concept developed by Mao was what can be called the concept of relative correlation of strengths and weaknesses, or relative correlation of forces.   Relative correlation of forces was probably derived from Sun Tzu. For example, Sun Tzu said:

> ...an army may be likened to water, for just as flowing water avoids the heights and hastens to the lowlands, so an army avoids strength and strikes weakness. And as water shapes its flow in accordance with the ground, so an army manages its victory in accordance with the situation of the enemy. And as water has no constant form, there are in war no constant conditions.[8]

Mao wrote: "the enemy forces, though strong (in arms, in certain qualities of their men, and certain other factors), are numerically small, whereas our forces, though weak (likewise in arms, in certain qualities of our men, and certain other factors) are numerically very large."[9] Elsewhere he wrote: "Japan's advantages lie in her great capacity to wage war, and her disadvantages lie in the reactionary and barbarous nature of her war, in the inadequacy of her manpower and material resources, and in her international support."[10]   In contrast, "China's disadvantage lies in her military weakness and her advantages lie in the progressive and just character of her war, her size and her abundant international support."[11]   Mao reasoned that time, or a prolonged or protracted war, was required to shift the balance in favor of his takeover of China. His argument was that: "the enemy's strength and our weakness have been relative and not absolute."[12]

To convince the skeptics, he wrote: "the fact is that the disparity between the enemy's strength and our own is so great that the enemy's shortcomings have not developed... while our advantages have not developed, and for the time being cannot develop to a degree sufficient to compensate for our weakness."[13] Favorable changes in the relative correlation of forces would occur over time as the Communists carried out the three strategic tasks, particularly the mobilization and organization of the united front against Japan. By accomplishing these tasks, China would cultivate its "advantages" as the war was drawn out.[14]   The task of the Communist military organization was to adopt the tactics that would best support the mobilization of the Chinese people. The key was flexibility. The three rules of flexibility were dispersal, concentration and shifting of position or movement.[15]

How to apply the rules of flexibility depended on the strategic phase of warfare that the conflict was in: strategic defensive, strategic pause and strategic counteroffensive. Mao identified three modes of warfare – guerrilla, mobile and positional – that roughly but not exclusively corresponded to the strategic phases. Flexibility meant being able to operate back and forth in the guerrilla, mobile and positional warfare modes seamlessly without major disruption. This was a revolutionary idea.

Mao said that ultimately military forces sought to become strong enough to hold terrain and fight conventionally in a war of positions. However, revolutionaries didn't want to do this in the early stages of the war, when forces were relatively weak, because that would play to the enemy's strengths and violate the rule of self preservation. Instead the revolutionaries organized guerrilla bands that could use their small size and local knowledge to move quickly and stealthily to harass and attack enemy vulnerabilities, such as supply and communications routes.

The military value of these attacks was marginal at best. The primary purpose was psychological: to demoralize the enemy by taking away the safety of their rear areas, but more importantly to energize and mobilize the people by showing them that resistance against the enemy was possible. It also served to mobilize international sympathy by portraying the guerrillas as righteous and heroic underdogs. Why not remain inactive, conserve strength and wait for the right moment? Because although counterintuitive, doing this would actually be counterproductive.[16] The guerrillas needed to remain constantly active, presenting at least the illusion of resistance, or the message would stagnate and mobilization of the people cease to occur. Constant combat activity was imperative, but for political and psychological reasons, not military reasons.

Mobile war was to be employed when the guerrillas were strong enough to form essentially conventional units that could take on the enemy in face-to-face battle, but did not fight to take or defend terrain except in a temporary manner, according to the tactical need of the moment. Military action acquired stronger forces because the objective of a particular action might be the destruction of a portion of the enemy's main forces, not just his vulnerable supplies and communications. However, mobile war was not conventional war, but essentially "large guerrilla war." Mobile columns were to apply guerrilla tactics of hit and run and harassment, but on a large scale. While the military value of the actions increased, the most important impact was still psychological and political to help consolidate the mobilization process. The message was to show that not only was resistance possible, but that it was possible to defeat enemy forces under certain conditions. It is important to note that Mao did not conceive of mobile warfare as replacing guerrilla warfare, rather as complementing it.

Guerrilla warfare was a means of preparing the battlefield for the mobile columns. Guerrilla warfare tied down, wore down, distracted and dispersed enemy forces so that they would be vulnerable to mobile warfare attacks. Depending on the local conditions, guerrilla actions or mobile actions could predominate. Flexible application of concentration, dispersion and movement were to be applied in all phases. Positional war was the final mode of combat adopted when all the conditions existed for the insurgents to fight the enemy in a conventional manner, head to head, and subsequently take and occupy territory. Again, mobile and guerrilla war did not cease to exist, but rather were coordinated to prepare the battlefield so the conventional forces could attack the enemy from a maximum advantage by having sapped his will and cut off his means of supply and communications before engaging in battle. The simultaneous combination of conventional, mobile and guerrilla warfare is known as the combination of all forms of struggle.

The strategic stages and their corresponding modes of battle were laid out in a very logical manner. However, a common error in the west has been to assume that these stages and modes occurred in a linear fashion. The Communists understood that the enemy is not a fool and that it, too, will act and react in its attempt to win the war. Thus, relative advantages can be gained by either side at different points of time in the war. There can be multiple strategic counteroffensives, because they can fail for multiple reasons. The insurgents may not have been as strong as they thought they were, or they were badly led, or the enemy was lucky and able to defeat them for various reasons. In other words, strategic phases were reversible, and the insurgents would have to start all over again. The Vietnam war offers a good illustration. In 1968 and 1972 the Vietnamese Communists attempted positional warfare and were beaten. Each time they moved back into guerrilla warfare mode, built up their forces, and attacked. It took the third try in 1975, for the Communists to triumph, this time as a conventional invasion of the North Vietnamese Army after the Americans had abandoned the South. A setback of a strategic phase does not mean defeat in war. It just means regression to the appropriate strategic phase.

We can see something similar occurring with Al Qaeda. The 9/11 attacks can be seen as a sort of peak for the organization. This was made possible by the existence of a secure base in Afghanistan and the experience of a series of successful attacks around the world. The United States' overthrow of the Taliban regime and subsequent counter-terrorist campaign, including disruption of financing operations, have hurt Al Qaeda. The response has been to regress to a more dispersed and cellular organization. In other words Al Qaeda applied Mao's rules of flexibility. After its rise and severe setbacks inside Iraq, the group is attempting to build its forces back up to continue the war on various fronts. Fighting the United States in Iraq offers them the opportunity to do so: to continue valuable media-friendly attacks on coalition and Iraqi forces, to invite made-for-TV counterattacks that can be used to inflame elements of the population, demonize the American public and their political leaders, and in general to maintain its profile as a visible enemy of the U.S. Mao is as applicable as ever today. What is important to note, however, is that the up and down fortunes in military phases and modes of operation were, and are, far less important than developments in other areas of struggle.

The second, and most fatal error committed by the west has been to assume that combat was the most important or principal activity of the insurgents. As we have pointed out, both guerrilla warfare mode and mobile warfare mode have the largely political objective of popular mobilization. It is only in the final positional warfare mode that military activity takes the fore in hopes of deciding the outcome of the war. If this is true, then prior to that the principal activity does not take place on the physical battlefield, but elsewhere.

This is where military and non-military, as traditionally seen, combine in the "all forms of struggle" concept. The North Vietnamese, specifically Truong Chinh, called it the "war of interlocking." In revolutionary warfare, all forms of struggle, political and military, are equally valid from the combatant's perspective. All occur simultaneously across the entire space of the territory being liberated (generally a country) and all contribute toward the triumph of the revolution. The form dominating at the strategic level depends on the strategic phase of the conflict. The form dominating at the local level is entirely dependent on local conditions. The ultimate aim is to provoke the uprising of the masses and for the insurgents to offer an organized vanguard to the masses that would ride the wave of the insurrection and guide it to victory. This could include protest marches, peace negotiations, propaganda, political organization and even participation in elections. If any combination of those means would move the organization forward and put the revolution in a better position, then they were just as valid, or better than combat. Mao is quoted ad nauseam as having written that the people are the water in which the guerrilla fish swim.[17] (While this isn't exactly what he said, it is close enough to convey his idea.) The concept is that the people are the support network of the insurgents and that without them the insurgency fails. While true, the problem with this understanding is that it portrays the people as playing a fairly passive and secondary role. The guerrillas are the active force who hide among the people, and get their logistics and recruits from them, but the people do little else besides being a "pond for the fish."

Under this presumption, the solution for counterinsurgency is easy: separate the insurgents from the people and they wither. However, reality is much more complicated than that; Mao envisioned a much more active role for the people. He noted: "The mobilization of the common people throughout the country will create a vast sea in which to drown the enemy, create the conditions that will make up for our inferiority in arms and other things."[18] This is a much more profound statement because here the people are assigned a more central role in the war. The people *are* the insurgency. This is not necessarily apparent because they are not, perhaps, armed and organized as an army. However, they don't just sit on the sidelines as auxiliaries; they are active combatants against the regime or dominant power. It is the people, organized, who shift the relative correlation of forces in favor of the insurgents and overcome the enemy.

History has proven that this concept can work well beyond Mao. In Cuba, 8,000 guerrillas defeated a government army of 60,000. In Nicaragua, 5,000 guerrillas defeated a government army of 30,000. Militarily these are ratios of 7.5 to 1 and 6 to 1 respectively. In each case the guerrillas advanced to the conventional forces stage and fought a war of positions to achieve victory. By itself this does not make sense as it is generally believed that conventional forces require a 2 to 1 ratio of superiority when attacking defending troops. The way it was accomplished in both cases was that the people actively rebelled, rose up, harassed, demoralized, isolated and trapped government forces, even if the masses were not highly indoctrinated in the insurgents' ideology. They made it impossible for the government to govern or exercise control over the country. Hezbollah appears to be following this strategy in Lebanon. This methodology allowed the guerrillas the ability to move around the country freely and concentrate superior forces at locations of their choosing, picking off government garrisons one by one.

The strategic importance of the non-military aspects of prolonged war are illustrated by a 1974 encounter between Colonel Harry Summers and North Vietnamese Colonel Tu. When Summers pointed out that the North Vietnamese had never beaten the United States on the battlefield, Colonel Tu's now famous reply was: "That may be true, but it is also irrelevant."[19] This is further reflected in the comparative casualties. American, South Vietnamese and allied combat deaths totaled 276,408. During the same period, the Communists lost 1,100,000,[20] an approximate 1 to 4 ratio, and yet the Communists won the war. This is because the non-military rather than the military actions proved to be decisive.

The second and third currents

So far, we have largely dealt with the first revolutionary task or current, the mobilization of the people, but the other two currents were also vital: the mobilization of the international allies, and the mobilization of internal opposition within the enemy power's own country. Mao is relatively silent on these tasks. When Mao was writing, the international community had already mobilized against Japan. Mao identified this mobilization as one of the Chinese relative strengths. Prior to 1941, most of the international community publicly denounced Japan and sold or gave weapons to China. During World War II, the United States and other Allies fought Japan directly and continued to provide the Chinese resisting Japan with large quantities of weapons and equipment, although most of it was not destined to the Communists. The bonus for the Communists occurred at the end of World War II when the Soviets turned over vast stores of weapons and equipment, including tanks and artillery, to Mao's forces. This equipment played a key role in the Communist victories during the civil war. Besides maintaining delegations in Moscow and other countries, the Communists had to do relatively little to mobilize international support; the Soviets were doing it for them. The situation was similar for Vietnam, as well. During the conflict with the U.S., the Soviets and Chinese played a similar role in supplying the Communist forces. Also, the threat of direct war with China if the United States invaded North Vietnam prevented the United States from acting, thus guaranteeing the territorial security of the Communists' base area.

The Chinese were never able to organize an internal Japanese resistance. However, the Allied war against Japan had the desired effect in that it weakened the Japanese homeland, and thus the Japanese ability and will to make war in China. The North Vietnamese were able to masterfully manipulate the internal U.S. opposition to the Vietnam War, a fact that played a strategic role in weakening the American national will to continue the fight. In the end, the U.S. defeat in Vietnam was due to the loss of domestic political will to continue the war rather than defeat in battle. The North Vietnamese leadership was explicit in acknowledging the important role that the internal U.S. opposition played in the Communist victory.[21] Other wars of liberation and revolutions have experienced similar success when wittingly or unwittingly they have successfully carried out the three tasks or currents posited by Mao. In Cuba and Nicaragua, revolutions were successful when the revolutionaries had mobilized the people for insurrection, obtained external support, and finally convinced the United States to remove, and/or block support from other countries for the government. Similar victories for the revolutionaries occurred in the former Portuguese African colonies of Angola, Mozambique and Guinea-Bissau.

In Afghanistan, a non-Maoist, non-Communist war of national liberation against the Soviets was successful because, whether by design or not, the three strategic tasks were accomplished. The *mujaheddin* were able to mobilize the population against the Soviets. The United States, several European countries, Pakistan and others were mobilized to both condemn the Soviet invasion and isolate Moscow diplomatically and economically, and provide hundreds of millions of dollars in military and humanitarian aid to the *mujaheddin* to fight the Russians. Finally, the failure and attrition in Afghanistan sharpened a political crisis in the Soviet Union that eventually led to Moscow's withdrawal in 1989. It is doubtful, given the nature of the Soviet system, that the *mujaheddin* or the United States were able to organize the anti-Afghanistan war movement in the Soviet Union the way the Vietnamese Communists were able to influence the anti-Vietnam war in the United States. However, the failures in Afghanistan coincided with an internal Soviet political crisis that the U.S. exploited with its political, military, and economic offensive designed to hasten an internal Soviet collapse. The system began to collapse of its own accord and along with it the will to continue the war in Afghanistan.

The case of El Salvador is worth mentioning here, because of the unique outcome, and because it took place at the same time as the Soviet war in Afghanistan. El Salvador had probably the most advanced insurgency in Latin American history. The insurgents, known as the Farabundo Marti National Liberation Front (FMLN) were able to mobilize people early in the war, and successfully able to gain international support.[22] However, although bitterly fought, they were unsuccessful in their attempts to get the United States to abandon El Salvador. Quite to the contrary, the United States heavily intervened on behalf of the government although political power in the United States was divided and a substantial percentage of the political establishment remained against U.S. policy in the country. The mobilized pro-FMLN element put sharp restrictions on what the United States could do to help the government, and thus its ability to defeat the FMLN.

However, despite the restrictions, the aid was crucial and allowed the government to counter-mobilize and take back a large part of the population in favor of the government (relative correlation of forces), although the FMLN was able to maintain a certain amount of the population mobilized for the revolution. With partial mobilization in El Salvador, full international support, and partial mobilization of internal opposition within the U.S., the war stalemated and ended in a negotiated settlement in which the FMLN survived as a viable political force. This is an interesting case because many of the challenges the United States face today are similar to the ones it confronted in the 1980's, with some of the same actors involved on both sides.

Relevance to today's wars

Red teaming partial internal U.S. opposition and partial popular mobilization in the host country can have a significant role as we attempt to find solutions to the insurgencies in Iraq, Afghanistan and the so-called War on Terror.

One example that illustrates the point is Iraq, where the insurgents have partially mobilized the population for insurrection. As of this writing, they are in the process of attempting to mobilize the rest. They have acquired some important international support, particularly from the Islamic street, although not from the majority of Muslim/Arab governments (at least not openly), though Iranian support has been considerable. Furthermore, although most of the world does not support the insurgents, it also fails to support the United States and its presence in Iraq. Finally, although it has not grown to the intensity of the Vietnam war, there is growing opposition in the United States to the war in Iraq. It is worth wondering what the situation will look like in year five or year ten of the conflict. These are good scenarios to red team, as they are likely to have an impact on United States strategic goals in Iraq and the conduct of operations. Al Qaeda's media strategy shows the traits of its Maoist training manuals. Understanding the Maoist framework can contribute to realistic solutions to present and future conflicts.

Red teaming since the Cold War

Red teaming has not kept up with the pace of warfare. Exercises have tended to focus on the military aspects of insurgent warfare such as guerrilla tactics. The political side has been ignored. Red teamers have been directed specifically not to include politicians in their gaming scenarios. In other words, we have dealt with the visible symptoms, but not the disease. While the United States became excellent guerrilla fighters in Vietnam, winning almost every military engagement, these skills were irrelevant to the strategic outcome of the war. The U.S. lost the war because it failed to understand the conflict *at the strategic level.* The lack of understanding of insurgent warfare continues to plague the United States thirty years later. While some fairly sophisticated analyses were done both during and since the conclusion of the Vietnam War, and U.S. experience in El Salvador reinforced these lessons, the military and the government essentially turned their backs on the lessons or failed to learn them at all. Small wars were messy and complicated. The strategic enemy was the Soviets and training focused on fighting a conventional war against the Soviets in Europe. All training and exercises were generally focused on defeating this foe. Red teaming meant knowing how the Soviet General Staff and its subordinate units operated. Careers were made by becoming experts on the conventional battle. Even with all the resources invested in red teaming the Soviets, the United States still avoided including Soviet strategic psychological warfare, known collectively as "active measures," as fundamental elements of their scenarios. Officers who focused on insurgency found their careers cut short.

The 1991 Gulf War only reinforced this tendency. Saddam Hussein foolishly chose to confront the United States in exactly the kind of battle the United States had spent twenty years training to win. The result was inevitable. The problem is that the victory in the Gulf War caused the United States to learn the wrong lessons. They learned that their focus on fighting massed armies had been right. Furthermore, because the Cold War was over, and there was no need to fight insurgents, they threw out the old manuals about small wars, insurgency and counterinsurgency. It became national policy not to "do counterinsurgency" any more. Conventional wisdom was that small wars and insurgency were just big wars in miniature. American leaders were soon to find out that they were not as right as they thought.

Shortly after the Gulf War it became painfully evident that the United States was unprepared to deal with other types of conflict. Communism collapsed and the Soviets disappeared as a strategic enemy. Numerous small but lethal wars broke out around the globe. Political decisions were made to intervene, and the institutions rushed to write new manuals to deal with the "new threat." The lack of institutional depth was reflected in all of the new names devised to describe the phenomenon of small wars over the past two and a half decades: Low Intensity Conflict (LIC), Counter-terrorism (CT), Military Operations Other Than War (MOOTW), Foreign Internal

Defense (FID), Internal Defense and Development (IDAD), Asymmetric Warfare, and one of the latest, Fourth Generation Warfare.

Until recently, it was generally the fact that most of the principles of these wars were very well covered in a forgotten Marine Corps manual published in 1940, known as the *Small Wars Manual*. This manual was based on the Marine Corps' experience in China and the Caribbean in the 1930's. Despite its age, the principles held true. The United States military is still struggling to define and understand this phenomenon and has reissued the *Manual*. But few analysts revisit Mao, which was evident in the multiple blunders the United States committed in Iraq after the initial invasion of the country.

However, despite the many failures since accomplishing the extraordinarily skillful mission of toppling the regime in March 2003, there have been some advances, albeit slow. The failure in Somalia and suboptimal solutions in the Balkans have pushed the military to advance red teaming. Slowly some of the non-military elements have found their way into war games. For example, an issue that began to have a serious impact on warfighting and military operations was the increasing involvement of non-governmental organizations as well as what became known as the "CNN effect." Non-government organizations included charities, humanitarian services, political organizations, media outlets and others that began to act in ways that affected military operations. The ability of CNN to broadcast in real time from conflict zones also impacted the way military operations were perceived and what troops could say or do. In ways that had never existed before, the actions of individual soldiers could have a strategic impact in real time because they could be seen live on CNN and produce political impact in the world and back home.

NGOs and CNN played a particularly important role in Somalia, where the site of Islamist mobs desecrating the bodies of American soldiers caused panic in Washington and led to a humiliating pullout. In fact CNN had been instrumental in pushing the United States and the International Community to make the decision to intervene in the first place by broadcasting images of a humanitarian catastrophe that cried out for the western democracies to do something. Realizing that they were out of their normal element, the military asked for help from the war gaming community. During and after Somalia, war games began to include players representing these nongovernmental groups. It took some time to figure out how to portray them. Were they friendly or were they enemy? The solution was to lump them together into their own team, often known as the Green Team. Green teams are essentially conceived as non-hostile forces that share some interests in common with Blue, but have their own agendas as well. In fact their separate agendas may even give them some incentive to cooperate with Red under the right conditions, or open them to infiltration, exploitation and manipulation. For example, a humanitarian NGO devoted to preventing starvation may feel that its best interests are to cooperate with Red in some areas, in order to be allowed to accomplish its objectives. Similarly, news reporters may collaborate with Red to get the story. This can have an impact on Blue's ability to achieve its mission objectives. However, Blue can't deal with Green the way it would with Red. The Marine Corps in particular did some very interesting work in the development of Green teams and their potential to be exploited by Red. In addition to CNN and NGOs it was found necessary to add cultural elements, actual citizens of the countries where the United States was operating that could accurately represent the political and cultural particularities of the scenarios. Host nation politics and forces have found their way into these Green teams as well.

One of the problems however, is the way Green teams are structured. Often there is a single green team, which is an amalgamation of basically everything that is not Red or Blue. The problem is that while convenient, this structure is inaccurate. There probably need to be multiple Green teams with multiple agendas that interact with each other and with the Blue and Red teams. Lumping them into a convenient single Green team means that they while they play they are often essentially ignored. They are there to pay lip service to the fact that they do play a significant role in real life, not to portray realistic and complex warfare.

Some military leaders have even instructed war gamers not to ruin their scenarios, as if to say, "Don't ruin a good war game with reality." This is an important problem because in the real world the complex relationships with the variety of entities that make up the Green team can have a significant impact on operations: both positive and negative. If war games are not realistic they don't accomplish the objective of preparing U.S. forces to deal with the type of small war situations they are likely to face. More realistic play would help commanders figure out how to have positive relationships with local cultures, humanitarian NGOs and the media, which would enhance the strategic success of their military operations. The United States is still too concerned with closing with and destroying enemies through kinetic action. While necessary, this is not sufficient to attain victory.

Sophistication of red teams

Red teams have also become more sophisticated. Now they often incorporate such elements as political structures, Red NGOs, mass movements, and propaganda. What is generally being played corresponds generally to an institutionalization of Mao's first task. However, there are three problems that hinder the development of truly robust Red teams.

First, because of the time periods portrayed in war gaming, events are usually not prolonged, lasting for a period of days, weeks, and occasionally months, but not years. For good reasons the United States prefers to fight quick and decisive conflicts. Current opponents are aware of this and appropriately plan and prepare for prolonged conflicts. Thus, war games become snapshots of things that might happen during a particular period of time (operational/tactical picture), but not a strategic picture that shows what will happen during a prolonged conflict. By approaching war gaming the way the U.S. would like things to be, practitioners play into enemy hands. All the enemy has to do is survive intact for a short period of time. Perhaps because of this, the second and third tasks or currents are never played and tested. However, as has been shown, for insurgents, the successful combination of all three over time is the basis for final victory.

Second, Blue always wins. Although Red may indeed develop a plan that would in reality frustrate Blue's objectives, since he always loses it doesn't matter. Red is always militarily inferior to Blue, which is not unrealistic, so it always loses. However, what is not tested is the non-military impact of Red's plan. How many of the people are mobilized? What is the effect of Red propaganda, Red civic action, Red psychological operations, etc? How do Red's operations attack political will back home? How can those operations be countered? These parameters are not measured. In the end, it is the number of fighters and weapons remaining in play that are measured. That's what is still important to the United States because too many officers still think that such quantification is the appropriate measure of victory. However, by reading Mao one easily understands that this is not what is most important to the insurgents. What is important to them is, rather, whether or not the people are more organized for insurrection than they were before. If they are, the insurgent military forces will regenerate and three, five, ten years down the road, they will be back. Perhaps by then America's will to intervene will fail and the insurgents will be triumphant.

This brings us to the final problem. In war gaming Red always reacts to Blue's concept of operations. Essentially, a scenario is created, values are pre-assigned to Red which is then expected to react to a Blue concept of operations. This immediately puts Red at a disadvantage. It also forces Red to play at an operational or tactical level, rather than the strategic level. Since the United States often intervenes in reaction to events generated by Red, the gaming approach is somewhat unrealistic, and therefore of little practical use to win the war.

These three problems mean that Blue never gets the full value of the Red team because it forces Red to play to Blue's strengths: short time, military forces, tactical level. As has been pointed out, the United States won just about every battle in Vietnam, and is currently doing so in Iraq, Afghanistan and elsewhere. Although Blue claims to value and understand the non-military aspects of warfare, it is still not incorporating them to their fullest extent. It prevents Blue from identifying its weaknesses and pretended that Red lacks the capabilities it really has to exploit those weaknesses. This needs to be changed. These exercises are useful to test tactical concepts, but they are not as useful in determining whether the United States and its allies can win complex asymmetric wars or small wars. Had the U.S. red teamed properly, it would have anticipated an insurgency in its Iraq war planning prior to the 2003 invasion. This is not 20/20 hindsight, but was foreseen by red teamers well before.

A proposal worthy of action was developed by Andrew Garfield, then a staff member of the Terrorism Research Center in Washington. He proposed that Red develop a strategy and have Blue war game Red's strategy in multiple scenarios. This would force Blue to get out of its comfort zone (quick, military, tactical) and deal with far more sticky issues (prolonged, political, and strategic). While Blue would likely fail repeatedly in the initial period, the experience would probably also force re-thinking and restructuring of the way we approach problems like Iraq, Afghanistan and the War on Terrorism. In the end, it can help us decisively win. All elements of strategic communication should be put to the red team test. Red teaming public diplomacy, political action, and political warfare will highlight the deficiencies in U.S. communication strategy and force the tough changes and seriousness of purpose that so far have eluded the public diplomacy community and others.

Our current problem is also reflected in how the United States misuses the word terrorism. Terrorism is not a strategy. It is a tactic. However, we discuss terrorism as if it were a strategy and as if it can be separated from the political, economic and social environment in which it is spawned. Speaking of it this way is highly convenient because it plays to United States strengths and gives the illusion that terrorists are somehow marginalized from society and can be surgically removed like a wart or a mole that then ceases to exist. Billions of dollars are spent on all kinds of technology and equipment to better locate and more cleanly excise terrorists from the earth. However, we continually fail to ask or answer the question of why they keep on coming back, with each generation a little more virulent and dangerous than the one before? It is because terrorism is a tactic that is linked to a political agenda or strategy. The strategies may not look much like the highly structured national strategies or concepts of operations developed by the United States military or public diplomats, but they are strategies nonetheless.

Conclusion

An understanding of Mao can begin to open understanding about why terrorists do what they do. Terrorism is the chosen tactical mode because the United States is strong and the terrorists are weak, thus terrorism avoids playing to the United States' strengths and exploits its many vulnerabilities. Terrorists are relatively resource poor, so this tactical mode also maximizes the resources at the terrorists' disposal. The main objective of the actions is not so much to cripple the United States, but to mobilize the terrorists' "home" population base and demoralize the American population.

As we can see, Mao's framework is very useful. Understanding the Maoist framework (even if the group is not Maoist per se) can greatly improve United States' ability to deal with terrorism by not only better finding and destroying the military cells, but by also properly identifying the non-military elements and adopting psychological and political policies that will neutralize these elements. This is the more difficult, but also more strategically important task. Robust red teaming can contribute to this process and prepare United States military and civilian decision-makers to know how to preempt and shatter the adversaries' strategies before they reach the battlefield. This task will fall heavily on those responsible for public diplomacy and strategic communication.

Notes

[1] In the Soviet system friendly forces were Red and enemy forces Blue.
[2] Williamson Murray, Ph.D., *Red Teaming: Its Contribution to Past Military Effectiveness* (Hicks & Associates, 2002), pp. 6-7.
[3] Ibid, p. 12.
[4] Mao Tse-Tung, *On Protracted War*, May 1938, in *Selected Military Writings of Mao Tsetung* (Foreign Languages Press, 1972).
[5] Ibid.

---

[6] Ibid.

[7] Mao Tse-Tung, "Problems of Strategy in Guerrilla War Against Japan," May 1938, in *Selected Military Writings of Mao Tse-Tung* (Foreign Languages Press, 1972).

[8] Sun Tzu, *The Art of War*, trans. Samuel B. Griffith (Oxford University Press, 1963), Chapter 6, verses 27-29.

[9] Mao Tse-tung, "Problems of Strategy in Guerrilla War Against Japan."

[10] Mao Tse-tung, *On Protracted War.*

[11] Ibid.

[12] Ibid.

[13] Ibid.

[14] Ibid.

[15] Mao Tse-tung, "Problems of Strategy in Guerrilla War Against Japan."

[16] History has borne this out. A good example of this is the Auténtico Party of Cuba that had far more organized people and resources than Fidel Castro's M-26 organization in the 1950s. However, while Castro and his small band acted, the Auténticos remained quiet, stockpiling their weapons and preserving their men for the "decisive" battle with the government. That moment never came because when the government began to collapse, and the people rallied to Castro, who had been visibly active. The inactive Auténticos were perceived as ineffective cowards.

[17] Mao Tse-tung, *On Guerrilla War.*

[18] Mao Tse-tung, *On Protracted War.*

[19] Harry G. Summers, *On Strategy: A Critical Analysis of the Vietnam War* (Presidio Press, 1995), p. 21.

[20] Jeffrey Record and W. Andrew Terrill, *Iraq and Vietnam: Differences, Similarities and Insights* (Strategic Studies Institute, U.S. Army War College, May 2004), p. 20. The figure represents five percent of the Vietnamese Communist population.

[21] J. Michael Waller, The Third Current of Revolution: Inside the 'North American Front' of El Salvador's Guerrilla War (University Press of America, 1991) pp. 2-3.

[22] Ibid. The FMLN relied heavily on Cuba, the Sandinista regime in Nicaragua, and East Germany for its organizational and direct military support. The insurgency could not have built a virtually instant international support network without the Soviet deployment of its international front organizations and controlled political parties.

17

A Comprehensive Approach to Information Operations

ANDREW GARFIELD

"Insurgencies are primarily concerned with the struggle for men's minds"
Sir Frank Kitson

Part I: The current situation

Information and influence are becoming more central to peace operations in general and counterinsurgency in particular. The U.S. Army has now recognized the importance of strategic communications and information operations (to include psychological operations, or PSYOP). Information is also one of the army's five critical logical lines of operation (LLO), those lines being a series of steps to solve a counterinsurgency challenge. The other critical LLOs are combat and civil security operations, host nation security forces, essential services, governance, and economic development.

The new Army *Counterinsurgency Field Manual* (FM 3-24) rightly states that in counterinsurgency operations, information operations (IO) are likely to be the most important LLO, and if not the most important, then certainly critical to the success of any of the other four. To quote directly from FM 3-24: "Arguably, the decisive battle is for the people's minds; hence synchronizing IO with efforts along the other LLOs is critical. Every action, including uses of force, must be "wrapped in a bodyguard of information."

This idea - that everything we do and say in a counterinsurgency operation should be "wrapped in a bodyguard of information" – is revolutionary for the U.S. military. Especially when one considers that as little as two years ago, most commanders saw IO and related tools of soft power as simply secondary functions designed to create the freedom of maneuver needed to facilitate combat operations.

By adopting the "bodyguard of information" concept, the U.S. Army will quickly deny our enemies a critical advantage. If we adequately explain our every word and action, we will gain far greater support from the local population; we will minimize the misunderstandings that can so easily arise when we do what we have to do; and we will significantly reduce an adversary's opportunities to distort, denigrate and deny our intentions, words and deeds.

However, while significant progress has been made over the last two years, we are not yet out of the woods. U.S. information operations remain but a shadow of those of our opponents, despite the investment of hundreds of millions of dollars annually. Overall, Coalition media strategies in both Iraq and Afghanistan have resulted in only limited success and it can be argued that our adversaries still maintain the information initiative.

Insurgent IO capabilities are advanced. Violence is their most effective propaganda tool. This is not a new strategy. For example, Johann Most, a nineteenth-century German pamphleteer, described terrorism as "propaganda of the deed." In both Iraq and Afghanistan, violence intimidates the uncommitted, undermines confidence in the authorities, demonstrates potency, and can provoke a disproportionate military response from both the authorities and the Coalition. When insurgents, terrorists, and militiamen do attack, they use multimedia to amplify their actions and convey sophisticated messages to multiple audiences.

The IO strategy of the other side is broad. Enemy forces employ low technology strategies to permeate their themes down to the grassroots and exploit mosques both to convey their point to the faithful and to suggest religious legitimacy. Extremist graffiti provides a constant reminder of their presence. In Iraq, Afghanistan and elsewhere, insurgents and militiamen utilize the arts, including paintings, poetry, and songwriting, and post flyers, distribute leaflets, author articles, and even publish their own newspapers and magazines.

Enemy forces are also proficient in using the information technology infrastructure that the U.S. and other Coalition countries have built. They use SMS text messaging and Iraq's telephone system to intimidate Iraqis and even Coalition members, and are well known for their video productions that they distribute widely within communities that U.S. forces and the Iraqi government seek to influence.

The insurgents, terrorists, and militiamen are adept at the art of manipulation. They need not rely only upon their own terrestrial and satellite stations but also use foreign journalists and media outlets to ensure that their messages and actions are conveyed to the widest possible audience. But perhaps their most important tool is the Internet. The Web provides not only a mass audience but also enables a quick response to Iraqi and Afghan government and U.S.-led coalition arguments.

How to overcome coalition shortcomings

In contrast to this sustained information onslaught on all contested audiences, there are significant shortcomings in the Coalition influence strategy. Fortunately, most of the problems are relatively easy to fix. These shortcomings include:

- a lack of central coordination,
- campaigns focused too much on abstract concepts without relevance for ordinary Afghans and Iraqis,
- too much investment in strategic advertising at the expense of far more effective grass roots campaigns,
- undue stress on generic audiences,
- a cumbersome approval process prior to product release,
- a shortage of qualified personnel,
- failure to effectively utilize and properly manage private contractors,
- metrics focused on performance rather than effectiveness,
- failure to develop local spokesmen, and
- a failure to convince the U.S. public about the importance of information operations and thereby secure the support and funds need to undertake effective IO.

In the face of these continuing shortcomings, how does one plan, organize, execute and properly measure the success of an effective IO campaign that will reach, be understood and positively impact key audiences in Iraq, Afghanistan and anywhere else? This chapter will outline an integrated approach designed to achieve this vital objective.

International public-private partnership

The development and execution of a successful public diplomacy, strategic communications, or information operations campaign requires an international public-private partnership. That partnership would combine American, international and local professionals consisting of experts in the development of Human Terrain Analysis and target audience selection; attitudinal research including polling, focus groups and structured interviews; the planning, creative development, testing, production and placement of multimedia products; and the comprehensive and impartial measurement of effectiveness and performance.

Success also requires an integrated methodology that combines the very best practice from academia, the public (information operations, PSYOP, public affairs and public diplomacy communities) and private sectors (advertising, marketing, public relations, crisis communications and political campaigning).

In order to better support U.S. government strategic communication effort, this writer has developed a unique approach to IO campaigning. The more comprehensive approach is designed to ensure that we are able to understand, reach and positively influence the attitudes and, ultimately, the behavior of any and all target audiences in support of our client's strategic objectives.

Three phase approach

The key to our approach is to provide clients with a genuinely full spectrum strategic communications and IO capability. This is achieved in three parallel phases: research, engagement and measurement.

The Research Phase begins with the development of an intimate understanding of the audiences we need to influence; our adversary's propaganda efforts; and the wider information environment in which we will operate. From this analysis, we are able to determine which specific audiences can and should be influenced and why. We are also able to determine, with considerable accuracy what they will and will not understand – the narratives they accept and use – and what means and medium to use to reach them.

Once this vital task is complete, we can then begin the Engagement Phase, which includes the creative development, testing, production and placement of multimedia products as part of an integrated IO or strategic communications campaign that exploits every possible tool of influence in order to reach the intended target audience and change attitudes and behavior.

The impact and success of Phases One and Two are assessed in the Measurement Phase, which involves the impartial assessment of both performance and effectiveness. This constant and consistent parallel review process ensures that each campaign remains precisely focused on achieving our client's objectives. The overall aim of our approach is to achieve understanding through research; engagement from understanding; and influence through engagement.

Essential prerequisites: Making the case for influence and information operations

"Everything we say, every thing we do, and everything we fail to say or fail to do, will have its impact in foreign lands."
President Dwight D. Eisenhower

Before one can commence an effective IO campaign, it is critical that operational commanders fully understand the strengths and weakness of IO and are willing to use it: a) as their primary line of operation or b) as an integrated part of every other operation.

If commanders do not understand that everything they do and say will determine the relationship that they will have with the local population, then no matter how effective the IO professional is, he or she can never be heard above the noise generated by other uncoordinated and often counterproductive operations, particular kinetic operations.

Every operation, even something as simple as driving between two forward operating bases can have a profound impact on how we are perceived by the local population. Running one Afghan or Iraqi driver off the road or forcing one proud and innocent Pashtu tribesman to the ground, hooded and cuffed, in front of his fellow tribesmen and family can undermine months of work designed to win hearts and minds and will often result in a kinetic response. In counterinsurgency operations, actions really do speak louder than words.

The successful commander must therefore understand that he or she is engaged in an influence operation that is designed to secure and hold the support of a growing percentage of the local population. Without that support the collection of intelligence becomes increasingly difficult and without intelligence our operations become even more unfocused and unnecessarily provocative. With local support anything is possible, as we have seen so vividly in al Anbar province over the last nine months. The first and perhaps most important task of the IO professional is therefore to influence his own command and commander, rather than the local population.

The IO professional must find ways to properly educate the commander and his staff regarding the impact of all actions undertaken by the unit or formation and how every solider or marine is in reality the front line IO warrior. This means finding creative ways of reminding commanders of some of the core principles of counterinsurgency as articulated in FM 3-24. These include the following:

- All operations will positively or negatively influence local attitudes;
- Sometimes, the more you protect your force, the less secure you may be;
- Sometimes, the more force is used, the less effective it is;
- Sometimes doing nothing is the best reaction;
- Some of the best weapons in counterinsurgency do not shoot;
- In counterinsurgency, relationships are everything.

Next the IO professional must explain what IO can and cannot do for the commander. Here are some examples:

- Manage the expectations of the local population by promising less and delivering more.
- Serve a tool to restore or bolster the morale of the local population, which has likely been stressed by years of conflict, depravations, and perceived and real slights.
- Open a dialogue with local population, perhaps over the heads of obstructive leaders.
- Build and reinforce relationships with individuals and communities.
- Inform local population about our intentions and explain our actions – something they deserve and have a right to expect. Doing so will significantly reduce misunderstandings and forestall enemy attempts to distort, denigrate and deny what we are doing and why.
- Apologize when we do something wrong as perceived by the local population. This is not a sign of weakness, but rather the appropriate response of an ally and friend.
- Respond to and properly publicize complaints and our effective response to those complaints.
- Highlight the vices of opponents and counter adversary propaganda on a 24/7 basis.

- Warn, threaten or deter in order to reduce the number of occasions when we must act aggressively and use force.
- Publicize the successes that the Iraqi government, local communities and individuals achieve, in the face our common enemies, and to selectively publicize our own success when appropriate.

The first and most important role of the IO professional is therefore to educate commanders, staffs and units so that they understand that they are the front line of the IO battle and that their actions and words are likely to have the greatest informational impact. Front line units can lead the IO battle in one of three ways - through communication, engagement and direct support.

Firstly, in the course of their normal duties units can deliberately exploit every opportunity to communicate with the local population – for example while on patrol, at checkpoints and during meetings. All soldiers can be given talking points to use with the local population.

Second, leaders and units can plan operations with the specific intent of engaging in a dialogue with a local leader or community. An example is to hold events and social gatherings designed simply to foster better relationships or by holding "town hall" meetings to explain actions or even to apologize.

Thirdly and perhaps most importantly, units can do things by providing direct support to a local community designed to build respect and trust. For example:

- Provide security and protection.
- Show respect and be courteous.
- Provide humanitarian assistance.
- Help rebuild communities, infrastructure and the economy.
- Assist and support the local government and security forces.

If the unit or formation that an IO professional supports understands their vital role in the influence battle then an IO campaign can be focused on exploiting and publicizing the success that will inevitably follow, and on attacking our enemies and countering their propaganda. If units do not fully understand their role on the IO frontline, then the IO campaign itself will likely be defensive and reactive. Failure to understand that every operation will influence will more than likely hand the informational initiative to our enemies.

While it is a significant challenge for IO professionals to convince the warrior of this reality, we can be sobered by this one thought. If we cannot convince our own commanders of this reality, how are we going to convince the Iraqi or Afghan populations to support their governments and the Coalition and resist a deadly and merciless insurgency?

Task order analysis

As with the planning of any success operation, planning for all information operations must   commence with a detailed review of each task order, to ensure that a client's requirements are fully understand, as well as any operational constraints. Such analysis is also needed to ensure that the full extent of all of the challenge that will be faced are identified and understood. This should be a formalized process that ensures that there is no ambiguity or misunderstanding and that all parties fully understand, from the outset, exactly what is desired and what is achievable. The questions/issues that the IO professional should seek to answer/confirm include the following:

- Overarching objectives (e.g. inform, warn, coerce, deter, motivate);
- Desired message themes;
- Intended/desired audience(s);
- Effects to be achieved;
- Success criteria;
- Timeframe;
- Resources;
- Task constraints;
- Coordination requirements (with other IO/public affairs activities).

This initial coordination and assessment process ensures that the IO professional is:

- Fully appraised of, and focused on, a client's desired goals, specific objectives and desired effects;
- Agile and has the awareness needed to quickly modify an ongoing campaign to meet changing operational requirement;

- Able to provide timely recommendations for future campaigns, products and measurable objectives.

Conduct rigorous self appraisal

Sun Tzu understood that it is vital to know both one's enemy and oneself in order to succeed in any conflict: "If you know the enemy and know yourself, you need not fear the result of a hundred battles. If you know yourself but not the enemy, for every victory gained you will also suffer a defeat. If you know neither the enemy nor yourself, you will succumb in every battle."

A rigorous self appraisal ensures that one's strengths are exploited to greatest effect and one's weaknesses can either be eliminated or protected. This effort requires an exceptional degree of honesty and introspection to ensure that no issue can emerge during a campaign that will deflect the IO professional from the core message or will undermine the confidence of an audience in the message or messenger.

Few problems are so severe that they cannot be overcome if identified in advance and measures taken immediately to mitigate or ameliorate negative consequences. Indeed, some issues can be turned into an advantage if dealt with well in advance. Also, few internal issues are likely to emerge that cannot be predicted well in advance through a careful self appraisal. In any conflict we can be certain of one thing: Our opponent will be conducting a thorough review of us to find any weakness in our armor, which they can and will ruthlessly exploit. Therefore, we seek to mirror image our enemy's review process in order to understand what they perceive to be both our strengths and weaknesses.

This self appraisal process does not take very long (typically a few of hours) but is vital to establish a baseline understanding of our strengths and weakness, as we perceive them, and as our adversaries and contested audiences perceive them. Listed below are examples of the questions that we ask ourselves and our clients:

- Who are we? (personal, collective and political identities)
- What do we stand for?
- What do we oppose?
- How are we perceived? (By allies, by opponents, by the uncommitted and third parties)
- Who are our allies and why?
- Who are our opponents and why?

- What are our public strengths & weaknesses? (As we see them, as our opponents see them, as the uncommitted and third parties see them)
- What resources do we have at our disposal?
- What are our constraints? (external, self imposed)
- What is our timeline?

This self appraisal process ensures that we begin the development of each new IO campaign with an objective understanding of ourselves and our strengths and weaknesses as we, our target audiences, and our adversaries see them. Sun Tzu understood that such knowledge is vital in order to succeed in any conflict. He is studied in U.S. military academies and universities, but his wisdom is seldom strategically applied.

Part II: Mastering the human terrain

Determine information gaps and develop collection plan

To ensure that an information operations (IO) campaign reaches and impacts the intended target audience, we must first collect all of the information needed to intimately understand our opponents and the various target audiences. Once all existing data have been collected and evaluated and information gaps have been identified, we must then develop a list of specific IO information requirements (IRs). Once these IRs have been determined, we should develop a coordinated information collection plan to ensure that all available resources are exploited. This collection effort ensures that the planning of an IO campaign—the selection of target audiences, messages, and media, and the assessment of effects—are underpinned by the best available intelligence drawn from the widest possible range of sources, quickly and at minimum cost.

Human terrain understanding and selection

In order to fully understand, select and engage the right target audience, at the right time, using culturally appropriate narratives and the right media, it is essential to conduct a detailed target audience assessment or human terrain analysis for each likely audience. This analysis must cover every relevant factor that influences a community or individual to behave in a particular way and/or is a source of their individual or collective identity. Key factors to review include the following, what we call the "human terrain":

- Ethnic and tribal background of the target audience (including kinship and descent)
- History and language
- Demographics (male/female, young/old, rich/poor, and urban/rural)
- Religion and superstitions, ideology, and belief structures
- Social structure (values, class and caste, symbols, artifacts, mores, traditions)
- Legal system (formal and informal, rule oriented and relationship oriented)
- Elites and traditional/nontraditional leadership systems
- Education system (How much can they understand/what have they been taught/who taught them and why?)
- Political system (parties, platforms, and personalities)
- Economic system (land rights and black market)
- Arts, entertainment, and sports
- Human factors (individual and collective psychology)
- Methods of communication (visual, verbal, or nonverbal)
- Prejudices, enmities, vendettas, and hatreds
- Security systems (state, tribal, familial, and political)
- General attitudes on key issues

The aim of this process is to develop a detailed, nuanced, and culturally attuned understanding of all potential audiences before we select specific segments to target.

Research methodology

The optional human terrain research methodology combines qualitative and quantitative research techniques organized around the proven intelligence collection cycle. This multidisciplinary approach uses specialists drawn from the intelligence community and relevant social sciences (e.g., history, politics, economics, sociology, anthropology, psychology); experts in the assessment of current attitudes using proven attitudinal research tools (polling, focus groups, and semistructured interviews); commercial market and political research experts; and media research professionals (broadcast, print, and new media). These specialists must fully cooperate with local subject matter experts drawn from the same disciplines.

Target audience selection

Once detailed human terrain research has been undertaken, we can begin to select the target audience. The IO professional should always resist attempts to define the target audience before this research process is under way. It is also vital that previously selected audiences be re-evaluated regularly, as their relevance, attitudes, and preferences can change over time. Proper research allows for the partition of the target population into segments based on the level of their anticipated support or lack thereof for our goals and objectives. Once the research effort is well under way, it is possible to decide which segments of the population to target using the appropriate narratives and media.

During the selection process, and in order to complete the research process, we must determine what the chosen target audience actually understands about the key issues that the campaign is designed to impact. In the author's comprehensive approach, these issues are known as "ground truths." The audience's perceptions on a range of issues are likely to be profoundly different from those of the IO professional. It is therefore necessary to establish what these ground truths are before developing the campaign. An IO campaign that is properly grounded by an intimate understanding of the world as it is, and not as we might like it to be, stands the greatest chance of success.

Adversary and propaganda analysis

Our enemies have shown themselves to be highly adept at releasing timely and effective messages that undermine support for our mission and that bolster their own reputation and perceived potency. They are quick to exploit Coalition failures and excesses, they respond rapidly to defend their own actions, and they are able to hijack Coalition successes and present them as proof that change occurs only as a result of their own violent campaign. It is vital to conduct an objective and comprehensive appraisal of each opponent before developing an IO campaign. This appraisal seeks to identify the opponent's strengths and weaknesses and determines who they are, what they have already done or will do to influence contested audiences, and what impact their campaign has or will likely have on these key audiences. Armed with this knowledge, it is possible to develop an IO campaign that avoids or mitigates an opponent's strengths and ruthlessly exploits their weaknesses.

Understanding the media environment

An expert from Voice of America once wrote that "if a message does not show, it does not sow." His point was that even a perfectly constructed and culturally attuned message will not achieve the desired impact if it is not seen, heard, or read by the right target audience. It is vital that we fully understand the media environment that we encounter in each area of operation (AO). This enables us to select and focus on those specific media channels that ensure that we reach and impact our chosen audience exactly as desired, thereby saving time and money. When conducting detailed media analysis, we should consider the following factors:

- Available media
- Ratings (broadcast, print, new media)
- Impartiality and/or bias of outlets
- Popular preferences
- Impact of each media on target audiences
- Popular and/or respected media sources and personalities

Nontraditional media sources

The overall aim is to develop and maintain a comprehensive overview of the multimedia environment in and around the AO, which can then be exploited to reach the most critical audience.

Summary

Having prepared properly, to include conducting detailed human terrain research, the IO professional is now optimally placed to begin the engagement and campaign measurement phases.

Part III: Effective engagement

The output of this comprehensive social science-based human terrain research phase should be the development of a detailed understanding of each likely target audience, to include the identification of those issues that matter to them; the narratives that can be exploited to impact them; and the most appropriate media that can be exploited to reach them. The IO professional is then optimally placed to partition the population into selected groups or segments based on the level of their anticipated support for ours or our enemies' goals and objectives. Having selected and evaluated these segments, these segments can then be effectively targeted. Armed with this extensive and comprehensive body of knowledge, the IO operator can then begin the process of developing and deploying effective multimedia campaigns.

Rather than explain the mechanics of how to commission, produce and deploy an effective information campaign, which should be well known to the IO professional, we will focus on certain ground truths that need to be fully understood to ensure effective engagement with all target audiences. Challenges and pitfalls that if ignored can derail in the most well planned effort.

'Locals know best'

At the beginning of a mission like Operation Iraqi Freedom, where direct access to the local population is denied, it is likely that the IO or PSYOP professional will need to rely on their own resources to identify and segment desired target audiences; determine the most suitable narratives and media that can be exploited; and produce and deploy the multimedia messages that will facilitate effective engagement. At the outset, it is unlikely that we will have access to the domestic media, although we may still be able to reach the target audience via satellite radio and TV stations, especially as satellite dishes continue to proliferate, even in countries such as Iran. At the outset however, efforts to reach the population are likely to be localized, using the military's own somewhat limited multimedia broadcast capabilities and the ubiquitous leaflet drop. (Private contractors can come in handy here with their own connections and resources.)

However, as soon as a locale has been secured, every effort should be made to engage and work with local experts, companies and media in order to achieve a sustained impact as quickly as possible. This recommendation is made because the author strongly believes that that the campaigns, themes and products that stand the best chance of resonating with the local population as desired, are those that are developed by the locals themselves.

Similarly, the messages that will achieve the most impact are those which address the issues that matter most to the local population and connect with them on a personal level – only they know with certainty what those issues are and how we connect with them. The role of the

IO professional should therefore be to exploit local knowledge, expertise and outlets in order to translate our desired effects, derived from our carefully selected lines of persuasion, into a form that can be absorbed, understood and will resonate with the local population.

The temptation of course is for the IO professional to develop his or her own Western based, English language ideas and concepts and translate them into the local language, expecting them to have the same impact in Arabic or Farsi that they might have in English. While senior commanders and lawyers easily understand these types of campaigns, rarely do the messages resonate as desired with the target audience. This process also works in reverse, as evidenced by the hugely successful Pakistani anti-terrorism pop song, "This is not Us –We Are Not That."

The lyrics of this charity song, recorded by top Pakistani pop stars, and sold or downloaded in huge numbers, have little meaning when translated into English. However, when performed in the native Urdu of the writer and performers, they have profound meaning to Pakistani Muslims tired of terrorism defining their country and faith. That is why companies like Ford and Coke do not use English speaking Madison Avenue-based advertising teams to sell their products in China or India. Instead, they use local advertising personnel to develop campaigns that resonate with the Chinese or Indian populations. To use a relevant analogy to illustrate this point - the IO professional should become, as quickly as possible, the impresario of the campaign delegating the duties of song writer, conductor and orchestra to local experts and companies rather than trying to trying to write the score and play the music themselves.

Keep it real

All too often IO campaigns and products are based on abstract concepts and Western ideals that have little relevance or are poorly understood by the local population. For example, as lines of persuasion go, the promotion of democracy, law and order or the local security forces are perfectly appropriate. However, they are too abstract if they fail to touch the daily life experiences of members of the target audiences. A Pashtu tribesman living in a rural community in southern Afghanistan does have a refined understanding of the concept of representative legitimate governance but in his case this is the traditional authority of village elders and tribal leaders rather than elected politicians. Similarly most Sunni tribal leaders in Western Iraq support the restoration of law and order and accept the need for an effective and reliable police force. However, many have great difficulty in accepting a Shia dominated police force, certain elements of which have participated in the torture and murder of hundreds of their fellow Sunni.

The key therefore is to connect our lines of persuasion to the issues that matter most to the local population, using narratives that they themselves understand and accept. "Keeping it real" for influencers and the population in general is absolutely the best way to achieve our desired objectives. Again this necessitates the use of local expertise not simply as subcontracted labor, controlled by English speaking foreign-owned prime contractors, but by drawing local vendors into the center of the IO planning and creative development process. Western media and advertising companies can facilitate this relationship but should not control nor dominate it, not least because if international vendors secure the main profits from these contracts, local capacity and capabilities will never expand or mature.

Think strategically but act locally

The largest concentration of IO professionals and resources is not at the brigade or battalion level where the greatest impact is achieved in counterinsurgency operations. Instead, it is at the corps and army level, where literally hundreds of personnel are deployed and hundreds of millions of dollars are spent.

The natural tendency when authority and resources are concentrated at the highest levels is for this assembled expertise to seek to develop a top-down national-level IO campaign rather than a bottom-up grassroots one. This mistake is compounded by an overreliance on expertise provided by international advertising and strategic communications companies similarly concentrated at the army and corps levels of command. These experts have focused IO efforts, especially in Iraq, on national and regional advertising campaigns deploying broad concepts aimed at a generic audience. The reality in places like Iraq is that we are not selling products and the audience is far more complex and diverse than those who might buy cars or soap powder. Rather, we are conducting simultaneous multifaceted national and local political style campaigns, undertaken in the midst of a major counterinsurgency operation.

Successful multi-issue political campaigns of this type – American presidential and congressional elections being an excellent example – are not won through national advertising campaigns. Not least, because there are few issues that the majority of voters can agree on as being most important, even those in the same political party. Instead, the candidates in these elections run grassroots focused campaigns reinforced by local and regional advertising and occasionally by national advertising. Such a campaign allows the candidates to deploy messages that connect with the issues that matter most in each state and congressional district, and even county by county and town by town in so-called swing states. Many of these messages are deployed by the candidates themselves at local events or by key local influencers who have message authority within a narrow community.

Similarly in places like Iraq, our IO effort needs to be focused at the grassroots level, where we can tailor our messages to focus on the specific issues that matter to the population in each community; reinforcing and amplifying the far more important actions and words of the Brigades operating in these areas. At this level, we can also enlist local influencers with real credibility and visibility within the community.

This grassroots approach to IO complements the main effort of COIN operations, which is at the brigade and battalion level, where the war is won individual by individual, street by street and community by community. The role of national and regional advertising should be to support the grassroots effort by focusing on those few issues that are common across communities and by broadcasting successes achieved at the local level. This begs the question - why then are hundreds of millions of dollars being spent at the national level in Iraq, while many battalions and brigades operate with insufficient experienced IO personnel and resources? Artillery would never be concentrated at the army or corps level to the exclusion of lower units and neither should IO personnel and budgets. The key to IO success is to "think strategically but to act locally."

Actions speak more loudly than words

Effective IO is not simply about what we say. It is far more about what we do. Our actions can say far more about who we are, what we want, and how we feel about the local population than any multimedia information campaign. Perhaps the greatest impact an IO professional can therefore have, is not in developing a kick-ass IO campaign or product but rather in assisting frontline commanders to develop and undertake combat and civil military operations that secure maximum positive influence with the local population; enhance trust in American and Iraqi government intentions; and discredit the arguments and actions of our adversaries.

IO professionals must deploy their intimate understanding of the local population to assist commanders to plan and conduct effective full spectrum operations designed take and hold local support, rather than undermine it. This reality is no different in the commercial world. The greatest advertising campaign will ultimately fail if the product it is promoting does not meet the needs of the market or fails to perform as promised. Ultimately a product must deliver to sell. No amount of snake oil can change that essential dynamic. By focusing on actions as well as words in order to help shape combat and civil military operations, IO professionals can quickly work themselves out of a job as the actions of the units they support win and hold the hearts and minds of the local population. That is, of course, their duty.

Entertain as well as inform

Many IO products are frankly rather dull, in the same way that most domestic public service announcements, while vital, do not exactly inspire or excite. There is absolutely no reason why this should be the case, other than a lack of ambition on the part of the IO practitioner and/or a lack of trust from commanders. It is possible to both entertain and inform. Indeed if one does not entertain the audience is far more likely that the messages will not stick.

Humor and ridicule can be effective weapons to disarm an audience and make them more receptive to our ideas. They are also highly effective at discrediting our opponents. Drama has long been a tool to convey political messages to audiences who might otherwise be unwilling to listen. The use of poetry, music and songs are highly effective ways to energize target audiences and have been used in Arabic and Afghan culture for centuries to inform, criticize and debate. These methods also tend to be more effective for crossing cultural, religious, and generation boundaries delivering subtle implied messages. Whether it is a pop song, the insertion of a character in a soap opera, a comedy show, a "Made for TV" movie, or a poem, entertainment is often the best way to reach and impact any audience.

Certainly western educated, English speaking IO practitioners are not going to be able to develop this type of programming themselves. But by working with local experts and vendors, it is possible to produce cost effective and culturally sensitive programs that will entertain and inform and do so in subtle ways that circumvent audience bias and preconceptions. Such subtle messaging is also more effective because it is "home grown" and properly respectful of cultural, family, and religious values, ensuring maximum impact with audiences that can easily detect and often dismiss non-locally developed messages and messengers.

Always seek independent second opinions

Even where local vendors are used to develop culturally sensitive creative concepts and prototype products, all should still be independently tested with representative sample audiences. At a minimum, this should include focus groups drawn from the same demographics as those the product is aimed at. Ideally products should also be shown to larger test audiences, although security considerations may sometimes preclude this.

Such research should not be undertaken by the same team or vendor that produced the concept or prototype product. That is because it is very difficult for the creators to objectively review their own products and because occasionally some vendors will chose the reviewers and reviews most likely to favor their designs and products. Seeking independent second opinions from individuals or audiences as similar as possible to the selected target audience will ensure that a campaign theme or product stands the best chance of being understood and of resonating as desired. The test audience will tell the IO professional if a concept does or does not work as long as the review process is properly undertaken and independently managed.

Summary

Of course IO professionals need to follow the campaign approach defined in official doctrine and outlined in their manuals and training. However, many pitfalls are not always reflected in the manuals and in training. Challenges can undermine the efforts of the uninitiated or inexperienced operator to reach and impact an audience. The author has tried to highlight some of the most important ground truths issues that need to be understood when developing and deploying a campaign with recommendations for how to overcome these challenges. This should enable the IO operator to facilitate effective communications with the local population regardless of culture, ideology or ethnicity. The fourth and concluding article of this series will focus on the most difficult task for the IO professional – the *reliable* measurement of performance and effectiveness – some might say the "holy grail" of successful information operations.

18

Synchronizing Rhetoric, Policy, and Action

JULIANA GERAN PILON

The ambassadors of peace shall weep bitterly.

Isaiah 33:7

Not all of those to whom we do good love us,
neither do all those to whom we do evil hate us.

Joseph Roux,
Meditations of a Parish Priest (1886)

Why should ambassadors of peace weep? Why do those one seeks to help sometimes fail to appreciate it? Fickle and inscrutable as humans are, evil may be perceived as strength, and all too often elicits respect, even awe. Though our intentions are good, we are – to paraphrase the classic song – Lord knows, misunderstood. "America has a serious image problem," concluded the Council on Foreign Relations' Task Force on Public Diplomacy in its June 2003 Report. "World opinion of the United States has dangerously deteriorated. Around the world, from Western Europe to the Far East, many see the United States as arrogant, hypocritical, self-absorbed, self-indulgent, and critical of others. American culture, language, and industry dominate the world stage in a way that many find discomfiting."[1] Hopeful that we will be able to convince the world, eventually, that "the United States can once again be trusted and admired," the Task Force states that success depends on our ability to "win hearts and minds."

Paradoxically, our culture, language, and industry dominate the world stage – and yet the world needs to be better acquainted with us. How can so many people be so demonstrably ignorant of our culture, policies, and activities? Is it even true that the majority of world opinion is increasingly anti-American? How can anyone know that for a fact, with any degree of certainty? Robert Satloff, for example, notes that public opinion surveys are often highly misleading.[2]

Much of what is demonstrated or perceived as anti-Americanism is more accurately expression of anger, disappointment, confusion and even anguish at U.S. policies, and anger or even hatred at U.S. political leaders, but not ideologically or viscerally against the United States as a nation.

It also is not clear whether those who find American power generally "discomfiting" are responding to what we tell them, to what they hear from their own media, or what they merely surmise about us based on little or no information. Given the wide spectrum of anti-American sentiments, what are the best strategies for winning "hearts and minds" of various shades, shapes, and sizes? Assuming that we really want to be liked more than being tolerated, feared or envied, how are image- or popularity-contests related to winning, pure and simple, in the marketplace and in the domain of national security? Are these goals always consistent, and if not, what should take precedence?

These questions range from the epistemological and practical to the strategic. The epistemological applies not only to assessing, with any accuracy, international public opinion regarding the effects of U.S. policies, rhetoric, and actions, but also to evaluating data related to the activities and intentions of other nations' populations and elites. Practical considerations include: traditionally limited financial resources allocated to foreign policy; bureaucratic infighting within the intelligence and foreign policy communities; political constraints resulting from pressure groups that include not only domestic special interest groups but also foreign governments, which engage in strategic diplomacy with the help of the best American lobbyists[3] money can buy, and bureaucratic fear of controversy and innovation. Finally, there are problems of a technological nature, sometimes the result of rapid advances, notably in the communication field, that require new and more innovative approaches to both gathering and disseminating information, as well as flexibility that governments are not generally known to be able to manage well.

America has always had difficulty thinking strategically. Adda Bozeman deplored the Western liberal assumption of the natural order of things as a state of peace which she argued is laudable in principle but is nevertheless a serious handicap in dealing with non-Western adversaries who generally believe the opposite.[4] As if echoing Heraclitus, the East finds everywhere strife, war, and struggle – ebb and flow of nature constant, change violent, and blind. To outwit the enemy requires skill, patience, discipline; peace is the brief, lucky lull between the storms, punctuating man's fate with mere moments of respite. In various Marxist, populist, and Islamist reincarnations, the philosophy of irrevocably, inevitably determinant, physical and moral struggle resurfaces – which explains the underlying framework of our enemies' strategic thinking, guiding both their policies and their actions.

This trinity of challenges – epistemological, practical, and strategic – provides the analytical framework for approaching the contiguous trinity of synchronicity between policy, rhetoric and action. The logical first step is to undertake a comprehensive, candid assessment of each of the many obstacles to designing strategically crafted policy; this cannot be done without a commitment to tackle each problem with imagination, flexibility, and consistency. The second step is to learn from our past mistakes, and resist the temptation to pick the most short-term, shortsighted solutions but measure the alternatives and choose the most effective course of action that is realistically possible. Concurrently, it is imperative to consider the manner in which those actions need to be communicated to a wide variety of both domestic and international constituencies. The ultimate responsibility of synchronizing the three elements of statecraft – policy, rhetoric, and action – requires adequate interagency communication, congressional and constituency support, and a clear signal from the administration and specifically the Commander in Chief himself. All of which can only happen if the principal actors are adequately trained to understand the challenges in the first place.

American foreign policy: The perils of exceptionalism

> *Anyone can hold the helm when the sea is calm.*
> Publilius Syrus, *Moral Sayings* (1st century. BC)

> *America is a large, friendly dog in a very small room.*
> *Every time it wags its tail, it knocks over a chair.*
> Arnold Toynbee (1954)

Foreign policy has not been America's game of choice. Crossing the Atlantic in rough weather convinced the colonists that navigating on calm seas is best, assuming one had to navigate at all. Having bravely left behind an Old World mired in what they considered degenerate prejudices and sclerotic traditions, they were bent on starting afresh, hoping to engage in foreign affairs only if necessary if at all. Feeling protected by the ocean and convinced of their moral superiority, they would do so on their terms, without apology. Benjamin Franklin charmed Paris while eschewing the latest fashions. John Adams did wonders in Amsterdam despite an unabashed, farmer's distrust of diplomacy. With a somewhat similar attitude, his son, John Quincy, elicited a frosty reaction in London. The haughty British reception, far from chastening, only fueled young Adams' antipathy to foreign missions.

It was not until the twentieth century that America, with Woodrow Wilson at the wheel, at last took it upon itself to sell its model abroad and pay greater heed to the impression it made on the global scene. In his quasi-religious "Fourteen Points," Wilson confidently declared that Americans were ready to commit their "lives, honor, and everything they possess" in the final war for human liberty. To his great surprise, the result was a storm whose thunder would last over a decade and arguably precipitated the devastating mid-century carnage of the Second World War.[5] America's new-found missionary zeal, far from eliciting instant praise, gave rise to resentment, even hatred. The reasons, to be sure, vary widely in different parts of the world.[6]

But this has not stopped Americans from believing themselves unique, convinced that America, with all its faults, has nevertheless demonstrated that a system of government based on a universalist concept of human rights is not only possible but preferable.[7] American foreign policy decisions have consistently been predicated on a semi-rational exceptionalism bordering on the self-righteous.[8] Thus convinced that our intentions are good, we have tended to assume that the Lord will help prevent our being misunderstood; but it hasn't turned out that way.

The consequences of American exceptionalist hubris have ranged from missing opportunities for effective communication to basing policy on flawed, even disastrously inaccurate, intelligence.[9] They have also obscured the need for clear, far-reaching planning and realistic evaluation of the financial implications of various policies. Idealism can also backfire when well-meaning policy turns out to be overly expensive, misdirected, or worse. Its abandonment in the midstream may lead to disastrous, unintended consequences. A case in point is the CIA-funded Afghan mujahideen. The U.S. abandoned them after the Soviet defeat in 1989, leaving moderate forces of Ahmad Shah Massoud and others vulnerable to the radical Islamist factions favored by the Wahhabis and the extreme fundamentalist Pakistani intelligence services which helped usher in the Taliban. Not that exceptionalism is going to be abandoned anytime soon: having catapulted to sole superpower status after the end of the Cold War, it seems even more plausible than ever.[10]

Its religious overtones come naturally to George W. Bush, whose choice of Michael Gerson as speechwriter guaranteed eloquent expression. Continuing the policies of his predecessor, President Bush merely reasserted the ideal of democracy and human rights as the cornerstone of American foreign policy, explicitly included in the National Security Strategy of the United States (NSS), released on September 17, 2002.

The NSS states unequivocally that the United States will, first and foremost, "champion aspirations for human dignity," and specifically "expand the circle of development by opening societies and building the infrastructure of democracy."[11] We will "use our foreign aid to promote freedom and support those who struggle non-violently for it, ensuring that nations moving toward democracy are rewarded for the steps they take"[12] by providing funding "for projects in countries whose governments rule justly, invest in people, and encourage economic freedom."[13] This policy, later not only reiterated but escalated with a (rhetorical) vengeance in the 2006 version, takes center stage in the 2004–2009 Department of State and USAID Strategic Plan as its first pillar: "To advance the growth of democracy and good governance, including civil society, the rule of law, respect for human rights, and religious freedom."[14] Ambitious enough policy, but the public rhetoric would prove even more ambitious still; the programs themselves – military interventions aside – considerably less.

Rhetoric: Too little too late, or too much too soon?

> A nation, like an individual,
> if it has anything to say, should simply say it.
> E. B. White, *One Man's Meat* (1944)

> A man makes no noise over a good deed,
> but passes on to another as a vine to bear grapes again in season.
> Marcus Aurelius, *Meditations* (c. 2nd century)

Americans have traditionally disliked and distrusted the habit of expatiating. George Washington embodied the stoic individualist who preferred deeds to verbiage. Subsequently, John Adams from modesty and Thomas Jefferson from ideological antipathy to vestigial trappings of monarchy, shunned the podium as well. Jefferson even resorted to sending Congress a humble, merely written "State of the Union" report. But in the age of television, democratic leaders are expected to articulate their nations' foreign policies on the world's electronic stage; self-effacement is not an option. Of American oration rituals, among the most widely watched is the Inaugural Address, when the Commander in Chief appeals to the virtual Coliseum. On January 20th, 2005, George W. Bush waxed more Periclean than many had expected, as he invoked the God-given rights of man, dignity and self-determination, pledging American leadership in bringing about a new dawn: "it is the policy of the United States to seek and support the growth of democratic movements and institutions in every nation and culture, with the ultimate goal of ending tyranny in our world."

It sounded good, almost too good, and many were rightly inspired. But speeches are notoriously unlike laser-guided munitions, their results far from predictable with any degree of accuracy. Ambiguity, vagueness, and hyperbole can slide into pomposity, and may elicit cynicism as easily as exultation. In the absence of clear implications for policy and action, rhetoric can backfire. So it was that on the inaugural morning-after, not only professional pundits wondered if America would indeed bear any burden and pay any price for the sake of liberty everywhere. The President felt that he had to clarify, explaining that his speech was designed to paint a picture of the (possibly distant) ideal; at the same time, he had wanted to emphasize that America's crusade for democracy was "not primarily the task of arms." What, then, was this a task *for*? The answer eluded many.

"But surely he was offering more than empty rhetoric" in his inaugural address, wrote Susan Rice hopefully, while skeptically pointing to the President's budget proposal to Congress which "does not even begin to match either his dream or the country's long-term security requirements."[15] The debate in the pages of newspapers and on talk shows seemed to have all the marks of public diplomacy gone badly. But perhaps that concept – public diplomacy – has never been fully understood, and America was no less comfortable with it than with an even minimally activist foreign policy.

Better known as "foreign information," the idea of formalized public diplomacy was created in the year the United States entered World War I, during the administration of Woodrow Wilson, who finally decided it worth pursuing systematically, at least for the duration of the conflict. Once the war ended, so did the perception that the U.S. needed to explain itself to the rest of humanity. Having found a messy world shockingly far from "safe for democracy," a nostalgic America tried to retreat to its former insularity and stay out of the international conversation. Remarkably, the United States would not revisit the idea until two decades later in 1938, with the establishment of a Division of Cultural Cooperation inside the State Department. After several identity crises and reorganizations, in the wake of Pearl Harbor the unit became known as Office of the Coordinator of Inter-

American Affairs (CIAA). Its unwittingly prescient acronym notwithstanding, the office was quite restricted in both scope and vision. Less than a year later, a more ambitious Office of War Information (OWI) was joined by an Office of Strategic Services whose mission was identified with debatably wise candor as "psychological warfare."

That bellicose resoluteness, however, was short-lived. Weeks after Japan's surrender, President Truman dissolved both OWI and the CIAA, replacing it by the Interim International Information Service, shortly thereafter absorbed into the International Information and Cultural Affairs. Renamed as the Office of International Information and Educational Exchange in the fall of 1947, it finally received at least nominal independence in 1953 as the U.S. Information Agency (USIA). The concept of "public diplomacy" had finally found a home. It was less clear whether it also acquire a clearly formulated or adequately understood mandate.

President Dwight Eisenhower, who understood well the importance of communication to the task of waging war perhaps better than any of his predecessors, did the best he could to set it in motion. Trained to think strategically in battle, he turned his superb military skills to the challenge of waging peace. He knew that the silence of guns could be – and usually was – deceptive, its comfort potentially dangerous. Eisenhower understood (even better than Harry Truman) that America, having won the Second World War by giving Stalin the benefit of a doubt he didn't deserve, was facing another kind of war, no less daunting for being frigid. The weapons would have to be adapted accordingly; USIA was to articulate the nature of the conflict by reflecting, as deftly as possible, America's belief that its method of government "in the long run will win out."

At the new Agency's inauguration, Eisenhower declared our system capable of defeating "all forms of dictatorial government because of its greater appeal to the human soul, the human heart, the human mind." A senior executive reportedly later recalled Eisenhower's private confession that he would have liked to increase USIA's funding "because it was such a force in the Cold War."

By contrast, reports the same executive, President Lyndon Johnson "never took it [USIA] seriously."[16] Curiously, it appears that Americans, among the most productive and innovative people in history, have trouble with diplomacy in general, whether public or private. For example, here is how one senator, Homer W. Caphart, described the job of USIA a few years after its creation: "to sell the United States to the world, just as a sales manager's job is to sell a Buick or a Cadillac or a radio or television set."[17] His good-old

American plain talk captures with laconic precision one of the reasons for the appalling failure of U.S. efforts in this domain. Even elite advocates of public diplomacy tend to focus on quantitative, institutional, and structural issues,[18] rather than scrutinize the very nature of the vision and strategy. Yet surely America is no Buick, nor are its leaders mere sales managers.

What "product," then, is public diplomacy supposed to deliver? The comforting simplicity of the Manichean struggle that defined the Cold War era was now gone. Defining an informational function for the U.S. government involves not only conceptualizing a new strategic vision, but undertaking a realistic evaluation of the state of the world on both a technical and cultural level. Our rhetoric must be matched by our actions; our policies must synchronize with the rhetoric required to effectively articulate them; and rhetoric itself should be complemented by other means of illustrating the rationale for our policies to other nations seeking to survive in a world that remains as Hobbesian as ever.

Imperceptibly, the over-hyped worship of technology and the prosperity resulting from a mostly unfettered market gradually seemed to undermine the lofty spiritual impetus that motivated many of the original settlers. The "closing of the American mind" deplored by University of Chicago historian Alan Bloom led not only to a decline of standards in institutions of higher education, with particular damage to liberal education, especially the humanities.

Partly to blame is modernity and our own globalizing popular culture. Traditionally reluctant to engage in deliberate, carefully crafted information dissemination that might be perceived as self-serving propaganda, we are, by default, leaving it up to Hollywood and Madison Avenue to forge the image of this nation. The most influential image-makers, therefore, are necessarily self-interested private companies and those who produce their content for pay. But the unwitting architects of our public-diplomacy-by-default, their eyes understandably fixed on box-office returns, cannot be expected to capture and do justice to the complex intricacies of our multi-faceted society.

The same goes for much of television. CNN anchor Judy Woodruff laments the deplorable effects of the ratings game on even the most watched news station in the world. Meanwhile, some of America's entrepreneurs, faced with anti-Americanism and cut-throat competition on the world market,[19] have resorted to disinformation.[20] For every patriotic Anhaeuser-Busch beer commercial at Superbowl half-time, there are many other, short-term profit-driven companies that appear not to be concerned whether or not they may be giving their country a bad name. It is heartening that a group of businessmen has voluntarily joined to shape a more positive perception of our culture, creating Businessmen for Public Diplomacy. Altruism and good citizenship aside, the group undoubtedly realizes that a negative image of America is patently not good for business. Still, it is obviously not their job to articulate their nation's policies. And that, after all, is what matters most in shaping international opinion about America as a state and not only as popular culture.

Accordingly, the academic literature on the relationship of rhetoric to official policy understandably focuses on the role of opinion makers and governmental actors. In many respects, political rhetoric is itself a form of political action. According to Kenneth Burke, a leading student of political discourse, rhetoric is designed "to sharpen up the pointless and blunt the too sharply pointed."[21] Sometimes the "points" of policy become not only sharper than anticipated but pointed in the wrong direction. Nevertheless, government officials have increasingly turned to rhetoric, including "image manipulation" and "photo-ops," as the most common forms of media outreach, especially after the Cold War gave rise to the "rhetorical presidency."[22]

Ronald Reagan, who established the White House Office of Communications, would play the rhetorician especially well, articulating with conviction themes that reverberated across the world at a particularly critical junction in history. But his natural abilities aside, he had the simple moral dialectic of the Cold War to work with, a luxury denied subsequent administrations. George Bush senior and Bill Clinton both faced the daunting task of adapting American exceptionalist rhetoric to far more diverse and diffuse global threats from a wider variety of political actors.[23]

America's current enemies are harder to describe in simple, headline-grabbing, sound-bites. The attempts by George W. Bush to reinvigorate the "good vs. evil," freedom-loving democracies vs. tyrannies, are sometimes seen as strained, disingenuous, even though those close to him agree that the president is genuine and sincere. Pericles himself, the Orator for All Seasons, would find it difficult to navigate the troubled post-communist ideological waters. As our enemies are less monochromatic, our weapons have to become more sophisticated. For that reason, when we overstate our goals we risk being considered hypocritical, arrogant, and worst of all, not taken seriously.

Actions: What works, what doesn't

We do not what we ought,
What we ought not, we do,
And lean upon the thought
That chance will bring us through,
But our own acts, for good or ill,
Are mightier powers.

Mathew Arnold, *Empedocles on Etna*

Lofty words cannot construct an alliance or maintain it;
only concrete deeds can do that.

John F. Kennedy,
address in Frankfurt, West Germany (June 25, 1963)

We have generally performed better in action than rhetoric, preferring concrete deeds to lofty words. We have been eager to help others – the American missionary zeal has a long history. Americans are also notoriously generous, having donated money, goods, and help on a massive scale, to promote the well-being of others. They dig deep into their own pockets. They voluntarily send more of their own people as troops on humanitarian missions than all the countries of the world combined, and at a colossal financial and human cost. Philanthropy aside, it was during the Cold War that we first engaged in a highly successful form of nonmilitary democracy assistance beyond development aid, mainly through Radio Free Europe and Radio Liberty, followed by covert aid to the Polish labor union Solidarity, and finally the establishment of the National Endowment for Humanities, IFES (formerly the International Foundation for Election Systems), and several other similar nonprofit groups designed to spread ideas, assist in elections, party building, and strengthening civil society. After the fall of the Soviet Union and its satellites, democratization programs expanded considerably, to the point that by the turn of the millennium they became institutionalized, and U.S. policy incorporated "democracy assistance" as a prominent pillar of its National Security Strategy (NSS).

Or so it might be expected. In conformity with the NSS, USAID published in 2002 an impressive report, a collection of research papers titled *Foreign Aid in the National Interest: Promoting Freedom, Security and Opportunity*. The compendium included a comprehensive section demonstrating the significance of democratization and the administration's commitment to promoting it.[24] But in fact, action and rhetoric have not matched. While most Americans believe that we spend a large percentage of our GNP on foreign aid, the actual amount far less – indeed, a mere fraction. Particularly small is the amount expressly designated for democracy-related projects. In FY 2003 for example, the budget of USAID's Office of Democracy and Governance (DG) – the office specifically dedicated to strengthening legal systems, political processes and elections, civil society, and good governance – was less than $13 million per year. In FY 2004, the same programs received a million less. Although $6.5 million was added to the total budget of the DG Office, its purpose was to strengthen the social, economic, and developmental status of vulnerable populations, which fits the description of humanitarian assistance rather than democratic governance. Funding later increased, but not in amounts commensurate with the stated national goals.

Not that investing in democratization programs guarantees democratic advances. Notoriously unlike Buicks or Cadillacs, these programs sometimes fail to drive in any gear but first, all too often disobeying the steering wheel and veering either left or right when supposed to go forward, and blowing tires on what, to the untrained eye, look like perfectly smooth roads. Particularly accident-prone are drivers whose vision is further impaired by rose-colored glasses. One major U.S. democracy-building organization admitted, for example, at a conference designed to assess the value of a multi-year grant to several institutions funded by the DG Office, that the activities in its domain of activity were not successful in a specific, quite sizeable, region. USAID itself readily recognizes with commendable candor that,

> there remains, within the community of both practitioners and analysts, profound uncertainty about how to best direct democracy assistance. USAID, like other donors, does not really know with any degree of certainty what works and what does not, or what works better, and what works less well, in any particular context – or in general, for that matter.[25]

The report then suggests that USAID "needs to rigorously examine its nearly two decades of experience" in this area. Officially started in 2004, the examination is purportedly still ongoing. It would be interesting to know what methodologies are currently being used to ensure more objective, insightful, and efficient conclusions than past, less rigorous USAID internal evaluation exercises, which have sometimes been known to drive contractors to desperation and worse.[26]

It should be noted, however, that while public sector assistance tends to be better known, the private sector has funded a far greater proportion of the democratization activities than is generally recognized, and with considerable success.[27] In any event, so long as democratization is indeed a pillar of national strategic policy, it behooves us to conduct these activities in the most effective fashion, and the taxpayers deserve to find out both what works and what does not and, if possible, why. Taxpayers certainly deserve to be informed: they foot the bill.

But that is where they are particularly short-changed. Ordinary Americans and even their representatives in Congress know next to nothing about the remarkable success of many (though by no means all) of these programs. Neither does the international community, and often times the beneficiaries themselves. One is hard-pressed to find information about the many success stories of American democratic assistance to people in the most remote corners of the world; the many lives that have been happily changed; the new-found respect by people who had never met an American before, in appreciation for the generosity of young and old, willing to risk much in order to make a difference in nations they would have previously failed to locate on a map.

This goes not only for USAID democratization programs but others, notably the Peace Corps, whose website would reveal virtually nothing about their accomplishments were it not for a list of publications by former Corps members, a unique insight into the richness and impact of their varied, admittedly sometimes politically slanted, but invariably significant experiences. Recently reinvigorated, the privately funded National Peace Corps Association, whose members are Corps alumni, intends to communicate better with the community at large – an effort the Peace Corps is well advised to encourage and facilitate, sharing data and in turn collecting lessons learned in an effort to improve current projects. Another example of effective publicity for the remarkable impact of democratization efforts, specifically those based on the principle of strategic nonviolence, implemented through U.S.-trained local civil society actors, is the highly-acclaimed PBS-produced movie, "A Force More Powerful: A Century of Non-Violent Conflict," still being shown throughout the world. Based on Peter Ackerman's research at Harvard on strategic nonviolent conflict,[28] the movie illustrates the stunning success of tactics predicated on the power of people who accomplish democratic ends through peaceful means. The list of democratization projects includes both government-funded[29] and a host of privately funded activities.[30]

The answer is not simply to advocate across-the-board endorsement of all self-described "democratization" programs; pretenders do not automatically qualify. Susan Rice's call for "a historic increase in funding for democracy promotion programs – a next-generation

Marshall Plan to build civil society, political parties and durable democratic institutions" is premature at best, considering the very mixed record of those programs. The U.S., in its infinite gullibility, has been known to train and assist people who turn out to be our enemies;[31] favor groups whose leaders speak English at the expense of other, more authentic entities; fund organizations that are politically well-connected in the U.S. and/or abroad rather than the most efficient; overlook personal corruption; to mention but a few of many problems.[32] Bad assistance is like bad medicine: it can make you sicker. The Hippocratic Oath should apply not only to those who would presume to cure the ailing body but equally, if not more, to those intent on treating the body politic: "First, do not harm."

Synchronicity: Matching policy to rhetoric, with action in tow

> *What you cannot enforce, do not command.*
>> Sophocles, *Oedipus at Colonus*

Like the *nebich* straight guys on HBO, is it really just a question of a radical image makeover, a foreign policy face-lift? The Council on Foreign Relations is hardly alone in blaming most of our problems on image; it's no use denying our infuriating, if occasionally endearing, legendary clumsiness in foreign company. Nor can we seem to want to shake the Buick-Cadillac model of diplomacy, whose latest casualty was the Under-Secretary for Public Diplomacy at the State Department, Charlotte Beers. She left, deeply disappointed, after discovering that her Madison Avenue skills resisted application to the job of selling American foreign policy. The position had been left unfilled for half a year, with an assistant secretary for educational affairs filling in as "Acting" – eloquent proof of either lack of interest in this critical function or confusion. Then after an interim came former State Department spokeswoman Margaret Tutwiler, who took the post only to quit after six months, in April, 2004, in order to pursue opportunities on Wall Street.

The U.S. went without a public diplomacy chief for nearly one-and-a-half years, in the heat of the wars in Afghanistan and Iraq, when Karen Hughes became undersecretary. Neither she, the Bush administration, nor the Senate appeared in any hurry to fill the job; the Senate confirmed Hughes in late July, 2005, and she was sworn in the following September.   By the time of the Hughes appointment it seemed as if no one would ever come forward who knew the difference between foreign policy and Cadillacs, let alone Buicks. Though hardly an expert in foreign policy, Mrs. Hughes had several assets – in addition to the president's confidence and Secretary Rice as an ally: a great deal of energy, enthusiasm, and willingness to listen. But above all, she is no Madison Avenue marketer. She had another talent, her hopeful supporters noted: political campaign and journalism experience that taught her how to fight and win through argumentation, persuasion and education.

Those qualities are critical. For one thing, it should be clear that even the best policies do not sell themselves. Outsourcing communication must be carefully handled lest they go astray, as evidenced by the recent outcry over hiring private PR firms to do the job for the Education Department and other agencies. Unable to recognize that it takes more than simply advertising who we are, pure and simple, for quite some time we have been shortchanging ourselves, wrongly assuming that since we have the know-how, prosperity in an unprecedented scale, and the best Constitution the world has ever seen, we can buy the world's admiration and be done with it.

With the U.S. image continuing to alternate between stagnation and downward drift as if without a floor, Hughes quit after just over two years on the job. As the Hughes debacle has shown, it will take more than getting our PR and public-diplomacy acts together. The warning by Comptroller General David M. Walker in a February 17, 2005, memo to federal agencies reminded officials that the law requires "appropriate disclosure" when government-produced. It seems that prepackaged news stories, sometimes known as video news releases, designed to resemble broadcast news stories, complete with narrators who can be easily mistaken for reporters, have become an increasingly common public relations tool. The obvious question is: why do government agencies resort to subterfuge when honest information will do? The good news is that federal agencies are interested in communicating with the rest of us; the bad news is that they had no idea how to do it.

The answer is not merely to become more slick propagandists. The problem is far deeper: we fail to appreciate the need to take our audience, indeed ourselves, more seriously. The president is right to aim high; American exceptionalism is here to stay, and so it should. But Susan Rice and other critics are right to ask that our rhetoric not sound empty, disingenuous, divorced from reality. Our shining city should not be stuck on a hill, basking in satisfied self-righteousness, while down in the valley the hard work awaits us.

To change this situation, it will take more than the president signing a bigger check for democracy programs or for public diplomacy. In the first place, no one leader can accomplish the task alone; a whole cadre of foreign policy actors stand in dire need of better preparation. The country with the best technology and information that money can buy should be capable of offering its diplomats and message-makers a more sophisticated education in strategic public diplomacy – not to be confused with its decoy "training," however comfortingly technocratic, mission-accomplished, and "professionalist," the latter may sound. It is not only necessary but practical to design a richer educational curriculum, a more sophisticated course of study, to as many members of the foreign policy community as possible, especially to those who are most likely to be involved in public outreach.

This course of study must include a rigorous approach to political communication and political warfare, but also a wide range of historical and humanistic texts in order to sensitize the foreign service corps member, the intelligence analyst, the foreign policy congressional legislative assistant, the USAID democracy officer, the cultural and educational exchanges program officer, the democratization project manager, not to mention the mighty ambassador and the all-powerful speech-writer, to the varied cultures of the world where the American message often lands with a strange, discordant sound, if it lands at all. It should include the idea of synchronicity itself, which rests on the notion of harmony – the very definition of civilization, the repudiation of chaos.   These critical people should be taught to understand synchronicity.

Complementarily

It should be obvious that policy and message will always complement each other. Sometimes rhetoric is best used to test the public waters with a proposal in its formative stages. Sometimes it has to justify the basis for a particular policy, preferably after ample and sufficient discussion of elements that may legitimately be brought into the public arena, allowing (if time permits) Congressional and expert – academic and professional – input. Finally, rhetoric should be used to offer appropriate explanations for the final decisions without either catering to the masses or, on the other hand, underestimating the public's intelligence.

Among its menu of recommendations for synchronizing policy and rhetoric, the Council on Foreign Relations Task Force is right to advise making the formulation of foreign policy more sensitive to public diplomacy, taking seriously Edward R. Murrow's request that policy-makers include public diplomacy officials at "the take offs, not just the crash landings." While most landings are smooth, all major policies and even minor ones run into unexpected bumps in the road. While human planning is necessarily imperfect, policy-makers should nevertheless be able to anticipate reactions to alternative scenarios, depending on outcomes, and prepare in advance alternative responses and messages in coordination with public diplomacy officials, in order to help public perception adjust to changing circumstances, to avoid the unnecessary impression that our policies are floundering.

Improving the public diplomacy coordinating structure is another good recommendation echoed by many other reports. It is definitely the most popular approach – as evidenced by members of the George Washington University's Public Diplomacy Council,[33] a noted Harvard professor,[34] and members of the United States Information Agency Alumni Association[35] – who are especially concerned with the effectiveness, structure, and size of the public diplomacy bureaucracy, and its relationship to other U.S. agencies.

One of the most often-heard demands was expressed in an editorial in the *Washington Post* on February 26, 2005, by four former directors of USIA (Leonard H. Marks, Charlez Z. Wick, Bruce Gelb, and Henry A. Catto) in the form of an open letter to the Secretary of State, for re-instituting the agency. Understandably, if somewhat anachronistically, they ask that USIA libraries be re-opened, the number of public affairs officers be brought back to former levels, and afford these officials the opportunity to advise, not merely report to, their superiors.[36]

But in fact none of these recommendations goes far enough: needed is also an administration-wide communication structure among the many democracy-promotion and other programs that involve activities beyond diplomacy more narrowly understood. Those programs now constitute a mystifying web, no less dysfunctional than the alphabet-soup isolated components of the intelligence community, though admittedly with less lethal repercussions. Internal coordination would definitely be a start, but as a next step we also need to incorporate the outside world more effectively – including private foundations, Congress, academics, and other experts. Indeed, as the Hudson Institute's superb study, *Global Philanthropy 2006*, written by Dr. Carol Adelmann, clearly demonstrates, the lion's share of what may be called "strategic outreach" is in fact undertaken by private rather than public actors.

Dialogue, however, implies listening. But if we are not very good at listening at each other, we are even worse at listening to our foreign "clients." Most suggestions for improving the U.S. capacity to "listen" to foreign publics, unfortunately, amount to recommending increasing – doubling, in fact – the resources devoted to foreign opinion polling, which is hardly the right approach. Again, quality rather than quantity is our main problem. What we lack is the knowledge of *how* to listen, to *whom* to listen, and *who* the listeners themselves should be. We do not know *what* they would wish to hear, how to make them understand what we want them to know about, and *why* it hasn't worked in the past if we did try. Oftentimes we do not known even *what* to ask in our polling. To some extent, USIA used to engage in some such research, although on a rather limited basis. There is no reason why this function cannot be outsourced to private organizations such as IFES, which has conducted some of the best foreign public opinion polling, and other nonprofits.

Similarly, the CFR suggestion to craft user-friendly messages, highlighting cultural overlaps between American values and those of the rest of the world, is far better delivered by groups *other* than the U.S. government. The best ambassadors for such messages are members of local media, co-religionists or members of the target ethnic or national groups. Highly skilled NGOs, such as IREX and Internews, both headquartered in the U.S., understand and apply this technique particularly well throughout the world. Specifically regarding the critical Muslim, Middle East, and especially Arab regions, experts point out the importance of training journalists who can deliver impartial news, working with existing Arab-language and Muslim media organizations that are credible and independent, and seeking every opportunity to present our point of view alongside others, welcoming debate and dialogue.

High on the agenda of "public diplomacy" improvements, beyond the rhetoric and the media, is enhancing exchanges. This too, like "democratization," is no "apple pie in the sky." There are bad, worse-than-nothing exchanges. But surely the people-to-people outreach that takes place among Americans and others all across the globe, by far the greatest number outside the government, as part of commercial, educational, voluntary and other service-oriented activities, account for much of the interaction that leads to the formation of images. When surveys indicate that America's image is negative based on its "government policies," however, the problem is clear: we have done a poor job of explaining that generally our government reflects the wishes of the people. In part this is due to the fact that we have failed to make our own people sufficiently aware of what we do. This does not mean engaging in "propaganda" – on the contrary.

Conclusion

Crass attempts at selling our culture and our policies are bound to backfire, to the point that even the truth becomes tainted if it is presented in a cheap one-sided way. If common sense doesn't suffice, Communist and most other varieties of officially cranked-out propaganda should have taught us that in the long run it doesn't work. Honest self-appraisal, not window-dressing, earns lasting commendation.   The very fact that so many of our policies are successful is reason for engaging in free, unfettered discussion. Not that everything should be in the open; some actions are best conducted without fanfare, for a variety of reasons, notably sensitivity to those we wish to help. For it will not do to advertise our wisdom and generosity in a boasting manner, when our main purpose is to empower others. Discretion is also required sometimes in order to avoid endangering or compromising those who venture to fight for freedom in perilous circumstances.   But the right information delivered to the right audience in the right way is not only a nice idea, it is wise policy – and it should be the rule, not the exception.

We seem not to know how to get it right. We engage in many important activities that we don't bother to talk about, or else we promise to do more than is possible and when the results don't match the rhetoric, we disappoint those we seek to help. Instead of winning friends we reap ridicule or worse. Much better would be to make sure first of all that policies are adopted only after serious debate, as inclusive and realistically possible, with clear appreciation of potential fall-out and alternative scenarios. Once policies are adopted, they must be presented, not sold – and certainly not oversold – with sensitivity, taking into consideration the nature and context of the audience, or rather, audiences. Finally, the actions – whether of a military or non-military nature – should both reflect the policies and serve to illustrate their impact. This, in brief, is the synchronicity.

Having identified the problem, however, the biggest challenge is how to implement a solution. It won't be easy; but we should be confident that we can eventually convince the world, and even ourselves, that our ideals are no less clear, and no less indispensable, than sunshine.

Notes

---

[1] *Finding America's Voice: A Strategy for Reinvigorating U.S. Public Diplomacy,* Report of an Independent Task Force. (Council on Foreign Relations, June 2003), p. 2.
[2] Robert Satloff, *Essays on U.S. Public Diplomacy in the Middle East* (The Washington Institute for Near East Policy, 2004), pp. 94 -98.

[3] Jarol B. Manheim, Strategic Public Diplomacy and American Foreign Policy: The Evolution of Influence, (Oxford: Oxford University Press, 1994).
[4] Adda Bozeman, *Strategic Intelligence and Statecraft* (Brassey's, 1992), "War and the Clash of Ideas," pp. 46-77.
[5] It did not help that Wilson's policy was not only unrealistic but inconsistent; see David Fronkin, *Kosovo Crossings*.
[6] Barry Rubin, *Hating America: A History* (Oxford University Press, 2004).
[7] Henry Nau, *The Myth of America's Decline* (Oxford University Press, 1990).
[8] Walter Lafeber, America's Age: U.S. Foreign Policy at Home and Abroad, 1750 to the Present (W. W. Norton. New York, 1994).
[9] Richard J. Heuer, Jr., "Limits of Intelligence Analylsis," *Orbis*, Winter 2005, pp. 75 -94. Also, Loch K. Johnson and James J. Wirtz, eds., *Strategic Intelligence: Windows into a Secret World – An Anthology* (Roxbury Publishing Company, 2004).
[10] Siobhan McEvoy-Levy, American Exceptionalism and U.S. Foreign Policy: Public Diplomacy at the End of the Cold War (Palgrave Press, 2001).
[11] *National Security Strategy of the United States*, "Overview of America's International Strategy," http://www.whitehouse.gov/nsc/print/nssall.html, pp. 3.
[12] Ibid., pp. 4.
[13] Ibid., pp. 13.
[14] http://www.state.gov/m/rm/rls/dossstrat/2004/23505.htm, 1.
[15] Susan E. Rice, "Money Talks," *Washington Post*, February 21, 2005, A27.
[16] See Leo Bogart, Cool Words, Cold War: A New Look at USIA's "Premises for Propaganda" (American University Press, 1995), xvii.
[17] Ibid.
[18] Examples: William A. Rugh, ed., *Engaging the Arab & Islamic Worlds through Public Diplomacy: A Report and Action Recommendations*, (Public Diplomacy Council, George Washington University, 2004); *Changing Minds, Winning Peace*, Advisory Group on Public Diplomacy for the Arab and Muslim World Report (State Department, October 2003; Joseph R. Nye, *Soft Power* (Princeton University Press, 2004); and the Council on Foreign Relations *Task Force Report*.
[19] Allyson Stewart Allen & Lanie Denslow, "Working with Americans"; Simon Anholt & Jeremy Hildreth, *Brand America: The Mother of All Brands* [London: Cyian Books, 2004).
[20] Remi Kauffer, Disinformation: American Multinationals War Against Europe (New York: Algora Publishers, 2001).
[21] Kenneth Burke, *A Grammar of Motives* (University of California Press, 1969), pp. 115.
[22] Jeffrey Tulis, *The Rhetorical Presidency* (Princeton University Press, 1987).
[23] Siobhan McEvoy-Levy, *op. cit.*
[24] Written by Hoover Institution Senior Fellow Larry Diamond, it is prominently featured as Chapter I of the Report, under the title "Promoting Democratic Governance," pp. 33 - 53.

[25] USAID, Bureau for Democracy, Conflict, and Humanitarian Assistance, Budget Justification to the Congress, FY 2004, section on Democracy and Governance.

[26] Among the evaluations cited in the USAID Report are Harry Blair and Gary Hansen's 1994 assessment of USAID's rule of law programs; the 1999 Working Paper by Derick Brinkerhoff and a subsequent article outlining the analytical framework he used in assessing the effect of political will on anti-corruption efforts; three case studies by Linda Carter described in her unpublished paper commissioned by USAID in 2000 on democracy programs' effect on political change; and several books by Thomas Carothers of the Carnegie Endowment, Guillermo O'Donnell and Philippe Schmitter, Juan Linz and Alfred Stepan. Not listed, because overlooked and much harder to obtain, are self-evaluations by implementing organizations (both USAID and non-USAID funded). Of great interest too is information about USAID's criteria for proposal success, supplemented by comments regarding unsuccessful bidders; this may be requested through procedures available under the Freedom of Information Act.

[27] See especially Kevin F. F. Quigley's excellent study, *For Democracy's Sake: Foundations and Democracy Assistance in Central Europe* (Washington: Woodrow Wilson Center Press, 1997).

[28] Peter Ackerman and Christopher Kruegler, Strategic Nonviolent Conflict: The Dynamics of People Power in the Twentieth Century (Praeger Publishers, 1993).

[29] Other government agencies involved in democratization programs include: the Department of the Treasury, customs security; the Department of Education, international education; the Department of Justice, police training; U.S. Trade Representative and Department of Labor, international labor affairs, anti-sweatshop programs, workers' rights; Department of Defense, civil-military projects; Department of State, women's rights, Middle East democratization projects, education and cultural exchanges; and others.

[30] Privately funded activities present their own challenges, as some mix humanitarian aid with political assistance that violate U.S. national interests, even acting as fronts for terrorist groups.

[31] Satloff, op.cit., Part II – "What We Do Wrong," pp. 19 - 30.

[32] Marina Ottaway and Thomas Carothers, eds., *Funding Virtue: Civil Society Aid and Democracy Promotion* (Carnegie Endowment for International Peace), esp. ch. 11.

[33] William A. Rugh, op. cit.

[34] Joseph S. Nye, Jr., Soft Power: The Means to Success in World Politics (Public Affairs, 2004).

[35] See the USIA Alumni Association website publicdiplomacy.org.

[36] "America Needs a Voice Abroad," *Washington Post*, February 26, 2005, A19

19

Wartime Message-Making:
An immediate-term approach

J. MICHAEL WALLER

Introduction

As the United States struggles to shape coherent messages to the world, it must also refine the means through which it delivers its ideas. The near-universal default is public diplomacy – the U.S. government's communication with the publics of the world – now combined with a larger evolving discipline called strategic communication. Yet policymakers and others lack a clear definition of how one relates to the other, or how either relates to present international political, diplomatic, military and security realities. And we are still fighting more to get the message out than waging a full-blown influence war against our enemies.

Our public diplomacy approaches and applications, while important in building long-term perceptions and relations, are inconsistent with the realities of the new international environment. Advances in information technology and the proliferation of electronic media outlets have leveled the battlespace between the U.S. and the world's small powers and non-governmental organizations. Even individuals can undermine Washington's carefully crafted messages rapidly and constantly, attacking in swarms and refuting, distorting and drowning out U.S. messages, and agitating increasingly shrill and influential opposition.

Against this background, the United States can and must reorient its approach to meet immediate-term wartime necessities. It need not wait for the crucial but time-consuming structural changes in the public diplomacy machine. Instead it can begin immediately by recalibrating its message strategy and modernizing the means of delivery.

We begin this process by asking the right questions. What are our core messages? What impact do we want to achieve? How effective have the messages truly been? How effective are they likely to be? What can we do to give those messages greater impact, right now when we need them, utilizing the people and resources we already have?

Certainly creative and capable use of information technologies can help make up for years of lost time since 9/11, and pull the nation out of its global political nosedive in a very short timeframe. That said, the technology is useless or worse (as our adversaries master it more cleverly than we in some cases) until we take a different approach toward how we communicate with the world and why. That is why victory in war depends on answering the questions above.

To succeed quickly, good public diplomacy and strategic communication in support of the war effort – and larger 21st century national interests – need an accelerant. Hence the central theme of this monograph: to reorient how we communicate with the world in the short-term, accelerating the tempo and intensity of the nation's conduct of the war of ideas.

Points of departure

In order to develop successful wartime messages, we must know first what we seek to accomplish and how we wish to achieve it. If we want to win a long-term global war, then we must secure and maintain a strategic influence presence around the world to support not only the current conflict, but other issues, present and future. However, we must also win perceptions victories here and now, while our troops need them, and before extremist movements can grow any further.

Our audience, therefore, is most of the entire world: allies new and old who need reinforcement, traditional allies who no longer support us and are drifting away, neutrals whose bias or genuine neutrality we must keep or regain in our favor, soft opponents who can be made softer, and hard opponents who can be calmed, cleaved or isolated, their militancy rendered ineffective. We begin with certain understandings:

- Terrorism is a form of political and psychological warfare; it is protracted, high-intensity propaganda, aimed more at the hearts of the public and the minds of decision makers, and not at the physical victims;

- The positive and gentle nature of traditional public diplomacy is not well-suited to neutralize or attack such psychological and political warfare;
- The gradual, patient, long-term approach of public diplomacy is a necessity for strategic purposes, but does little to address the most pressing, near-term national needs;
- Explaining U.S. policies and culture, and non-offensive messages about American ideals, are vital but insufficient for current realities;
- Some U.S. policies and statements inadvertently benefit the enemy;
- We cannot credibly sell a bad policy, no matter how it is packaged;
- There are some issues, good and bad, that we simply cannot convince people to support, yet we must pursue them nevertheless;
- There are many other issues that people will support as long as the United States is not the messenger;
- Despite profound differences and antipathies, the U.S. and most of the Islamic world do share common interests and causes, which, it must be remembered, includes worshiping the one God, a core issue that we ignore at our peril;
- We cannot afford to wait for the cumulative effect of traditional public diplomacy to work because we have lost several years; our information initiative and our troops need the support now, and we risk running out of time in current war zones and other parts of the world.

Universality of ideology

People buy into an ideology, irrespective of its hue, for broadly the same reasons. Ideology provides people with a unifying identity and sense of community. It gives them a cause they can identify with. It provides a sense of purpose, meaning and shape to their lives. Ideology also provides someone else to blame for a people's misfortunes, and building up an image of an enemy to fight. Perhaps most importantly, ideology offers the hope that direct action will make for a better future, either in this life or the next.

Experience has shown that if we properly understand the tenets and nuances of a particular ideology, we can employ all of the tools of influence to expose the absurdity of an ideology's precepts. We can dispel the myths and lies on which the ideology is based. We can destroy the ideology's credibility and lure its supporters away by offering more tangible and realistic alternatives (even if those alternatives do not fit snugly with our own worldview). The bottom line is that an ideology such as Islamist extremism is built on foundation of sand which can be easily undermined by the right ideas and arguments, delivered via the appropriate channels. We have fought and won this type of warfare before and can do so again.

Islamism: a political ideology, not a religion

First, let's dispense with a self-made dilemma that has crippled U.S. message-making. We are not targeting a religion. Radical Islamism is an extremist political ideology. It is the politicized mutation of a religion. Radical Islamists are political extremists who seek to change or destroy an established political order by intimidation, terrorism and subversion: classical means of ideological warfare that the U.S. and other countries have successfully fought and defeated in the past.

Therefore the U.S. can combat radical Islamism freely without being concerned about fighting a religious battle. Radical Islamists work to influence international politics, foreign governments, and the internal workings of the United States government. Like any political movement, radical Islamism emphasizes the shaping of public opinion in the course of changing the political and constitutional orders of countries around the world. Radical Islamists are diverse in their theological and political ideologies – far from monolithic and at times in murderous conflict with one another.

The 1979 revolution in Iran and the rise of the Taliban militia in Afghanistan are representative examples of two different types of radical Islamism manifested into political power. Some movements have the stated goal of reestablishing a caliphate – a political system under the control of an ideological vanguard to govern populations in specific geographic territory.

Others have the goal of subverting or overthrowing established constitutional governments and use their politicized interpretations of the Qur'an as the basis of a new constitutional order, with Shar'ia as the law. This type of political system, formerly used by the Taliban and still the basis of the hard-line Wahhabi government of Saudi Arabia, takes a holy book that Muslims believe is divinely inspired, and turns it into a political manifesto of men and not God. In recognizing the regime of Saudi Arabia, the United States officially recognizes the political nature of the Qur'an as the Saudi constitution. Thus official U.S. policy already differentiates between the Qur'an as a theological document and as a political one.

Thus clerics and theologians who pursue political power must be regarded, for practical purposes, in their temporal roles as political leaders and operators. Such figures do not require the deference due to purely spiritual religious leaders.

Approaching radical Islamism as a political force can liberate American policymakers from the self-imposed, paralyzing angst that many suffer about the religious aspects of the conflict. This anxiety is as strong within the Department of Defense and uniformed services as anywhere else. It is a form of unilateral disarmament that gives the enemy more time, more insights into what we can and cannot do to them, ultimately more freedom of action, and aids their attrition campaign against us. It is the type of unilateral disarmament that gets our own forces, those of our allies, and innocent civilians senselessly maimed or killed.

Here at home, radical Islamists seek the overthrow of the Constitution of the United States. They may actively seek its destruction, or say simply that the Qur'an should replace it. Every U.S. government official – civilian and military – is legally bound to protect and defend the Constitution against such foreign and domestic enemies. Thus the need for something between public diplomacy and military force becomes more apparent as an immediate wartime tool. Such a tool can be applied precisely and decisively to reduce our reliance on the blunt instrument of military power.

Another artificial barrier that hinders the fight

The twin devil of our inability to fight the enemy as it should be fought is the defeatist interpretation of an obsolete law aimed against the legacy of President Franklin D. Roosevelt. That law is now invoked to prevent warfighters, diplomats and other government officials from running effective information campaigns against the enemy. A tiny clause of the U.S. Information and Educational Exchange Act of 1948, known as the Smith-Mundt Act, forbids certain government officials and agencies from disseminating information in the U.S. that is intended for recipients abroad.

In fact, many legal and ethical ways exist to prevent Smith-Mundt disciples from shutting down effective messaging operations, even if Congress is unwilling to change the law. When the widespread use of the Internet showed policymakers that technology had made the old laws obsolete, the Clinton Administration found an easy way around the obstacle. Legally, and with no objection or challenge, the administration circumvented Smith-Mundt by hosting Voice of America websites on servers physically located in foreign countries.

That precedent remains in force, but is not used as widely as it might be. Public affairs officers (PAOs) often veto military information operations (IO) designed to exploit terrorist websites, on the grounds that Arabic-speaking American citizens might see the U.S.-sponsored content and thus cause the military to be in violation of Smith-Mundt.

The executive branch should obtain a realistic legal opinion of the application of Smith-Mundt and its limitations. The administration must instruct PAOs to abide by the letter and spirit of the up-to-date legal interpretation. It must provide government-wide political support to give practitioners as much latitude as possible to do their hearts-and-minds work abroad. It must also ask Congress to modernize the law.

The necessity to follow these recommendations is simple and obvious. We cannot fight and win a war of ideas by denying ourselves the primary means of engaging this adversary and by muting our influence warriors. Not when our enemy uses these same tools so effectively to mobilize its support base, intimidate opponents and discredit and disparage us. We cannot concede this key terrain to our adversaries who then use it directly and indirectly to influence our domestic population, our politicians and our judges. We can and must contest this space. The enemy is already doing their best to deny these tools to us. We do not need to be complicit in this strategy.

Public diplomacy: building on – and breaking with – the traditional approach

The idea of public diplomacy and the official definition of the term have changed over time and often vary according to the perspectives of those who view the mission. At one end, it can be psychological and political warfare. On the other, it is passive "soft power."[1] Both tools are important, but neither is sufficient in itself.

Message warfare

The demise of the U.S. Information Agency and public diplomacy is well documented elsewhere, and a study group of The Institute of World Politics will make its own modalities proposal in a monograph to accompany this volume. Going back to our nation's roots, it becomes clear that scrappy, low-budget political warfare – attacking the target with negative messages, combining these attacks with overt and covert political organization and agitation, and offering positive alternatives – was a fundamental element of the American war of independence from Great Britain. These activities understandably carried a compelling sense of urgency about them.[2]

The U.S. has episodically waged such efforts internationally in support of its interests through the 19th and especially through much of the second half of the 20th century. Such strategies were not necessarily instinctive to diplomats or public diplomats, yet both recognized the need and knew how it integrated with their missions. After the National Security Act of 1947, a permanent government entity, the CIA, existed to provide the intellectual, legal, political and material tools to carry out covert political operations abroad. Those tools practically do not exist any more at the national strategic level.

Though the passage of time and changing attitudes to statecraft give it an almost archaic air, no other terms properly describe the third way between diplomacy and armed combat: political and psychological warfare. U.S. national security culture fostered careful study and practice of global psychological warfare strategy in order to resolve or win conflicts around the world without escalating to all-out war. President Truman created a Psychological Strategy Board under the National Security Council to plan, coordinate and approve global psychological operations. The U.S. has had nothing quite like it since.

Political warfare and psychological operations

Veteran practitioner and historian Wilson Dizard traces U.S. public diplomacy's origins to the Office of War Information of World War II, and unabashedly calls public diplomacy a function of ideological warfare.[3] Public diplomacy's tactical military cousin is psychological operations (PSYOP), a discipline that the Department of Defense defines as "Planned operations to convey selected information and indicators to foreign audiences to influence their emotions, motives, objective reasoning, and ultimately the behavior of foreign governments, organizations, groups, and individuals."[4]

"Hearts and minds," for want of a better term, refers specifically to the psyche. Yet we tend to run away from the true meaning as we try to rebuild our strategic communication capabilities.

A fighting spirit need not compromise the discipline's integrity as long as public diplomacy is a component of, instead of an umbrella for, a larger communication strategy. A 1989 National Defense University study offered an integrated view of how public diplomacy fits into the American defense arsenal:

> Public diplomacy is a form of international political advocacy
> directed openly by civilians to a broad spectrum of audiences... It is
> aimed at civilians and is confined in the main to forms of advocacy
> available to host governments. It seeks to elicit popular support for

solutions of mutual benefit that avoids threats, compulsion, or intimidation. It is not a form of political warfare, although it may be used in combination with political warfare.[5]

Political warfare is the art and practice of waging and winning international conflicts by non-military means. Political warfare is explicitly aggressive and hostile in intent. Many public diplomacy practitioners are uneasy with or even hostile to the idea of strategic political warfare, as are many government public affairs professionals. And for good reasons.[6] Credible public diplomacy depends on openness and trust, and strong firewalls to separate it from the tougher disciplines.[7] However, the reality of ideological conflict is its heavily psychological nature. But political warfare, like PSYOP, is an important, non-lethal weapon that can work where public diplomacy and other forms of communication cannot, and can complement or even substitute for military action. The nation's short-term messaging needs to call for a punchier approach.

Fighting on the psychological defensive

Waging a psychological form of siege warfare, some of the world's top terrorists and their supporters believe that their opponents will lose heart if the conflict is sufficiently drawn out. Since antiquity, militarily inferior forces successfully have drawn superior foes into a protracted conflict in a sound politico-military strategy. "Victory is the main object in war," ancient Chinese military philosopher Sun Tzu warned in 500 B.C., adding, "If this is long delayed, weapons are blunted and morale depressed... When your weapons are dulled and ardour damped, your strength exhausted and treasure spent, neighboring rulers will take advantage of your distress to act."[8] Terrorists and insurgents can win by simply not losing. Governments and armies generally cannot.

Modern democratic societies are especially vulnerable to a highly motivated enemy that can manipulate public opinion and the perceptions of their leaders, and erode and break national will. Armed with a fanatical motivation that welcomes death, the extreme Islamist enemy is comfortable with the concept of diminishing the target's will to fight – not necessarily at the combatant level on the battlefront, but on the political level in the targeted societies. Indeed, most enemy combat operations are designed to achieve a political and psychological impact rather than an attritional or physical impact.

Captured al Qaeda manuals show that the radical Islamists have made careful studies of the writings of Mao, the campaigns of other Islamist terrorist organizations including Hizbollah, and the conduct of the Vietnam War. They perceive the Vietnam War as a classical case of how a militarily and politically inferior force can defeat a quantitatively and qualitatively superior force by undermining the will of that force's home population and political leadership. The U.S. military's new counterinsurgency doctrine emphasizes the political nature of the conflict and the Al Qaeda manuals and methods show natural expertise in manipulating images and emotions to exploit democratic policymaking processes in the United States and elsewhere.[9]

Al Qaeda leader confident that U.S. will lose the will to fight

The enemy's delivery system channels images and messages into the eyes and ears of the world public and especially those who make and shape policy and opinion. The enemy monitors American public opinion closely. Osama bin Laden explained this directly, addressing the American public in a recording aired through Aljazeera in January 2006:

> What prompted me to speak are the repeated fallacies of your President Bush in his comment on the outcome of the U.S. opinion polls, which indicated that the overwhelming majority of you want the withdrawal of the forces from Iraq, but he objected to this desire and said that the withdrawal of troops would send a wrong message to the enemy.

Bin Laden noted the daily roadside bombings in Iraq whose attrition of U.S. and coalition military personnel has become the greatest catalyst to the erosion of support for the war effort there. He attempted to draw parallels between U.S. soldiers in Iraq and Vietnam:

> The Pentagon figures indicate the rise in the number of your dead and wounded, let alone the huge material losses, and let alone the collapse of the morale of the soldiers there and the increase in the suicide cases among them.

> So, just imagine the state of psychological breakdown that afflicts the soldier while collecting the remnants of his comrades' dead bodies after they hit mines, which torn [sic] them. Following such [a] situation, the soldier becomes between two fires. If he refuses to go out of his military barracks for patrols, he will face the penalties of the Vietnam butcher, and if he goes out, he will face the danger of mines.

So, he is between two bitter situations, something which puts him under psychological pressure – fear, humiliation, and coercion. Moreover, his people are careless about him. So he has no choice [but] to commit suicide.

While bin Laden missed the mark about the American soldiers' choices, he understands the effect of attrition campaigns. The al Qaeda leader focused not merely on the psychological effect of the roadside bombs on U.S. troops in Iraq, but on the American public back home. The results of American public opinion polls seemed to reinforce bin Laden's confidence: "To go back to where I started, I say that the results of the poll satisfy sane people that Bush's objection to them is false." A third time in the Aljazeera broadcast, bin Laden commented on "the substance of the results of opinion polls on withdrawing the troops" from Iraq.[10]

Bin Laden offered a truce and threatened similar terrorist campaigns in the United States. He hinted that the Americans lack the patience to win:

- "Do not be deluded by your power and modern weapons. Although they win some battles, they lose the war. Patience and steadfastness are better than them."
- "...we will take revenge... until your minds are exhausted and your lives become miserable."
- "...our situation is getting better, while your situation is getting worse."
- "We will remain patient in fighting you."[11]

Could the al Qaeda leader have a point about American resolve? Weeks after Aljazeera aired the bin Laden recording, a wealthy American antiwar activist commissioned a prominent polling company to survey the views of U.S. military personnel deployed inside Iraq. (Why U.S. commanders allowed the pollsters access to the troops is unclear.) The poll purportedly found that the majority of American troops in Iraq felt that the U.S. should pull out within 12 months, thus contradicting official government and Pentagon statements, and appearing to ratify bin Laden's analysis.[12]

The American psychological fatigue that the terrorist leader observed is indeed occurring. The quartet of suicide bombers, roadside bombs, TV and the Internet appear to be working well for the insurgents and terrorists. This is something that public diplomacy, by its long-term nature, is not intended to fix. So here is a vulnerability gap that needs to be closed and soon. We need to break the psychological siege not only by trying to win the wide middle of the undecided and softer opponents, but by directly attacking the enemy's own circles of support – and even the terrorists' cadres – on the intellectual and emotional fronts.[13] If we cannot get the enemy with kinetic actions, we can strike them with psychological weapons. Part of that means viewing television and the Internet as weapons – not merely for command and control or delivering munitions to targets, but as delivery systems to drop content on targets that we cannot physically locate.

Turn the tables: Bring the fight to the enemy

Here is where we ought to adapt traditional public diplomacy to current realities: to promote American ideas and ideals in a positive way, and also to bring the political and ideological fight to the enemy by using public diplomacy instruments and related resources as means of attack. This approach has many precedents since the American Revolution. Founding documents such as the Declaration of Independence offer a model: present uplifting goals and beliefs to take the moral high ground, and attack the enemy mercilessly. In the words of Samuel Adams, the message must always "keep the Enemy in the Wrong." The message-makers under Presidents Wilson, Roosevelt, Truman, Eisenhower, Kennedy and Reagan followed the Founders' model. They ably combined gentle and sometimes passive public diplomacy with political and psychological warfare to confront and attack, instead of merely defend against, the adversary's propaganda and ideological warfare.

Note the simple wartime message-making formula: a soft policy to tell the world of our intentions and what we stand for in positive and hopeful tones, in the appropriate linguistic and cultural settings, with the punch of a simultaneous strategic influence offensive to discredit and ultimately destroy the enemy as a political, moral and psychological force. Public diplomacy and strategic communications in general are thus back in balance. The tools now assume far more vitality than mere auxiliaries for diplomatic support. They become strategic weapons.[14]

Subdue the enemy's will

If the war of ideas is a clash of wills, and human will is centered in the brain, then the target in this war is the mind. Politics, diplomacy and warfare all involve bending and at times breaking the will of an opponent. From a military perspective, the brain is therefore a legitimate military target. However, our traditional military approach has not been to influence that target, but to destroy it.

That might work in fast, short-term operations against known targets where persuasion is impossible or undesirable. But it can seldom produce desired results in a lengthy military occupation or a protracted conflict. For our purposes, rather than breaking hostile will by killing terrorists, we should find situations that produce equal or superior results through a larger concentration of politics and psychology. Many of our enemies are not mere inanimate entities requiring either our defeatist coexistence with them or their physical destruction. They are living beings with their own willpower that can be broken, subdued, or in many cases, positively influenced.

The situation will vary from country to country, within countries, and over time and circumstance. In Iraq, for example, we unwittingly turned people against us when they could have been our allies. A recent study of British military attitudes toward U.S. conduct in Iraq states:

> The lack of cultural awareness has prevented the Coalition from fully exploiting traditional and nontraditional leadership, tribal loyalties, and the Arab honor code in order to encourage the local population to isolate itself from the insurgents. The Coalition has also consistently failed to counter enemy propaganda, allowing the insurgents to promote themselves as the providers of hope, to discredit the Coalition, and to intimidate wavering communities. Coalition actions including the excessive use of force and indiscriminate and poorly targeted cordon-and-search operations have actually encouraged communities to embrace the terrorists, if not because of a belief in their cause, then for revenge.[15]

So how can we work to subdue the hostile will that we helped create? Col. Richard Szafranski USAF (Ret.), an early information warfare theoretician, argued more than a decade ago, "if the object of war truly is *to subdue hostile will or to make the opponent comply with our will*, then we must consider enemies not just as systems, but as organisms with will. Likewise, if weapons are *means used to coerce an adversary's will*, then our understanding of weapons must go beyond tangible things, implements or tools."[16] As a battlefield commander in World War II, Dwight D. Eisenhower intimately understood the power of psychological warfare to undermine an enemy's morale and actively supported the development of a robust U.S. Army PSYOP capability. As president early in the Cold War, Eisenhower took the military psychological skills he developed against the Nazis and applied them as a civilian leader against the Soviet Union and communism, taking the fight to the enemy in every corner of the planet.[17]

The emphasis today, though, has been on subduing and destroying the will's host – the adversary's physical brain – instead of subduing the will itself, which is governed by the mind that resides in the neocortex. Szrafranski continues:

> Because we believe that the entity 'will' is existential and brain-centered, we concentrate our attention on the existence of brains, not on the nature of will. In so doing we may have mistakenly identified the *craft* of war as the *art* of war. By that I mean that our science of war is not so much the study of subduing will as it is the means of devising and applying progressively more elaborate means and methods for destroying brains. Destroy enough brains, or the correct brains, our studies seem to encourage us, and 'will' necessarily dies along with the organism.

That approach arguably has encouraged the overkill that our British allies worry about.[18] In a prolonged conflict it appears to be militarily unsound. With huge communication resources, it is usually immoral. The 2006 *Counterinsurgency Field Manual*, which lays out a revolutionary change in military doctrine, recognizes those concerns, advising that at times, "the more force is used, the less effective it is," and that "some of the best weapons for counterinsurgents do not shoot."[19]

Peeling the onion

We create deadly problems for ourselves when our nation's actions unite people against us. When they unite extremist factions that direct their violence away from each other and at our own forces, the problem is far worse. So our message strategy must be designed to be as divisive to our foes as possible.

We can compare the physical universe of opposition to an onion: a three-dimensional, roughly spherical universe consisting of concentric layers. At the center is the hard core of the most intransigent opposition. At the outermost layers, the opposition is the weakest. Our divisive strategy is to peel away the outer layers of opposition, getting down as close to the core as possible with a minimum of lethal force. Each layer we peel away is a layer that no longer identifies with the enemy and starts to realize it has a vested future in our success. The closer we get to the hard core, the more difficult it is to peel away the most benighted layers of hard-core activists and terrorists or insurgents. At that point the use of military power becomes necessary, accepted and effective.

It is here that our attempts to divide will be the most challenging. They might also be the most important, as they will focus on breaking up personal networks and provoking resentments, suspicions, fear and paranoia, and ultimately generating betrayals and defections, allowing the U.S. to identify and destroy the most intransigent targets.

The layered-onion metaphor presents a challenge to advocates of democratization. We are attempting, as we peel away layers, to win anti-democratic and very hostile elements away from the hard core. We are not trying to persuade them of the virtues of democracy, the liberation of women, or alternate lifestyles. We are not necessarily trying to make them our friends. We don't expect expressions of gratitude. We are simply appealing to their own interests as the enemy of their enemy.

Once we establish the enemy-of-your-enemy relationship, we will succeed in reducing hostility against us and allow us to form some sort of temporary alliance or working relationship. That uncomfortable alliance of convenience, for the short-term, will be sufficient to help us isolate and subdue the most intransigent. Over the long-term we will have to keep splitting, isolating and destroying the successively most extreme remaining elements while avoiding radicalization of the healthy outer layers. Historically we have often succeeded with this strategy when we applied it in counter-insurgency.

Immediate-term approach: Messages on two fronts

We can summarize traditional public diplomacy's message-making approach with the following basic themes:

- tell America's story;
- engage in dialogue (not monologue) with the rest of the world;
- resolve misunderstandings;
- build international relationships; and
- work together in a spirit of friendship and common purpose.

Shorter-term approaches must be calculated:

- to divide our opposition, wherever it is, even of and within our traditional allies in the industrialized democracies;
- isolate the enemy;
- coerce and subdue hostile will; and
- ultimately eliminate those who would do harm.

Note the important distinctions between "opposition" or "adversary" on the one hand, and "enemy" on the other. Our opposition and even adversary might be a normally close ally or important partner. It need not be a belligerent. The opposition or adversary could be a legitimate, mainstream political party or politician in a given country. Even so, the persuasion component directed at an adversary must be part of a counterterrorist or counterinsurgency strategy.

We can illustrate the new approach as a stylized addition formula, showing how the traditional public diplomacy approaches in the left column, plus the wartime accelerant on the right, add up in the war of ideas:

Public diplomacy		Added accelerant
Long-term relationships	+	*Immediate-term needs*
Promote our image	+	*Attack enemy's image*
Tell our story	+	*Discredit enemy's story*
Engage in dialogue	+	*Take control of language*
Discuss differences	+	*Discuss common enemy*
Resolve misunderstandings	+	*Reach proper understandings*
Build relationships	+	*Divide critics and foes*
Raise hope and morale	+	*Break hostile will*
Become friends	+	*Become 'enemy of enemy'*
Cooperate (as friends)	+	*Collaborate (as allies)*

This dual approach is the heart of an immediate wartime message strategy. Its development and implementation require no legislation or bureaucratic reorganizations. With a simple directive, the president can create an interagency task force and appoint and empower his own staff to call and run the meetings and ensure the compliance of all relevant agencies. Strong and successful precedent exists for such an entity.[20]

Conclusion

Deployment of a simple immediate-term message strategy will accelerate the shaping of international perceptions, opinions and behavior about the United States and its enemies for wartime purposes. It must combine the positive vision and soft approach of traditional public diplomacy with an assertive and relentless political and psychological campaign designed to subdue the enemy's will and prevent others from developing the will to terrorize, while providing optimism and developmental and economic assistance to sustain and build morale at home and abroad.

The immediate strategy provides the intellectual and political spadework toward building a new, more energetic and more creative public diplomacy and strategic communication system. This system anticipates rather than reacts. When it must be reactive, it is dynamic and flexible. It accepts a diversity of new approaches and functions. And it is opportunity-oriented to take immediate advantage of rapidly changing situations.

Notes

[1] Joseph S. Nye, Jr., Soft Power: The Means to Success in World Politics (Public Affairs, 2004).

[2] For discussion of American revolutionary public diplomacy and political warfare, see Chapter 1 of this text, J. Michael Waller, "The American Way of Propaganda." Also see Gladys Thum and Marcella Thum, "War Propaganda and the American Revolution: The Pen and the Sword," in Garth S. Jowett and Victoria O'Donnell, eds., *Readings in Propaganda and Persuasion: New and Classic Essays* (Sage, 2006), pp. 73-82.

[3] Wilson P. Dizard, Jr., Inventing Public Diplomacy: The Story of the U.S. Information Agency (Lynne Reinner, 2004), pp. 2-3.

[4] Department of Defense Dictionary of Military and Associated Terms, Joint Pubs 1-02, 1994.

[5] Paul A. Smith, *On Political War* (Washington: National Defense University Press, 1989), p. 7.

[6] Such unease is nothing new; even proponents of psychological warfare felt uneasy about the term when developing the discipline after World War II. Then, as now, many practitioners and policy professionals have trouble using the world "propaganda" to define influence activity, when as a neutral term propaganda is exactly what public diplomacy, political warfare and, for that matter, marketing and advertising, is all about.

[7] Building firewalls between public diplomacy, political warfare and other strategic communication while integrating each element is an ongoing subject of study and debate. Se Bruce Gregory, "Public Diplomacy and Strategic Communication: Cultures, Firewalls and Imported Norms," paper presented to the American Political Science Association Conference on International Communication and Conflict, August 31, 2005.

[8] Sun Tzu, *The Art of War*, trans. Samuel B. Griffith, II:3-5.

[9] See Chapter 15, David E. Spencer, "Red-Teaming Political Warfare." Spencer is a professor at the National Defense University.

[10] Osama bin Laden, "Text – Bim Laden Tape," BBC, January 19, 2006.

[11] Ibid.

[12] Al Pessin, "Poll Indicates U.S. Troops in Iraq Favor Withdrawl," Voice of America, March 1, 2006. The federally-funded LeMoyne College Center for Peace and Global Studies commissioned Zogby International to conduct the poll.

[13] The 2006 *Counterinsurgency Field Manual* FM 3-24 stresses the need to split the enemy as an early order of business. By contrast, the Voice of America did not help the war effort in the way it covered the March 1 poll of troops in Iraq. The poll was the lead story on VOA's English-language online service, and VOA did not mention that a wealthy American antiwar activist paid for the survey until the last sentence of the 15-paragraph story. VOA did not cover comments by analysts across the American political spectrum who found fault with the polls methodology.

[14] Strategic communications could assume a role as a peer to classical diplomacy and military power, much as the Bush administration has elevated foreign development and humanitarian assistance (on paper, at least) as pillars of national security. Such a role implies entirely new conceptual, structural and procedural changes that go beyond the scope of this monograph. The Defense Science Board has taken the lead in this area, with the State Department starting a strategy about two years later.

[15] See Andrew Garfield, Succeeding in Phase IV: British Perspectives on the U.S. Effort to Stabilize and Reconstruct Iraq (Foreign Policy Research Institute/GlobalSecurityMedia, 2006).

[16] Richard Szafranski, "Neocortical Warfare? The Acme of Skill," *Military Review,* November 1994, pp. 41-55. Reprinted in John Arquilla and David Ronfeldt, eds., *In Athena's Camp: Preparing for Conflict in the Information Age* (RAND Corportation, 1997), pp. 395-416. Emphasis in original.

[17] See Blanche Wiesen Cook, The Declassified Eisenhower: A Divided Legacy of Peace and Political Warfare (Doubleday, 1981); and Kenneth Osgood, Total Cold War: Eisenhower's Secret Propaganda Battle at Home and Abroad (University of Kansas Press, 2006).

[18] Garfield, op. cit.

[19] *Counterinsurgency Field Manual* 3-24, pp. 1-150, 1-152 and 1-153.

[20] The Reagan Administration's public diplomacy coordination model is a useful example, as formed by National Security Decision Directive 77, "Management of Public Diplomacy Relative to National Security," January14,

1983. For a first-person account of the success of the Reagan interagency working group to counter Soviet active measures, see Chapter 9, Herbert Romerstein, "The Interagency Active Measures Working Group," in this volume.

About the Contributors

Note: The views expressed by the contributors are theirs alone, and not necessarily those of their employers or associates.

Stephen C. Baker is a former researcher at the Center for Security Policy and a Special Agent with the Federal Bureau of Investigation (FBI). He holds a Master's degree from the Institute of World Politics.

Angelo Codevilla is a professor of international relations at Boston University. He served as a U.S. Navy officer, a foreign service officer, and professional staff member of the Select Committee on Intelligence of the U.S. Senate. His books include *No Victory, No Peace* (Rowman & Littlefield, 2005) and *Seriousness and Character: The Intellectual History of American Foreign Policy* (Yale University Press, 2006).

Michael Cohn is a civilian social scientist working in support of U.S. Army combat operations in Afghanistan. He holds a Master's degree from The Institute of World Politics, where he wrote his chapter in this book as a graduate research paper.

Andrew Garfield is a founding partner of Glevum Associates, an international communication consulting firm. A British army veteran and former senior advisor to the Ministry of Defense, Garfield has designed and carried out information operations in Afghanistan and Iraq. He is a Senior Fellow at the Foreign Policy Research Institute, and a faculty member of the Leader Development & Education for Sustained Peace program at the U.S. Naval Postgraduate School.

John Lenczowski is founder and President of the Institute of World Politics, a school of national security and international affairs in Washington, D.C. His government service includes a senior State Department position where he specialized in public diplomacy. He served for seven years as director of European and Soviet Affairs on the National Security Council.

Carnes Lord is Professor of Military and Naval Strategy at the U.S. Naval War College. He served as director of international communications and information policy on the National Security Council under President Reagan, and was assistant to the vice president for national security affairs. His books include *The Modern Prince* (Yale University Press, 2003) and *Losing Hearts and Minds? Public Diplomacy and Strategic Influence in the Age of Terror* (Praeger, 2006).

Jennifer Marshall is director of domestic policy studies and director of the Richard and Helen DeVos Center for Religion and Civil Society at The Heritage Foundation. She oversees Heritage research in education, welfare, marriage and the family, and religion and civil society. She holds a Master's degree from the Institute of World Politics.

Juliana Geran Pilon is a Research Professor of Politics and Culture at the Institute of World Politics. Her extensive public diplomacy experience includes service as vice president of the International Foundation for Electoral Systems. A member of the Council on Foreign Relations, she holds a Ph.D. from the University of Chicago. Her latest book is *Why America is Such a Hard Sell* (Rowman & Littlefield, 2007).

Robert R. Reilly is a veteran public diplomacy practitioner, an international broadcaster who became the twenty-fifth Director of the Voice of America. He served in the White House Office of Public Outreach during the Reagan Administration and in a diplomatic post in Switzerland before moving to VOA. After the 9/11 attacks, he served in the Office of the Secretary of Defense, and later became a Senior Advisor to the Ministry of Information in Iraq.

Herbert Romerstein is an adjunct professor at the Institute of World Politics. From 1983 to 1989 he headed the Office to Counter Soviet Disinformation at the United States Information Agency. From 1978 to 1983 he was a Professional Staff member of the House Permanent Select Committee on Intelligence. From 1965 to 1975 he was an investigator and later Minority Chief Investigator for the House Committee on Un-American Activities/House Committee on Internal Security. His work as a professional staff member of the Permanent Select Committee on Intelligence for the U.S. House of Representatives included a lead role in exposing Soviet forgeries and active measures campaigns. He is co-author, with the late Eric Breindel, of *The Venona*

Secrets: Exposing Soviet Espionage and America's Traitors (Regnery, 2001).

David E. Spencer is Professor of National Security Affairs at the Center for Hemispheric Defense Studies at the National Defense University. A specialist in counterinsurgency who provided support for a variety of products for the United States Southern Command (USSOUTHCOM), he holds a Ph.D. in political science from the George Washington University.

Hampton Stephens is a journalist who covered Congress for States News Service, and covered the Department of Defense as managing editor of *Inside the Air Force*, he has written for *Air Force* magazine, the *Boston Globe*, and *Foreign Policy*. He was founder and editor of WorldPoliticsReview.com. He holds a Master's degree from the Institute of World Politics.

John J. Tierney is the Kohler Professor of International Relations at the Institute of World Politics. He is a former foreign affairs officer at the U.S. Arms Control and Disarmament Agency and was executive director of the Congressional Caucus on National Defense and the National Security Research Group of the U.S. House of Representatives. Tierney holds a Ph.D. from the University of Pennsylvania and served as chairman of the politics department at the Catholic University of America. His most recent book is *Chasing Ghosts: Unconventional Warfare in American History* (Potomac Books, 2006).

J. Michael Waller is the Walter and Leonore Annenberg Professor of International Communication at the Institute of World Politics. He was a political communications trainer for U.S.-backed insurgent and counterinsurgent forces, and teaches influence operations to the U.S. military as a faculty member of the Leader Development & Education for Sustained Peace program at the Naval Postgraduate School. His is author of *Fighting the War of Ideas like a Real War* (IWP Press, 2007) and editor of *The Public Diplomacy Reader* (IWP Press, 2007). He holds a Ph.D. in international security affairs from Boston University.

www.ingramcontent.com/pod-product-compliance
Lightning Source LLC
Chambersburg PA
CBHW062152270326
41930CB00009B/1512